Africana Islamic Studies

THE AFRICANA EXPERIENCE AND CRITICAL LEADERSHIP STUDIES

Series Editors: Abul Pitre, PhD
North Carolina A&T State University

Comfort Okpala, PhD
North Carolina A&T State University

Through interdisciplinary scholarship, this book series explores the experiences of people of African descent in the United States and abroad. This series covers a wide range of areas that include but are not limited to the following: history, political science, education, science, health care, sociology, cultural studies, religious studies, psychology, hip-hop, anthropology, literature, and leadership studies. With the addition of leadership studies, this series breaks new ground, as there is a dearth of scholarship in leadership studies as it relates to the Africana experience. The critical leadership studies component of this series allows for interdisciplinary, critical leadership discourse in the Africana experience, offering scholars an outlet to produce new scholarship that is engaging, innovative, and transformative. Scholars across disciplines are invited to submit their manuscripts for review in this timely series, which seeks to provide cutting edge knowledge that can address the societal challenges facing Africana communities.

Titles in this Series

Survival of the Historically Black Colleges and Universities: Making it Happen
    Edited by Edward Fort
Engaging the Diaspora: Migration and African Families
    Edited by Pauline Ada Uwakweh, Jerono P. Rotich, and
    Comfort O. Okpala
Africana Islamic Studies
    Edited by James L. Conyers and Abul Pitre

Africana Islamic Studies

Edited by
James L. Conyers Jr. and Abul Pitre

LEXINGTON BOOKS
Lanham • Boulder • New York • London

Published by Lexington Books
An imprint of The Rowman & Littlefield Publishing Group, Inc.
4501 Forbes Boulevard, Suite 200, Lanham, Maryland 20706
www.rowman.com

Unit A, Whitacre Mews, 26-34 Stannary Street, London SE11 4AB

British Library Cataloguing in Publication Information Available

Library of Congress Cataloging-in-Publication Data

The hardback edition of this book was previously cataloged by the Library of Congress
as follows:

Names: Conyers, James L., editor. | Pitre, Abul, editor.
Title: Africana Islamic studies / edited by James L. Conyers and Abdul Pitre.
Description: Lanham, Md. : Lexington Books, [2015] | Series: The Africana
   experience and critical leadership studies | Includes bibliographical
   references and index.
Identifiers: LCCN 2015047368 (print) | LCCN 2015048346 (ebook)
Subjects: LCSH: Black Muslims. | Nation of Islam (Chicago, Ill.) | Elijah
   Muhammad, 1897-1975. | X, Malcolm, 1925-1965. | Islam—United
   States—History.
Classification: LCC BP222 .A37 2015 (print) | LCC BP222 (ebook) | DDC
   297.8/7—dc23
LC record available at http://lccn.loc.gov/2015047368

ISBN 9780739173442 (cloth : alk. paper)
ISBN 9781498530392 (pbk. : alk. paper)
ISBN 9780739173459 (electronic)

♾™ The paper used in this publication meets the minimum requirements of
American National Standard for Information Sciences—Permanence of Paper
for Printed Library Materials, ANSI/NISO Z39.48-1992.

Printed in the United States of America

Contents

Introduction

Abul Pitre

On September 11, 2001, Islam became a topic of discussion worldwide. Shocked by the horror of the events that took place in New York, the American populace began to seek more understanding about Islam and Muslims. The aftermath of September 11 also, however, brought to light the vast ignorance that most of have of the faith. Islam is not a new phenomenon in American life and in fact has played a major role in shaping American jurisprudence. However, the light of Islam and the role that it has played in American life has been underplayed.

Some of the first Africans to arrive in the United States to be made slaves were Muslims. Herbert Berg writes, "Many Africans who made the Middle Passage were Muslims. The story of how their religion was all but extinguished in the United States is a remarkable one."[1] During a sixty-four-year period these Muslims were stripped of their religion and culture, creating what was termed a "Negro." Negro comes from the word *necro* and when the *c* is genuflected it becomes *g*. Negro means someone who has been made dead, someone who has lost the knowledge of self, like an amnesia victim. Akbar (2003) writes, "Negro comes from the same origin as 'necro' and 'nekro' [translation: "dead"].[2] In Greek there is no difference between these words. Some wise and devious white scholar knew what he was saying when he decided to call Black people Negro (or "Necro"). "The necro refers to a mentally, socially and culturally dead person."[3] The majority of Blacks brought to the United States were forced to separate from their traditional religious beliefs with the majority being made Christians. Berg cogently writes, "The vast majority of slaves were stripped of their names, their religion, and their culture."[4]

The presence of Islam in America does not only include the first Africans who were involuntarily brought to American shores. The early writers of the

Declaration of Independence along with those shaping the American constitution were students of Islam. They studied Islam in secret societies. A visit to the George Washington shrine reveals the names of numerous Muslim countries. Tynnetta Muhammad disclosed that Islam influenced the American founding fathers and paved the way for them to create the U.S. Constitution, which was based on principles they learned from their study of Islam.[5]

These founding fathers never acknowledged Islam but studied it in their secret societies. In places like the Masonic order the students are tasked with moving through various degrees and once reaching the 33rd degree are given a Holy Quran. What is contained in the Holy Quran? It contains the highest knowledge that if studied properly catapults the student into spiritual science. Here spiritual science means a knowledge that is supreme in helping the reader of its contents to observe or see new realities. In addition, it is a book of light containing more than knowledge—it awakens the student to the inner voice, awakening the divine essence in human beings. Thus Islam has been a carefully guarded secret by those who rule the masses.

September 11 cast a veil over Islam that made it look obscene; it became America's worst nightmare. Most Americans knew only a little about Islam through persons like Malcolm X and Louis Farrakhan. However, one of the greatest leaders in American history was Elijah Muhammad. Born in Sandersville, Georgia, Muhammad was a rural farm boy who moved north after witnessing firsthand the lynching of Blacks along with other atrocities.[6] Saying that he had seen enough of the White man's brutality to last him 26,000 years,[7] he moved to Detroit in the 1930s to seek better living conditions.

In Detroit he met Wallace D. Fard, whom he believed to be the long-awaited returned Christ. He studied with Fard from 1931 to 1935 and, along with Fard, established the Nation of Islam during this period. When his teacher departed, he left Elijah with the task of raising Blacks in America to a new level of consciousness.

The Nation of Islam under the leadership of Elijah Muhammad flourished, especially during the tumultuous 1950s and 1960s. Black consciousness was being raised, and several of Muhammad's students began to gain national attention. One of those most recognized is Malcolm X an eighth-grade dropout who had been arrested for larceny. While serving time Malcolm began studying Islam under the teachings of Elijah Muhammad. After leaving prison he became a national spokesperson for the Nation of Islam and was later catapulted into the national spotlight.

In 1959, Mike Wallace and Louis Lomax aired a documentary titled "The Hate That Hate Produced," which was promoted on national news. The documentary sought to frame the Nation of Islam as a hate group. This image was later reinforced when the FBI began to place news editorials in papers that painted the Nation of Islam in a negative light. One editorial, "The Black Merchants of Hate" by Alex Haley and Alfred Balk, became the template that would guide the majority of writings about the Nation of Islam. To date this template is still being used as the basic narrative to describe the Nation of Islam. In the context of defining the Nation of Islam Haley and Balk raised the question, "How does this fanatical doctrine fit in with the tenets of the orthodox Muslim faith, which has 500,000,000 followers throughout the world."[8] To answer this question they quoted Ahmad Kamal who declared, "Elijah Poole's teachings, his dogma and doctrine of hatred are utterly non-Muslim." Even within the pages of this volume this narrative continues to dominate how writers frame their discussion of the Nation of Islam.

Prior to the article "The Black Merchants of Hate," Eric Lincoln wrote his 1960 dissertation titled "Black Muslims in the United States."[9] Black Muslims became the basic terminology to identify Muslims under the leadership of Elijah Muhammad. It's important to note that before the publication of Lincoln's book the followers of Elijah Muhammad never referred to themselves as Black Muslims. There are those who argue the term "Black Muslims" was an attempt to separate the members of the Nation of Islam from mainstream Islam or suggest that Muslims under the leadership of Elijah Muhammad were not real Muslims. Other writers like Essien-Udom (1962) in *Black Nationalism: The Search For An Identity* wrote about Elijah Muhammad and the Nation of Islam without an agenda to disparage the Nation.[10]

Despite these challenges, Elijah Muhammad has done more than any Muslim leader with regard to making Islam known in America. Berg is insightful in highlighting the significance of Elijah Muhammad in the twenty-first century:

> Moreover, in light of ongoing concerns about a clash between Western and Islamic civilizations, it is ironic that hundreds of thousands—if not millions—of Muslims living in the United States were directly or indirectly converted to Islam via the uniquely American formulation of this religion by Elijah Muhammad. . . . Its leader for over forty years, Elijah Muhammad, was therefore arguably the most important person in developing Islam in America, eclipsing other prominent figures such as Noble Drew Ali, Wali Fard Muhammad, Malcolm X, Louis Farrakhan and Warith Deen Muhammad (originally known as Wallace D. Muhammad).[11]

Daniel Pipes argues, "it does not take much imagination to see that, should Islam in fact replace Christianity as the primary religion of African Americans, this will have vast significance for all Americans, affecting everything from race relations to foreign policy, from popular culture to issues of religion and state."[12] He notes that should this take place, the credit or blame should go to "the squeaky little man teaching hate," Elijah Muhammad. One could argue that Elijah Muhammad's teachings appeared to be hate because they disrupted White supremacy causing him to receive negative labels by those who were White supremacists. Statistics disclose that Islam is indeed a permanent fixture in America, with a growing population of African Americans returning to the faith.[13] Moreover Elijah Muhammad's teachings highlighted the cultural clashes that are now engulfing the whole world and the interplay of Islam and Christianity in these monumental changes.

As a result of these iconic changes universities are now taking center stage in the study of Islam. In a large number of research universities degree programs are being offered in the study of Islam, whereas in historically Black colleges and universities degree programs on Islam are virtually absent. For those in positions of power, Blacks gaining knowledge of Islam is threatening because it could create a cultural revolution among a population that has historically been deprived of knowledge that would free them from oppression. Now, even students in predominately White universities are provided with opportunities to study Islam through the rich history of the African American experience in the United States.

In fact, this project came together as a result of a symposium held by the African American Studies Department at the University of Houston. The symposium brought together various scholars who were studying varying aspects of Islam as it related to the African American experience. Its twelve chapters cover a wide range of topics, including ten chapters focusing exclusively on some aspect of Elijah Muhammad, Malcolm X, and the Nation of Islam.

In chapter 1, "'Raising Her Voice': Writings by, for and about Women in *Muhammad Speaks* Newspaper, 1961–1975," Bayyinah Jeffries focuses on women in the Nation of Islam. The chapter highlights the significant role that women played in the Nation of Islam by examining the journalistic contributions made to the organization's *Muhammad Speaks* newspaper. Highlighted in this chapter are issues around health, education, Black world affairs, and standards of beauty as they related to Black women.

In chapter 2, "Take Two: Nation of Islam Women Fifty Years after Civil Rights," C. S'thembile West discusses her personal experiences with women in the Nation of Islam while growing up in Harlem, New York. She then presents an ethnographic study of women in the Nation of Islam who were actively involved in the Black community's struggle for justice and equality. Echoing the words of Elijah Muhammad to "elevate the Black man and woman to their original greatness," the voices of women in the Nation of Islam are raised to prominence as West revisits women who were active in the Nation of Islam during the civil rights and Black Power movement in

America. She highlights their ongoing activism in the continued struggle for equality and justice and explores gender roles and economic choices by women in the Nation of Islam.

In chapter 3, "Elijah Muhammad, Multicultural Education, Critical White Studies and Critical Pedagogy," Abul Pitre explores Elijah Muhammad's teachings in the context of critical educational theory. He argues that Elijah Muhammad's primary mission was the reeducation of Blacks in America. Drawing parallels between contemporary educational discourse in multicultural education, critical White studies, and critical pedagogy, he discloses how these contemporary frameworks are not new but were predated by the teachings of Elijah Muhammad. For example the emerging field of critical White studies and the examination White identity development were frameworks that Elijah Muhammad explored prior to the development of critical White studies as an academic field. Moreover the chapter examines Elijah Muhammad's critique of black education in the context of critical pedagogy, in which critical educational theorists ask questions about knowledge construction.

In chapter 4, "Bismillah—Message to the Blackman Revisited: Being and Power," Jinaki Abdullah continues this investigation into the African American Muslim leaders' development of the core principles of what became critical race theory. She explores the leadership of Elijah Muhammad in articulating a counternarrative to the White supremacist social structure that had enslaved the psyche of human beings. Highlighting Elijah Muhammad's book *Message to the Blackman in America* she discloses how this classic text sought to explain the Black man's being in the world. She draws from writers like Martin Heidegger to explore the Black man's being in the world in relationship to God. The chapter highlights the contemporary shootings of Black men across the United States and the prophetic words of Elijah Muhammad regarding the election of the first African American president. She concludes by pointing out that Elijah Muhammad's analysis of racism in America "has come to be accepted norm in the form of critical race theory."

In chapter 5, "The Nation of Islam: A Historiography of Pan Africanist Thought and Intellectualism," James Conyers highlights that the Nation of Islam could be considered one of the most meaningful black organizations in the twentieth century. Conyers draws from concepts in Pan Africanism, historically tracing its concepts to a theoretical framework coined *Ujimma*, meaning collective work and solidarity. With an emphasis on historiography this chapter proceeds to disclose parallels of Pan Africanism with the Nation of Islam. It includes a discussion of leaders like Marcus Garvey and Noble Drew Ali and their roles in the Black nationalist movement. It also briefly covers an historical overview of the Nation of Islam and concludes that future scholars should explore the tools from the organization and how they can be applied in a technology-driven society.

In chapter 6, "Understanding Elijah Muhammad: An Intellectual Biography of Elijah Muhammad," Malachi Crawford uses Kawaida theory to develop an intellectual biography of the Elijah Muhammad. The chapter has four key constructs, which include social organization, political organization, economic organization, and historical organization. Under each of these constructs comparisons are made to the life and work of Muhammad, reviewing his early life experiences and how they shaped his ideological views about social, political, and economic concerns. Crawford discusses the Nation of Islam's appeal to the most downtrodden Blacks in the American society and contends that the Nation of Islam was the hope and vanguard for countless Blacks who had been placed on the margins of society. Elijah Muhammad, he argues, was able to make religion applicable to the needs of Blacks.

In chapter 7, "The Depiction of Slavery in Steven Barnes's *Lion's Blood* and *Zulu Heart*," Rebecca Hankins explores how these two novels use an Islamic framework. She discusses an interview with Barnes in which he discloses that Islam was used because it is a unifying religion. The chapter then proceeds to discuss characters in the novels in the context of Islam. Hankins also explores science fiction, fantasy, and speculative fiction with regard to exploring new approaches to the study of Islam.

In chapter 8, "Islam in the African Literary Tradition," Christel Temple discusses Islam in the context of Africana literary tradition. She begins by defining and making a distinction between Africana Islamic literature verses Islamic literature. The chapter provides a long list of Africana literary writers who have produced Islamic literature. She highlights Marvin X, who is considered the father of Muslim American literature, continuing the lineage of Edward Blyden, Duse Muhammad Ali, Noble Drew Ali, Master Fard Muhammad, and Elijah Muhammad. She then points out works like *The Autobiography of Malcolm X* and Louis Farrakhan's "Orgena" and his classic song "White Man's Heaven Is a Black Man's Hell." Other works like Amiri Baraka's "A Black Mass" are referenced as well as other Africana Islamic literary writers such Sonia Sanchez.

In chapter 9, "Martin L. King Jr. and Malcolm X," Charles Allen discusses the similarities and differences in both men's philosophies for equal rights for Blacks in America. The chapter reviews King's famous "I Have A Dream" speech and Malcolm X's "Message to the Grassroots." What emerges from the chapter is how those in positions of power have engineered the ideologies of both men to fit their interest. Highlighted in the chapter is the virtual absence of Malcolm X from textbooks used in schools and universities.

In chapter 10, "Elijah Muhammad's Nation of Islam: Separatism, Regendering, and a Secular Approach to Black Power after Malcolm X (1965–1975)," Ula Taylor examines the Nation of Islam and its primary leaders Elijah Muhammad and Malcolm X with regard to developing the foundation for Black nationalism. The chapter begins by discussing the negative media images that have sought push to people away from Elijah Muhammad and the Nation of Islam. It then explores Malcolm X as one of the most significant spokespeople in the Nation of Islam and how Malcolm's rise to stardom led to an increase in Nation of Islam membership. The chapter also explores the Nation of Islam's position on land as the basis for economic independence, reparations, the terminology around the word Africa, and gender roles. The chapter includes narratives from members of the Nation of Islam as it relates to their conversion to the practice of Islam under the leadership of Elijah Muhammad.

In chapter 11, "'My Malcolm': Self-Reliance and African American Cultural Expression," Tonya Conston and Emile Koenig explore the Nation of Islam's ability to create a do-for-self philosophy among its members. They discuss Malcolm's ideas about education and land ownership, highlighting the number of African American students that are majoring in agribusiness. Citing Malcolm's arguments regarding land they point out that the Nation of Islam's current leader Minister Louis Farrakhan continues the Nation of Islam's legacy of encouraging Blacks to seek land. During Minister Farrakhan's recent tours to various historically Black colleges and universities he has raised the question around the need for more students to major in agriculture. The chapter concludes by exploring Malcolm X's role in artistic expression as a means to self-empowerment.

In chapter 12, "Dr. Martin Luther King Jr. the Modernist and Minister Malcolm the Postmodernist?: An Analysis of Perspectives and Justice," Kelly Jacobs illustrates how Dr. King's views aligned with modernist thinking and Malcolm X's ideas reflected postmodernist thinking. The chapter discloses how both men made significant contributions to the Black struggle for equality in America. The author points out that both men played a significant role in shaping black identity to the benefit of humanity.

In this volume, we have attempted to begin a conversation with regard to this area of study. There are still many topics to explore: the dynamic interplay of Islam as it relates to the Africana experience, the role of Louis Farrakhan in the dynamic intersectionality of religion on world affairs, and the importance of Clara Muhammad, Tynnetta Muhammad, Nobel Drew Ali, and Imam Warith D. Mohammed—all significant leaders in the formation of Islam in America. It is our hope that this volume will serve as a first step in addressing all of the people, perspectives, and movements that have contribute to Africana Islamic studies.

NOTES

1. Herbert Berg, *Elijah Muhammad and Islam* (New York: NYU Press, 2009), 9.

2. N. Akbar, *Akbar Papers in Black Psychology* (Tallahassee, FL: Mind Production, 2003).

3. Berg, *Elijah Muhammad and Islam,* 100.

4. Ibid., 10.

5. Tynnetta Muhammad, *The Million Man March: Women in Support of the Million Man March.* (Chicago, IL: Final Call, 1995).

6. A. Pitre, *An Introduction to Elijah Muhammad Studies: The New Educational Paradigm.* (Lanham, MD: University Press of America, 2009).

7. Claude Andrew Clegg III, *The Original Man: The Life and Times of Elijah Muhammad* (Chapel Hill: University of North Carolina Press, 2014).

8. A. Haley, and A. Balk, "The Black Merchants of Hate" (1963), http://www.alex-haley.com/alex_haley_black_merchants_of_hate.htm.

9. E. Lincoln, *Black Muslims in the United States* (Ph.D. dissertation, Boston University, 1960), ProQuest Dissertations and Theses database (UMI No. 6003466).

10. Essien U. Essein-Udom, *Black Nationalism: The Search for an Identity* (Chicago: University of Chicago Press, 1962).

11. Berg, *Elijah Muhammad and Islam,* 2.

12. D. Pipes, "How Elijah Muhammad Won." Middle East Forum (2000). www.danielpipes.org/341/how-elijah-muhammad-won, 36.

13. J. A. Banks, *An Introduction to Multicultural Education,* 5th ed. (Boston: Pearson, 2014).

Chapter One

"Raising Her Voice"

Writings by, for, and about Women in Muhammad Speaks *Newspaper, 1961–1975*

Bayyinah S. Jeffries

The ability to effect significant change in a society requires the courage to raise one's voice to advocate for radical reform. The Nation of Islam (NOI) used the *Muhammad Speaks* newspaper to do just this. Under the direction of Elijah Muhammad, the NOI believed in the potential of the Black press; they held that the Black press was the best weapon Black Americans could use to make a blow against the repressive grip of white supremacy.[1]

Since 1827, there have been well over four thousand Black newspapers and magazines published.[2] These included a variety of literary, political, and religious publications such as the *Freedom's Journal*, *The Messenger*, *The Detroit Tribune*, *Crisis Magazine*, *The Chicago Defender*, and the *Pittsburgh Courier,* to name a few.[3] The early Black press helped communicate the plight of and advance the cause of African American people on many fronts, from civil rights to education to political know-how. By the 1940s, the Black newspaper industry had the reach and purpose to significantly impact public viewpoints, particularly concerning race relations within the United States.

Although the Black press routinely represented diverse perspectives, many publications tended to champion one of two dominant worldviews with respect to political and racial matters; one view was conciliatory and, some would argue, placating, while the other was critical and controversial. This dichotomy was most obvious during times of war, and perhaps never more so than during World War II. The war had a tremendous impact on all public media but more so on Black newspapers as the government consistently monitored and scrutinized them for any critical remarks concerning U.S. foreign policy and the state of race relations that could wittingly or unwittingly aid the enemies of those in power.[4] The targeting and censorship of the Black press was brought about by several factors including the growing popularity of communism among a number of African Americans, the prevalence of Black conscientious objectors to the war, and the empathy demonstrated by African Americans for the Japanese being held in detention camps.[5]

Because the Black press was suspected of being used as a platform to spread communist' propaganda within U.S. borders, government officials sought to restrain any publications that appeared too disapproving of the United States and its policies. Newspapers that covered lynching and other Southern horrors were accused of being unpatriotic and working against democracy. White Americans, placed in a precarious situation, fought for the values and ideas of democracy abroad while withholding those same rights from African Americans who were their neighbors and battled beside them. Historically outspoken editors of newspapers received enormous pressure to curtail their messages; and many capitulated out of fear of being labeled communists, communist supporters, or simply un-American. Some editors even went so far as to eliminate any negative coverage of the U.S. government. Yet, despite these pressures of censorship, a few Black newspapers and publishers remained steadfast in their criticisms of the government; and their writings poignantly held it accountable for failing to "[fulfill the] promise[s] made during World War I and World War II to end the oppression of its Black citizens" who had fought alongside whites to make "the world safe for democracy" for everyone.[6]

These acts of defiance in the face of political pressure and censorship placed these publications in the small yet persistent activist-journalist tradition here in the United States. One of the most uncompromising publications during the post–World War II period was *Muhammad Speaks*. The newspaper provided a forum for both trained and untrained writers to contribute to the wider dialogue concerning the Black liberation struggle. Most interestingly—and in stark contrast to their white counterparts and smaller activist-journalist community—*Muhammad Speaks* offered a stage for a great many African American Muslim women to have their say.

This chapter critically examines the contributions of African American Muslim women to the NOI and the larger media stage.[7] It explores the largely unacknowledged philosophical perspectives and sociopolitical ideas embraced and espoused by African American Muslim women as they navigated the NOI during the civil rights–Black Power era. The findings presented here reveal that these women were not "silent and passive bystanders."[8] Instead we see in their contributions to *Muhammad Speaks* how they made their voices heard by critically raising and responding to topics and issues most significant to them at home and abroad.[9]

This chapter is comprised of three segments. The first section provides a brief overview of the history and goals of the NOI's newspapers and the sociopolitical milieu in which women "raised their voices."[10] The second section explores the selection of broader themes that NOI women commonly engaged in their writings. And the third section explores how *Muhammad Speaks* provided women with a platform to participate in the dialogue concerning the local and global Black liberation agenda.

ORIGINS AND BACKGROUND
OF THE NATION OF ISLAM NEWSPAPERS

In 1934, the NOI created and distributed its first publication, titled *Final Call to Islam*. Though it did not enjoy a long run, over the years there would be several other attempts to get the Nation's message out. In the 1950s, the Nation's message was disseminated through other Black newspapers such as the *Pittsburgh Courier* and *Los Angeles Herald Dispatch*. There were also several local attempts at publishing newspapers to extend the message and increase membership in the Nation, such as *Mr. Muhammad Speaks* in Harlem, New York, and *Salaam* in Philadelphia. These early attempts helped the Nation to gain a foothold in the consciousness of African American people by publicly establishing its goals and agenda: to spread the socioreligious message of Elijah Muhammad to a larger audience (domestically and internationally); to provide a written record of the atrocities and crimes of whites in America; to help immortalize the community life and accomplishments of the NOI; and as part of a larger economic plan to maintain ownership and operation of all industries (including the press) within the community.[11]

In 1960, Elijah Muhammad appointed Dan Burley, former editor of both the *Chicago Defender* and the *Chicago Crusader*, to produce and edit a national publication for the NOI.[12] Although not a member of the Nation, Burley was a supporter of the group, its message, and its reform efforts.[13] The year 1961 marked the debut of *Muhammad Speaks* as a nationally, and eventually internationally, distributed paper, and women were determined to participate in its production.[14] While there were no women appointed as editor of the monthly newspaper from 1960 to 1975, a solid team of male and female journalists made the paper one of the most popular publications of the 1960s and 1970s, having a circulation of over five hundred thousand.[15]

Once *Muhammad Speaks* began, the Nation mandated men and encouraged women to get the paper, and therefore the message, out to the masses of Black people. The instructions given to women concerning the paper indicates just how important every member was to the Nation's growth:

> Sister when you take it upon yourself to help the brothers sell this paper, *Muhammad Speaks*, you're helping to resurrect the dead bones, the dry bones that

Ezekiel spoke about in the valley. So get behind your newspaper sister and remember it bears the name of God, and contains that which our people are so vitally in need of. You are actually carrying the word of God. When you help sell this paper you are bearing witness there is no God but Allah and the HONORABLE ELIJAH MUHAMMAD is his last and greatest Apostle.[16]

During its first few years, *Muhammad Speaks* was referred to by its editors as a "militant monthly dedicated to Justice for the Black Man."[17] After a little more than a year, it began its circulation on a weekly basis, with its motto changed to "Dedicated to Freedom, Justice and Equality for the So-Called Negro." The twenty- to-thirty-page publication covered both national and international news concerning not only NOI activities but also events in the wider community and throughout the African-Asian Diaspora. Both Muslims and non-Muslims, men and women, African Americans and other nonwhite groups, contributed to, were featured in, and purchased the periodical. Contributors to *Muhammad Speaks* covered a number of issues associated with the teachings and programs of Clara and Elijah Muhammad and provided articles about and related to Black history, Black pride, the civil rights movement, police brutality, and international affairs. In addition, the paper included notices for self-determinist initiatives including employment opportunities and promotions for Black businesses and products like "Joe Louis" milk. It also featured model Muslim families and highlighted individual triumphs, including Muslim children who won awards or excelled in school. Interestingly, the paper even provided a platform for disparagers of the movement—letters, editorials, and articles from detractors, particularly people who opposed the Nation's separatist' agenda.

Muhammad Speaks featured images critical to communicating the subtext of the Nation and how they viewed the political scene of the period. Additionally, every issue contained a number of positive and uplifting messages to the wider African American community, such as "We must make jobs for ourselves"; "We Respect and Love Our Women"; "We Must Control Our Neighborhoods"; "Children Must Be Prepared"; "The Black Woman is the Mother of Civilization"; "We Must Have Some Land"; "Know Yourself"; and "We Must Go For Self."[18] These slogans of Black consciousness and nationalist ideology were used to help facilitate the reenvisioning and reeducation of the "mentally dead so-called Negroes." These slogans were again taken up in the late 1960s and 1970s by advocates of Black studies and independent Black schools.[19]

Many of the Nation contributors to *Muhammad Speaks* offered materials meant to provide an analysis of the current social conditions of people of African descent. For instance, in an article titled "We Charge Genocide," the writer quoted Articles II and III adopted by the United Nations on December

9, 1948 for the "Prevention and Punishment of the Crime of Genocide."[20] The reporter accused the Los Angeles Police Department, and by extension the U.S. government, with committing crimes of genocide against Black people by highlighting recent inhumane injustices, with detailed records of offenses, against African Americans. Other article titles included "Starvation Still Stalks Half of World's 3 Billion Population"; "Black Man Not Safe in Civilized U.S."; "Exempt Negroes from Taxes"; and "Will the U.N. Stop Race Murders in South West Africa."[21]

BLACK CONCERNS IN THE ERA OF *MUHAMMAD SPEAKS*

For the greater part of the first half of the twentieth century, the masses of African American people lived under the constant shadow of poverty and despair—the result of centuries of discrimination and oppression. As a community they faced crisis on numerous fronts: health, employment, housing, and education.[22] Across the country, particularly in large cities in the North and Midwest, disease, drug use, unemployment, urban squalor, and crime soared.[23] These issues and controversies proved to be catalysts for a number of articles and editorials written by, for, and about women in *Muhammad Speaks*.

Health

During this period matters related to African American health were coming sharply into focus. One of the most devastating controversies was the Tuskegee syphilis experiment, a study sponsored by the U.S. Public Health Service at the Tuskegee Instituted from 1932 to 1972.[24] This experiment permitted large numbers of Black men infected with syphilis to go untreated even when a cure became available. The "syphilis study is but one stop on a long journey of pernicious medicine involving African Americans that reaches back to experimentation on slaves to eugenics [sterilization] practices in the second half of the last century."[25]

This type of abuse and mistreatment contributed to the growing suspicions embraced by African Americans of the medical field and therefore helped to erect psychological barriers that would prevent many members of the community from taking proper steps in health prevention, care, and maintenance. Tuskegee would prove to be an obstacle to medical reform for decades. As part of their health activism and reform, the NOI refused to include any announcements in *Muhammad Speaks* of products they believed contributed to the downward spiral of the African American community, such as advertisements for pork, cigarettes, liquor, or any other products deemed harmful to

African American health. African American Muslim women, who were front-line reformers in terms of the dietary health of their families, wrote a number of articles that addressed "the kitchen as a medicine cabinet."

Reproductive Rights

The negative impact of the Tuskegee experiment did not confine itself to generic health matters. Soon family planning issues, namely medically induced contraception, were implicated, and the distrust of the medical profession heightened even more as a seemingly targeted effort to limit the birth rates of African American women emerged. Indeed, Planned Parenthood efforts were generally directed toward poor Blacks.[26] Viewed as an assault on the Black family, and thus the future of the Black race, the idea of the threat of genocide by birth control was considered in a number of publications during the civil rights and Black consciousness period. This sentiment was highlighted throughout *Muhammad Speaks* and elsewhere, such as the 1969 essay by Toni Cade Bambara called "The Pill: Genocide or Liberation?," which considers the rift between men and women over the underlying function of birth control in the Black liberation movement.[27] Bambara addresses the means and methods of Black genocide by way of reproductive repression. Birth control was positioned in opposition to self-determination by Black people as a group and was often seen as a limitation on "Black sexual autonomy."[28] For Muslim women in the Nation this was a particularly alarming issue, as it signified a coordinated effort by the white establishment to curb the growth and proliferation of Black families, which was anathema to a community working hard to strengthen and develop itself.

Education

After the 1954 Supreme Court ruling in *Brown vs. the Board of Education*, educational opportunities for Blacks appeared to worsen. The bussing of African American children to majority-white schools, which was initiated in an effort to speed the process of integration, presented significant problems for African American children, their families, and communities.[29] Issues included a curriculum that was unabashedly biased and racist, the dramatic decline of African American teachers and administrators being hired by school boards, and the alienation and attacks by hostile white students.[30]

The sheer depth and breadth of the issues affecting the African American community during this era was substantial, often disproportionately affecting African American women. NOI women discussed and debated their sociopolitical concerns loudly and confidently and added their voices to the chorus of those engaged in the dialogue that rang across the Black Diaspora in terms of liberated education.

World Affairs

A fourth area of concern during this time period was international affairs. Nation policy strongly encouraged NOI women to "keep an interest in politics and world affairs."[31] Although the decolonization of Africa began after World War II, white economic domination of the world remained a reality. As a result, the 1960s and early 1970s was a critical time in Black history not only in the United States but throughout the Black Diaspora. As an organization looking for powerful alliances outside of the borders of the United States, the NOI dispatched delegations and *Muhammad Speaks* reporters to extend well wishes and plant the seed of the possibility for future global partnerships with newly independent countries and their leaders. Likewise, the NOI attempted to build possible global bridges to enhance their socioeconomic ambitions with other nations. While men were the editors of the paper, numerous women were correspondents and reporters reporting on domestic and international affairs. Three of the more prominent writers in terms of the international discourse were Tynnetta Deanar, Harriett Muhammad, and Bayyinah Sharieff. The global Black consciousness movement toward self-determination helped to further legitimize and popularize Clara and Elijah Muhammad's community as maintainers of that legacy within the United States. Their self-determinist economic and educational success played a role in helping to build worldwide relationships while producing a small international following.[32]

WOMEN AT *MUHAMMAD SPEAKS*

The Nation's publication, *Muhammad Speaks*, served as a major driver of the discourse concerning how Black people would confront the issues involving Black people with solutions generated and enacted by Black people. As engaged members of the Nation and frontline drivers of this journalistic enterprise, women contributed to the newspaper from its inception; "each . . . became both a journalist and . . . activist, using her position to advocate . . . for her race, for her sisters, and for humankind."[33] The newspaper functioned as a platform that made Nation women most visible to the wider African American community and documented their participation in the global struggle for liberation.

Although numerous women played a part in the newspaper throughout its history, only a few consistently wrote over a significant period of time, such as Bayyinah Sharieff and Harriett Muhammad. Several columns and types of features were regularly written by women, such as "Women in Islam," "Muslim Women in History," "News & Notes About Women," "News Briefs From

Around the World," "For and About You," "Portrait of A Professional," "Natural Beauty," "Let The Buyer Beware," "What the Muslims Want and Believe," and "What Islam Has Done for Me."[34] Subjects explored by NOI women were extremely diverse, ranging from "pearls to pampers," local to international, and cooking to safety. In many ways, they took a holistic approach to the issues facing African Americans in both the public and private sphere.

Most of the women who wrote for *Muhammad Speaks* were not formally trained as journalists. However, they became part of a long tradition of African American women journalists active in the U.S. These included Ida B. Wells-Barnett, editor and writer for the *Free Speech* and later the *New York Age*; Maria Stewart, who wrote for the *Liberator*; Josephine St. Pierre Ruffin, founder of the publication the *Women's Era*; Amy Jacques Garvey who wrote for the *Negro World*, the mouthpiece for the Universal Negro Improvement Association (UNIA); and countless others.[35] Women who wrote for *Muhammad Speaks* shared a "community first" worldview and focused on issues they felt to be a priority to secure social justice—especially the development of the sociopolitical and economic success of Black people through unity, self-determination, and collective work.[36] The following sections look at the themes written by (and for) women most consistently: identity, education, health and home, Black history, religion, and international affairs. Though men also wrote on many of these issues as well, it was the women who primarily addressed these core-value areas.

"Love the Skin You're In": Black Women and Issues of Identity

Black identity was extremely significant and one of the most recurrent themes in *Muhammad Speaks* newspaper. African American Muslims sought to carve out their own distinct personality to present to the wider Black world. While white women had historically been the standard model of beauty in the United States, and one many African American women aspired to accept, NOI women placed themselves in active opposition to these normative ideas of womanhood and attractiveness. Essentially, Nation women discarded normative white standards of beauty and sought instead to elevate the natural beauty of African American women. They attempted to push beneath the physical and attach character, dress, moral fortitude, and intellectual astuteness to the conceptualization of beauty. Learning to "love the skin you're in" was one of the most important aspects of being a NOI woman. For some African American women entering the Nation, it was very difficult to cover their hair, limit their makeup, wear long attire, and conform to a beauty that required inner strength rather than outward markers of attractiveness.[37] The shift toward natural Black beauty was extremely challenging because African

American women had been surrounded by a dominant culture that put their beauty continuously in question.

Because of these concerns, both women and men at *Muhammad Speaks* targeted the issue of Black consciousness as it relates to conventions of physical appearance, dress, intelligence, and the like. For instance, an article titled "Are Fashion and Beauty the Same? Fashion is Seasonal but Beauty is Eternal," the author asserts:

> It would seem that the desire of most women is to be admired for her beauty. So we see the result in the indiscriminate dash for fashion. . . . [Yet] all Black women were endowed with the basic material for a true beauty. A mind, heart, and body already fashioned by the Perfect Creator. We have only to develop them to their fullest beauty. . . . Not distort or disregard them so much that they change seasonally with Paris. You may argue that the mind does not enter into it, but it certainly does. . . . You do not need fashion. . . . You as a Black woman need only a few basic rules to be beautiful . . . cleanliness internally and externally at all times for cleanliness is next to Godliness. Modesty is a woman's most valuable asset. It makes her far more noticeable and interesting then [sic] does the frequently almost naked fashion we see in the streets daily. Last, but not least, naturalness.[38]

The writer of this editorial suggests that African American Muslim women, like other women, are and remain preoccupied with image and matters of self-esteem. This was not a new fixation. African American women had long struggled with the pressures of living in a white dominant culture. Some scholars have pointed out the legacy of Madam C. J. Walker, a beautician and entrepreneur who became the first female self-made millionaire in the United States. She developed a product line and beauty school focused on African American women's grooming.[39] However, some scholars have argued that it was her company that pressured African American women to adopt white standards of beauty.[40] Black culture responded with the "Black Is Beautiful" movement of the 1960s. But even before then, NOI women were resocialized and came to understand and embrace their natural beauty and by extension their identity, which encompassed the physical, mental, and spiritual, moving them ideologically away from the normative white models of beauty that privileged and elevated the physical.[41] Although Madam Walker's products and methods may be critiqued as supporting white standards of beauty in some ways, in other ways she was very much aligned with the philosophy of Nation women. Walker argued that "to be beautiful . . . does not refer alone to the arrangement of the hair, the perfection of the complexion or to the beauty of the form. . . . To be beautiful, one must combine these qualities with a beautiful mind and soul; a beautiful character."[42] Throughout their writings, NOI women attempted to promote the sentiments offered here by Walker while simultaneously responding to the overwhelming and persistent stereotypical images of Black females as unattractive, unfeminine, aggressive, lazy—in other words, unworthy of womanhood.[43]

By rejecting the taxonomy of white normative modes of beauty, Nation women created their own Black identity and ideas of attractiveness emphasizing character and skill. Their responses took the form of writings geared toward influencing other women's perceptions about image and self-esteem as illustrated in dress, behavior, and mindset. Featured titles of formal writings and poetry that enforced this theme included "For Blackwoman Beauty is a Standard"; "The Muslim Woman is Model Personality"; "The Beauty of Being Black"; "Through Islam Confidence Replaces Her Uncertainty"; "Black Beauty"; and "Black Woman Most Beautiful Woman in the World."[44] These writers understand that while the issue of beauty may seem inconsequential, "when considered in light of constant white supremacist assaults on notions of black beauty, it is of profound significance."[45]

It appears that almost every issue of *Muhammad Speaks* from 1961 to 1965 included an ongoing column titled "Natural Beauties or Natural Beauty." This column attempted to reinforce and promote positive self-images of African American women. The writers of "natural beauty," although unknown, identify both non-Muslim and Muslim women who readers believed fit the concept of a natural beauty as prescribed by the NOI. One caption reads, "The beauty of the Black woman is the standard of the world. Women, the world over desire to copy the beauty of the Black woman. . . . The Black woman puts herself in a lower state when she continues to copy after the White man who greatly resents her God-given beauty."[46]

The beauty of the African American woman has been scrutinized for centuries, and the overwhelming responses offered by both Nation women and men demonstrate that during this period of black consciousness, from 1965 to 1975, the theme still resonated with readers. In addition, editorials that focused on character as related to beauty reflected Nation women's desire to create their own ideas of beauty interwoven with Islamic mandates of modesty, whereby clothing became not only a political statement but also an outward illustration of a prideful identity. Muslim women exclaimed, "Unity in dress meant unity in mind."[47] Although Elijah Muhammad mandated that the length of the dress must come well pass the knee, it was NOI women who created their own uniforms, which included various colors and styles.[48] Nation women referred to their attire as "our divine garments" and, unlike historian Ula Yvette Taylor, who describes their uniforms as confining, Nation women declared that their dress was "designed for a queen who must be able to sit high on her throne and also prepared to go to battle for her Nation."[49] The diverse attire inspired by Nation women aided them in their ability to create new fashions and ideas of attractiveness and to make reality what Madam C. J. Walker articulated, that beauty was more than the physical; it encompassed the character and spiritual growth of the individual of which their dress attempted to communicate.

"Education or Indoctrination": Black Women on Education

The NOI was a pioneer in terms of Muslim education for Black children but also in terms of providing a different narrative of U.S. race relations to Black children. As early as the mid-1930s NOI adherents had fought for the minds of their children by illegally pulling them out of public schools and providing their own educational institutions unsanctioned by the white establishment.[50] By the 1960s and 1970s the NOI had become an alternative to both white majority–run public and Catholic schools.

The period of Black educational consciousness, from 1965 to 1975, was a turning point in the education of African American children. In the mid-1970s, in the name of integration, African American children were removed from the safe and nurturing environments of their local neighborhood schools with teachers and staff who looked like them. They were transferred to new schools with a majority of white teachers and students who were often times hostile to them. In these newly integrated schools, administrators implemented rigorous "tracking" systems of African American children and other tactics to undermine desegregation efforts.[51] To critique traditional education and the growing educational inequities and as a method of educational activism, NOI members—particularly women like Audrey 3X, Claretha X, Christine Muhammad, Tynnetta Deanar, and Harriet Muhammad, to name a few—began to write about education in *Muhammad Speaks.* They contributed articles such as "What Have You Taught Your Child Today"; "Our Children Among Most Beautiful"; "How Well Do You Know Africa?"; "We Need Our Textbooks"; "University of Islam Graduating Tomorrow's Leaders"; and "Dr. Thomas Patrick Warns Against Television Slavery."[52]

Sister Claretha X, a public school teacher in Fernando, California, addressed the education African American children receive in the white public school system. In her article "Whoever Controls School, Controls Future,"[53] she made a connection between chattel slavery and the current mental condition of African Americans. She argued that African American children "are educated to accept their condition and inferior status and therefore do not desire to do anything for themselves but instead desire to labor for the benefit of their oppressor." Because of her experiences working within the white public school system, Sister Claretha maintained that there is a great need for Black people to invest in the education of their children because without their involvement their children will continue to be indoctrinated into a sense of inferiority. She believed that Elijah Muhammad's University of Islam—a network of private schools established by the NOI—is the "only place where Black children could get a thorough knowledge of themselves." Moreover, she argued, "If your friend controls your education, your friend controls your future. If your enemy controls your education, your enemy controls your future. If YOU control your education, YOU control your future."[54]

Sister Christine was another frequent writer on education. Trained as a public school teacher, she was a regular contributor to *Muhammad Speaks* as well as director and principal at the University of Islam in Chicago, Sister Christine published the first formal textbook for the University of Islam, titled *Muhammad's Children: A First Grade Reader.*[55] This reader was extensive and included readings from and about Carter G. Woodson, W. E. B. DuBois, J. A. Rodgers, and distinguished Blacks within the United States and abroad. The textbook also covered a range of relevant topics, including "How Africans Came to America," intra-Black relations, a biography of Alexander Pushkin, and the history of the University of Islam—much of which would most likely be considered above the grasp of a typical five- or six-year-old even today. She also penned the poignant essay "We Need Our Textbooks," in which she exposed the continued inclusion of historical fabrications in public school textbooks.[56] She maintained that the narrow and one-sided white history that impressionable children continued to receive had harmful and long-term consequences. As a result, Sister Christine argues, "there is a need for textbooks written by and about Black people."[57] Some of her other works included "Education of Relief Clients: Why Is Chicago Afraid?"; "Self Help or Oblivion for the Negro"; and "Islam School's Expanding Role: Announcing New Adults' Program."

Christine Muhammad advocated not only the creation of textbooks but also adult education and the teaching of Black history to all Black children. She explained the importance of these measures:

The social sciences and history books used in our schools are "primers in white supremacy," and the longer the child continues in school the more his mind is patterned after his slavemaster, and by the time he completes training for his bachelor's or master's or Ph.D. degrees, he is a complete replica of his master and has no desire or incentive to change. Therefore, if we are to ever break away from our masters and the spell they've cast upon us, we must act now and start teaching our pre-school and early school age children ourselves. Let them see black, brown, cream and yellow faces when they open their books. Let them become accustomed early in life to the ideas, that he has something to strive for. Let them realize early that they have a history with meaning, and not a meaningless, nebulous something about "Negro history and how much progress we have made since slavery." Tell them, with conviction and assurances on your part, about their history "all the way back to Africa, when the white man lived in caves and was a savage," then we won't have to waste time trying to re-educate fools with degrees.[58]

Sister Velma X composed the article "Education or Indoctrination." In her critique she urged parents to take a more active role in their children's education by helping them understand that everything they read and learn in school, particularly for those unable to attend a Muhammad's University of Islam, should be rigorously questioned, as should their teachers when those teachers continue to misconstrue information, specifically history. She writes, "parents must take the time at home to separate the lies from the truth. . . . We must qualify ourselves to help our children by gaining a knowledge of ourselves. . . . We must take an active part in the affairs of our children, and the schools which they attend."[59]

Many other NOI women wrote on education. Sister Audrey Ali wrote an important article regarding children and education. In "Our Children Among Most Beautiful," Ali maintained, "what child can be beautiful if he or she has no respect for his parents, friends, or other people's property."[60] She goes on: "train and show your children from the beginning . . . early training molds them into fine men and women. . . . A young mind is the most receptive to learning."[61] Sister Harriett Muhammad, based in Los Angeles, California, wrote the editorial and advice column called "For and About You." The feature highlighted national and international news and provided both men and women with advice on education, relationships, marriage, the rapport between Africans and African Americans, parenting, laws regarding desertion, and child custody rights. She also added to the education debate with "Children Now, Black Self-Determination Committee Brings African History to L.A. Schools."[62]

The critique of educational indoctrination offered by NOI women outlined here remained a lynchpin for Nation's educational philosophy, which asserts:

> There is, and has been, in America a national conspiracy to indoctrinate our children with "white supremacy" propaganda. This conspiracy operates quite openly; it is condoned by most parent organizations, officially approved by school boards and subsidized by Federal, state and local governments. It reaches every school child in the country with its insidious "white supremacist" literature. I refer to the textbook used in our schools for our children.[63]

Yet, in spite of the preconditioning of not only African American children but also many of their parents, countless women, like Harriett and Christine Muhammad, raised their voices about the education of African American children and the vigilance parents must have in order to counter any destructive information imparted to African American children. Nation women maintained that education was a critical site for resistance, and they used it as a vehicle of activism to help foster a strong, Black, conscious Nation.

The "Most Powerful Unit in Islam": Black Women on Health and Home

The Nation community saw health and home as interconnected as there were particular physical illnesses associated with Black life. The NOI laid out a program to combat these disorders by instructing followers "how to eat to live." Diet played a vital role in maintaining healthy families, and Nation members believed a combination of the right foods prepared in the correct manner prevented severe illnesses that plagued the African American community such as cancer, diabetes, and high blood pressure.[64] *Muhammad Speaks* had several regular columns that addressed health awareness: "Science and Medicine," "The Kitchen Is Our Medicine Cabinet," "Let The Buyer Beware," and "Muslim Cookbook." In these columns, the journalists discussed diverse topics related to African American health such as "Death from Heart Disease Drops among Females"; "What Is Bronchitis?"; "All about Stomach Ulcers"; "We Need Medical Plan to Aid Poor"; "Poor Diets in Mothers Bring Children Trouble"; "Negro Cancer Rate High"; "Avoid Accidents in the Bathroom"; "Life Span of Negro Baby Boy in U.S. Some 13 Years Less Than White Girl"; "Fad Diets Can Cause Malnutrition, Scurvy and Death, Physicians Warn"; "How to Fight 'Flu' Viruses"; "Common Cold a Costly Mystery"; and "How Will Power Will Pull Weight Down."[65] In an effort to correlate proper diet with health and wellness Sister Ann 3X posits:

> Is there a cure for arthritis, cancer, high blood pressure, etc.? Which one of these gives you the most trouble? You probably have all three and some others that you are not aware of. What is the CAUSE? There can be only one answer: POOR DIET. Mr. Elijah Muhammad teaches us that the kitchen is out medicine cabinet.[66]

In the sphere of the home, women offered a great deal of helpful suggestions to maintain healthy families. Advice on how to keep the house safe was typically featured under household hints; for example, one column covered which cooking utensils could be harmful when cooking such as aluminum. Women gave healthy cooking tips and recipes in order to improve quality of life and to encourage fitness. The column's target audience was often African American women who not only worked outside of the home but also made time to cook and take care of the family. Home care in general was included in every issue. Editorials included "Handy Shopping Hints Save Time," "Keep New Look in Bath Towels," and "Save Fees On Repairs for Appliance and Packaging."[67] Though the author names were sometimes absent, we may speculate since the Muslim program appointed women as primary maintainers of the home environment that women were doing the research and providing the information around these themes.

Women readers in the NOI were interested in hygiene, proper child care, homemaking, decorating, cleaning hints, budgeting, and food storage and preparation. They saw home building as a lost art and science that needed to be recaptured, recentered, and refined. Nation members claim that women received "scientific training in these areas" during Muslim Girls in Training and General Civilization Class, (M.G.T. and G.C.C.) instruction. By focusing on areas such as how to cook, educate and discipline children, and eliminate hazards in the home, women were trained to provide a safe, clean, and nurturing environment for the entire family.

From the beginning, the family unit was the center of the home-building initiative in the minds of all Nation members. To this end, Sister Tynnetta Denear Muhammad (writing as Sister Tynnetta Denear), a longstanding *Muhammad Speaks* columnist, penned the article "Family Most Powerful Unit in Islam." She wrote:

> In Islam there is no stronger more binding working unit than the family.... The Muslim marriage ... is ... a serious matter in Islam ... it forms the base of the Muslim family. It must be carried out with the utmost sincerity and dedicated efforts of both parties to bring about a successful union."[68]

Nation of Islam women and men believe only the correct training, such as the honing of skills in home building, usually taught in M.G.T and the young men's class, Fruit of Islam (F.O.I), could produce a successful and strong home and family, and by extension well equipped, intelligent, and healthy citizens for the Nation.[69]

While not formally trained in journalism, Tynnetta Deanar became the most common writer of the paper's "Women in Islam" column. Moreover, she contributed to NOI newspapers for well over thirty years, including both *Muhammad Speaks* and the *Final Call*. In her early career, Deanar usually wrote about women's issues in the United States and abroad. For example, she composed the editorials "Dress Should Identify Black Woman" and "Whites Reject Islam, Indian Woman Told."[70] Deanar's editorial titled "Muslim Women in History" traced the history of Muslim women and also highlighted modern Muslim women in an effort to eliminate the thinking that the Muslim woman was backward "when history proved otherwise." Denear argued that her column provided what she called "an intelligent approach to the study of Muslim women."[71] Her other writings in *Muhammad Speaks* included "Invitation to Black Woman," "What Is Cultural Refinement," and "Beauty of Nature Reveals How Black Man Underestimates Self."[72]

These authors saw health and home as integral to maintaining a safe, physically fit, and happy family—a cornerstone of building a strong Nation and one for which women were vital.

"On Common Ground": Black Women and Black History, Religion, and International Affairs

The NOI "places a great emphasis upon black consciousness and racial pride, claiming man cannot know another man until he knows himself."[73] With this in mind, writers at *Muhammad Speaks* also addressed the Black Diaspora and the global Black experience in which NOI women participated, particularly the struggle against white social, economic, educational, and political hegemony. Through their writings, Nation women aided in the establishment of common ground for alliances and coalitions with the wider Black Diaspora. By including their struggles in the paper, sending delegations, correspondence, hosting, and employing members of the global black community, the intersecting dialogues of the specifically NOI women, and people of African descent impacted Black consciousness, identity, and culture on both a national and international level. People of African descent experienced racial oppression through colonialism, chattel slavery, and imperialism; NOI adherents saw this as a point on which to build solidarity. By examining these intraracial dialogues from the perspective of self-determination, the NOI was very much in step with Asian and African countries attempting to secure economic, political, educational, and social autonomy during the 1960s and 1970s.

The global movement toward Black self-determination, of which the Nation was arguably a pioneer in the post–World War II era of Black consciousness, was in some ways oppositional to the discourse of integration. For example, while many integrationist groups were focused almost solely on carving out a space for African American people within established white enclaves, NOI correspondents strongly encouraged the building of institutions *by* and *for* people of African descent. They wrote strident articles about colonialism and white imperialism that celebrated the independence of their Diaspora brethren by asserting, "no longer does the African here 'praise the wise rule' of England; if anything at all, he wants the British out from his homeland, and to keep them out," a sentiment the Nation embraced and desired for their own community.[74]

During this heightened period of Black consciousness, global Black leaders, like the Nation, began to unmask and openly attack white colonialism, imperialism, and hegemony.[75] Black consciousness and self-determination became common ground on which to stand in order to solicit Black Diaspora support and coalitions. The NOI sought to draw on these loosely defined and informal partnerships, especially from the Muslim world. According to C.

Eric Lincoln in his groundbreaking work *The Black Muslims in America*, as of 1961, "there were scarcely 33,000 Moslems in North America, compared with 345,000 in South America, 12½ million in Europe and more than 400 million in Africa and Asia."[76]

It is within this broader community that the Nation actively attempted to align itself. The Nation was rumored to have the support of the United Arab Republic, which extended invitations to NOI Muslims to visit Egypt under the leadership of President Gamal Abdel Nasser.[77] Moreover, Elijah Muhammad was alleged to have had Japanese support during the early days of the Nation in the late 1930s and 1940s.[78] Likewise, a number of teachers and other individuals from abroad were associated with the Nation including Sheikh Diab of Palestine, Abdul Basit Naeem of Pakistan, Theodore Rozier of Haiti, Professor Ali Baghdadi of Egypt, and many others.[79] Abdul Basit Naeem's writings drew correlations between the work of the NOI and what he observed as the "ultimate solution to the world's cumbersome, persistent and perplexing problems." He goes on to describe the Muslim program under the Nation as "the panacea for all ills afflicting humanity."[80] C. Eric Lincoln argued that "The Muslim leader [Elijah Muhammad] . . . had powerful friends abroad to sponsor and receive him, and this extended to his followers."[81] Muhammad Ali, world heavyweight champion and Nation adherent, also helped to expand the Nation's popularity within international Muslim and non-Muslim communities. At the Savior's Day address of 1975, Professor Ali Baghdadi announced to the Nation adherents:

> The Nation of Islam is connected to 600 million Muslims in the East. Elijah Muhammad touched many lives. His loss was felt in the Middle East and their hearts are with the faithful followers of the Honorable Elijah Muhammad. The success of Islam was carried by him. We are one Body and all the body feels pain and reacts. We love you because you love Islam. You have become the Freedom Fighters of Islam—Soldiers of Allah. Muhammad Ali stood in that ring and put Islam on the map internationally.[82]

When it comes to the Diasporic relations between Black Americans and the rest of the nonwhite world, Black Muslims in America posits that

> Islam recognize[s] complete equality of Brotherhood; a Muslim is truly the brother of another Believer, regardless of how black the skin or how kinked the hair. He is welcomed with sincere and open arms and recognized by his light-skinned or copper-colored Arab brother. He is also recognized in the same way by his brown or yellow-skinned Japanese, Chinese, and Indian brothers.[83]

The NOI used its Islamic platform of "freedom, justice and equality" for all Black people to help build coalitions with Jamaica, Egypt, Bermuda, Peru

and the like. In 1974, Charles 67X and Alonzo 4X report on the NOI delegation visit to Jamaica, writing,

> More than 200,000 Jamaicans lined the streets of Kingston as a 20 car motor-
> cade twisted through the capital city to an official welcoming ceremony at the
> government's National Arena. During the ceremony Prime Minister Manley
> lavishly praised the works of Mr. Muhammad, [stating] "The Honorable Elijah
> Muhammad leads one of the most remarkable movements in the world." . . . We
> are proud of his work. And you let him know that this prime minister of this
> proud country would be very honored to welcome him as our guest at any time.[84]

In 1956 and 1957, the NOI was featured in the international magazine *The
Moslem World and the U.S.A.,* edited by Abdul Basit Naeem. By 1975, the
Nation had adherents, sympathizers, and supporters in Bermuda, China, England, Egypt, British Honduras, and Japan; and Nation delegations had been
sent all over the world extending the greeting from Muhammad in an effort
to build international alliances.[85] Subsequently, a more critical assessment of
the relationship between the NOI and other nonwhite nations is important to
explore. The NOI saw the struggle of the Black man in America inextricably
tied to the fate of all nonwhite people, particularly Muslims, in the rest of the
world.

Throughout this apex of black consciousness, members of the Nation had
strong interests in African affairs and were greatly concerned with the political climate of various African and Asian countries. In the 1940s, the NOI was
designated as a pro-Japanese sect by government enforcement agencies.[86] In
the 1950s, Elijah Muhammad sent two of his children in addition to other Muhammad University of Islam students to study Arabic in Cairo, Egypt, thus
paving the way for a coalition with a critical Muslim regime under President
Abdel Nasser. In the 1960s, the NOI sent a delegation to Ghana following
its independence. The extent of the relationships between the NOI and newly
Black liberated societies is unclear, but what is certain is they both shared the
same objective concerning the elimination of European American sociopolitical and economic imperialism.

In this atmosphere of joint struggle with other Black and Muslim communities worldwide, NOI writers reached out to cover world events in their
publications. Clara Muhammad traveled abroad in the late 1960s to Egypt.
Bayyinah Sharieff, an African American columnist for *Muhammad Speaks*,
wrote about her experiences in Sudan for over three years under the editorial title "Life in the Sudan." And Harriett Muhammad traveled abroad and
interviewed people from all over the world for her column "For and About
You." Nation literature is replete with references to Africa and other parts of
the Afro-Asian world, particularly Egypt, Ghana, Sudan, and Tanzania.

Although their messages at times seemed mixed, for the most part it appears Nation women respected, admired, and felt a connection with women of African descent throughout the African-Asian Diaspora. For instance, in the article titled "Afro-Asian Women in UN," the author discusses women in the United Nations and maintains that although these "Asiatic" women were from a variety of countries, they did not allow language, customs, or other obstacles to get in the way of working together for a similar cause—the eradication of discrimination and oppression. The author also acknowledges several African women from Nigeria and Niger for their work and contributions in the United Nations on behalf of all Black women. In the July 1962 article, the journalist champions the first woman, Ella Koble Gulama, to hold a cabinet post in Sierra Leone.[87] In the August 31, 1966, issue of "Women's News and Notes," the author discusses the rising support of women by male leaders in Egypt, chiefly as a result of President Abdel Nasser. The president, the critic argued, opposed the more conservative views of his contemporaries regarding women's public roles. The author contended that Nasser was supportive of Egyptian women's rights and encouraged women to become more active in social and political activities. In the remainder of the text, the writer discusses women's newly politicized views and their increased organizing efforts, perhaps taking cue from Nation women.[88]

An editorial titled "Women of Africa in America" in "Notes and News about Women," discussed women in New Guinea, calling attention to the growing public roles of women in Africa. According to the writer, Guinea, a former French colony, was one of the "fastest-advancing nations in the world" and had raised the educational and health standards for all it citizens, especially women.[89] In "Women of Africa in U.S. Part II," published in April 1964, the writer notes the works and achievements of various women in African countries, as well as their UN efforts to end racial discrimination throughout the world. The author acknowledges Judith Imru of Ethiopia and Florence W. Addison of Ghana for their "sympathy and encouragement to their Negro brothers and sisters who are struggling in America for freedom, justice and equal opportunities."[90]

The attention to international affairs was evident in many other articles that were either written by or about women. These include "Tanganyikan Students Speak of Women in Zanzibar"; "16 Nigerian Women in U.S."; "First Women Officers in Sierra Leone Army"; "Portrait of A Crusader: Highest Ranking Woman in Egypt, Dr. Hekmat Abou Zeid"; "Women: Africa's Unsung Heroes"; "Men of Africa Pledge Aid in Negro's Fight for Freedom"; "Women Fighters in Asia"; and "Women in Africa Seek Closer Ties With Sisters in America."[91] In this last article, author Harriett Muhammad's attitude is representative of Nation women's writings about Africa in general, and the Black world in particular, when she writes:

> The increasing empathy, and understanding between Africans and Afro-Americans is one of the emerging political factors which the West now must contend with. The artificial separation which existed between Negroes and their African brothers maintained by divisive White supremacy, is now being swept aside by the obvious respect both have for the struggles for freedom being waged by the other.[92]

CONCLUSION

From 1961 to 1975 *Muhammad Speaks* addressed many issues of concern to women and featured many prolific women writers in its pages. But the role of women in the newspaper evolved. In the early years of its publication women wrote about a variety of topics, from traditional subjects like home and family to international topics like the Black Diaspora. However, in the later 1970s this began to change. Nation women's commentary began to appear only in a few sections of the paper, chiefly in the column "Women in Islam." There were also more writings under this heading directed toward the topic of femininity.

Several factors may have contributed to this apparent shift. From a cultural point of view, it may be that the newspaper editors deemphasized the role of women in their publications in response to the growing women's movement of the 1970s, so as not to appear to be aligned with the movement. Also, the community was beginning its shift toward a more orthodox Islam, which pushes Muslim women from visibility to invisibility in the public arena. From an evidentiary point of view, it's also worth noting that a significant number of the NOI newspapers from this period were not archived and are thus no longer available for study. So the count of articles by and about women is based on a reduced number of samples, which makes determining any shift in emphasis difficult. Second, many of the articles were published without bylines, making it hard to determine just how many were penned by women.

Despite a somewhat reduced profile starting in the late 1970s, it is clear that both Muslim men *and* women traveled abroad as successful models of what Muslims in America had accomplished even under the burden of social, intellectual, economic, and religious oppression. Their growing international popularity was made possible by not only Clara and Elijah Muhammad's message and economic success but also ministers like Louis Farrakhan, Malcolm X, and Muhammad Ali. Muhammad Ali became an international giant in the 1960s assisting with the promulgation of Islam. Ali's popularity helped build the alliances the NOI wanted to develop with leaders of the nonwhite world in addition to small delegations and the utilization of *Muhammad Speaks* newspaper. The publication was successful at parading the success of the Nation's education and economic programs. Women as contributors to the newspaper also assisted with solidifying sought-after alliances. Black women provided information on their synopsis of what was occurring in the world concerning people of African descent and helped correlate the work of the NOI with other nonwhite nations in the rush for self-determination.

The writings by Nation women undoubtedly help enrich our understanding of the NOI community and the significance of women within it. They offer some critical insight into how women thought about the issues they believed hampered the African American community during the civil rights and Black Power era. Their writings discussed not only traditional subject but international affairs, covering news in places like Ghana, South Africa, Nigeria, Sudan, Egypt, and the wider Black world. Given the political environment of the 1960s and 1970s, *Muhammad Speaks* stood out from other Black publications because of its nonconformity, outspokenness, and political aims.[93] *Muhammad Speaks* was perhaps the most successful Black newspaper in the post–World War II era, providing women of all socioeconomic and educational backgrounds with the opportunity to raise their voices for the cause of Black liberation at home and abroad.

From 1961 to the 1970s the issues that plagued the African American community—health, police brutality, white supremacy, disparities in education, and international affairs—remained center stage and fundamental to the writing of Nation women. Through their prose, Nation women established common ground for alliances and coalitions with the wider Black Diaspora (i.e., the elimination of white hegemony and the advancement of Black self-determination). By engaging in these dialogues, Nation women were able to perhaps impact black consciousness, identity, and culture on both a national and international level. By examining these intraracial dialogues from the perspective of self-determination, we have observed the NOI women being serious contributors to and also very much in step with their Asian and African sisters, attempting to secure economic, political, and social autonomy during the 1960s and 1970s.

NOTES

1. African Americans utilized the press to garner support for their causes: Frederick Douglass in his writing in several publications about the institution of slavery and abolition, Josephine Pierre Ruffin *Women's Era*, and Ida Bill Wells in terms of her antilynching campaign.

2. Charles A. Simmons, *The African American Press, with Special References to Four Special Newspapers, 1827–1965* (Jefferson, NC: McFarland & Company, 1998), 2–3; Armistead Scott Pride, "The Names of Negro Newspapers," *American Speech* 29, no. 2 (May 1954): 118, www.jstor.org/stable/453331 (accessed April 3, 2009).

3. Pride, "Names of Negro Newspapers," 118.

4. Karl Evanzz, *The Messenger: The Rise and Fall of Elijah Muhammad* (New York: Vintage, 2001), 58, 106.

5. Ibid.

6. Simmons, *African American Press*, 81.

7. There are no full manuscripts published that definitively address the contributions of women to the NOI. There is one article written in the *Final Call* by Askia Muhammad that briefly addresses the history and importance of the *Muhammad Speaks* newspaper.

8. Farah Jasmine Griffin, "Ironies of the Saint: Malcolm X, Black Women, and the Price of Protection," in *Sisters in the Struggle: African American Women in the Civil Rights–Black Power Movements*, ed. Betty Collier-Thomas and V. P. Franklin (New York: NYU Press, 2001), 218–19; Sonsyrea Tate, *Little X: Growing up in the Nation of Islam* (Knoxville: Tennessee University Press, 2005), 86.

9. The great majority of scholars who have written about women in the NOI—including Ula Yvette Taylor, "As-Salaam Alaikum, My Sister, Peace be Unto You: The Honorable Elijah Muhammad and the Women Who Followed Him," *Race & Society* 1, no. 2 (1998): 183–84, 187; Andrew Claude Clegg, III, *An Original Man: The Life and Times of Elijah Muhammad* (New York: St. Martin's Press, 1997), 29, 101, and 242; and C. Eric Lincoln, *The Black Muslims in America* (Boston: Beacon Press, 1961), 31 and 55—have only considered Muslim women under the leadership of Elijah Muhammad as it relates to their involvement in the domestic sphere. In addition, they see women's roles as oppressive, one-dimensional, and restrictive compared with their male counterparts. Cynthia S. Thembile's work provides a more expansive way of viewing Nation women, though she too maintains "Black Muslim women were encouraged to stay home." See "Revisiting Female Activism in the 1960s: The Newark Branch Nation of Islam," *The Black Scholar*, 26, no. 3–4 (1996/1997): 41.

10. Rodger Streitmatter, *Raising Her Voice: African-American Women Journalists who Changed History* (Lexington: University Press of Kentucky, 1994), 14.

11. *Muhammad Speaks* newspaper was banned from many countries because it was believed it would cause racial discord where many believed none existed. For one such example see Quinto Swan, *Black Power in Bermuda: The Struggle for Decolonization* (New York: Palgrave Macmillan, 2009), 19.

12. Richard Durham, "another widely respected" journalist, followed Burley as editor of the paper, then John Woodford, who had been a writer for *Ebony Magazine*. After Woodford, came author and professor Leon Forrest, and finally Askia Muhammad who took control in the late 1960s and now writes periodically for the *Final Call.* Askia Muhammad, "*Muhammad Speaks*: A Trailblazer in the Newspaper Industry," *Final Call*, March 10, 2000.

13. A "Special Edition" issue was released under *Mr. Muhammad Speaks* in September 1960. According to Curtis, "although the Nation of Islam owned and distributed their own paper they employed a majority non-Muslim staff in 1960." See Edward E. Curtis IV, *Black Muslim Religion in the Nation of Islam, 1960–1975* (Chapel Hill: University of North Carolina Press, 2006), 191.

14. *Muhammad Speaks*, September 1960.

15. Clifton E. Marsh, *From Black Muslims to Muslims: The Transition from Separatism to Islam, 1930–1980* (Metuchen, NJ: Scarecrow Press, 1984), 62; According to Askia Muhammad, in the *Courier* and the *Crusader* the column was called "Mr. Muhammad Speaks," and in the *Amsterdam News* it was titled "The Islamic World." The *Observer* printed the teachings of Mr. Muhammad in a series called "White Man's Heaven Is Black Man's Hell." Before *Muhammad Speaks*, these newspapers were sold door-to-door and on street corners throughout the country by Nation followers. Askia Muhammad, *Black Muslim Millennium: A Brief History of the Nation of Islam* (Drewryville,VA: Kha Books, 2002), 9–16.

16. Muhammad's Mosque of Islam, "The *Muhammad Speaks* Newspaper," in *M.G.T. & G.C.C.: Your Orientation Brochure.*

17. *Mr. Muhammad Speaks* was the original name of the editorial featured in a number of Black newspapers in the 1950s. It later changed to simply *Muhammad Speaks*. *Muhammad Speaks*, 1961–1963 (front page). Because of the quality of the microform, some page numbers were unidentifiable. Where page numbers were readable, they are included. When available a full date is given. Many of the articles in the publication were unsigned. If an author is listed I provide the name. When no author is listed I give title and date or any information provided.

18. These "plaques" are throughout *Muhammad Speaks*, 1961–1975.

19. Elijah Muhammad, *Message to the Blackman in America* (Newport News, VA: United Brothers Communication Systems, 1965), 39–43.

20. "We Charge Genocide," *Muhammad Speaks*, June 1962; "Pawns in a Pattern That Points toward Genocide," September, 30, 1962, 12; "Northern Leaders Verify Mississippi Genocide against Blacks," July 21, 1967, 4.

21. *Muhammad Speaks*, October 1962, June 1962, July 1962, and September 15, 1962.

22. Thomas J. Sugrue, *The Origins of the Urban Crisis: Race and Inequality in Postwar Detroit* (Princeton, NJ: Princeton University Press, 1996), 25–27, 37–40, 174–75, 211.

23. Ibid.

24. Robert G. Weisbord, "Birth Control and the Black American: A Matter of Genocide," *Demography* 10, no. 4 (1973): 571–90.

25. Michele Goodwin, *Black Markets: The Supply and Demand of Body Parts* (New York: Cambridge University Press, 2006), 28. Jean Heller, "Syphilis Victims in U.S. Study Went Untreated for 40 Years," in *Tuskegee's Truth: Rethinking the Tuskegee Syphilis Study*, ed. Susan M. Reverby (Chapel Hill: University of North Carolina Press, 2000), 116–18.

26. Joyce A. Ladner, *Tomorrow's Tomorrow: The Black Woman* (Garden City, NY: Doubleday & Company, 1971), 254; Jennifer Nelson, *Women of Color and the Reproductive Rights Movement* (New York: NYU Press, 2003), 57–58.

27. Toni Cade, "The Pill: Genocide or Liberation?" in *The Black Woman: An Anthology*, ed. Toni Cade Bambara (New York: Washington Square Press, 1970), 203–12.

28. Weisbord, "Birth Control and the Black American," 572.

29. Roy L. Brooks, *Integration or Separation: A Strategy for Racial Equality* (Cambridge: Harvard University Press, 1996), 30–31; Tom Wicker, *Tragic Failure: Racial Integration in America* (New York: William Morrow, 1996), 93–94 and 124; Martin Schiff, "Community Control of Inner-City Schools and Educational Achievement," *Urban Education* 11, no. 4 (1976): 415–28.

30. For example of backlash from *Brown vs. Board* decision on Black children is most evident in autobiographies from young people involved in the movement. See Melba Patillo Beals, *Warriors Don't Cry: A Searing Memoir to Integrate Little Rock's Central High School* (New York: Pocket Books, 1994), xvii, 1, 22–28; Peter H. Irons, *Jim Crow's Children: The Broken Promise of the Brown Decision* (New York: Penguin Group, 2002), 184–87.

31. Muslim Girls in Training List of "Do's and Don'ts."

32. Swan, *Black Power in Bermuda*, 19–20, 111.

33. Streitmatter, *Raising Her Voice*, 3.

34. *Muhammad Speaks*, 1962–1964.

35. Streitmatter, *Raising Her Voice*, 5–7, 151; Pride, "Names of Negro Newspapers," 114–15; Armstead S. Pride and Clint C. Wilson II, *A History of the Black Press* (Washington, DC: Howard University Press, 1997), 93–95, 173–174.

36. Marcus Garvey made the assertion in the early part of the twentieth century that the agenda of Blacks must begin with Black solidarity or "race first" irrespective of socioeconomic status. See Tony Martin, *Race First: The Ideological and Organizational Struggles of Marcus Garvey and the Universal Negro Improvement Association* (Dover, MA: The Majority Press, 1976), 3.

37. Sister Dela, interview by author, Atlanta, GA, March 2008.

38. "Are Fashion and Beauty the Same?" *Muhammad Speaks*, April 1962, 22.

39. A'Lelia Perry Bundles, *Madam C. J. Walker* (New York: Chelsea House, 1990), 66–67.

40. Donna Franklin, *What's Love Got to Do with it: Understanding and Healing the Rift between Black Men and Women* (New York: Touchstone, 2000), 105.

41. Tynnetta Deanar, "Why No Makeup? Cosmetics Produce Two People in One: Not for Our Women," *Muhammad Speaks*, January 1962, 24. See also Edwin Moss, "Wallace Muhammad Says Women Not Forbidden to Make up," *Mr. Muhammad Speaks*, September 1960.

42. Bundles, *Madam C. J. Walker*, 67.

43. J. Betsch Cole and B. Guy-Sheftall, *Gender Talk: The Struggle for Women's Equality in African American Communities* (New York: Ballantine Books, 2003), 200–1; George E. Cunningham, "Derogatory Images of the Negro and Negro History," *The Negro History Bulletin* 27, no. 6 (1965): 126–42.

44. Tynnetta Deanar, "Muslim Woman Is Model Personality," *Muhammad Speaks*, January 1962; "Beauty of Being Black," *Muhammad Speaks*, July 1962; Sister Mary X McCalm, "Through Islam Confidence Replaces Her Uncertainty," *Muhammad Speaks*, July 1964; Sylvester Leaks, "The Natural Look Is Reborn in Brilliant New

Show Beauty of Negro Womanhood Theme of Naturally '63' Hair Fashion Revue," *Muhammad Speaks*, February 1963.

45. Cole and Guy-Sheftall, *Gender Talk*, 220.

46. "Beauty of a Black Woman," *Muhammad Speaks*, July 1963.

47. *Muhammad University of Islam Yearbook*, 1968, 290.

48. Former NOI members, group interview by author, Philadelphia, PA, January 2008.

49. Taylor, "As-Salaam Alaikum, My Sister, Peace be Unto You," 185, 187; Sister Lt. Deborah 9X, "Our Divine Garment," *M.G.T. Bulletin*, September 1974.

50. Clara Muhammad along with other parents was arrested for contributing to the delinquency of minors. Nation schools, under the network of Muhammad University of Islam, were featured in newspapers as being shut down by government and school officials in Detroit, Chicago, and Washington, DC, for attempting to take control of educating their own children.

51. Andrew Hacker, *Two Nations, Black and White, Separate, Hostile, Unequal* (New York: Scribner, 2003), 191–92.

52. Sister Wilma Ann, "What Have You Taught Your Child Today?" *Muhammad Speaks*, 1962; Audrey 3X, "Our Children among Most Beautiful," *Muhammad Speaks*, April 1962; "How Well do You Know Africa?" *Muhammad Speaks*, July 1962, 16; Sister Christine, "We Need Our Textbooks," *Muhammad Speaks*, April 1962; "University of Islam Graduates Tomorrow Leaders," *Muhammad Speaks*, April 1962, 13; Sister Audrey 3X, "Dr. Thomas Patrick Warns against Television Slavery," *Muhammad Speaks*, February 1962.

53. Sister Claretha, "Graduation Address: Whoever Controls School, Controls Future," *Muhammad Speaks*, April 1962, 12.

54. Ibid.

55. Christine Muhammad, *Muhammad's Children: A First Grade Reader* (Chicago: University of Islam Press, 1963), table of contents, 1–5.

56. Christine Muhammad, "We Need Our Textbooks," *Muhammad Speaks*, April 1962. Also see Stanley Axelrod, "The Treatment of the Negro in American History School Textbooks," *The Negro History Bulletin* 29, no. 6 (1966): 135.

57. David L. Elliott and Arthur Woodward, eds. *Textbooks and Schooling in the United States* (Chicago: The University of Chicago Press, 1990), 44.

58. Elliott and Woodward, *Textbooks and Schooling in the United States*; Sister Christine, "Self Help or Oblivion for the Negro," *Muhammad Speaks*, February 1962.

59. Velma X, "Education or Indoctrination," *Muhammad Speaks*, July 1962, 16.

60. Audrey 3X, "Our Children among Most Beautiful," 24.

61. Ibid.

62. Sister Christine, "Self Help or Oblivion for the Negro," February 1962. "Education of Relief Clients: Why Is Chicago Afraid?" May 1962, 20; "Islam School's Expanding Role: Announcing New Adults' Program," *Muhammad Speaks*, April 1964, 18; Harriett Muhammad, "Children Now, Black Self-Determination Committee Brings African History to L.A. Schools," *Muhammad Speaks*, May 1965.

63. Sister Christine, "Self Help or Oblivion for the Negro."

64. Elijah Muhammad, *How to Eat to Live, Book 1* (Phoenix, AZ: M.E.M.P.S., 1967), 7–9.

65. *Muhammad Speaks*, August 1962; May 1962, 27; June 11, 1964; June 9, 1967; October 1962; July 15, 1962; March 18, 1963; June 1962; September 11, 1964.

66. Ann 3X, "Kitchen is Our Medicine Cabinet," *Muhammad Speaks*, May, 1962.

67. Louis Walker, "Packaging," *Muhammad Speaks*, October, 1962; July 1962.

68. Tynnetta Denear, "Family Most Powerful Unit in Islam," *Muhammad Speaks*, May 1962, 8.

69. Tynnetta Denear, "Women in Islam," *Muhammad Speaks*, February 4, 1963.

70. Denear, "Women in Islam," April 1962, 12; July 1962, 27.

71. Ibid.

72. *Muhammad Speaks*, May 1962, 23.

73. J. Herman Blake, "Black Nationalism," *Annals of the American Academy of Political and Social Science* 382 (1969): 15–25, www.jstor.org/stable/1037110 (accessed December 18, 2007).

74. "Africans Stop Praising Wise Bossism of British Masters!" *Muhammad Speaks*, February 1962, 5.

75. Nation of Islam, *Accomplishments of the Muslims* (1975). Michael Manley praises Elijah Muhammad and NOI for their work. Richard Daley, mayor of Chicago, also praises the work of the Muslims, as do several other state officials throughout the country. President Abdel Nasser and Abdul Basit Naeem all give the NOI praise for their work given the highly racial and violent milieu of the United States.

76. Lincoln, *The Black Muslims in America*, 223.

77. Ibid., 225.

78. Evanzz, *The Messenger*, 130–34; Claude Andrew Clegg, *An Original Man: The Life and Times of Elijah Muhammad* (New York: St. Martin's Press, 1997), 29 and 82.

79. Lincoln, *The Black Muslims in America*, 26; Herbert Berg, *Elijah Muhammad and Islam* (New York: NYU Press, 2009), 107; Brother Lovell, interview by author, Philadelphia, PA, December 2007.

80. Abdul Basit Naeem, "Sees Divine Purpose in the Trials, Humiliation, Suffering of Muslims," *Muhammad Speaks*, July 7, 1967.

81. Lincoln, *The Black Muslims in America*, 226.

82. Ali Bagdadi Savior's Day Address, The Nation of Islam, "Saviour's Day," DVD, February 1975.

83. Elijah Muhammad, *The Supreme Wisdom*, vol. 1 (Atlanta: M.E.M.P.S., 1957), 37.

84. Charles 67X and Alonzo 4X, "Jamaica Government Host Muslim Delegation," *Accomplishment of the Muslims* (1975): 24.

85. "Nation of Islam Mourns Elijah Muhammad," *Ebony Magazine*, March 1975, 79; "Nation Mourns Muslim Leader," *Jet Magazine*, March 13, 1975, 14–15.

86. Evanzz, *The Messenger,* 134–35; Lincoln, *The Black Muslims in America*, 26.

87. "Afro-Asian Women in UN 'Language, Custom Not a Barrier to Understanding One Another,'" *Muhammad Speaks*, December 30, 1962.

88. *Muhammad Speaks*, December 30, 1963; "African Nation Names Woman to Cabinet Post," *Muhammad Speaks*, July 1962; "Nasser's Advocacy of More Freedom for Egypt Women Opposes Old Time," *Muhammad Speaks*, September 15, 1962.

89. "Women of Africa in America," *Muhammad Speaks*, March 27, 1964.

90. "Women of Africa in U.S.—Part II," *Muhammad Speaks*, April 10, 1964.

91. Harriett Muhammad, "Tanganyikan Talks of Fossil Fuels," *Muhammad Speaks*, May 8, 1964; June 19, 1964; August 1965.

92. Harriett Muhammad, "Men of Africa Pledge Aid in Negro's Fight for Freedom," *Muhammad Speaks*, April 24, 1964; *Muhammad Speaks*, May 1964, May 22, 1965, and July 1964.

93. Askia Muhammad, *Black Muslim Millennium*, 8–10.

Chapter Two

Take Two

*Nation of Islam Women
Fifty Years after Civil Rights*

C. S'thembile West

My interest in the experiences of women in the Nation of Islam (NOI) grew out of living in Central Harlem during the formative years of the organization and experiencing its presence in the community. Many of my friends became active in the ranks of the NOI, while others participated in more conservative civil rights organizations like the National Association for the Advancement of Colored People (NAACP) and the Congress for Racial Equality (CORE). A few of my peers and I were active in efforts by the communist party (CP), particularly a galvanization of a critical mass around the candidacies of Angela Davis and Jarvis for vice president in the 1980s. Moreover, breakfast programs initiated by the Young Lords (YL) and the Black Panther Party (BPP) were telling features of Harlem during the activist 1960s. Coming to adulthood in Harlem in the 1960s catapulted many young people, like myself, into grassroots, social/political organizations.

THE PREHISTORY OF THE NATION OF ISLAM IN HARLEM

My own experience growing up in Harlem provides a glimpse at the community culture in which the Nation of Islam flourished in the 1960s and 1970s. Born in a Harlem hospital in the late 1940s, I am the child of a teenage mother and a father who held a blue-collar job. Both second-generation Harlem residents, they were the progeny of struggling, working-class parents. My paternal grandfather's entrepreneurial spirit led to home ownership at the tail end of the Great Depression. He was known for his weekly treks to Hunt's Point market to buy vegetables and fruits that he sold on local streets.

Grandpa's industrious ventures never sullied the respect that he earned and claimed within the family of Harlem's freemasons.

On the other hand, my maternal grandmother worked in domestic service for working-class, Jewish households in the Forest Hills neighborhood of Queens, New York. I often accompanied her to these two- and three-bedroom apartments in brick buildings that line Queens Boulevard. People of color were rarely seen there in 1955. Nevertheless, African Americans broke the boundaries—effects of discrimination and redlining—to homeownership, when they moved into single-family homes in southeast Queens for the first time during the 1950s.

The street that I called home, 138th Street, and the larger Harlem community comprised a nexus of vibrant artistic, educational, and social networks that supported activism. The Harlem of my youth, adolescence, and adulthood generated an eclectic array of lived experiences that interfaced with life-changing political events *up-South*[1] and in the burgeoning civil rights movement of the South. In sum, the community networks, along with the national movements for equity across ethnic and class boundaries, offered a critical foundation for development of activism among youth. Protests, marches, and picketing by young people, even elementary school children, like the adolescents at the progressive, Brooklyn community organization known as *The East*, were the rule rather than the exception within working-class, underemployed enclaves in Harlem.

During the tumultuous 1960s, Harlem provided some of the most momentous and distinctive life-changing features of my existence. The following institutions, all within walking distance of home, became sites for awakenings of *consciousness* as a young, black woman: Countee Cullen Public Library on 136th Street and the Schomburg Center for Research in Black Culture on 135th Street, both just west of Lenox Avenue; the New Lafayette Theatre on the southeast corner of 138th Street and Seventh Avenue (Adam Clayton Powell Boulevard today); and the famed Apollo Theatre on the north side of 125th Street between Seventh and Eighth Avenues (now Malcolm X Boulevard). A ten-minute walk or short bus ride away lay the Nation of Islam's Mosque No. 7 under the leadership of Minister Malcolm X at the southwest corner of Lenox Avenue and 116th Street.

Every Saturday at 3:00 pm, First World lectures—programs offered by a black think tank and community resource that provided a national forum for intellectual and civic empowerment among African Americans—were held at the Church on the Hill, at the northeast corner of 145th Street and Convent Avenue. Technically, the Church on the Hill and its idiosyncratic, canary yellow facade lay in the Hamilton Grange area of the city, but close enough to central Harlem that residents rarely made a distinction. Open only to people of African descent, notable conversations on the hill laid a foundation for mass organization and activism on behalf of black communities nationwide. Drs. Wade Nobles, Frances Cress Welsing, Richard King, Leonard Jeffries, Rosalyn Jeffries, Molefi Kete Asante, Yosef Ben-Jochannan, Marimba Ani, and Malana Karenga were among the eclectic and quite remarkable array of national speakers, whose theories and strategies illuminated the varying contexts of the social conditions of African Americans.

In addition, the plethora of small jazz clubs like Smalls Paradise, two doors from 135th Street, on the west side of Seventh Avenue; Snookie's Sugar Bowl, a local ice cream parlor and sandwich shop; and Wells, the home of chicken and waffles, comprised local watering holes for relaxed but exuberant conversations among community members. The Renaissance Ballroom, which preceded the New Lafayette Theatre (1967), like the famed Savoy Manor Ballroom, served as a home for "happy feet." Although discourse on the civil rights period rarely highlights the impact of entertainment in the dissemination and spread of information or the maintenance of political momentum, these local gathering spots provided ongoing electrical chargers for the protest journey. In the relaxed environment of a club or eatery, one might be ambushed by a local politico. Moreover, you were expected to know the discourse about what was happening in Harlem.

Living in Harlem provided myriad opportunities to learn from others across age, socioeconomic, and gender divides. For example, five-story, brick, walk-up apartment houses dotted the landscape. Roomers—those who clandestinely rented one or two rooms in a four- or five-bedroom apartment from leaseholders independent of management—like my grandmother and mother—abounded. These roomers, who lived in close proximity to blood relatives and strangers alike, acquired an education in the interdependence, people politics, and ongoing support necessary to sustain critical, mass action.

This pervasive sense of community provided an anchor of connectedness in Central Harlem during the sixties and into the seventies. We knew neighbors in ways that twenty-first-century residents often complain about today. Where my family lived from 1955 to 1962—10-12 W. 138th Street—twenty-nine other tenants shared the six-story tenement with five apartments per floor. We played jacks in the tiled hallway, borrowed sugar, flour, and other sundry supplies from our neighbors.

One day, when my brother and I argued about whose turn it was to lock the sixth-floor apartment door, heroin addicts, who lived on the landing that led to the tarred roof, scolded us: "You know you'd better lock that door." Although I defiantly ran down the steps, my brother sullenly went back to secure the door. Even indigent members of the community possessed valuable traits and, curiously, did not seek to steal, abuse, or batter us. No one in our building was ever robbed or attacked. My little turf of Manhattan felt safe.

Of course, my descriptions here do not erase statistics that support incidents of vandalism and theft within the community. However, such acts were rare, and generally people knew each other and held each other accountable for their daily behavior. Moreover, in the context of national events, solidarity among people of color was a palpable presence in Harlem and in other black communities like Bedford Stuyvesant and Crown Heights, Brooklyn, Southeast Queens, and the South Bronx.

It was also a time when other people chastised and even spanked neighbor children with impunity. "Voices of rumor" spread from one block to another like wildfire. For example, one time when I was ten or eleven, I raised my eyebrows to an elder. That act was considered brazen and "fresh." As a result, I was chastised by the elder whom I offended and, before I journeyed the four or five short blocks to my house, I was repeatedly reprimanded by an extended family of neighborhood residents. Then, strangely enough, by the time I crossed the threshold of our apartment, my mother had already learned of my indiscretion and stood, one hand anchored on her hip, ready to chastise me yet again. The community raised children and held them accountable to an extensive network of area residents.

The 1960s represented a time of ferment, deconstruction, reconstruction, persistence, and imagination. Longstanding concepts of inferiority as well as white supremacy, internalized among blacks, were scrutinized, challenged, and turned topsy-turvy to, in the words of Elijah Muhammad, elevate the black man (and woman) to their "original greatness." Harlem, like Detroit and Chicago, constituted a site of transformative self-development strategies within the Nation family and turbulent, reconstructive, social activity.

Models for activism that I witnessed included the stand-off at the 32nd police precinct on 135th Street, between 7th and 8th Avenues. It was impressive to see a flock of impeccably dressed black men stand in military formation, three or four rows deep, in front of the steps of the precinct. These men, whom I saw individually every day during the early sixties, typically in bow ties, starched white shirts, and navy or black pants and jackets, were the *Fruit of Islam*. These black men silently yet forcibly confronted the police. They, led by Minister Malcolm X, provided a show of force—a "we-will-not-be-moved" stance reflected in biblical references from black church hymns—a metaphorical demonstration that defied de facto discrimination and white supremacy at work in black neighborhoods across the United States.

Organized black men, standing in defense of a position, in a country where enslavement and *Jim* and *Jane Crow* legislation were crafted to sustain second-class citizenship for people of color, left an indelible imprint on me that day in Harlem. Their defiance and the response of the police, mostly white, in a majority black community, whom I had never seen challenged, marked a critical shift in me personally and in the community.

Consequently, events that occurred in Harlem, New York, and the lessons from those events have remained a critical point of analyses and questioning. The present study emerges from a lingering perception that ongoing, unsettling tension exists among black women activists, particularly those, like myself, who were born and raised in Harlem. Despite the changes in life conditions for a sizeable number of contemporary, urban, middle-class African American women who came of age in the throes of civil rights protest, nationalist, and Black Power movements, a nagging unrest remains a palpable feature of life. Even today, more than fifty years after *Brown v Board of Education*, the height of the Nation of Islam (NOI) project, and the birth of the Black Power movement, there is an unsettling silence that sparked me to revisit the women who were active in the NOI during this turbulent period in U.S. history.

Despite that we are the beneficiaries of the educational, political, and social shifts on the U.S. landscape, since the later sixties and early seventies, it is increasingly evident that a consistent, ongoing, long-term social project is still needed to sustain and promote equity within African America. The following voices of black women, all of whom participated in the social project identified with the Nation of Islam in the sixties and seventies, bear witness to the unfinished work of the civil rights movement and the women's movement.

THE ORIGINS OF THE NATION OF ISLAM

In the early twentieth century, Noble Drew Ali initiated a movement among African Americans called the Moorish Science Temple of America (MSTA). Though little known today, this movement led to the development of the social, political, and economic enterprise known as the Nation of Islam (NOI) under the leadership of Elijah Muhammad.[2] The NOI constituted a *home-grown* version of Islam to service the specific, sociopolitical and economic needs of African Americans.[3] The NOI—under the leadership of Elijah Muhammad and subsequently that of Louis Farrakhan—created a network of rules and regulations that would encourage behaviors that not only led to highly organized and efficient day-to-day existence but also helped to build economically viable pockets in urban black communities.

THE WOMEN OF THE NOI IN THE 1960s AND 1970s

In the 1990s I conducted interviews with diverse, urban, female participants in the social project instituted by Elijah Muhammad. The ethnographic insights of women who chose to join the Nation family and to adhere to its tenets in the sixties and the seventies provided a heretofore unexamined, gender-specific perspective of African American women's choices. In 2012, I conducted follow-up interviews with some of these same women to see how they perceive and understand the changing face of a contemporary United States with respect to civil rights, gender, and economics.

The women in this group lived and worked in New York City during the 1960s and 1970s. Some moved on, like the educator who moved to Atlanta and continues to offer workshops on pedagogy after her retirement from the school system there. Other have continued to live the bulk of their lives in New York, like the former teacher and board of education administrator who has owned several businesses in Harlem—clothing, antique furniture, real estate—and traveled extensively, lending her thoughts a pan-African perspective. All of the women have remained involved with grassroots community projects throughout the past thirty to forty years as educators and activists in formal and informal settings: public and private schools, home tutoring sessions, community health environments, and local as well as national political campaigns. Moreover, each has contributed to the cultivation and enhancement of an African-centered identity among black children and community members. Collectively, they have raised children who have entered numerous professional arenas: education, engineering, filmmaking, marketing, medicine, and performance. The women are grandmothers, who engage their grandchildren in activities that range from discussions of African heritage and self-definition to film, dance, and music performances, family reunions, and travel. Although they have officially retired from their professional work, they all continue to work in arenas that significantly contribute to the well-being and sustenance of Africans in the diaspora. Their focus centers on the black communities in which they live.

TAKE TWO: FROM THEN
TO NOW—BLACK WOMEN REFLECT

The State of the Civil Rights Movement

One of the key questions I asked of the interviewees when I first interviewed them in the 1990s was whether they felt that the meaning or context of the civil rights movement had changed since the 1960s and 1970s. Their responses were telling. In particular, they felt that the discussion of civil rights had broadened in the ensuing decades. One of the original respondents, a retired elementary and middle school educator, responded, "No, the meaning of civil rights has not changed, but the context has changed somewhat to include more homosexual discrimination and unfair practices. . . . I believe the emphases on ethnic studies, multiculturalism, and gender issues have impacted rights for African Americans." Although this broadening of the context for civil rights in some ways led to a de-emphasis on blacks specifically, the respondent noted the benefits of the expanded focus, for example for girls. There are, she noted, more programs like the "Southeastern Consortium for Minorities in Engineering (SECME), Black Girls Rock, and a host of programs geared for girls to enter engineering or programs for African American girls [so that they] can be successful, no matter what they pursue." This respondent, along with her husband, are both recently retired master teachers who worked continuously with African American youth in their home to improve the kids' science, mathematics, and computer skills. At one point in the 1980s, she ran a preschool in their apartment home, and her husband has been involved with martial arts education for black youth in the community for over thirty years. Their partnership in community projects continues today.

Another respondent discussed the impact of the civil rights period in the context of lineage: "I am a direct descendent of the Mitchellville Settlement on Hilton Head Island, South Carolina [the Gullah]. We have the only original Creole [community] in the United States of America. We have been here since the 1700s. The struggle for our civil rights has and remains ever present in our lives. The spiritual fiber in our communities plays a crucial role in that struggle."

Another interviewee was a Harlem native who has remained active in the family of Muslims, although she engages traditional Islam, not the NOI under the leadership of Minister Louis Farrakhan. She emphasized the continuing connections between civil rights, Islamic practice in the African Diaspora, and her own personal experience. She wrote: "There have always been Islamic practices in our communities. It has been documented that many Muslims came to these shores, before the slave ships. Many Muslims [also] came on these ships. It was easy to recognize those elements in my family and in the community [of Harlem] after becoming a Muslim." In making connections between the civil rights movement and contemporary, activist consciousness among African Americans, this sister[4] notes: "My view of the civil rights movement has metamorphosized with the times. In fact, it seems that we have catapulted backwards. We [African Americans] being victimized by the system [of white supremacy] are now fighting many of the same basic battles from the bygone days."

There is an unsettling, telling anger and disappointment that pervades this sister's conversation. Her words became more heated as she poignantly illuminates some of the pressing concerns in African America that are even more pronounced than they were in the sixties:

Mass incarceration—the new plantations—an inferior Educational System [her emphasis], which fosters mass unemployment. Now, there is a constant pool of bodies for the privatized penal system. . . . Poor health care provides a dumping ground for the paramedical industry. Pandemic, police brutality—KKK mentality. The lynching of our youth, particularly our males—guns have replaced the noose, justified by official talking heads. The disenfranchisement of voting rights.

The contrasts that the respondent makes between enslavement, Jim Crow, and present-day policies resoundingly echoes not only the ongoing fervor of black women activists in the social project of the Nation of Islam forty years ago, but also their continued concern for the well-being of African Americans in multiple social arenas. This grandmother of two has had several businesses in Central Harlem, owned a brownstone, and remains rooted in that community as well as in the Carolinas. She lends her voice to numerous community endeavors as she creates visual art for exhibition internationally. Aware of the multiple ways that people of color are impacted by institutional structures, she continues to assert: "Massive dumping of drugs into our communities—to add insult to injury! The chronic character assassination of all the victims by the corporate media! The constant propaganda machine, which goes undetected by the sedated masses." It is clear that the work begun during the civil rights movement must continue.

The interviewees also emphasized the difference between legal progress and cultural progress. Despite legislation like the Civil Rights Act of 1964 and Title IX that opened door to federal jobs to diverse workers, prejudice continues. One respondent noted, "Just because the laws are legally on the books, it doesn't change the hearts of some people who may not want you [blacks] to have that position or job." Changing the hearts of people remains the fundamental goal of present-day equity battles.

The interviewees' comments on the continuing dynamics of racism call to mind the words of civil rights activist, Rev. C. T. Vivian, who led sit-ins at lunch counters in from the 1940s to the 1960s. At the 2012 Dealing With Difference Institute held at Western Illinois University, he spoke eloquently about the lessons of the 1960s movement for contemporary civil rights efforts:

> The whole civil rights struggle was a struggle against violence. Not to get rid of racism, but to get rid of violence. Because if you don't get rid of violence, racism is going to be there. And if you don't get rid of racism, you allow the dehumanization of man. And, if you allow the hate to continue, it will, in fact, penetrate the best of the *conscience* [my emphasis] of all of us, because we won't have enough courage to stand-up against it.

The civil rights movement achieved significant success in eradicating the disenfranchisement of Africans in the diaspora. However, the work of the movement is by no means finished: to affect conscience such that people will stand on the side of justice and peace.

Women's Dress and Hijab

A second topic that the NOI women discussed was the role of dress in the 1960s culture of the NOI. They spoke in particular about wearing the hijab, a traditional Arab cloth that covers the head and parts of the face. Wearing the hijab was fairly common among African American NOI women during the 1960s and 1970s. When they were first interviewed in the 1990s, they spoke with conviction about the role of hijab in traditional Islamic countries versus the United States in the 1960s. Whereas wearing the hijab was an embedded cultural practice in Islamic countries, in the United States it was intended to reshape the images and attitudes toward black women in the social structure.

In the 1960s there was much discussion among black Muslim women as to whether black women were more respected when veiled or unveiled. Some felt that veiling had nothing to do with the measure of respect shown toward black women. Others felt that the hijab provided a method of identification that many black Muslim women liked. Veiled, uniformed black Muslim women could be easily identified, and the men of the NOI knew whom they were expected to protect. This prominent identification signaled their expectation of respect but also could draw unwanted attention.

The responses of former black Muslim women in 2012 did not vary significantly from those who spoke to this issue in the nineties. One woman responded, "*Hijab* is an Arabic custom. Most African Americans do not want to attract attention to themselves. Wearing *hijab* would attract attention." Although some black Muslim women understood that the uniform of the early NOI period was intended to identify them as well as encourage a measure of respect, many never covered their faces.

A former teacher who was active in the NOI for two decades, also emphasized the specifically Arab nature of the hijab: "African Americans [in Islam] prefer to adopt the African customs of wrapping the head with a scarf or gelee." She never covered her face in the sixties and seventies, although she wore the prescribed dress: long skirts, a squared, long-sleeved tunic-like top, and head covering in matching solid colors. In the eighties and nineties, she wore African fabrics and gelees. Even today, she wears traditional African dress as well as pants. In fact, modest dress—that which does not inordinately hug the body—remains a staple of the women that I spoke to in 2012. African garb and loose fitting, A-line dresses or mid-calf length skirts and blouses comprise the bulk of their wardrobes.

Another interviewee, an artist, also spoke of *hijab* among Islamic women internationally in contrast to African Americans. She had this to say:

> The hijab has not been a part of the African American Muslim community for the most part. We have our own unique style just as most Muslims internationally

do. One must be careful not to apply a monolithic stamp on the Muslim community. Often times, that which is culture has little to do with religion. Even the
African Muslims have a different attire from the Arab populations.

Making distinctions between customs adopted in varying cultures and those
mandated by religious practice provides a window into the diverse ways that
Islam has been incorporated into social structures worldwide.

This artist went on to articulate:

> We [Muslims] are to be modestly dressed. The hair is covered in many ways,
> including hats, and [covering is] mandatory for prayer. There are many who
> cover for prayer in their private spaces. The confusion about Islam has led many
> to shed their cultural garments completely. The desire is to assimilate to stay out
> of harms way. Even in the NOI, we did not wear our—long long—or uniform
> to the work place. They were for the Temple.

The diverse interpretations of the hijab were as prevalent in the 1960s as
they are today. These questions of dress are closely related to questions of
female status. One of the most fascinating aspects of black women in the
NOI (and those who have moved on to more traditional Islamic practice) is
their sense of agency and autonomy. One interviewee asserted, "The women
I knew, many were like me: independent, free-spirited in terms of ideals and
things that we were gonna do or not do; no, we were not submissive like that."
Her recollection mirrors my personal experience among friends who participated in the Nation project during the sixties and seventies in New York. And
the present-day respondents continue to validate and support the thesis that
although some black women were submissive—holding their heads down and
not looking into men's eyes during conversations—a significant number of
NOI women confronted and opposed patriarchal models.

Another respondent, an educator and grandmother of four, noted, "In terms
of clothing, many followed the lead [of the NOI]. Many defied it as well."
She laughed and shared that she was one of those women who defied the
Nation's lead. Yet her perception of choosing her own path within the organization demonstrates an alternative reading of black women's behaviors, not
only then, but also now, in the twenty-first century. With fervor and conviction, she emphasized: "The Nation wanted you to be submissive: to hold your
head down and all this other stuff. You want me to do that for you and I don't
even do that for my husband, whom I cook for at home? You know that's
not gonna work! . . . I need to see what your eyes are saying and you need
to see what my eyes are saying. So I'm just not gonna do that!" She recalled
one male's response to her stance: "Sista', you're being rebellious." "No, I'm
being real," she said. "I can't talk like that [i.e., with her head down]. I'm so
sorry." She went on to say, "I never stopped being me! Fortunately, people

allowed me to be me." But she clarifies: "Some people, whatever the rule or suggestion was, they just did it. . . . I wasn't being rebellious just to be rebellious. I just couldn't do that!" Apparently, a strong sense of self, confidence, and independence trumped mandates that seemed unimportant and impractical to some black women in the Nation family.

Repeatedly, in both the 1990s and 2012 interviews, black Muslim women and former NOI practitioners recalled their insistence on autonomy, despite organizational expectations for women. Moreover, these contemporary women demonstrated over and over again that they think for themselves, determine the feasibility and appropriateness of diverse behaviors, and then choose for themselves: self-agency.

Economics: Helpmates and Work

During the sixties and seventies, black Muslim women were encouraged to pursue traditional roles as wives and mothers within the Nation family. Concurrently, rhetoric extolled husbands who took care of their spouses by fulfilling conventional responsibilities as the breadwinner. Although many black Muslim men attempted to live out conservative male role models, despite lack of access to employment that would make those expectations feasible, many women worked as well.

When asked about employment among black Muslim women, one respondent replied, "Due to increasing economic pressure, a lot of my Muslim friends had to go to work instead of sitting home with the children. More Muslim women are sharing the load with their husbands and they want to." Even during the apex of NOI activity in Harlem, this respondent worked in the public school system. She shared: "I was a teacher and I came in already with a degree. They came seeking me! They knew I was teaching. They came to my class in the public school." Yet she understood and continues to assert that work is necessary within African American, two-parent homes, which is rarely highlighted today. Too often scholarship on African Americans focuses only on examples that support so-called pathological behaviors and patterns, like the disproportionate numbers of households headed by black females. What are left out are the complete demographics. These single female heads of households typically have only a high school degree or less and face other obstacles like underemployment, poor self-esteem, and histories of abuse.

When she spoke of why NOI women wanted to work, this former school teacher emphasized: "They see the need for income. Opportunities that the family may need. I don't necessarily think gender is related to what they want for their children." In response, I asked her if she didn't have to work, would she want to work? To this she replied: "I'm one of these independent people who want to have their own money, even though my husband could give it to me." She continued: "I like travel. That was more important to me than getting things. Because I have an adventurous spirit and I wanted to see the world."

Other Nation women who responded in the first round of interviews shared that they were pressed to provide opportunities for children in the sixties and for some well into the nineties. However, as the children have left the nest, many of the women have traveled extensively to places as diverse as Belize, Ghana, Nigeria, and Panama.

A second informant offered a different perspective on women and work within the NOI. She declared:

> Muslim women in the NOI have always been free to work. Our history in the country almost dictated that we work. Our men often needed the combined effort. Even if we remained at home, the African American woman, like all others worldwide, had their way of getting additional funds in the house. They sewed, baked, sold vegetables, had *Sou sous,*[5] did hair, babysat, went to universities, trade schools, got jobs. We have always worked. A few were privileged to stay home because their partner could afford to keep them there.

As this respondent asserted, black women have a long history of working outside the home in the African Diaspora.[6] In fact, the continuum of working black women dates back to African antiquity and thereafter. Entrepreneurial market women abound in West African countries as well as in places like Zimbabwe and Botswana.

CONCLUSION

A second round of interviews with black women who participated in the Nation of Islam in the 1960s allowed them to look back on the impact of their involvement in the NOI, the civil rights movement, gender roles, and economic choices.[7] It is clear that black Muslim women's choices, in light of social and political impediments during the sixties and seventies, reflected diverse perspectives. There was no monolithic response to the Nation's policies and mandates, just as no one-shoe-fits-all formula reveals the stories of African American women who chose routes other than the Nation. The ideas of NOI women were not significantly different from those of black women outside of the Nation.

The NOI women did share some similar perspectives, however. The women continued to express the same kind of defiance to structural barriers like racism, white supremacy, and biased employment practices. The model of self-determination that I found among the participants in the 1990s continues: Former activists persist in fashioning lives that speak to the needs of African American communities. The women that I have engaged in conversation and whom I revisit herein displayed the kind of tenaciousness that serves as a reminder of the remarkable, undaunted willfulness of African American women. In the words of Alice Walker, in *In Search of Our Mother's Garden*, "they love themselves regardless."

NOTES

1. Locations in the north to which African Americans migrated during diverse historic periods—the Great Migration, after the Spanish American War—from the southern United States were referred to as "up-South." In the Harlem community of the fifties and sixties, "up-South" constituted a vernacular expression that many residents used frequently to denote that many of the prejudices endemic to a bifurcated South, remained telling presences in the North: New York City, New Jersey, Connecticut.

2. Claude Andrew Clegg III, *An Original Man: The Life and Times of Elijah Muhammad* (New York: St. Martin's Press, 1997); Aminah Beverly McCloud, *African American Islam* (New York: Routledge, 1995); Jeffrey Ogbonna Green Ogbar, *Black Power: Radical Politics and African American Identity* (Reconfiguring American Political History) (Baltimore: John Hopkins University Press, 2005); Richard Brent Turner, *Islam in the African-American Experience*, 2nd ed. (Bloomington: Indiana University Press, 2003). Martha Lee, *The Nation of Islam: An American Millenarian Movement*. (Syracuse, NY: Syracuse University Press, 1996).

3. Cynthia S'thembile West, "Nation Builders: Female Activism in the Nation of Islam, 1960–1970" (Ph.D. dissertation, Temple University, 1994).

4. The term, *sister/sista'* was used frequently during the sixties and seventies among African Americans. The term lingers among old school activists of the era.

5. *Sou-sous* refers to groups of black women who run businesses in the Caribbean, Africa, and the United States and who band together, volunteering to designate a specific dollar amount be collected from each member. Then each month the money is given to one woman in the group. This process helps to promote entrepreneurship among the women. The informant was not sure of the etymology of the term.

6. La Frances Rodgers-Rose, ed., *The Black Woman* (Beverly Hills, CA: Sage, 1980), is a seminal volume that notes that longstanding tradition of financially independent black women.

7. For more on these topics, see C. S'thembile West, "Revisiting Female Activism in the 1960s: The Newark Branch Nation of Islam," *The Black Scholar* 26, no. 3–4 (Fall–Winter 1996): 41–48, and C. S'thembile West, *Veiled Thoughts* (unpublished manuscript).

Chapter Three

Elijah Muhammad, Multicultural Education, Critical White Studies, and Critical Pedagogy

Abul Pitre

Elijah Muhammad—most notably known as the teacher of Malcolm X—has been studied from a wide range of social science perspectives. However, very few have undertaken the study of his educational ideas. Scholars in education have explored Malcolm X. Universities offer Black studies courses on Malcolm X and Martin Luther King Jr., and the University of California Los Angeles even offers a course titled *The Pedagogy of Malcolm X* by educational theorist Peter McLaren.

But while these are noble and admirable undertakings, scholars still don't seem to acknowledge that Elijah Muhammad has shaped much of the cultural landscape that we are currently experiencing in the postmodern multicultural world.[1] For example, they have failed to discuss the role of Elijah Muhammad in making Malcolm X an intellectual giant.[2] The courses offered in universities along with the prevailing discussion of Elijah Muhammad has been centered on contributions to Black studies, particularly history, sociology, and political science. Indeed these disciplines provide some understanding of this great historical figure. However, it could be argued that Muhammad's mission was centered on education. It is in the study of education that Elijah Muhammad's teachings elicit a deeper and more thoughtful study.

A study of this controversial figure will reveal that his teachings about education were similar to those found in critical educational theory, and it is from these teachings that educators may very well be able to construct a new education—one that has never experienced before. This chapter discusses Elijah Muhammad's teachings in relationship to critical educational theory regarding multicultural education, critical pedagogy, and critical White studies.

BIOGRAPHICAL SKETCH OF ELIJAH MUHAMMAD

Born Elijah Poole in Sandersville, Georgia, in October of 1897 to William and Mariah Poole, Elijah was one of thirteen children. The Pooles were sharecroppers in the Sandersville area. The name Elijah was given to him by his grandfather who had jokingly noted the biblical significance of the name.[3] His mother, however, felt the name accurately depicted the future greatness of the child that she had carried for nine months. Mariah had visions in which she was shown the future greatness of the child that she was carrying.

His childhood was centered on the family's work as sharecroppers. He was a unique child who had the ability to resolve differences between his siblings. His father was a Baptist minister in the local area, and as a result he found himself listening, reflecting, and studying writings found in the Bible. The early education he received, like that of most Black people during that time period, was rooted in the teachings of the Bible. In *The Theology of Time*, he talked about his reluctance to join the church at the age of fourteen because he didn't want to tell a lie by saying that God had told him to join.

It seems as though he was born with a yearning for scriptural knowledge that would uplift his people from the cruelties of racism, hatred, and suffering inflicted upon them as a result of White supremacy. Elijah witnessed firsthand the brutal legacy of White supremacy in the form of lynching. One of those experiences included an evening walk where he heard voices in the woods. He assumed that the sounds were his brothers who were out looking for him. As the voices got closer he realized that this was not his brother but in fact a group of White men who were leading a Black man into the woods with a rope around him. Elijah fearfully observed the lynching of this man who attended his father's church.[4] This along with the daily abuse by White supremacists probably caused Elijah to yearn for more knowledge, a knowledge that would provide a way out of the oppression suffered by Black people.

This terrible lynching experience along with other experiences would follow him into Macon, Georgia. When he was sixteen years old, he moved to Macon in search of work. There he worked for the Cherokee Brick and Tile Company. In 1915, he met Clara Evans. Clara was one of three children in the Evans family. Clara's sister Rose recalled that Elijah, dressed in a blue suit, would visit their house on Sundays. After two years of courtship, Elijah married Clara on May 2, 1917.[5]

Although he witnessed the physical abuse of Blacks, Whites had never physically abused him directly. Louis Farrakhan, in a speech titled "What a Friend We Have in Jesus," mentions what may have been a dispute between Elijah and his employer.[6] According to Minister Farrakhan the dispute was serious enough to cause him to leave the South. With jobs in short supply, he moved his family to Detroit, saying, "I have seen enough of the white man's brutality in Georgia to last me 26,000 years."[7]

Elijah could never have imagined what awaited him when he reached Detroit. Like most Blacks who had journeyed north to find a better of way of life, he was confronted with the false promises of a better life. He had assumed that it would be relatively easy to find work and when this did not materialize he found himself drinking.[8] His drinking perhaps grieved his wife Clara as she reflected on the hopes that were unrealized, only to find themselves alone in a strange city. His drinking was so bad that she would sometimes have to get him out of the alley where he had unconsciously fallen. Reflecting on his life experience, he said that when God found him, only his eyeballs were out of the mud.

It was his wife Clara who first attended a meeting to hear the speaker Wallace D. Fard. She later urged Elijah to come out and listen to this man; he replied that he was not interested in hearing heathenism, referring to Islam. He was a devout Christian, son of a Baptist minister, student of the scriptures and assumed that he could never listen to a subject on Islam. Reluctantly, after being given more information he decided to attend the meeting at the urging of family members.

On September 22, 1931, despite some reservations, he attended a lecture by Fard.[9] As he listened, he reflected on the scriptural teachings that he had studied over the course of his entire life. He felt immediately that this was the man that the scriptures said would come in the last days. According to Jabril Muhammad, Fard disclosed the measurements of the earth and the origin of things.[10] It could be argued that immediately after hearing these teachings, he fell in love with W. D. Fard.

Scholars have pointed out that part of Elijah's acceptance of Fard's teaching was a result of his experiences in the South. This is a plausible conclusion as those experiences were providing him with a love for the man that would come to be known to him as "the Saviour." At the close of the meeting it was customary for Fard to shake hands with his listeners. As Elijah shook hands with the man who would become his teacher, he replied "I know who you are; you are the one the Bible says would come in the last days under the name Jesus." Fard replied, "Yes, but who knows this except yourself? Be quiet." One has to question what Muhammad must have felt like on this night; perhaps he had come to realize that the yearnings that he felt since a child were now coming to pass. He had met the man who could provide knowledge that would uplift his people. Reflecting on his experiences, he later wrote, "Ever since he's [himself] been in his boyhood he's been craving to see someone come to the rescue of his people."[11]

Within a month Fard sent a message out to Muhammad that he could begin teaching in the Hamtramck area and that he would see him soon.[12] The two eventually started having private meetings where Fard taught Muhammad supreme wisdom. Muhammad studied under the man he referred to as "Master Fard Muhammad" for more than three years. Regarding his experience with "Master Fard Muhammad," he wrote, "He began teaching us the knowledge of ourselves, of God, and the devil . . . the history of the two nations, black and white that dominate the earth. . . . He said . . . My name is Mahdi: I am God, I came to guide you into the right path that you may be successful and see the hereafter."[13]

This relationship with Fard would spark a new beginning for Elijah Muhammad. For the next three and a half years, Fard would teach him on several topics ranging from theology, history, and education, to science and numerous other topics. Regarding his experiences with Fard he declared, "We used to sit sometimes from the early part of the night until sunrise and after sunrise."[14] Fard, according to Elijah Muhammad, was born on February 26, 1877, in Mecca. Fard told him that his father was in the circle of Gods who had come to the realization that some members of their family had been involuntarily been brought to the United States of America. Fard's father, being of a very dark complexion, realized that he could not get among the people of America because the country was mostly White. As a result he went into the Caucasus Mountains to find a "White woman" to bear a son who could blend in among diverse groups of people: "He said his mother was a white woman. He said my father went up in the mountains to choose my mother in order to get a child that looked like the people that had this particular member among them, so that he could get among them more successfully, and that he was the one. His mother he said was a white woman, and his father was a black man."[15]

Fard had visited America for twenty years before making himself known. He studied and taught at the University of California at Los Angeles and he had enrolled at several other universities.[16] Education was extremely important to Fard. Elijah Muhammad stated, "He studied every educational system in the civilized world and that he could speak sixteen languages and write ten of them. . . . He said that he had been studying for us, what he meant to teach us, and reform us for forty-two years."[17]

The educational work of Fard became the foundation of Elijah Muhammad's educational philosophy. Fard, in studying educational systems and what he intended to teach Blacks in America (and eventually the whole human family) handed down to Elijah Muhammad a mission—to build up the kind of knowledge that would raise the consciousness of people in America. Speaking about his missions Muhammad declared, "My work from him was to teach my people these facts, and reform them and make them what they should be; as they are children, the bible teaches, from God but they are lost in evil and practice evil."[18] He reiterated his mission by recalling what Fard had told him earlier: "Tell them that I will walk up in a mountain forty miles to teach just one of them. Tell them I love them."[19]

Elijah Muhammad's passion for education led to a major encounter with law enforcement officials. In the early 1930s he established what was initially called the University of Islam, a network of Nation of Islam–affiliated primary and secondary schools. The Michigan State Board of Education was fearful of the impact an independent Black educational system would have on the development of Blacks in America. In 1934, the teachers at the school were arrested, and when Elijah Muhammad was made aware of these arrests he committed himself to jail and was charged with contributing to the delinquency of minors. The court gave him six-months' probation and ordered that the Muslim children attending the schools be placed back in public schools. Realizing the significance of education he did not adhere to the court order and later moved to Chicago.[20]

Elijah Muhammad clearly believed proper education was the pathway to freedom. He did not see education simply in terms of technical skills. For him the purpose of education was making Blacks aware of their divine essence, which would allow them to live on a higher spiritual plane. He argued that the education of Blacks in America should begin with the knowledge of self. Writing on the knowledge of self, he contended that the education of Blacks in America was not designed to truly free them.

Exploring concepts in history and using deconstruction, he argued that those shaping the educational agenda that did not provide Blacks in America with a knowledge of their history, origin, and purpose. He critiqued the organization of Black colleges after the Civil War and referred to the congressional debate regarding funding for Howard University. During the debate a senator questioned why they should fund a Black university since they were not going to teach students the sciences needed to be free peoples. This caused Elijah Muhammad to write, "This shows the slave-master has been very successful in dominating us with an education beneficial to him."[21] His critique of Black education predated contemporary critical educational theorists who ask whose knowledge infuses the curriculum. Elijah Muhammad not only critiqued the educational system but offered a body of knowledge outside of the sphere of those ruling the society.

Those entering the Nation of Islam were given an X to symbolize the unknown. Elijah Muhammad's teaching sought to destroy every element of slavery that placed Blacks in the inferior position. Hilliard, speaking about the issue of naming, echoed Elijah Muhammad's teachings: "At the conscious level, naming was a strategy to commit 'cultural genocide,' a strategy to destroy ethnic family solidarity, a strategy to place emphasis on individual rather than family behavior, or a strategy to confuse Africans about their ethnic identity."[22] Similarly Dr. John Henry Clarke wrote, "It is impossible to continue to oppress a consciously historical people."[23] In the context of understanding Elijah Muhammad, one must understand that his work reflected an educational process that would be truly transformative.

To really grasp the teachings of Elijah Muhammad one has to delve into the background of his teacher, W. D. Fard. Some writers have painted Fard as a criminal who tricked Elijah Muhammad in his scheme to make money. *The Los Angeles Herald Examiner* in 1963 released an article along with a picture which they claimed was Wallace Dodd Ford who also went under the name Wallace D. Fard.[24] The article highlighted that Wallace Dodd Ford had been arrested for drug use and several other crimes in California. Dr. Wesley Muhammad (known as True Islam) has painstakingly researched these claims in his book *Master Fard Muhammad: Who Is He? Who He Is Not?* True Islam carefully studied the FBI documents relating to the case and concluded, "The story was hoax."[25]

Despite the controversy that has followed Muhammad's teachings, there is no question that his educational program has been able to transform lives. And many of his educational ideas have taken hold in the field and study of education. One of the more obvious areas of influence is the Afrocentric tenet of exemplar scholars.[26] In accordance with this principle, Afrocentric schools have emerged to provide extraordinary learning opportunities for African American students. Scholars have been slow to acknowledge this influence. Watkins has briefly touched on the Nation of Islam's impact on contemporary Black education.[27] But attention has otherwise been scant, a problem I documented—and tried to rectify—in my own volume *The Educational Philosophy of Elijah Muhammad: Education for a New World*, in which I juxtapose the ideas of Elijah Muhammad with those of multicultural education and critical pedagogy.[28] Muhammad's ideas offer a compelling possibility to transform the entire educational system—possibly creating a new universal system of education one that might usher in a New World.

MULTICULTURAL EDUCATION

The multicultural education movement in America was birthed as a direct result of the country's civil rights movement and Black leaders' ideas about justice and equality. One of the leaders who played a significant role in advancing the civil rights and multicultural movements was Elijah Muhammad. Eric Lincoln, a long-time scholar on the Nation of Islam, named Elijah Muhammad as a major contributor to the multicultural development of the United States saying, "We in America can thank Mr. Muhammad for the major role he played in helping us to understand and prepare for what lies ahead in the multi-culture, where religion is so basic to human understanding and cooperation."[29]

Lincoln's perspective suggests that there is something to be explored in Elijah Muhammad's teachings that should be studied from the context of multicultural education. James Banks, a leading scholar and considered by some as the initiator of multicultural education, noted that multicultural education is premised on the ideals of freedom, justice, and equality. It is just this idea of education that Elijah Muhammad advocated decades before; in fact, examining Banks's earlier texts in the 1970s, it seems clear that he had studied some aspects of Elijah Muhammad's teachings.

Contrary to those who think multicultural education is a feel-good approach that makes everyone get along, scholars have used it to raise a wide range of critiques regarding the inequities in education. With regards to curriculum issues Banks notes that most view multicultural education from an additive prospective writing the, "cultural content, concepts and themes are added to the curriculum without changing its basic structure, purposes and characteristics."[30] The additive approach to multicultural education is in contrast to the approach of radical or critical multicultural theorists, who argue that multicultural education should address equity and social justice.[31] Critical multicultural scholars assert that the additive approach is "too watered down" and thus lacks the substance needed to change the horrendous conditions of inequality that exist in schools and the larger society.

In one of his lectures, Minister Farrakhan disclosed the multicultural dimension of the Nation of Islam to include critical White studies when he proposed that W. D. Fard came to save White people. Indeed, the multicultural education movement, when examined properly, is beneficial to people of European descent; it gives them the ability to self-reflect and view the world from the diverse perspectives. More importantly, multicultural education is about the destruction of White supremacy that distorts and hides the truth; it is an exploder of myths.[32] Strands of Elijah Muhammad's teachings can be seen woven throughout the fabric of contemporary ideas on multicultural education.

James Banks, who is considered the founder of the multicultural education movement, has pointed out that multicultural education is a reform effort centered on the idea of equality. Banks highlights, "It grew out of the civil rights movement grounded in Western democratic ideals such as freedom, justice, and equality."[33] One could argue that freedom, justice, and equality are not

Western ideals but are founded in the very principles of life. According to Elijah Muhammad, the notions of freedom, justice, and equality were rooted in the makeup of the universe; in order to really observe these principles at work, one simply has to look at the signs—the sun, moon, and stars—that exist in the heavens. The sun represents freedom, as it gives light, energy, and life freely to all people. The moon represents equality, in that it balances the water from overtaking the land. And the stars represent justice in that each of us is justified in our existence. To illustrate his point, he used the example of the star-shaped badge worn by law enforcement officials who rightfully administer justice.

Elijah Muhammad argued that Blacks wanted freedom, justice, equality, and independence. While his ideas are similar to those of Banks, they go much deeper into universal laws that must be understood in order to develop an effective educational system that would provide freedom, justice, equality, and independence. Such a system would require the sun to represent the gifts and talents that each individual provides humanity freely, the moon to represent an education that would help us to find balance in life, and the stars to represent education that helps us to justify our purpose for existence. This concept of education would in turn require us to rethink one's view of society, education, and school.

The first step in changing our thinking about society, education, and school is to require instruction that does not sugarcoat the historical racism and inequality that serve as the foundation for American life. Most American students have been taught a mythical history of the United States that serves the purpose of maintaining White supremacy and world hegemony. It is quite amazing to attend all-White schools and witness how White students view other cultures as being savage and inferior. Responsibility for this view lies partly with the teachers and textbooks that have been Europeanized to support White supremacy. This has had a deleterious effect on the nonwhite masses. For some Blacks, it has led to a mindset that the ultimate goal is to be as White as possible with regard to behavior and thinking.

However, despite best efforts to become White by some people of so-called color, full access to White privilege has still been denied. Banks explains this phenomenon: "Some individuals of color, such as many African Americans, Native Americans, and Puerto Rican Americans, in their effort to assimilate and participate fully in mainstream institutions, become very Anglo-Saxon in their ways of viewing the world and in their values and behavior" (p. 4). The educational system should be credited for this type of thinking, as it was a part of the ideology used to teach Native Americans: "kill the Indian and keep the man." Thus, the multicultural education movement as an exploder of myths asserts that "the truth about the West should be told, that its debt to people of color and women be recognized and included in the curriculum, and that the discrepancies between the ideals of freedom and equality and the realities of racism and sexism be taught to students."[34]

Long before scholars of critical educational tackled these subjects, Elijah Muhammad attacked the White supremacist teachings taught to the masses and shocked the world when he pronounced "the white man is the devil." Ultimately, what Muhammad was doing went beyond the multicultural education movement into the origin of whiteness. While some Whites were extolling their standard of beauty (previously the only culturally acceptable model), Elijah Muhammad was saying that Black is beautiful and the White standard is the devil. This forced Whites to reexamine their standard through the lens of equality and freedom in comparison to the darker-skinned peoples of the earth; suddenly, the White standard was not necessarily the most beautiful. Thus, the mind of White supremacy was attacked with a force and power more than equal to the thought that brought White supremacy into existence.

The masses could not accept this exegesis of whiteness, having been indoctrinated to see Whites as superior. A key goal of Elijah Muhammad's teaching was to give Black people a way of deconstructing the White supremacist mindset that had been placed in them. Just as important, this type of teaching would also break the mindset of White supremacy so thoroughly ingrained in White people. As one of my students pointed out, multicultural education is really for White students. Banks explained, "A key goal of multicultural education is to help individuals gain greater self-understanding by viewing themselves from the perspective of other cultures."[35] This certainly applies to White students, as they are afforded what Howard called the "luxury of ignorance." Howard noted, "Individuals from the dominant group are usually unaware of their own power and can carry on the daily activities of their lives without any substantial knowledge about, or meaningful interaction with, those people who are not a part of the dominant group."[36] Howard explained that this luxury is not afforded to other groups whose "lives demand expertise in translation and transition between their own culture and the culture of dominance."[37] Multicultural education opens the door for the destruction of the miseducation of the masses by teaching multiple perspectives of the world that move beyond the Eurocentric view.

Today, scholars openly talk about whiteness; much of the credit for this belongs to Elijah Muhammad's teachings. In talking about racism, Peter McLaren highlights the following:

> The specific struggle that I wish to address is that of choosing against whiteness. Yet is it possible for us to choose against whiteness given that, historically, the practice of whiteness has brought about such a devastating denial, disassembly, and destruction of other races? One would think that such a choice against

whiteness would be morally self-evident. However, precisely because whiteness is so pervasive it remains difficult to identify, to challenge, and to separate from our daily lives. My message is that we must create a new public sphere where the practice of whiteness is not only identified and analyzed but also contested and destroyed. For choosing against whiteness is the hope and promise of the future.[38]

It could be argued that the hope for the destruction of whiteness (not White people) and the creation of the New World lies in the ideas espoused by Elijah Muhammad. McLaren highlights that in moments of despair movements such as the Million Man March offer a possibility of hope. The Million Man March was a powerful sign of the impact of Elijah Muhammad's teaching in contemporary times. The march demonstrated what Shor and Freire call an educational endeavor that should be examined as "liberating education."[39] Freire writes, "there is another place for the existence of and the development of liberating education which is precisely in the intimacy of social movements."[40] The Million Man March has had a deep impact on life in America. Schools and school systems have purposely limited discussion of this movement. Unknown to most is the role that Elijah Muhammad played in planting the idea for the Million Man March in Minister Farrakhan, who convened it.

CRITICAL PEDAGOGY

McLaren notes, "Critical pedagogy asks how and why knowledge gets constructed the way it does, and how and why some constructions of knowledge are legitimated and celebrated by the dominant culture while others clearly are not."[41] Critical understanding of the relationship between power and knowledge is essential for Blacks in America who have been dominated by European education.

Some scholars have argued that the educational experiences of Blacks in America have resulted in miseducation.[42] Historians of Black education highlight that the education of Blacks was specifically designed for the purpose of making slaves.[43] They contend the education process was designed to make Blacks servants of those who held dominant positions. In his book, *Message to the Blackman in America*, Muhammad quotes Edwin Embree: "We have as far as possible, closed every avenue by which light may enter the slaves' mind. If we could extinguish the capacity to see the light, our work would be complete; they would be on a level with the beast of the field and we should be safe."[44] Embree's light mentioned here represents knowledge. The cutting or depriving of knowledge was a prerequisite for maintaining White rule over Black people. Watkins notes how White philanthropists scripted Black education for seventy-five years after the Civil War:

> From the onset the white architects of black education understood the power of ideas. They carefully selected and sponsored knowledge, which contributed to obedience, subservience, and political docility. . . . Colonial education had to be fitted to the American south. This undertaking required the efforts of both the ideologists and the financers. Corporate philanthropists joined forces with racial sociologist to design seventy-five years of education for blacks.[45]

Elijah Muhammad, knowing the importance of knowledge and proper education, challenged the foundation of the White supremacist construction of black education. This challenge in educational terms is called *critical pedagogy* and is the junction at which the relationship between power and knowledge is examined. Elijah Muhammad raised several points related to critical educational theory, and, more importantly, he provided knowledge to overcome the curriculum prescribed by those who rule. He raised the following points regarding power and knowledge:

> Certainly the so-called Negroes are being schooled, but is this education the equal of that of their slave masters? No. . . . After blinding them to the knowledge of self and their own kind for 400 years, the slave masters refuse to civilize the so-called Negroes into the knowledge of themselves of which they were robbed.[46]

Muhammad brilliantly points out that the "so-called Negro" is being "schooled" but not educated. In his book, *Too Much Schooling, Too Little Education,* Shujaa distinguishes the difference between education and schooling.[47] Shujaa explains the process of schooling, in which Black students are taught to fit into the dominant society, versus the process of education, in which students are taught to understand their potential. Therefore, Muhammad is correct when he says that Blacks are being schooled as opposed to being educated. The schooling process of Black people in America is not bringing out the genetic power that lies dormant within the individual because the schooling process put to death the creative power of self. Asante asserted that he has never "found a school in the United States run by Whites that adequately prepares Black children to enter the world as sane human beings."[48] Freire believes this version of education actually turns Blacks into "beings for others," which can be interpreted to mean that the oppressed are schooled in the interests of those who oppress them.[49] Woodson concurs:

> When you control a man's thinking you do not have to worry about his actions. You do not have to tell him stand here or go yonder. He will find his proper

place and will stay in it. You do not need to send him to the back door. He will go without being told. In fact, if there is no back door he will cut one for his special benefit. His education makes it necessary.[50]

The miseducation of African American children can be seen in visiting what are called "inner-city" schools and communities. These institutions represent what is manifest to the eye as social decay. Upon closer examination, it is apparent that this miseducation is not limited to the inner city; it is also a reflection of what is taking place in the minds of those who rule.

In this statement Muhammad raised issues with contemporary education and civilization. The educational system, having been designed by those interested in maintaining white supremacy, is an excellent example of how some minority populations have been improperly civilized and denied access to equal knowledge. The system does not give those populations the education needed to be free peoples. Muhammad discusses the 1920s debate over Black education and the type of education that would have actually been necessary for Blacks to have been declared free. In this debate one senator said there was no point in educating Blacks because they would not be taught the science of modern warfare or chemistry or any of the knowledge needed for free people to protect and advance themselves.[51]

Today, nothing has changed; in fact, schools have become more equipped to perform this function of domination. The No Child Left Behind Act of 2001 (NCLB) and the Race to the Top program are evidence of this dominating function of education that has been beneficial to the world shapers. NCLB has resulted in the restructuring of schools and have made them more oppressive for historically underserved students resulting in what some have called *being black in school*—the intentional targeting or removal of some Black students in order to raise the overall test scores of a particular school. Elijah Muhammad and Carter G. Woodson argued that the education of Blacks is left completely in the hands of those who have enslaved and oppressed them. Asante writes, "Whites are accustomed to being in charge of ideas circulating in the American academy."[52]

Speaking on education under outside control Elijah Muhammad wrote, "Today with all of our white civilized schooling, we have not been taught our own. They will never teach us of our own."[53] Woodson concurs: "Negroes have NO CONTROL of their education and have little voice in their other affairs pertaining thereto."[54] Asante asserts, "The little African American child who sits in the classroom and is taught to accept as heroes and heroines individuals who defamed African people is being actively decentered, dislocated, and made into a nonperson, one whose aim in life might be to one day shed that 'badge of inferiority,' his or her Blackness."[55] Our nation's educational history has only proven them right. A clear example of this phenomenon is the school board in Lafayette, Louisiana, which voted 7–2 against incorporating Black history in the school curricula. This is just one example of the continued white dominance of Black education.

The disastrous results of standardized testing as the right arm of white supremacist education have caused educational scholars to ponder what is needed to create the best educational program for all children—and has resulted in a number of studies related to closing the achievement gap between Black and white students in particular. Scholars and educators who are concerned with issues of social justice and educational equality have brilliantly identified problems with the education of nonwhite students. Problems such as racism, inequitable school funding, the lack of diversity in a Eurocentric curriculum, biased standardized tests, and a majority white teaching force are some factors that contribute to the so-called gap. However, a major part of the problem in Black education also lies in what Woodson called "education outside of the control of Black people." Woodson eloquently stated, "The education of the Negroes, then, the most important thing in the uplift of the Negroes, is almost entirely in the hands of those who enslaved them and now segregate them."[56] Even in cases where Blacks seem to be in control of the educational system, they are often educated to maintain or oversee public schools—the modern plantation. Woodson accurately describes this problem:

> With mis-educated Negroes in control themselves, however, it is doubtful that the system would be very much different from what it is or that it would rapidly undergo change. The Negroes thus placed in charge would be the products of the same system and would show more conception of the task at hand than do the whites who have educated them and shaped their minds as they would have them function.[57]

CONCLUSION

Woodson's description of the complexity of Black education is even more applicable today than at the time of its writing. In fact, the new standardization of education has resulted in lack of vision about approaching the problems of Black education. Too many schools have continued to use European philosophy as the basis for all education and Black teachers, while realizing something is wrong with the educational system, have not been able to accurately pinpoint the problem:

> Negro educators of today may have more sympathy and interest in the race than the Whites now exploiting Negro institutions as educators, but the former have no more vision than their competitors. Taught from the same books of the same

bias, trained by Caucasians of the same prejudices or by Negroes of enslaved minds, one generation of Negro teachers after another has served for no higher purpose than to do what they are told to do. In other words, a Negro teacher instructing Negro children is in many respects a White teacher thus engaged, for the program in each case is about the same.[58]

This should raise questions regarding the role of education in domesticating Black consciousness. Questions like, what should be included in the curriculum to stimulate the creative mind in Black students? Woodson argues, "Real education means to inspire people to live more abundantly, to learn to begin life as they find it and make it better, but the instruction so far given Negroes in colleges and universities has worked to the contrary."[59]

Elijah Muhammad argued, "Knowledge is the result of learning and is a force or energy that makes its bearer accomplish or overcome obstacles, barriers and resistance."[60] It could be argued that a reexamination of Elijah Muhammad's teachings along with his leadership could potentially result in a new educational system that encompasses human beings across the planet. A careful study of his teachings reveals that he was a forerunner to critical educational theorists; however, he has been locked out of the educational discourse because his critiques offer a true path for liberation and freedom for oppressed peoples.[61] We need to rectify this omission in order to create the best educational opportunities for Black students.

NOTES

1. D. Muhammad, "Scholar C. Eric Lincoln dies at 75." *Final Call,* May 30, 2000, retrieved from www.finalcall.com/national/c_eric_lincoln5-30-2000.htm; A. Pitre, *The Educational Philosophy of Elijah Muhammad: Education for a New World*, 2nd ed. (Lanham, MD: University Press of America, 2008).

2. P. McLaren, *Life in Schools: An Introduction to Critical Pedagogy in the Foundations of Education*, 6th ed. (Boulder, CO: Paradigm Publishers, 2015). W. Watkins, J. Lewis, and V. Chou, *Race and Education: The Roles of History and Society in Educating African American Students* (Boston: Allyn and Bacon, 2001). J. E. Morris, "Malcolm X's Critique of the Education of Black People." *The Western Journal of Black Studies* 25, no. 2 (2001): 126–35, T. Perry, *Teaching Malcolm X* (New York: Routledge, 1996).

3. C. Clegg, *An Original Man: The Life and Times of Elijah Muhammad* (New York: St. Martin's Griffin, 1998).

4. M. Halasa, *Elijah Muhammad: Religious Leader* (New York: Chelsea House Publishers, 1990).

5. Ibid.

6. L. Farrakhan, *What a Friend We Have in Jesus* [videotape] (Chicago: Final Call, 1996).

7. Halasa, *Elijah Muhammad*, p. 29.

8. E. Curtis, *Islam in Black America: Identity, Liberation, and Difference in African American Islamic Thought* (Albany, NY: SUNY Press, 2002); Farrakhan, *What a Friend We Have in Jesus*. VHS. (Chicago: Final Call, 1996).

9. J. Muhammad, *This Is the One: The Most Honored Elijah Muhammad, We Need Not Look for Another*, 3rd ed. (Phoenix, AZ: Book Company, 1996).

10. Ibid.

11. N. Hakim, *The Black Stone: The True History of Elijah Muhammad, Messenger of Allah* (Atlanta: M.E.M.P.S. Publications, 1997), 27.

12. Hakim, *The Black Stone*.

13. E. Muhammad, *Message to the Blackman in America* (Chicago: Final Call, 1965).

14. Hakim, *The Black Stone*.

15. Ibid.

16. T. Muhammad, "The Cultural Revolution Begins: In Search of the Messiah," *Final Call*, June 14, 2011, retrieved from www.finalcall.com/artman/publish/printer_7934.shtml.

17. Hakim, *The Black Stone*, 44.

18. Ibid., 46.

19. Ibid., 54.

20. E. Muhammad, *Message to the Blackman*; Hakim, *The Black Stone*.

21. E. Muhammad, *Message to the Blackman*, 40.

22. A. Hilliard, "Race, Identity, Hegemony, and Education: What Do We Need to Know Now?" in W. H. Watkins, J. Lewis, and V. Chou, eds., *Race and Education: The Role of History and Society in Educating African American Students* (Needham Heights, MA: Allyn and Bacon, 2001), 7–33.

23. Cited in Hilliard, "Race, Identity, Hegemony, and Education."

24. Hakim, *The Black Stone*; T. Islam, *Master Fard Muhammad: Who Is He? Who He Is Not?* (Atlanta: All in All Publishers, 2007); J. Muhammad, *This Is the One.*

25. Islam, *Master Fard Muhammad*, 25.

26. Molefi Kete Asante, "The Afrocentric Idea in Education," *Journal of Negro Education* 60, no. 2 (1991): 170–80.

27. W. Watkins, "Black Curriculum Orientations: A Preliminary Inquiry," *Harvard Educational Review* 63, no. 3 (1993): 321–38.

28. Pitre, *The Educational Philosophy of Elijah Muhammad.*

29. D. Muhammad, "Scholar C. Eric Lincoln Dies at 75," p. 6.

30. J. A. Banks, *An Introduction to Multicultural Education*, 5th ed. (Boston: Pearson Education, 2014), 53.

31. Sleeter is cited in J. Noel, *Notable Selections in Multicultural Education*, 2nd ed. (New York: McGraw Hill, 2008); McLaren, *Life in Schools.*

32. J. Kincheloe and S. Steinberg, *Changing Multiculturalism* (Buckingham, PA: Open University Press, 1997).

33. Banks, *Introduction to Multicultural Education*, 10.

34. Ibid., 11.

35. Ibid., 3.

36. G. Howard, *We Can't Teach What We Don't Know: White Teachers in Multiracial Schools*, 2nd ed. (New York: Teachers College Press, 2006), 63.

37. Ibid., 62.

38. McLaren, *Life in Schools*, 198.

39. I. Shor and P. Freire, *A Pedagogy for Liberation: Dialogues on Transforming Education* (Westport, CT: Bergin and Garvey, 1987).

40. Ibid., 38.

41. McLaren, *Life in Schools*, 133.

42. M. K. Asante, *Race, Rhetoric, and Identity: The Architecton of Soul* (Amherst, NY: Humanity Books, 2005); C. G. Woodson, *The Mis-education of the Negro,* 11th ed. (Trenton, NJ: First Africa World Press, 1999; 1st ed. orig. published 1933).

43. W. Watkins, *The White Architects of Black Education: Ideology and Power in America 1865–1954* (New York: Teachers College Press, 2001); D. Spivey, *Schooling for the New Slavery: Black Industrial Education 1868–1915* (Trenton, NJ: Africa World Press, 2006; 1st publ. 1978).

44. E. Muhammad, *Message to the Blackman*, 186.

45. W. Watkins, *The White Architects of Black Education*, 41–42.

46. E. Muhammad, *Message to the Blackman*, 44–45.

47. M. J. Shujaa, ed., *Too Much Schooling, Too Little Education: A Paradox of Black Life in White Societies* (Trenton, NJ: Africa World Press, 1994).

48. Asante, *Race, Rhetoric, and Identity*, 65.

49. P. Freire, *Pedagogy of the Oppressed* (New York: Continuum, 2000).

50. Woodson, *The mis-education of the Negro*, xii.

51. E. Muhammad, *Message to the Blackman*, 40.

52. Asante, "The Afrocentric Idea in Education."

53. E. Muhammad, *Message to the Blackman*, 48.

54. Woodson, *The Mis-education of the Negro*, 22.

55. Asante, "The Afrocentric Idea in Education."

56. Ibid., 22.

57. Ibid., 23.

58. Woodson, *The Mis-education of the Negro*, 23.

59. Ibid., 29.

60. E. Muhammad, *Message to the Blackman*, 41.

61. For additional reading, see N. Hakim, ed., *The Theology of Time*, 3rd ed. (Atlanta: M.E.M.P.S. Publication, 1997); S. Nieto and P. Bode, *Affirming Diversity: The Socio-Political Context of Multicultural Education*, 6th ed. (New York: Longman, 2012); A. Rassoull, ed., *The Theology of Time* (Charlotte, NC: Conquering Books, 1992).

Chapter Four

Bismillah—Message to the Blackman Revisited

Being and Power

Jinaki Abdullah

Before the coining of the term "critical race theory," African American Muslim leaders were conceptualizing many of its components. One component was a counternarrative that opposed the white-centric history of American culture; the Honorable Elijah Muhammad and his mentor W. D. Fard began by defining a new reality for black people and their relationship to whites with a counterstory of creation referred to as Yacub's history, wherein they posited that the white man was derived from the black man. Another component was structural determinism; Mohammad and Fard as part of their daily analysis pointed out to their audiences the inherent racism within America and the evil of white privilege, which was personified when they called the white man "the devil." Not only did they verbally attack white power and privilege, they criticized the alliance, during the civil rights era, between African American elites and liberal whites by highlighting the disingenuous nature of interest convergence and the empathy fallacy. They even went further in seeking solutions by asking for separate states within America where they could build a just system of economics, education, and politics for themselves. These leaders transformed illiterate, oppressed, and silent people into activists with voices who wrote and published their own narratives about oppression and African American life through their newspaper *Muhammad Speaks*. And collectively they gained influence, unity, self-pride, and respect among the masses of African American people; amassed property in the form of businesses and farmland; and were inspired to improve themselves and their communities.

Message to the Blackman in America (1965) by Elijah Muhammad is a book that expresses the ontology of the black man in America. According to

Martin Heidegger, *Dasein*—the concept of being there/here—is the experience of an individual for whom being is an issue. Elijah Muhammad sought to explain the *Dasein*—the being-in-the-world—of the black man from a metaphysical perspective. "Who am I?" and "Why are we here?" are questions that have plagued humankind from ancient times. Yet Muhammad's book has not been given the analysis that it warrants. Written during the civil rights era, *Message to the Blackman in America* proposed separation instead of integration into the society of European Americans. This was the antithesis of the leading voices of that day. Moreover, it encouraged Black people to relinquish Christianity—the religion of Europe—and become Muslims. More than forty years have passed since the book was first published, and integration has become the law of the land, yet the question of being-in-the world of the black man in America remains a paradox.

"Who am I?" "What is my place in the world?" and "Does God exist?" are universal questions that have been asked for centuries and are still relevant for African Americans today. In the book *Message to the Blackman in America*, Elijah Muhammad addressed those questions, not in a scholarly manner or in the rhetoric traditional religious discourse but in a way that attests to the cognizance of mind and being of the individual as well as a nation of people. African Americans are a new race of people. They were created during the slave trade, with the first of them arriving in Virginia in 1619. As the slave trade increased, tribes from different parts of the African continent, possessing different languages and cultures, were brought to the Americas to be sold as slave labor. When they arrived, hybridization occurred. The intercourse between Africans, Europeans, and Native Americans brought about the creation of a new people, a new race, and a new destiny.

This new race of people evolved at the behest of modern man. Western civilization had already derived its theories on life, labor, and language, and the three great religions had already been revealed; but all three religions, according to their scholars, characterized the black man as cursed by God. That is a terrible psychological and sociological burden—to bear the stigma that the Creator himself has created you to be on the lower rung of humanity as the servants or slaves of other humans. Moreover, this religious doctrine was supported by pseudoscience that postulated the natural inferiority of Africans. African Americans had lived with these debilitating social and psychological barriers until the arrival of Elijah Muhammad and the advent of the Nation of Islam. Muhammad gave blacks in America, for the first time, a sense of pride in being black. He provided a myth or narrative of black creation to explain the peculiar circumstances of black life within America and the world, and his teleological ideas elucidated the polarity of black and white that had plagued the soul of every African American. Proclaiming a Manifest Destiny for the black man in America, Muhammad's rhetoric was labeled as racists and absurd. But was it more absurd than the language of European, Jewish, and Arab religious and academic scholars who had relegated black people to be the wretched of the earth?

In matters of the metaphysical, the Enlightenment tradition of logic and reason was unable to bring humans knowledge of the Omniscient. Yet *The Message to the Blackman in America* uplifted the moral, intellectual, and economic life of the poor black man and prepared him for entry into the universal teachings of Al-Islam. Not only did the teachings of the Nation of Islam uplift the black man socially and spiritually, but they placed him in a position to critique the white man's world; this was something that many African American scholars and leaders had attempted to do, but the Muslim perspective provided a completely new level of analysis to white supremacy. Leaders such as Marcus Garvey, Noble Drew Ali, W. E. B. Dubois, and Martin Luther King Jr. sought to separate from or integrate into the white man's milieu, but they did not dare to make the bold claims about black ontology that the Nation of Islam espoused unequivocally: that the black man was God and the white man was the devil. It was this paradigm shift that attracted many followers to the Nation at that time because the white man had visited many societies with atrocities that surely only a "devil" could do. And although the black man was on the bottom rung socially, his long suffering under the oppression of white supremacy inculcated within him the "god-like" qualities of a prophetic people, producing a long line of wise leaders like Nat Turner, Harriet Tubman, Sojourner Truth, Frederick Douglass, Booker T. Washington, W. E. B. Dubois, Marcus Garvey, and others. And the Nation of Islam was a progression of that heritage, producing great Muslim leaders whose strategy was controversial in its implementation yet remarkable in its results.

This chapter will look at the ways in which *Message to the Blackman in America* anticipated some of the most important ideas of critical race theory: counternarrative, structural determinism, and white supremacy.

THE QUESTION OF
BEING AND CREATION OF A NARRATIVE

The essential question that Elijah Muhammad sought to answer was: What is Being for the Black man in America? An ancient Egyptian proverb states, "Know Thyself." That is the beginning of being or the defining of one's existence. History records the path of humans as they struggle to understand themselves in the world. This record or narrative recounts our individual and collective efforts to know and understand our destinies as individuals as well as nations. Before the advent of writing and widespread literacy, many of these records were told orally in the form of myths. All people have a story of their creation and purpose, which is to ennoble and inspire. Yet until the middle of the twentieth century, African Americans possessed no such myths.

It was this lack that Muhammad addressed in *Message to the Blackman in America*. Myths speak from a metaphysical perspective in their intent to describe humans' existence in the world in relation to themselves, others, and things. The myth of Romulus and Remus, twin boys raised by wolves who as adults discover Rome, describes the origin of the Roman people. The Navajo origin legend is a myth that speaks of the importance of corn and wind in the unique creation of the Navajo. *Message to the Blackman in America* posited a narrative that made the black man the original man—"the mighty, the wise, the best, but do not know it."[1] Elijah Muhammad said that God came Himself in the form of a man named W. D. Fard to deliver the Lost Found Nation of Islam from the wilderness of North America. Muhammad said, "It is Allah's will and purpose that we shall know ourselves. Therefore, he came Himself to teach us the knowledge of self. Who is better knowing of who we are than God, Himself? He has declared that we are descendants of the Asian black nation and of the tribe of Shabazz."[2] Muhammad added that they were the original tribe that came with the Earth sixty-six trillion years ago when a great explosion divided the planet into two parts, the earth and the moon:

Allah has decided to place us on the top with a thorough knowledge of self and his guidance. We are the mighty, the wise, the best, but do not know it. Being without the knowledge, we disgrace ourselves, subjecting ourselves to suffering and shame. We could not get the knowledge of self until the coming of Allah. To know thyself is to know all men, as from us came all and to us all will return. I must keep warning you that you should give up the white race's names and religion in order to gain success. Their days of success are over. Their rule will last only as long as you remain asleep to the knowledge of self.[3]

This is the narrative of the origin of the black man in America. It attempted to explain his origin with the language and references of modern times that addressed the reality of his existence. First, the narrative gave the people a tribal name, which comes from the Creator. Giving the loosely connected blacks a tribal name invested them again with all of the social advantages that belong to a race of people. A tribal name would identify them as a united people sharing the same language, culture, and history. Similarly, European Americans are descended from such tribes as Anglo-Saxons and Slavs, and Africans have tribal names such as the Ashanti and Bantu.

Second, this counternarrative made them aware of their longevity on Earth and the origin of their kinky hair, which is a source of mystery among black men and women as well as other races. Kinky hair has always been a matter of contention among blacks. A great deal of money is spent yearly in an attempt to straighten, perm, curl, or extend kinky hair so that it will be "good" like white folks' hair. However, the counternarrative made one appreciate the strength and durability of black people and kinky hair.

Finally, the narrative made blacks aware of the importance of having knowledge of self or being and its ramifications on social relationships. When *Message to the Blackman in America* was written, blacks had been living in America for 346 years. Their relationship with their fellow white citizens was as subordinates, with white supremacy being a major factor in the customs and behaviors of both races. Such association, maintained by fear, ignorance, poverty, and intimidation, was bound to make blacks overly dependent upon whites. Moreover, this dependence made blacks vulnerable to abuse and underdevelopment, yet it perpetuated an unnatural relationship wherein the blacks came to despise themselves and love everything white.

CREATION OF A COUNTERNARRATIVE

Elijah Muhammad's counternarrative concerning the origin of the black man stood in direct opposition to the accepted master narrative of the Judeo-Christian religion. In the master narrative, blacks were subject to the "Curse of Ham," which stated that the descendants (Canaanites) of Ham (Africans), the youngest son of Prophet Noah, were to be the servants of his brothers Shem (Asians) and Japheth (Europeans). This master narrative was used to justify the enslavement of Africans during the slave trade, and even today, in some circles, it is the reasoning for racist behavior toward Africans and the presumption of innate African inferiority. The curse consisted of three elements:

> (1) that black skin is the result of God's curse and is therefore a signal and sign of the African's cursedness to slavery; (2) that Africans embodied this cursed nature through hypersexuality and libidinousness; and (3) that these sinful and cursed Africans were also uncivilized brutes and heathens who were helped by slavery because they were exposed to culture and the saving Gospel of Jesus Christ. At the close of the seventeenth century, the Curse of Ham evoked a single racist image of a black skinned, hyper-sexualized, pagan slave.[4]

And that image persisted well into the twentieth century when W. E. B. Dubois remarked, "The problem of the 20th century is the problem of the color line."

Elijah Muhammad's counternarrative employed the stratagem of duality. The dual complement to a white god would be a black devil, so the complement to a black god would be a white devil. During the time of Elijah

Muhammad, whiteness was associated with everything good and blackness with everything bad. The ultimate privilege of whiteness during the time of Elijah Muhammad and still existing today is its association with the divine. For example, the white man portrayed his image as divine in religious icons of the Christian religion and promoted the curse of Ham as proof of black inferiority and wickedness. Furthermore, his power and prestige throughout the world seemed to validate his status as the "chosen" of God, while denigrating nonwhites. The counternarrative of the white man being the "devil" served as an opposition to white hegemony in the teachings of Black Muslims.

COUNTERNARRATIVE AND STRUCTURAL DETERMINISM

In the counternarrative, whites are created by Yacub, one of the gods of the original black people who was dissatisfied with the status quo. Yacub started studying the life germ of man to try making a new creation, a new man. It was prophesized that Yacub would produce a new race of people who would rule the original black nation for six thousand years until the original black nation gave birth to one whose wisdom and knowledge would be recognized worldwide, and he would destroy Yacub's world and restore the original black nation into power. Yacub discovered the power of magnetism—opposites attracting each other—and theorized that "an unlike human being, made to attract others, [could], with the knowledge of tricks and lies, rule the original man—until that nation could produce one greater and capable of overcoming and making manifest his race of tricks and lies, with a nation of truth."[5]

Social determinism as espoused by Yacub was the genetic annihilation of the black race, which means that structural determinism is present not only institutions and culture but also in sexual behavior. Yacub's plan, the creation of the white race (devils), required that the whole structure of society be designed for this purpose. Dark-skinned blacks could not marry among themselves; they had to marry lighter-colored spouses in order to achieve the desired result. The elite rulers who were a part of the planning and management of the society and the masses who vicariously participated in creating the white race were complicit in creating an order that would bring about the white man's rule over the black man and other people of color. According to Muhammad, this rule or white privilege was also the divine will of Allah, who allowed Yacub's plan to come to fruition, allowing whites to dominate blacks and the entire world until one with greater knowledge than Yacub was born. This counternarrative possessed the knowledge of being for the black man and provided an explanation of the white man's global hegemony and the enmity between the two races. This was appealing to Nation of Islam followers according to Acevedo, Ordner, and Thompson, for several reasons:

> The NOI founders not only inverted and rejected ideological/moral assumptions about African American's racial heritage and destiny, but also created completely new moral distinctions out of traditional Christian moral codes. The NOI mixed basic Christian moral assumptions with a novel "un-supposed" mythology to construct a hybrid moral code centered on the African American experience in America. In this sense, the NOI's narrative inversion represents a re-appropriation and inversion of moral codes . . . to produce a unique moral code designed by and for African Americans.[6]

Acevedo and coauthors claimed that a counternarrative can also invert the master narrative "so that commonly held beliefs lead to the creation of completely new ideological belief systems."[7] However, it was an affront to the efforts of civil rights leaders whose goal was the integration of blacks into white society, which NOI followers believed would continue the process of destruction through further miscegenation.

WHITE SUPREMACY, WHITE POWER, WHITE PRIVILEGE

Critical race theory claims that white power or white privilege permeates American society even though the masses of people within society, especially whites, perceive it as normal. And for such a ubiquitous structure to exist, it must be an inherent part of the social framework (matrix) and psyche of its members.

The structural framework for a racial hierarchy or criminalization of blacks can be evidenced in the outcomes associated with the Thirteenth Amendment to the Constitution, which ironically abolished slavery and at the same time reestablished it for posterity. Stating that slavery is abolished except if one is convicted of a crime, Southerners established Black Codes or Jim Crow laws that led to the imprisonment of African Americans in large numbers for crimes as miniscule as vagrancy based upon the premise of the Thirteenth Amendment. And these convicted freedman were sold to businesses and farms through the convict leasing system. Sadly, thousands of African Americans were forced to rebuild the South during the Reconstruction period under conditions that were considered to be worse than slavery, for now these workers were not the legal property of anyone, so they could be worked literally to death. This system established the criminalization of the black image, which persists today in the minds of many Americans and is revealed through police brutality, racial profiling, "stand your ground" laws, inequity in sentencing, and more. In *Message to the Blackman*, Muhammad acknowledged that injustice has been commonplace in the exercise of white supremacy, power, and privilege: "You should be ashamed of yourself today to lynch and kill so-called Negroes while you have an army full of Negroes helping you to fight and protect and maintain the government. You should be ashamed of it. Especially when that same man's father slaved for your fathers for nothing."[8]

According to the counternarrative allegory/satire of Yacub, the purpose of the white race was to dominate and destroy the black race in this conflict or struggle for power and survival. Dr. Frances Cress Welsing corroborated this phenomenon (white supremacy) in her book *The Isis Papers: The Keys to the Colors*:

> The local and global power system structured and maintained by persons who classify themselves as white. . . . The ultimate purpose of the system is to prevent white genetic annihilation on Earth—a planet in which the overwhelming majority of people are classified as non-white (black, brown, red and yellow) by white-skinned people. All of the non-white people are genetically dominant (in terms of skin coloration) compared to the genetically recessive white-skinned people.[9]

This explanation by Dr. Cress Welsing of white genetic survival parallels and inverts the counternarrative. Yacub worked to create whiteness by weakening the power of the dominant black gene until he achieved a state of albinism/ whiteness. In contrast, Dr. Cress Welsing stated that uncontrolled sexual contact with nonwhites is a paramount concern among white supremacists because they know that the offspring of a nonwhite and white will be nonwhite. This phenomenon is most acutely seen in the physiognomy of the first "black" president of the United States, Barack Obama.

Furthermore, George Yancy (2004) asked, "Is it possible that whiteness embodies a historically concrete form of hatred toward the Other, that is, nonwhiteness? Is it therefore parasitic upon nonwhiteness? Whiteness, on this score, then, is life-denying not only in terms of the erasure of nonwhite Others, but in terms of self-erasure."[10] Yancy's remarks signal a paranoia of whites toward nonwhites and also that the white being or ontology is predicated on the existence of the nonwhite. Another perspective stated by Foucault was that in the second half of the nineteenth century bloodlines and sexuality worked in tandem to develop and maintain white power:

> Racism . . . was then that a whole politics of settlement (peuplement), family, marriage, education, social hierarchization, and property, accompanied by a long series of permanent interventions at the level of the body, conduct, health, and everyday life, received their color and their justification from the mythical concern with protecting the purity of the blood and ensuring the triumph of the

race. Nazism was doubtless the most cunning and the most naïve . . . combination of the fantasies of the blood and the paroxysms of a disciplinary power.[11]

Elijah Muhammad understood completely the dynamics of power (race, sex, subordination, identity) whether by whites or by blacks when he said, "Many so-called Negroes despise and hate 'Black Supremacy' without having knowledge of what this means, and yet they support and believe in 'White Supremacy.' If you say you do not either, then you are neutral. But nay— some must rule over the other. It is the law of nature."[12] And that is the crux of white supremacy. It is the imperative to world domination over nonwhites and especially the genetically dominant black man. This paranoia or local and global power system is in operation today and was clearly defined during the Reconstruction period of American history. After Africans were freed, Vann Woodward, author of *The Strange Career of Jim Crow*, claims that Southerners tried several options in their quest to normalize relations with the newly freed man, but all of the options pursued caused rifts in white unity, both politically and socially, until they settled for the baser solution—white supremacy.[13]

WHITE SUPREMACY AND MISCEGENATION

In *Message to the Blackman in America,* Muhammad's views on miscegenation or the politics of race were not as unorthodox as one might think. Neely Fuller Jr. stated that white supremacy/racism is a global and unjust phenomenon practiced by white people. And based upon this observation he posited that there are four basic motivating factors in human behavior: (1) racism (white supremacy), (2) reaction to racism, (3) sexual expression, and (4) reaction to sexual expression.[14] Therefore, sex and race(ism) are dominant factors in the socialization process of Western thought, and concomitantly they can innocuously lead to white genetic annihilation within a cosmopolitan setting.

Furthermore, well-known European Americans, such as Thomas Jefferson, have stressed the importance of separating the races due to the dangers of miscegenation. When he compared slavery in Rome with slavery in America, Jefferson made it clear that the blood of the African was not to be taken lightly: "Among the Romans emancipation required but one effort. The slave, when made free, might mix with, without straining the blood of his master. But with us a second is necessary, unknown to history. When freed, he is to be removed beyond the reach of mixture."[15] Although Jefferson had no qualms about contaminating the blood of Sally Hemings, his female slave, and their offspring, he spent many years of his life working toward the emigration/ colonization of Africans from America in the eventuality of their freedom.

Although Yacub's history speaks of a rebellious black scientist who intentionally creates the white race, history attests to the fact of white men whitening the societies of indigenous people as they became their rulers/masters and elevating their bastardized offspring above their dark mothers in status.

Thomas Jefferson feared the inevitability of blacks and whites mingling on equal footing within society, and his solution was the colonization of freed blacks to amenable parts of the globe, which according to Michael Vorenberg was the prevailing thought of a "former generation's conservative approach to slaves and free blacks."[16] This idea prevailed up to the presidency of Abraham Lincoln, who also made plans and actually emigrated five hundred out of a proposed five thousand free blacks to Vache Island, a small island off the coast of Haiti privately owned by land developer Bernard Kock in 1862.[17] Yet Lincoln's colonization plan did not happen on the scale proposed, and the remaining settlers of Vache Island, "350 malnourished and raggedly clad black men, women, and children," returned to America on March 21, 1864.[18]

Even though colonization proved to be a disastrous endeavor, the reasoning behind the return of the émigrés and a newfound awareness regarding the state of free blacks was based upon another aspect of white supremacy— *interest convergence.* Leading politicians of that day saw some benefit in keeping the black man in America, and it was not because Frederick Douglass and other anticolonizationists opposed emigration.

> Blacks had taken a key role in the army, and the notion of sending abroad potential warriors against the Confederacy ran counter to common sense and military strategy. Moreover, alternatives to colonization outside the United States had proved more successful than any of Lincoln's schemes. Such efforts as Eli Thayer's military colonization in Florida and Lorenzo Thomas's refugee program in Mississippi may have given Lincoln a sense that blacks could have a future in this country.[19]

So when whites perceived some tangible benefit from the freeing of the slaves and allowing them to stay in the United States, they then modified the system of power and dominance in order to maintain control. They employed strategies such as Jim Crow laws in the South, the mass immigration of European workers as competition in the North, and the freeing of former slaves with nothing but the clothes on their backs, which forced them to return to their former slave owners for work, food, and shelter. Impotent and completely at the mercy of white Americans, blacks were again relegated to a subordinate status while whites in solidarity strengthened their power over them by "maintaining, expanding and refining white supremacy."[20]

NATIONALISM VERSUS INTEGRATION

Integration and nationalism are also aspects of critical race theory. During the civil rights movement, there was a desire on the part of black leadership to integrate into white society. This idea seemed to be the solution to discrimination, poverty, and injustice, yet Muslim leaders were not in agreement with integration; their answer to the social injustices faced by African Americans was nationalism—more clearly, the establishment of a separate state or territory of their own, either on this continent or elsewhere.[21] According to Essien-Udom, author of *Black Nationalism*,

> The Nation of Islam shows the black nationalists' desire to free themselves from the exploited image of blackness and hence from the deep feeling of self-rejection, cultural alienation, and social estrangement which pervade and corrupt the personalities of the Negro masses. It expresses the nationalist's need to attach himself in a positive way to something worthy and esteemed, some center of power, some tradition and, generally, some "central ideal" capable of endowing his life with meaning and purpose. It offers hope in a future, one in which blackness will no longer be despised. In part, this vision of the future inspires the Muslims to pursue their life activities with courage and unbending determination.[22]

The Nation of Islam attracted the masses of poor blacks, not the middle class or highly educated, for it spoke to their need for dignity and exposed the hypocrisy of white America. This unapologetic example of courage contrasted sharply with the patient, cautious, multiracial approach of integration. Dr. C. Eric Lincoln explained that dichotomy in *The Black Muslims in America* (1961):

> Like their counterparts in the middle class, the Blacks furthest down are impatient with the arguments for "education and negotiation." They cannot see why people as well educated as the white man is alleged to be can't tell the difference between right and wrong. It seems to be obviously wrong that people who are not white should be treated differently from those who are, especially in a country where all are supposed to be equal under the laws of the land. They reject the half-hearted explanations about "white moderates" and "men of good will." They do not understand how a "handful of Ku Klux Klan congressmen from Georgia and Mississippi can make the North, the East, the West, the Mid-West and all the rest of the country" conform to their style of racist practices. They are inclined to doubt the alleged good will of any white man, and they tend to be ready to accept Muhammad's allegation that the white man's tricknology has brainwashed the black leaders and bought them out with iced tea and worthless promises.

The followers of Marcus Garvey are represented in the Muslim temples in substantial numbers, as are the Moorish Scientists. But there are also thousands of Muslims who have had no previous contact with black nationalism. What they have had is a sustained contact with enduring corrosion of prejudice, white hatred, and discrimination—and they are looking for a way out. Any way out.[23]

The black leaders and white supporters of that day were exclusively focused on integration/assimilation as the solution to the Negro problem. Church leaders and the NAACP were the major forces in determining a plan of action for acquiring full citizenship rights and equal protection for blacks under American law, and they were of the opinion that these rights could not be gained without the assistance of whites and therefore they acquiesced to their insights. The *Los Angeles Herald-Dispatch* reported that the Jews "have infiltrated the NAACP" and the organization has been "sidetracked by the Jews into a struggle for integration."[24] Due to the influences of whites and Jews in promoting integration as the solution for blacks, Elijah Muhammad charged the black leaders of his day with being reckless: "The most foolish thing an educator can do is to preach [integration]. It shows the white man you want to be white. . . . Our children should be trained in our own schools, not dropped into the schools of the enemy where they are taught that whites have been and forever will be world rulers."[25] Integration included assimilation into the white world, absorption of black people into the larger society, yet the physiognomy of the blacks made assimilation/integration into white society impossible, especially with America's "one drop" rule as a definition of blackness, coupled with the threat of white genetic annihilation.

E. Franklin Frazier, sociologist, educator, author, and scholar, claimed that integration/assimilation was the only option the civil rights leaders were willing to accept because most of them had become the leaders of the black masses by default. As free blacks during slavery, they had been educated by their former slave masters or fathers, and after slavery, their counterparts were mentored by missionary-minded whites. Both scenarios created a sense of paternalism between prominent black leaders and their white benefactors, which continued to manifest itself during the civil rights movement and culminated in the struggle for integration/assimilation. Frazier said, "Integration involves the acceptance of Negroes as individuals into the economic and social organization of American life. This would imply the gradual dissolution of the Negro community, that is, the decline and eventual disappearance of the associations, institutions and other forms of associated life in what constitutes the Negro community."[26]

In contrast, Muslim leaders did not trust whites with the well-being and future of blacks. Muhammad had declared that they were a race of devils and were not to be trusted. He encouraged blacks to trust in themselves and unite, and he criticized the civil rights leaders concerning their loyalty and blind love for their oppressor:

> The offer of integration . . . is made by those who are trying to deceive the black peoples into believing that their 400-year-old open enemies of freedom, justice, and equality are, all of a sudden, their "friends." . . . If the white people are truthful about their professed friendship toward the so-called Negro, they can prove it by dividing up America with their slaves.[27]

Moreover, Muhammad did not absolve the masses of blacks from their responsibility as free men and women. He encouraged them to not only think independently but act independently as well. He understood that a true movement or revolution must grow from the bottom and extend upward: "You must start thinking and working in the way of independence. . . . Get away from that childish way of thinking that the white man forever owes it to you to provide for you the necessities of life."[28]

EMPATHIC FALLACY

The empathic fallacy of critical race theory is the mistaken belief that the telling of racial incidents from the perspective of the oppressed creates empathy within the oppressors, causing them to implement incremental or sweeping social reform. However, the reality is that most people empathize with that which is significant to them, and empathy has not proven itself powerful or persuasive enough to overcome the oppressive structures of a society. Historically, when African Americans such as Frederick Douglass told their stories of oppression in their slave narratives, abolitionists identified with these stories because they supported their contention that American slavery was morally wrong and, consequently, would bring about the fall of America, so their empathy was due to their concern for the future of America, not the condition of Africans. Likewise, their opposition to slavery was of minimal importance in ending slavery; it was the secession of Southern states from the Union that caused the Civil War and ultimately ended slavery.

The impotence of empathy can be seen further in the example of the Union troops' withdrawal from the South during the Reconstruction period. The implementation of Jim Crow laws did not evoke an immediate response from the federal government nor a mass insurrection from principled people in the North. African Americans faced a reign of terror for nearly seventy years before European Americans took measures to stop it, and that was predicated upon interest convergence again. American leaders concerned with the U.S. image abroad during World War II made structural changes so that opponents of democracy, like fascism and communism, would not find it so easy to expose the hypocrisy within American democracy.[29] Yet black leaders of that day thought that exposure to the truths of racial oppression—such as the intransigent racial hatred of Bull Connor (commissioner of public safety for the city of Birmingham, Alabama, who gained notoriety as the international symbol of racism during the period)—on the evening news influenced American leaders to do the right thing. This was false. Elijah Muhammad asserted, "The so-called Negroes are disgracing themselves lying at the feet of the white man and begging him to accept them as equals. . . . It is against the very nature and disposition of the slave-master to accept his once slave as his equal."[30]

Proof of the limitations of empathy are seen today in the phenomenon of microaggression, which critical race theory defines as small encounters with racism, usually unnoticed by members of the majority group. Wilson describes this behavior:

> The ultimate force in the world is the force of mind. When that force is defeated all is lost. Dominant Whites have used words and symbols to violently and unrelentingly attack oppressed Blacks in a thousand and one nefarious ways, including the projection of dehumanizing stereotypes and caricatures of them; the falsification of their history and culture; the miseducation of Blacks; and the engaging chronic derisive media attacks on their morals, behavior, intelligence, ways of life, sexuality, physical features, motives and values.[31]

The limits of empathy were also evident to Muhammad in white America's reaction to even the mild resistance of the mainstream civil rights movement. When *Message to the Blackman in America* was written in 1965, the system of Jim Crow and segregation were the norm within America, so daily assaults on the minds and bodies of black people were commonplace. And Elijah Muhammad did not expect the tactics to intimidate and control blacks to change even under integration. He warned:

> If the white race were for peace they would thank God for raising up in their midst a peaceful people who do not desire to make any mischief among them. Here we have the NAACP, CORE and various other organizations before our eyes, who attempt to try achieving their aims [. . .] without weapons, without anything harmful. . . . only to be kicked and stamped upon.[32]

CONCLUSION

Elijah Muhammad wrote *Message to the Blackman in America* at a time when much racial animosity existed and the American government was complicit in maintaining the racial hierarchy. Since then, much has changed in the social relationships between blacks and whites, and many other races, such as Latinos and Asians, have become a growing part of the American landscape. African American Muslims have continued to progress within American society, and many immigrant Muslim communities also call America their home. And in 2008 Americans elected an African American president, the son of a Kenyan man and Caucasian American female. Muhammad doubted Kennedy's claim that in forty years a Negro man would become president.[33] Unfortunately, it has been under President Barack Hussein Obama's administration that white supremacy has been most visible since the civil rights movement. High-profile shootings of unarmed black youth like Travon Martin, Oscar Grant III, Jordan Davis, Jonathan Ferrell, Renisha McDaniels, Michael Brown, and many more by police or pseudo-police have made Americans and the world aware that the life of blacks in America is still precarious. Furthermore, African Americans are still largely a dependent people with a small showing in business and community development. Public education has gotten worse, with many African American males dropping out of school or incarcerated, and the African American family is in shambles.

But despite these social ills, integration, the panacea to segregation, is the law of the land. There are no governmental barriers to what a man or woman of color can do in America, but structural barriers within society persist. Critical race theory acknowledges that these barriers exist as functioning aspects of power executed by the powerful. Derrick Bell, one of the founders of critical race theory, was also executive secretary of the Pittsburgh branch of the NAACP during the controversial rise of the Nation of Islam[34] and later became a civil rights lawyer in the South. He was very optimistic about the goals and objectives of the NAACP, which he believed would lead to the eventual eradication of white supremacy and racism in America. But his ideals had been eroded by the 1970s

> as a number of lawyers, activists, and legal scholars across the country realized, more or less simultaneously, that the heady advances of the civil rights era of the 1960s had stalled and, in many respects, were being rolled back. Realizing that new theories and strategies were needed to combat the subtler forms of racism that were gaining ground, Derrick Bell, Alan Freeman, and Richard Delgado put their minds to the task.[35]

Before his passing in 2011, Bell asked his supporters to consider the "proposition" that racial oppression in America is permanent:

> Black people will never gain full equality in this country. Even those herculean efforts we hail as successful will produce no more than temporary "peaks of progress," short-lived victories that slide into irrelevance as racial patterns adapt in ways that maintain white dominance. This is a hard-to-accept fact that all

history verifies. We must acknowledge it, not as a sign of submission, but as an act of ultimate defiance.[36]

It is a paradox that Elijah Muhammad's analysis of racism in America has come to be accepted in the form of critical race theory. By teaching black Muslims the truth about racism/white supremacy and power through the use of myth and the ennoblement of an identity and purpose for black existence in America, African American Muslims were buttressed against the vicissitude of American political leadership and its weaker elements. Upon the passing of Elijah Muhammad, his son W. D. Mohammed became the leader of the Nation of Islam and transitioned it from a nationalistic, provincial eschatology to acceptance of the universal message of Al-Islam. W. D. Mohammed pointed out that belief in God is greater than race and nation, and Al-Islam offers what African Americans and their ancestors have been searching for since slavery:

A Muslim is obligated first to live his Muslim life as Allah revealed it in the Qur'an and as demonstrated in the life of our Prophet Muhammad. Al-Islam was before the United States and will be after the United States. Believe me, African Americans do want to grow up more. We have to latch on to something bigger than the United States. Latch on to something that has more permanence than politically formed systems. Latch on to something that has a higher principle, a higher value than political systems. Do that and we will become the best citizens. The best citizens of the United States are those who have a high principle ruling over their behavior. Such people live in worlds bigger than geographical boundaries.[37]

NOTES

1. E. Muhammad, *Message to the Blackman in America* (Philadelphia: House of Knowledge Publications, 1965), 32.

2. Ibid., 31.

3. Ibid., 31–32.

4. D. Whitford, "A Calvinist Heritage to the 'Curse of Ham': Assessing the Accuracy of a Claim about Racial Subordination," *Church History and Religious Culture* 90, no. 1 (2010): 25–45, 27, doi:10.1163/187124110X506509.

5. Muhammad, *Message to the Blackman in America,* 112.

6. G. A. Acevedo, J. Ordner, and N. Thompson, "Narrative Inversion as a Tactical Framing Device: The Ideological Origins of the Nation of Islam," *Narrative Inquiry* 20, no. 1 (2010): 124–52, 132, doi: 10.1075/ni.20.1.07ace.

7. Ibid., 131.

8. Muhammad, *Message to the Blackman in America,* 167.

9. Frances Cress Welsing, *The Isis Papers: The Keys to the Colors* (Chicago: Third World Press, 1999), ii.

10. G. Yancy, "A Foucauldian, Genealogical Reading of Whiteness: The Production of the Black Body/Self and the Racial Deformation of Pecola Breedlove in Tony Morrison's *The Bluest Eye*," in *What White Looks Like: African American Philosophers on the Whiteness Question,* ed. G. Yancy (New York: Routledge, 2004), 107–42, 113.

11. M. Foucault, "Right of Death and Power over Life," in *The Foucault Reader*, ed. P. Rabinow (New York: Random House, 1984), 258–72, 270–71.

12. Muhammad, *Message to the Blackman in America,* 130.

13. Van Woodward, *The Strange Career of Jim Crow* (3rd ed.) (New York: Oxford University Press, 1974).

14. Neely Fuller Jr., *The United Independent Compensatory Code/System/Concept* (Author, 1971), 23.

15. T. Jefferson, "Thomas Jefferson's Thoughts on the Negro, Part 1," *Journal of Negro History* 3, no. 1 (1918): 55–89, 57, retrieved from www.jstor.org/stable/ 2313794.

16. M. Vorenberg, "Abraham Lincoln and the Politics of Black Colonization," *Journal of the Abraham Lincoln Association* 14, no. 2 (1993): 22–45, 23, retrieved from www.jstor.org/stable/20148897.

17. Ibid., 41.

18. Ibid., 44.

19. Ibid., 43.

20. Fuller, *The United Independent Compensatory Code,* 13.

21. Muhammad, *Message to the Blackman in America,* 161.

22. Essien U. Essien-Udom, *Black Nationalism: The Search for an Identity in America* (Chicago: University of Chicago Press, 1962), 123.

23. E. C. Lincoln, *The Black Muslims in America* (New York: Kayode Publications, 1961), 173–174.

24. Ibid., 157.

25. Muhammad, *Message to the Blackman in America,* 171, 272.

26. Cited in Khalid Abdullah Tariq Al-Mansour, *Betrayal by Any Other Name* (San Francisco: First African Arabian Press, 1993), 471–72.

27. Muhammad, *Message to the Blackman in America,* 163–64.

28. Ibid., 301.

29. Douglas A. Blackmon, *Slavery by Another Name: The Re-Enslavement of Black Americans from the Civil War to World War II* (New York: Anchor, 2009); Woodward, *The Strange Career of Jim Crow.*

30. Muhammad, *Message to the Blackman in America,* 207.

31. A. Wilson, *Blueprint for Black Power: A Moral, Political, and Economic Imperative for the Twenty-First Century* (New York: Afrikan World Infosystems, 1998), 11–12.

32. Muhammad, *Message to the Blackman in America,* 214.

33. Ibid., 208.

34. Lincoln, *The Black Muslims in America,* 155–156.

35. R. Delgado, and J. Stefancic, *Critical Race Theory: An Introduction,* 2nd ed. (New York: NYU Press, 2012), 40.

36. D. Bell, *Faces at the Bottom of the Well: The Permanence of Racism* (New York: Basic Books, 1992), 12.

37. W. D. Mohammed, *Al-Islam Unity and Leadership* (Chicago: The Sense Maker, 1991), 152.

Chapter Five

The Nation of Islam

A Historiography of Pan Africanist Thought and Intellectualism[1]

James L. Conyers Jr.

INTRODUCTION

This chapter looks at the development of Pan Africanist thought in the Nation of Islam. Throughout the history of African Americans—from the era of enslavement to the contemporary period—African Americans have exhibited a posture for spiritual solemnity and pilgrimage, one that has allowed them to unearth a voice and perspective of cultural autonomy (e.g., pan Africanist, cultural nationalist, Black nationalism, and Afrocentric perspectives).

These cultural perspectives have been in contrast to the white perspective that has pervaded American history and culture. As Charles H. Wesley has noted,

A consistent and continuous effort has been made during the history of the United States to present the American Negro as inferior beings and as a folk different from the normal American stock. Their biological inferiority and racial inequality have been readily accepted because they have been so treated by so many American thinkers. From the earliest colonial periods through the Civil War to the present time, one general belief has been dominant in the mind of the American people concerning the Negro. Conclusions have been drawn from differences in color, physique and other apparently inherited or acquired characteristics, which have been regarded as inescapable. Then, too, with variations in these physical evidences of race, the question remains unanswered as to what is a Negro. Even some of those who were the friends of the Negro people regarded them at times with the hopeful assurance, often reemphasized by religious convictions based upon revivalism, that they would ultimately improve and make progress during the advancing years."[2]

It was to counter this white racism that the Nation of Islam developed its own strand of Pan Africanist thought and intellectualism. The Nation of Islam was one of the most meaningful Black organizations to have taken up these ideological schools of thought in the twentieth century. Aminah Beverly McCloud writes about its popularity, in the following manner: "The Nation of Islam, an indigenous African American Islamic expression founded by Wali Fard Muhammad and developed by Elijah Muhammad, became the American media prototype of Islam in the African American community. The core philosophy of the Nation was characterized by a combination of messianism and form of chiliasm."[3] The chapter draws on definitions, theoretical paradigms, and methodology to examine the role of the Nation of Islam in the development of Pan Africanist thought and analysis on themes such as retention, residual, and reflexivity of an continental African composite of culture "sifting" to Africans throughout the diaspora. Cultural "sifting" is "the fomenting of unity among peoples of Africana descent going across barriers of land, history, and culture."[4] Staples refers to this concept as "revolutionary Pan Africanism," which operates on three levels: (1) cultural; (2) economic, and (3) political.[5]

To study these strands of Pan Africanism, we will draw on historiography, which studies how and why history written in the manner in which it unfolds.[6] Historiography attempts to interpret cultural attitudes by examining what variables are addressed and what data and information is omitted in the writing of history. One aspect of historiography is the role of language in the social construction of race. Evelyn Brooks Higginbotham offers a generative point discussing metalanguage, noting "its powerful, all-encompassing effect of the construction and representation of other social and power relations, namely, gender, class, and sexuality." She comments: "We must recognize race as providing sites of dialogic exchange and contestation, since race has constituted a discursive tool for both oppression and liberation."[7]

The organizational structure of the NOI came about between two important periods in Americana historiography. The organization was founded in 1930 by Wallace Fard (i.e., sometimes referred to Farad Muhammad) in Detroit, Michigan. Immediately prior to its founding, during the mid- and latter parts of the 1920s, African Americans were engaged in the process of redefining and reexamining themselves, under the auspices of the concept "New Negro" and the sociopolitical movements of the Harlem Renaissance, the Great Migration, and the early civil rights movement. This period was saw the emergence of the ideological schools of existentialism and phenomenology, and the Muslim League was in formation by the early 1900s, which established the base for the formation of Pakistan. The founding of the NOI was bookended on the far end by World War II, another important moment for historiography. The NOI soon became an important voice in the discourse of race in midcentury America.

Despite the importance of the Nation of Islam in the intellectual developments of the twentieth century, few studies have addressed the role the NOI
played in the rehabilitation of African Americans ethos, memory, and logos.
Many studies have been conducted on the NOI, but they are consistently situ-
ated within a conflict perspective. This chapter takes a different perspective:
to use analytical research tools to show how the NOI addressed the crucial
questions of African American identity in the twentieth century: What does
it mean to be African? What does it mean to love African people? And how
do we maintain a pro-African perspective within the constraints of a hostile,
racialist-racist society?

The conceptual paradigm used in this study is the *ujimaa* model. Ujimaa
is the Kwanzaa principle of collective work and social responsibility. In this
case, the emphasis is on examining the historiography of the Nation of Islam
using meta-analysis and qualitative methodologies. It draws upon secondary analysis as the primary design of collecting data and information, while
simultaneously using tools from historical methods, content analysis, and
ethnography.

HISTORICAL OVERVIEW
OF THE PAN AFRICANIST MOVEMENT

The conceptual analysis of Pan Africanism lends itself to addressing issues
and schema of self-determination and cultural agency for people of Africana
decent. Leaders such as Martin Delany, Sylvester Williams, W. E. B. DuBois,
and Marcus M. Garvey consistently agitated for these actions to be articulated
to the masses of Africana people. Yet despite the Nation of Islam's teachings
on Pan Africanism in the United States, scholarly studies tend to focus solely
on the NOI as a Black Nationalist organization.

Perspectives on the NOI often fall into the three categories outlined by
Steven Tsoukalas: (1) Fard a Moor; (2) Fard is Ford; and (3) Fard a Fraud.[8]
These reductionist views ignore that the organization has its contextual base
of ideological repertoire in a global Pan Africanist perspective.[9] Equally
important, some critics address the shortcomings of an orthodox practice of
religion employed by Farad and Elijah Muhammad of African Americans in
the West. Instead, when we engage in a process of discovery research, we see
that Elijah Muhammad was part of a growing theological-spiritual movement
in America in the late 1890s and early 1900s that grew out of a structural Pan
Africanist philosophy of liberation. Tsoukalas discusses this issue further:

> The Nation of Islam (NOI) is a product of the times. The movement, which be-
> gan in 1930, did not appear within a vacuum. Several cultural, anthropological,

and theological influences from the nineteenth and early twentieth centuries spawned it. Consequently, the movement cannot be understood without mention of slavery and the attitude it birthed among certain black people or without a study of a few key black leaders who promoted black nationalism and who proceeded the rise of the NOI.[10]

Malcolm X himself offered comments to support the validity of global Pan Africanism:

Many of us fool ourselves into thinking of Afro-Americans as those only who are here in the United States. America is North America, Central America, and South America. Anybody of African ancestry in South America is an Afro-American. Anybody in Central America of African blood is an Afro-American. Anybody here in North America, including Canada, is an Afro-American if he has African ancestry—even down to the Caribbean, he's an Afro-American. So when I speak of the Afro-American, I'm not just speaking of the 22 million of us who are here in the United States. But the Afro-American is a large number of people in the Western Hemisphere.[11]

Richard Brent Turner addressed the intellectual and praxis development of Pan Africanism and Al-Islam in the West.[12] He wrote specifically of the importance of Edward Wilmont Blyden, a Liberian educator and diplomat who advocated a Pan African politics:

It is impossible to understand fully the transition between the "old Islam" of the original African Muslim slaves and the "new American Islam" of the early twentieth century without giving some attention to nineteenth century Pan Africanism, which formed the ideological bridge between these phases of Islam in the United States. Moreover, the Pan Africanist ideas of Edward Wilmont Blyden (1832–1912) are key to understanding the racial particularism and signification that was endemic to global Islam in the nineteenth century. Blyden, who is sometimes called the "father of Pan Africanism," used the example of Islam in West Africa as the paradigm for racial separatism and signification in his Pan Africanist ideology and ultimately argued that as a global religion for blacks, Islam was preferable to Christianity. These ideals were destined to have a profound impact on black nationalist and Islamic movements in America in the twentieth century.[13]

Blyden wrote in the late 1880s, a period during which Pan Africanism in the United States was growing as a movement of self-definition, autonomy, and acquisition of power. As such, a number of nationalist organizations embraced the idea of Africana cultural autonomy. Many of these individuals and organizations had a direct influence on the NOI: Blyden, the economic philosophy of Marcus Garvey, the Moorish Science Temple, the Temple of

Islam, and many others. They became the basis of the NOI's religious and economic nationalist ideology.[14]

Adib Rashad also wrote about the role of Garveyism and Black nationalism on the foundation, context, and practice of Islam by African Americans. Equally important, Duse Muhammad Ali is often times referred to as a mentor to Marcus Garvey, in his development of the Universal Negro Improvement Association (UNIA).[15] Still, it appears the concept of Pan Africanism, which in many ways can be transmitted as Afrocentricity, is the cultural basis and context for the alternative interpretative analysis of the Africana experience, with emphasis on North America.[16] Historically, the Ahmadiyya movement in India during the late 1880s provided dialogue and a base for engagement on Islam in the West. Turner points out that the World's Fair of Religions held in Chicago in the 1890s provided the forum for the introduction of Islam in the West, with advocates such as Mohammed Alexander Russell Webb, born in 1846 and credited as the first white man in America to convert to Islam.[17] Rashad expostulates this subject in a standardized manner:

> [Garvey's] objective was the redemption of Africa for Africans at home and abroad. He believed that if Africans in the United States were economically viable and independent they would be able to redeem the African continent and establish a world wide confraternity of African people. More importantly, he believed that Africans of the world once united by the consciousness of race and nationality, [they] could become a great and powerful people once again. Even though Garveyites continued to use the term "Negro" they passionately identified with their African origins. Garvey frequently used Ethiopian as a symbolic term for all of black Africa.[18]

Karl Evanzz wrote about what he considered to be the naïve nationalism and prophecies of Pan Africanism of the Nation of Islam under the leadership of Wallace Farad Muhammad and Elijah Muhammad. But Evanzz fails to take into account the conditions in which the NOI emerged in the 1930s. These tendencies in the NOI can be explained on the basis of two points: (1) the Great Migration of blacks from the Deep South to Northern metropolises created the advent of participation in activist organization espousing a rhetoric of Africana agency; and (2) the NOI was influenced by the social ecological attributes of Freemasons, the Jehovah's Witnesses, Baptist fundamentalism, and the theological tenets of Reverend Frank Norris.[19] From a historical perspective, the NOI joined the teachings of Islam with elements of religious nationalism in order to meet the needs of the people in that specific place and time.

The concept of Pan Africanism continued to gain prominence in the twentieth century. Samuel Livingston cites Maualana Karenga's analysis of the cultural needs of African Americans that might contribute to the rise of Pan Africanism:

> Karenga's Kawaida concept situates political thought as an essential area of cultural reconstruction, which is essential to any notion of liberation. He suggests that Americans of African descent are plagued by a form of "ideological deficiency," a general lack of culture specific perspectives, paradigms and ideologies. One particular aspect of this ideological deficiency is false consciousness, the tendency to assume the perspectives and ideological stances of dominating groups. Although the adoption of Eurocentric perspectives is the dominant form of false consciousness, Americans of African descent have adopted the point of view and, at times, the identity of other cultural—political entities.[20]

This misidentification of African Americans with the dominant culture is exactly what the concept of Pan Africanism was meant to counter. Part of Pan Africanism's counternarrative has been to reinterpret the very meaning of being a black Muslim. Even now, most of the biographical or sociological studies conducted on this topic present African American Muslims and their movement as a practitioners of a polytheistic dogma of terrorism or as naïve nationalists who are antiwhite. These studies center too much attention on descriptive analysis and less on the memory of cultural norms, values, and mores of African Americans. Black Muslims continue to battle these narrow descriptions and to self-define, aligning themselves with the sacred evolution of African Americans to achieve conciliation with the will of Allah and acceptance of the teaching and foundations of Islam.

In contemporary times, too many academics ignore the development of the African American Muslim movement in the United States in favor of focusing on the civil rights movement. This narrow focus has left critical issues unexamined, issues such as the cultural aspects of Islam that have proven key to understanding the repression and, conversely, progress of African people. Without studying Black Muslims throughout their sojourn and epoch of bondage through the antebellum era, we cannot understand their identification with socialism and nationalism, along with Islam, as implements of analysis for their sacred and secular understanding of memory and belief.

Table 5.1 is a comparative historiographical charting of Americana and African American historical events starting from 1892 and going up until 1914. The illustration of linkages between major events both in the United States and in African American historiography provide an analysis to examine black life in the United States from a macro perspective.

NATION OF ISLAM

As noted earlier, the Nation of Islam, although known popularly for its nationalist tendencies, was in actuality an important participant in Pan Africanist thought in the twentieth century. This section will offer a working analysis of Pan Africanist intellectual thought and provide a historical overview of the Nation of Islam.

Pan Africanism has two main pillars (1) the unification of Africans on the continent of Africa and (2) the unification of Africans in the diaspora. These conceptual foundations of Pan Africanism took shape during the late 1800s and early part of the 1900s Specifically, in the 1900s, visionaries such as Edward Wilmont Blyden, Sylvester Williams, Anna Julia Cooper, and W. E. B. DuBois were key leadership figures in the vanguard of the Pan Africanist movement.[21] Leading up to the 1920s, African Americans were engaged in redefining and reexamining themselves under the auspices of the "New Negro" movement, centered in the Harlem community. Still by the1930s, the Negritude movement was an augmentation of Pan Africanist thought being practiced in Paris.[22] Despite these developments, Moses points out, "From the mid-1930s to the mid-1960s, black intellectual leadership was overwhelmingly committed to intergrationism."[23] Nonetheless, the conceptual foundation for Africana cultural autonomy was taking root in the Americas. Indeed, reclamation of culture would be identified as one of the key variables in the adjustment of memory and ethos of a African-centered perspective.

Wallace Fard Muhammad founded the Allah Temple of Islam—the precursor to the Nation of Islam—in Detroit, Michigan, in 1930. Prior to the founding of the NOI, there were at least four African American Islamic movements already established in the United States: (1) The Moorish Science Temple founded by Noble Drew Ali in 1913 in Newark, New Jersey; (2) the Ahmadiyya movement of Dr. Mufti Muhammad Sadiq in 1921 in Chicago; (3) the Universal Islamic Society of Duse Muhammad Ali in 1926 in Detroit; and (4) the Islamic Propagation Center of America, founded by Shaykh al-haj Daoud Ahmed Faisal in 1928 in Brooklyn, New York.[24] There were other Islamic organizations emerging elsewhere in the Americas as well; Clyde-Ahmad Winters cites the 1880s activism of Jose Paraiso as well as the African Islamic movements in Brazil at Port Novo, led by a Yoruba trader named al-Haji–Mouterirou Soule.[25] Still, Richard Brent Turner cites the Ahmadiyya movement's recruitment of African Americans as proselytes and evangelists. There is also documented information that Sadiq gave lectures periodically at Garvey's UNIA meetings.[26] Of these movements, the first acknowledged is the Moorish Science Temple of Allah, founded in Newark, New Jersey, in 1913, by Noble Drew Ali. In some cases, these organizations were re-creations of earlier ones, when members left a group to establish another.[27]

Table 5.1. Historiographic Timeline of Americana and Africana History and Culture[1]

Year	Americana	Africana
1892	Populist party wants reform and picks James Weaver to run for president of the United States. Benjamin Harrison is elected as the 23rd president of the United States on the Republican Party ticket. Also, in 1890 Wyoming is admitted to the Union as the 44th state on July 10, 1890.	Southern Lynch Law; Ida Wells Barnett publishes her exposé on "Southern Horrors: Lynch Law in All Its Phases."
1895	Austrian psychologist Sigmund Freud founds the field of psychoanalysis.	Booker T. Washington delivers his Atlanta Compromise Speech.
1896	Supreme Court makes the decision that segregation is not against the Constitution. Utah becomes the 45th state of the Union.	Mary Church Terrell becomes president of the National Association of Colored Women. *Plessy v. Ferguson* landmark decision of the Supreme Court allows "separate but equal" public facilities.
		Ethiopian emperor Menelek II defeats the Italian army at the Battle of Aduwa in 1896, making Ethiopia the only African nation to maintain its independence from colonial domination.
1899–1902	In the South African Boer War, Dutch settlers fight to maintain domination of South Africa. First Peace Conference is held in Hague, Netherlands; 26 nations meet to discuss issues such as arms reductions and conditions of warfare. The United States annexes Hawaii.	Composer Scott Joplin publishes the song "Maple Leaf Rag."
1900	Jazz gains popularity in Europe. Existentialism and phenomenology are the two leading schools of philosophy in Europe.	First Pan African Congress meeting is held in London.
1901–09	Theodore Roosevelt assumes presidency of the United States after the assassination of William McKinley. The Roosevelt administration is aggressive in progressive reform and intervention in Panama, with the construction of the Panama Canal.	Booker T. Washington dines with President Roosevelt, amid criticism based on segregation and Jim Crow Laws.

1903	Orville and Wilbur Wright make the first successful flight of an airplane at Kitty Hawk, North Carolina, traveling nearly 37 miles.	W. E. B. DuBois publishes *The Souls of Black Folk*.
1905	The Niagara Movement is organized and assembles in Niagara Falls, Ontario.	Niagara Movement led by W. E. B. DuBois and Monroe Trotter. DuBois coins the term "The Talented Tenth" to refer to college-trained African Americans who could step into leadership positions to advance the cause and status of African Americans.
1906	President Theodore Roosevelt gives the order for 167 Black infantrymen to be given dishonorable discharges based on the conspiracy of a white citizen in Brownsville, Texas. Muslims in India choose the Muslim League to represent them in negotiations against the British.	Alpha Phi Alpha fraternity is incorporated at Cornell University, creating the first African American student Greek lettered fraternity. John Hope becomes the founding president of Atlanta Baptist College.
1907	The so-called Gentlemen's Agreement is drafted to limit Japanese immigration to the United States. Theodore Roosevelt ends segregation of Japanese school children and provides limited protection for Japanese immigrants.	Black Primitive Baptist congregations—formed by emancipated slaves during the post-Civil War era—becomes known as the National Primitive Baptist Convention.
1908	Ottoman military officers from the Committee of Union and Progress (CUP)—formed in 1899 and known as the Young Turks—call for a restoration of the Ottoman constitution; they advance the idea of a new national identity based on Turkish culture.	In a race riot in Springfield, IL, several thousand whites attack the black community, and two elderly blacks are lynched.
1909	William H. Taft is elected as the 27th president of the United States on the Republican Party ticket.	W. E. B. DuBois begins research on the *Encyclopedia Africana*. The NAACP is founded.
1911	Carl Jung founds the field of analytic psychology.	The National Urban League is founded in New York City.
1912	U.S. troops are sent into Cuba.	The African National Congress (originally called the South African Native National Conference, or NNC) is founded.
1914	Europe goes to war after the assassination of Austria's Archduke Franz Ferdinand and his wife.	Great migration of African Americans from the South to Northern metropolises begins.
1914	World War I begins, eventually involving 32 nations.	Marcus Garvey founds the UNIA.

1 Encarta Encyclopedia CD Rom, Britannica Encyclopedia of Black Profiles, *For the People, By the People* (Paterson, NJ: The People's Publishing Group), 1998, 283, 301, 356–57, 376; Robert Divine, T. H. Breen, George M. Fredrickson, and R. Hal Williams, *America Past and Present*, 2nd ed. (Glenview, IL: Foresman, 1987).

Nonetheless, it is clear that a general African Islamic movement was gaining steam in the United States and elsewhere in the Americas.

The Nation of Islam was part of this general movement. It was founded in 1930 by Wali Fard (Farad) Muhammad, who began with just a few committed aspirants. E. U. Essien-Udom explains the development of the NOI in the following manner: "Historically, the Nation of Islam has much in common with the separate Negro church and associations, and more directly with the nationalist movements led by Noble Drew Ali and Marcus Garvey, but it differs from the earlier traditions in that its ideology is intensely chiliastic and buttressed by racial doctrines."[28] William Banks writes about the early foundations of this organization in the following:

> Wallace Fard's teachings varied significantly from those of traditional Islam, which promotes brotherhood among people of all races. His religious movement, in fact, had more in common with Marcus Garvey's black nationalism and Noble Drew Ali's Moorish Science Temple of America. As a result, he attracted to the Nation of Islam many of the same people who had been drawn to Garvey and Ali. Fard's "lost sheep" subsequently became known as Black Muslims.[29]

Clifton Marsh adds the following information:

> During the summer of 1930, W. D. Fard Muhammad, often referred to as Professor Fard, appeared in the Paradise Valley community of Detroit, Michigan, claiming to be Noble Drew Ali reincarnated. His mission was to gain freedom, justice, and equality for people of African descent residing in the United States. Master Fard proclaimed himself the leader of the Nation of Islam with remedies to cure problems in the African American community: social problems, lack of economic development, undisciplined family life and alcoholism.[30]

One of the priorities of the organization was to locate the Lost Found Nation of Asiatics in the west. Often referred to as the Lost Tribe of Shabazz, African Americans represented the downtrodden masses of African Americans misplaced in the wilderness of North America.[31]

Fard's organization was called the Allah Temple of Islam from 1930 to 1933.[32] By 1933, because of internal and external strife in the Detroit community, as well as the departure of Fard and Ugan Ali—two of the early ciphered figures of leadership in the Allah Temple of Islam—the labor of instruction and management of this assembly was transmitted to one of Fard's disciples, Elijah Muhammad, who changed the organization's name to the Nation of Islam.[33] From this period up until the 1940s, the organization went through ideological transition. By the early 1950s, the Nation of Islam was identified as one of the largest Black businesses in America, while simultaneously being referred to as a threat to the internal security of the United States.[34] By this time Elijah Muhammad was referred to as a patron saint in the history and structure of the organization.[35]

Despite its focus on Africans in America, the Nation of Islam already had a clear Pan Africanist perspective. Minister Tynnetta Muhammad describes the symbolism of the Nation of Islam writing, "The Flag of Islam with the symbols of the Sun, Moon, and the Stars, represent the Universe and is also a Banner of Universal peace and harmony. Our Holy Temples of Islam were established in America as sanctuaries of peace and higher learning into the Knowledge of the Oneness of God."[36]

The Nation of Islam arose at a time when blacks were querying the validity of a Eurocentric hegemonic perspective. Scholars and thinkers like Edward Wilmont Blyden believed that Islam would be the religion to provide liberation for African Americans by providing an alternative to that Eurocentric hegemonic perspective. Turner writes:

> The Pan Africanist ideas of Edward W. Blyden (1832–1912) are the key to understanding how and why the racial particularism and signification of black American Islam became linked to racial separatism and signification that was endemic to global Islam in the nineteenth century. Blyden, who is sometimes called the "father of Pan-Africanism," used the example of Islam in West Africa as the paradigm for racial separatism and signification in his Pan Africanist ideology and ultimately argued that as a global religion for blacks, Islam was preferable to Christianity. These ideas were destined to have a profound impact on black nationalist and Islamic movements in the twentieth century.[37]

Furthermore, the social ecological landscape of 1930 provided an impetus for the establishment and development of the Allah Temple of Islam. With emphasis on labor history, Joe Trotter writes about the African American population who moved in great numbers, as part of the Great Migration, to urban areas in the northern metropolises. The black population in northern cities increased from

> forty-four percent in 1930 to nearly fifty percent during the depression years. The black population in northern cities increased by nearly twenty-five percent; the cities with black populations of over 100,000 increased from one in 1930 to eleven in 1935. Public social services played an increasing role in decisions to move. . . . The increasing migration of blacks to cities intensified the poverty of established residents.[38]

Table 5.2 is a social ecological screen showing social movement events that led up to the foundation of the Allah Temple of Islam.

During this time period, the concept of Orientalism was associated with the teachings of Islam, African history, and metaphysics of spirituality. C. Eric Lincoln writes about this topic regarding Noble Drew Ali:

> Drew never seems to have had formal education, but at some point he apparently had been exposed to Oriental philosophy. He was particularly impressed

Table 5.2.   The Social Ecology of African American Social Movements[1]

Year	Social Movement
1895	Booker T. Washington delivers his Atlanta Compromise speech.
1896	*Plessy v. Ferguson* decision by the United States Supreme Court establishes the "separate but equal" doctrine.
1900	The first Pan African Congress meeting is held in London.
1903	W. E. B. DuBois publishes *The Souls of Black Folk*.
1905	The Niagara Movement is founded.
1908	The Springfield race riot takes place, killing seven.
1909	The NAACP is founded.
1913	The Moorish Science Temple by Noble Drew Ali is founded in Newark, New Jersey.
1911	The National Urban League is founded.
1914	The Great Migration of African Americans out of the Deep South to Northern metropolises begins.
1915	Carter G. Woodson organizes and founds the Association for the Study of Afro-American Life and History.
1916	The Universal Negro Improvement Association is founded.
1919	The so-called Red Summer of racial riots against blacks causes death and the destruction of black neighborhoods.
1920	Harlem Renaissance takes off in New York.
1926	Carter G. Woodson establishes Negro History Week.
1930	The Allah Temple of Islam is founded.

[1] Sources are taken from the chronology in William R. Scott and William G. Shade, eds., *Upon These Shores: Themes in the African American Experience 1600–Present* (New York: Routledge, 2000), xxv–xxvi.

by the lack of race consciousness in Oriental religious thought and saw in it a possible answer to the Negro's plight in a color conscious America. If Negroes could somehow establish an identity with the Oriental peoples, whose religious philosophies either knew nothing of the curse of Canaan or else found it irrelevant, they might become less susceptible to the everyday hazards of being everyday-Negroes in America.[39]

Unfortunately, because of the United States's internal security during both World Wars I and II, the concept of Orientalism—with an accent on language, theology, history, and vernacular—was perceived in many cases as anti-American. Henceforth, with such allegations, came surveillance and counterintelligence ploys used as mechanisms to dismay and misdirect the foundation and purpose of African American Islamic organizations.

Despite these barriers, the Nation of Islam thrived in the midcentury. One important organizational thrust was the effort to transform language, as African Americans were equipped to communicate a system of etymological, cosmological, and axiological autonomy. As noted earlier, Brooks-Higgonbotham pointed out the NOI's emphasis on metalanguage as a means

Table 5.3.   Definition of Terms in the Nation of Islam[1]

Term	Definition
As Salaam Alaikum	Arabic greeting meaning "Peace be unto you."
Asiatic	Name used to identify the international representation of people of Africana descent.
Bililian	Name given to identify the orthodox posture and representation of African Americans' belief in the religion of Islam. The name is taken after Bilal, the first Mu'adhdhin of Islam (caller of prayers for prophet of Muhammad).
Black Muslims	Term referring to African Americans who practice an unorthodox form of Islam. This practice of religion combines elements of nationalism and Islamic lessons.
bori	Soul dominion among the Hausa.
Fruit of Islam	The semimilitary unit of the Nation of Islam. Members are trained in hand-to-hand combat (i.e., martial arts).
hajj	A pilgrimage to the holy city of Mecca.
imam	The leader of Islamic prayers within the community.
Islam	The religion that identifies with submission to the will of Allah.
polygyny	The belief and practice of having more than one wife.
jama'a	Community, often used to refer to agrarian villages.
Lost–Found	The name given to a black American who visits Muhammad's mosque for the first time.
mganga	Swahili term for liturgy authority or healer.
mwalimu or walimu	Swahili term for teacher of any kind.
Muslim Girls Training	Also known as General Civilization Classes, the training program that prepares women in the areas of nutrition, family science, and family health care.
Registered Muslims	Financial and active members of the Nation of Islam.
The "so called Negro"	The name by which members of the Nation of Islam refer to African Americans who are perceived as assimilationists without a consciousness of being black.
The "X"	A symbol representing membership in the Black Muslim program.

[1] Walter Dan Abilla, "A Study of Black Muslims: An Analysis of Commitment," Ph.D. Dissertation, Case Western Reserve University, January 1972, 44–45; McCloud, *African American Islam*, 193–97; Nehemia Levtzion and Randall L. Pouwels, eds., *The History of Islam in Africa* (Athens: Ohio University Press, 2000), 575–77.

of transforming the African experience. Table 5.3 is a listing of terms and definitions used throughout the literature that describes and evaluates the Nation of Islam. These terms offer a historical understanding of the Nation of Islam through its use of language. Equally important, the list shows the NOI's use of an etymological cohort of African American vernacular theological terms, Kiswahili words, and Arabic terms. These terms provide context and synthesis for the divine messages and method of articulation of the Islamic conversion of African Americans.

Table 5.4 is a selected listing of African Americans participation in the Islamic faith from the period of 1312 to 1889. This compendium shows how,

Table 5.4.   African American History with the Islamic Faith[1]

Year	Event
1312	African American Muslims (Mandinga) arrive in the Gulf of Mexico for exploration of the American interior using the Mississippi River as their access route. These Muslim were from Mali and other parts of West Africa.
1530	African slaves arrive in America. During the slave trade, more than ten million Africans were uprooted from their homes and brought to American shores. Many of these slaves were from the Fulas, Fula Jallon, Fula Toro, and Massina as well as other areas of West Africa. These areas were governed from their capital, Timbuctu. These slaves were sent to Mexico, Cuba, and South America. More than 30 percent of these ten million slaves were Muslim. They became the backbone of the American economy.
1732	Ayyub ibn Sulaiman Jallon, a Muslim slave in Maryland, is set free by James Oglethorpe, founder of Georgia, and provided transportation to England. He arrived home (Boonda, Galumbo) from England in 1735.
1807	Yarrow Mamout, an African Muslim slave, is set free in Washington, DC, and later becomes one of the first shareholders of the second chartered bank in America, the Columbia Bank. Mamout may have lived to be more than 128 years old, the oldest person in American history.
1809	Al Hajj Umar ibn Sayyid is enslaved in Charleston after running away.
1870	The Reverend Norman, a Methodist missionary, converts to Islam.
1889	Edward W. Blyden, noted scholar and social activist, travels throughout the eastern and southern parts of the United States proclaiming Islam. In a speech before the Colonization Society of Chicago, Blyden tells his audience that the reasons Africans choose Islam over Christianity is that "the Qur'an protected the black man from selfdepreciation in the presence of Arabs or Europeans."
1893	The American Islamic Propaganda Movement is founded by Mohammed Alexander Russell Webb. He is regarded as one of the earliest white American converts. In that same year on September 20 and 21, M. A. Webb appears at the First World Congress of Religions and delivers two lectures: "The Spirit of Islam," and "The Influence of Islam on Social Conditions."

[1] McCloud, *African American Islam*, 10, 69, 91; Richard Brent Turner, "Islam and Black Nationalism," in *Microsoft Encarta Africana 2000*, ed. Henry Louis Gates and Anthony Appiah (1993–1999); Marsh, *From Black Muslims to Muslims*, 81; Turner, *Islam and the African American Experience*, 64, 120, 125–26, 225, 232–34; Lincoln, *The Black Muslims in America*, 220–21; P. Chike Onwuachi, *Black Ideology in African Diaspora* (Chicago: Third World Press, 1973), 58; Islamic Information Office of Hawaii.

through the process of voluntary and involuntary migration, African people retained a composite of spirituality; religion; and cultural norms from their ancestral homeland. Even more important, the process of adaptive vitality enabled Africans to be somewhat reflexive and to envisage liberation and sovereignty through instruments accessible within the complicated system of politics and economics in America.

Table 5.5 is an illustrative analysis of African American Islamic movements in the United States. The first movement began in 1913 with the Moorish Science Temple, under the leadership and direction of Noble Drew Ali. Occasionally organization names were changed or there were ideological transitions, moving from a nationalist to an orthodox practice of religion with residual crevices of traditional West African culture. Further, the movement of Islam of African Americans in the West is a relatively recent phenomena, starting in earnest in the late 1890s. Awareness of these movements outside the realm of conventional Eurocentric doctrine provided an alcove for African Americans to redefine themselves, as they relate to the advancement of Blacks in a collective capacity. Indeed, as a result of African Americans being involuntary migrants, their quest for spiritual sobriety and cultural transmission exhibited itself in the practice of alternative religious doctrines outside of Anglo-Saxon Protestantism.

The twin currents of Pan Africanism and black nationalism continued in the Nation of Islam's development under Elijah Muhammad. By 1935, Muhammad left the city of Chicago and began to travel across the United States amid a period of internal strife and rival factions in the NOI.[40] This transitory lifestyle continued up to the 1940s, when, in 1942, Muhammad was arrested for resisting to matriculate for the draft and convicted to five years of incarceration in a federal correction institution in Michigan. It is not until 1946 that he resumes his role in a leadership capacity of the Nation of Islam.[41] In 1949, Malcolm X converted to Islam and accepted the teachings of the Honorable Elijah Muhammad while in confinement. This conversion led to him replacing his last name Little with the designate of X.[42] By the 1950s, Elijah Muhammad had solidified his leadership of the NOI, and the organization had grown with great mass appeal. The NOI reached out to college campuses and local Black communities, and new leadership came from these areas. With its expansion, the NOI began to attract the attention of the media, for better and worse. A low moment was the 1959 documentary *The Hate That Hate Produced*, which was produced by Mike Wallace and Louis Lomax and aired nationally; the documentary provided the American media and public with an unfortunately biased view of this African American Islamic organization.[43]

The NOI came most strongly into the spotlight during the1960s as part of the national civil rights movement in America. It distinguished itself by

Table 5.5. African American Islamic Movements

Name	Year	Location	Founder
American Muslim Brotherhood[1]	1892–1893	New York, NY	Mohammed A. Webb
Moorish Science	1913	Newark, NJ	Noble Drew Ali
Temple Ahmadiyyah Movement in Islam	1921	India (Chicago in the United States)	Mirza G. Ahmad
Universal Islamic Society	1926	Detroit, MI	Duse Muhammed Ali
First Muslim Mosque of Pittsburgh	1928	Pittsburgh, PA	Walter Smith Bey (Master Teacher in the Movement)
Islamic Mission Society (also known as the Islamic Mission of America; the organization changed its name from the Islamic Brotherhood to the State Street Mosque and then to the Islamic Mission Society)	1929	New York, NY	Sheikh Daoud Ahmed Faisal
Allah Temple of Islam (originally the Allah Temple of Islam; under Elijah Muhammad, the organization changed its name to Allah Temple of Islam in 1933)	1930	Detroit, MI	Wallace Fard Muhammad
Addeynu Allahe Universal Arabic Association	1930s		
Nation of Islam	1933	Detroit, MI (moved to Chicago in 1934)	Elijah Muhammad
Fahamme Temple of Islam and Culture (the organization was also known as the Fahamme American Ethiopian Temple of Islam and Culture)	1930s	St. Louis, MO	Paul N. Johnson (also known as the Ra-Rasool, the Culture Prophet, the Sheik Ahmad Din, the Prophet of Amun-Ra, the Ro-baitu-Ha, and the successor of Kem; he was also possibly a member of the Ahmadiyya Movement in 1922 and the Moorish Science Temple)

Organization	Year	Location	Founder
African American Mosque	1945	Pittsburgh, PA	Founded by a group of African Americans individuals
Islamic Center of Washington, DC	1957	Washington, DC	
Hanafi Madh-Hab Center	1958	Washington, DC	Hammas Abdul Khaalis
Darul Islam (Abode of Islam)	1962	Brooklyn, NY	Y. Abdul-Kareem
Muslim Mosque Incorporated	1964	New York, NY	Malcolm X Shabazz
Five Percent Nation of Islam (founded on the premise that 5 percent of the population is prepared to save the population of African Americans, 85 percent is wandering through the hell of North America deaf, dumb, and blind, and the remaining 10 percent of the population are selfish opportunists; much of this same doctrine is taken from W. E. B. DuBois concept of the talented 10th)	1964	New York, NY	Clarence 13X
Ansaaru Allah Community	1970	Brooklyn, NY	A. M. A. Mahdi (Al Hajj Al Imam Isq Abd Allah Muhammad Al Mahdi)
Islamic Party of North America	1971	Washington, DC	Yusuf M. Hamid
World Community of al-Islam in the West	1976–1981	Chicago, IL	W. D. Muhammad
Nation of Islam	1977	Highland Park, MI	John Muhammad
Nation of Islam	1977	Chicago, IL	Louis Farrakhan
Lost Found Nation of Islam	1977	Atlanta, GA	Silas Muhammad
American Muslim Mission	1981–1985	Chicago, IL	W. D. Muhammad
The Ministry of W. D. Mohammed (this Second Resurrection of the Nation of Islam adopted the name World Community of al-Islam in the West and then in 1978 the American Muslim Mission; it focused on an orthodox form of practicing Islam until the 1980s when the national organization was terminated and organization focused on a council of imams in state and regional areas)	1981–1997		

(continued)

Table 5.5. (continued)

Name	Year	Location	Founder
The Islamic Society of North America (ISNA) (now an umbrella organization for many active Islamic groups seeking to further the cause of Islam in the United States)	1982	Plainfield, IN	
Naqshabandiyyah	1986	key urban areas	Maulan Shaykh Nazim Adil Qubrusi
African American Shiite Muslim Community	1987	Los Angeles, CA	P. Q. Halifu
Muslim American Community	1990s	Chicago, IL	Warith D. Mohammed
Islamic Moorish Empire of the West Incorporated	1990s		
Muslim American Society	1997– Present		

For more information, see Martha Lee, *The Nation of Islam: An American Millenarian Movement* (Syracuse University Press, 1996).
[1] McCloud, *African American Islam*, 10, 69, 91; Turner, "Islam and Black Nationalism"; Marsh, From Black Muslims to Muslims, 81; Turner, *Islam and the African American Experience*, 64, 120, 125–26, 225, 232–34; Lincoln, *The Black Muslims in America*, 220–21; Onwuachi, *Black Ideology in African Diaspora*, 58; Islamic Information Office of Hawaii.

providing an alternative analysis of the condition of African Americans from a Black perspective. Organizationally, the 1960s were a time of transition and advancement: Malcolm X established the weekly newspaper *Muhammad Speaks* and was appointed as national spokesperson for the NOI. There was a decline in the physical health of the Honorable Elijah Muhammad, who was the target of allegations of infidelity. Malcolm X was eventually suspended from public lectures, left the organization, and was shortly thereafter assassinated. There were even a number of internal rival factions involved in shootings and murder.[44]

When Elijah Muhammad died in 1975, his seventh child, Imam Warith Deen Muhammad, was named as his father's successor. Under the new leadership, the organization took an orthodox shift. Nyang notes, "The history of the movement from 1975 to 1985 is thus a history of gradual but fundamental changes effected by Imam Muhammad in order to bring his followers to the mainstream of the Islamic umma."[45] This project was complicated by the fracturing of the leadership; as illustrated in table 5.5, by 1977 there were three separate factions claiming the legacy of the NOI.

The historiography of the organization has been affected by the huge changes that have come about since the mid-1960s. Some earlier detractors began to attack the validity and effectiveness of the organization's religious, economic, and sociopolitical teachings. Imam Mohammed's conversion of the organization to a form of orthodox Islam became a rich field of research inquiry and constructive engagement. Still, many scholars and independent writers have apprehensions about writing about the NOI. So much so that it was not until 1997 that the first biographical study of Elijah Muhammad appeared: Claude A. Clegg's *An Original Man: The Life and Times of Elijah Muhammad*.[46] The lack of scholarly attention up until then may have been related to the inaccessibility to sources, the lack of communication with former members of the NOI, and even the fear of physical harm from zealous members of the NOI wary of defamation of Muhammad's character.

The publication of Clegg's biography created a groundswell of demand for scholarship on NOI topics. Ironically, this subject, which was formerly met with intensity and fear, has now become one of great interest and is seen as vital to gain knowledge and information about African Americans movement inside the faith of Islam. The historiography of the NOI has undergone a number of transitions: early writings labeled it as a Voodoo cult in the 1930s, later writers characterized it as an advocate of Black nationalism, there were periods of disinterest, and still later writers portrayed it as an integrationist protest organization, especially around the time of the Million Man March in 1995.

Despite the fact that important work is being done from a mixture of ideological views—from integrationist and nationalists schools of thought—

scholarship has still not fully addressed the concepts of Black cultural agency and autonomy that the NOI engaged in and developed. Possibly with the study and research of the array of information on this issue, scholars will attempt to examine as many variables as possible in describing and evaluating this organization and its role in the social protest movements of African American historiography.

CONCLUSION

This chapter aimed to address historiography, intellectual thought, and Pan Africanism with emphasis on the Nation of Islam. Credited with being one of the most influential organizations in the intellectual tradition of African America, the NOI was able to attract those members in our society who most institutions and individuals had given up on. Using metaphors and analogies of redemptive suffering of Africana people during physical bondage and institutional enslavement, the NOI was able to reinterpret this causation of suffering as a point of perseverance for collective memory and to use this memory and ethos for the liberation of Black people in the United States.

Taking the moral high ground allowed the NOI to help African Americans to see their own faults but simultaneously address the "categorical intentionality" of the Eurocentric hegemonic perspective. The term *categorical intentionality* refers to how we "predicate, relate, collect, and introduce logical operations into what we experience."[47] The era of slavery caused the systematic subordination of Africana people on a global level. Still, even as we were cognizant of the cruelties of this era, African Americans had not engaged this topic from a Black perspective. Elijah Muhammad and the NOI provided a lens and analysis for the fusion of the teachings of Islam, Africana historiography, and religious-economic nationalism.

One of the primary advantages of historiography has been the flexibility of interpretation. Indeed, the NOI used the concept of interpretation for examining religious, philosophical, historical, and political texts. This attention to the uses and abuses of language was one of the strong points of the organization. The NOI believed that the choice or selection of alternative religious practices of African Americans was key to their future. The practice of these types of customs and rituals exhibits the quest and sojourn for Black cultural autonomy, despite the fact that African Americans' embrace of these alternative practices often brought forth the repercussions of white hostility, as the dominant culture feared a loss of privilege and an alternate to their systematic subordination of people of Africana decent.

The Nation of Islam has continued to evolve in the twenty-first century. Perhaps the role of future researchers and activist intellectuals will be not to replicate the golden years of the NOI but rather to study and examine what tools from this movement can be used in an info-tech society, to aid and assist in the cultural, political, economic, and social liberation of Africana people.

NOTES

1. This chapter originally appeared in *Engines of the Black Power Movement: Essays on the Influence of Civil Rights Actions, Arts, and Islam*, edited by James L. Conyers, Jr. (Jefferson, NC: McFarland & Company, 2007). Reproduced with permission of McFarland & Company, Inc., Box 611, Jefferson, NC 28640. www. mcfarlandpub.com.

2. Charles H. Wesley, "The Concept of Negro Inferiority in American Thought," *Journal of Negro History* 25 (1940): 540–41.

3. Aminah Beverly McCloud, *African American Islam* (New York: Routledge, 1995), 27.

4. Schomburg Center for Research in Black Life and Culture, New York Public Library, *African American Desk Reference* (New York: Wiley, 1999), 63.

5. Robert Staples, *Introduction to Black Sociology* (New York: Oxford University Press, 1988).

6. See James L. Conyers Jr. and Alva Barnett, eds., *African American Sociology* (Chicago: Nelson Hall Publishers, 1999), essay on Charles H. Wesley and historiography.

7. Evelyn Brooks Higginbotham, "African-American Women's History and the Metalanguage of Race," in *We Specialize in the Wholly Impossible: A Reader in Black Women's History*, ed. Darlene Clark Hine, Wilma King, and Linda Reed (Brooklyn, NY: Carlson Publishing, 1995), 3–4.

8. Steven Tsoukalas, *The Nation of Islam: Understanding the Black Muslims* (Phillipsburg, NJ: P & R Publishing, 2001), 21–22.

9. Karl Evanzz, *The Messenger: The Rise and Fall of Elijah Muhammad* (New York: Pantheon Books, 1999), 33.

10. Tsoukalas, *The Nation of Islam*, 1.

11. Bruce Perry, ed., *Malcolm X: The Last Speeches* (New York: Pathfinder Press, 1989), 152–53.

12. Richard Brent Turner, *Islam in the African American Experience* (Bloomington: Indiana University Press, 1997), 47–48.

13. Ibid., 47.

14. Clifton E. Marsh, *From Black Muslims to Muslims: The Resurrection, Transformation, and Change of the Lost–Found Nation of Islam in America, 1930–1995* (Lanham, MD: Scarecrow Press, 1996), 9.

15. Amir Nashid Ali Muhammad, *Muslims in America: Seven Centuries of History, 1312–1998* (Beltsville, MD: Amana Publications, 1998), 42.

16. Ronald W. Walters, *Pan Africanism in the African Diaspora: An Analysis of Modern Afrocentric Political Movements* (Detroit: Wayne State University Press, 1993), 46.

17. Adib Rashad, *The History of Islam and Black Nationalism in the Americas* (Beltsville, MD: Writers' Incorporated, 1991), 61.

18. Adib Rashad, *Elijah Muhammad and the Ideological Foundation of the Nation of Islam* (Hampton, VA: U.B. and U.S. Communications Systems, June 1994), 121.

19. Tsoukalas, *The Nation of Islam*, 31.

20. Samuel T. Livingston, "NOI: Divided We Stand," *The International Journal of Africana Studies* 5 (December 1999): 50–51.

21. Wilson Jeremiah Moses, "From Booker T. to Malcolm X: Black Political Thought, 1895–1965," in *Upon These Shores: Themes in the African American Experience 1600–Present*, ed. William R. Scott and William G. Shade (New York: Routledge, 2000), 208.

22. "Pan Africanism," in *The Oxford Companion to African American Literature,* ed. William L. Andrews, Frances Smith Foster, and Trudier Harris (New York: Oxford University Press, 1997), 558–59.

23. Moses, "From Booker T. to Malcolm X," 215.

24. Amir Nashid Ali Muhammad, *Muslims in America*, 47–48.

25. Clyde-Ahmad Winters, "Afro-American Muslims—From Slavery to Freedom," *Islamic Studies* 17, no. 4 (Winter 1978): 187–203, 200.

26. Richard Brent Turner, "The Ahmadiyya Mission to Blacks in the United States in the 1920s," *The Journal of Religious Thought* 44, no. 2 (Winter–Spring 1988): 59–60.

27. For additional discussion on the intermerging of leadership, see Marsh, *From Black Muslims to Muslims*; Evanzz, *The Messenger*; Turner, *Islam in the African American Experience*.

28. Essien U. Essien-Udom, *Black Nationalism: The Search for Identity in America* (Chicago: University of Chicago Press, 1971), 18.

29. William H. Banks Jr., *The Black Muslims* (Philadelphia: Chelsea House Publishers, 1997), 35.

30. Marsh, *From Black Muslims to Muslims*, 37.

31. Minister Tynnetta Muhammad, "A Brief History on the Origin of the Nation of Islam in America: A Nation of Peace and Beauty," www.noi.org/noi-history.

32. Evanzz, *The Messenger*, 94–95. Evanzz discusses the strategic plan of operation by which the organization of Islamic converts changed for ideological, political, and law enforcement reasons.

33. Zafar Ishaq Ansari, "W. D. Mohammed: The Making of a Black Muslim Leader, 1933–1961," *The American Journal of Islamic Social Sciences* 2 (1985): 245–62, 248.

34. See Evanzz, *The Messenger*. Evanzz provides an interesting journalist's analysis of the life and organizational structure of the Nation of Islam and draws attention to Ugan Ali's role in the early formation and structure of the Nation of Islam.

35. *Elijah Muhammad*, videotape from the biography series African American Achievers.

36. Minister Tynnetta Muhammad, "A Brief History on the Origin of the Nation of Islam."

37. Turner, *Islam in the African American Experience*, 47.

38. Robin D. G. Kelley and Earl Lewis, eds., *To Make Our World Anew* (New York: Oxford University Press, 2000), 410.

39. C. Eric Lincoln, *The Black Muslims in America* (Boston: Beacon Press, 1961), 51.

40. Banks, *The Black Muslims*, 121.

41. Ibid.

42. Ibid.

43. Ibid., 122.

44. Ibid., 122–23.

45. Sulayman Nyang, "A New Beginning for the Black Muslims," *Arabia,* 1985, 50–51.

46. Claude Andrew Clegg, *An Original Man: The Life and Times of Elijah Muhammad* (New York: St. Martins Press, 1997).

47. Robert Sokolowski, *Introduction to Phenomenology* (New York: Cambridge University Press, 2000), 88.

Chapter Six

Understanding Elijah Muhammad

An Intellectual Biography of Elijah Muhammad¹

Malachi Crawford

The objective of this chapter is to delineate the political, social, and economic ideologies of Elijah Muhammad. While acknowledging the importance of such factors as social ecology, the focus of this analysis is not primarily concerned with the beliefs of Muhammad's predecessors; it speaks to the productions of Muhammad, instead of his producers.

This study makes use of a comprehensive and comparative framework from which to view and engage the research. In order that the depth and breadth of this analysis be better served, the historical and philosophical beliefs of Elijah Muhammad are placed next to current and past issues in Black America's fight for independence. This arrangement allows for a rather lucid understanding of today's Black leadership by observing the political, cultural, social, religious, and economic implications taken from the writings and interviews of Elijah Muhammad. Kawaida theory is used to understand and categorize the data under consideration (see table 6.1).

Triangulation addresses the use of more than one research design in a study. Both historical analysis and ethnography are employed here, with the former being the lead design of the project. Historical analysis is a research design that undertakes the collection of primary source data in order to discover the true beliefs of the subject. There are both internal and external flaws with applying this design, one of which is the internal bias of the author. Through employing the method of historical analysis, this work attempts to answer two queries: (1) What are the essential beliefs espoused by Muhammad? and (2) Is there systematic refinement in the strategies employed by Black leaders to gain Black independence?

Table 6.1. Theory and Methods

Theory: Kawaida	Method: Historical Analysis	Format: Intellectual Biography
Key Constructs	Nguzo Saba (Dependent Variables)	Measures (Independent Variables)
Social Organization	Unity	Education, morality, responsibility
	Creativity	Use of religion
Political Organization Unity	Unity	Group consciousness, leadership
	Creativity	Relation to government
Economic Organization	Unity	Business cooperation and etiquette
	Creativity	Business diversity
Historical Organization	Unity	Circumstance, identity
	Creativity	Use of mythology

The strategic appeal of the Nation of Islam resulted from the circumstances surrounding northern Black communities during the 1930s. Lawrence Levine notes a rising distinction between the sacred and secular aspects of Black life that began with the abolition of slavery.[2] Freedom for slaves led Blacks to partially accept white culture and marginalize Black culture. American education, for example, led to the decline of spirituals and those things associated with slave culture. Daniel A. Payne, a well-known bishop in the African Methodist Episcopal Church during the mid-nineteenth century, went from one city to another decrying Blacks' use of ring shouts.[3] Freedmen were increasingly of the general opinion that no power existed in acting Black. Therefore, an apparent distinction in Black culture between sacred and secular led to changes in Black religious structure and song. This dichotomy formed the backbone of the disputes between Holiness and Spiritualist churches, the former accepting the ways of the past while the latter rejected them. Musically, with its focus on the afterlife, gospel music placed humans in a position solely dependent on God. Blues, a highly personal musical genre, centered on depicting the day-to-day conflict in Black social interaction. Specific fields within Black culture failed to address the sacred and secular needs of the Black community together.

The Nation of Islam's (NOI) use of religion in combating the social, political, and economical powerlessness of Blacks in America was—at the time—culturally dissonant. Unsurprisingly, accusations against Black Christian preachers that Christianity failed to liberate Blacks resounded in this climate. Elijah Muhammad's focus on the enslavement of Blacks in America combined the sacred and secular components of the NOI's ideology. Muhammad's main contribution to the NOI, Black identity, and nationalism, rests in the attention that he placed on slavery. After being released from prison in 1946, Elijah Muhammad's decision to call for Black separation within the United States resulted from this change in ideology and had a dramatic influence on Black humanity.[4]

THE BIRTH OF MUHAMMAD'S PHILOSOPHY

On October 7, 1898, Elijah Muhammad was born Elijah Poole in Sandersville, Georgia.[5] His life in Georgia as a sharecropper influenced his later thinking in life to an extraordinary degree. Muhammad's experience with sharecropping caused him to be a leading proponent of Black equity and economic independence among Black leaders of the twentieth century.

The American institution of sharecropping (and its predecessor) led to similarities in the platforms advocated by other Black leaders who have been directly affected by these institutions, for example, Booker T. Washington. Given the fact that Elijah Muhammad was born in Georgia, it's easy to understand why he found moral discipline essential to uplift the Black race. Similar to the Washingtonian school of Black social thought, which has its origins in the Deep South's social conditions, Muhammad believed that Blacks must come to have good public behavior, to be at all times good, honest, decent, upstanding members within the community.[6] The institution of sharecropping was one that pitted Blacks without any land, money, and ownership of anything but themselves against a system of perpetual indebtedness. Muhammad believed that the institution of industry did the same and expressed his indignation at that social reality: "I have lived with you all my life. . . . I have looked upon the evil treatment of our people day and night. . . . No justice whatsoever."[7]

Another instrumental experience influencing the ideology of Elijah Muhammad was the fact that his father was a minister.[8] Muhammad came to see the hypocrisy in the treatment of Blacks in America and white America's professed adherence to the principles of Christianity. This led to his disillusionment with Christianity and its viability as a means to the achievement of Black independence. When Fard Muhammad introduced Elijah Muhammad to a modified form of Islam, Fard made his mark on a man with longstanding experiences of American institutionalized racism.[9]

Muhammad certainly was influenced by Farad Muhammad and by doctrines such as those of the Universal Negro Improvement Association and the Moorish Science Temple. The founder of the Moorish Science Temple,

Table 6.2.   Organizational Comparisons between Moorish Science Temple and Nation of Islam

	Moorish Science Temple	*Nation of Islam*
Nationality	Moorish Americans	Asiatic-Black
Prophet	Noble Drew Ali	Elijah Muhammad
Religion	Islam	Islam
Land	No desire for separate state, psychological separation through Moorish status	Separate
Sacred text	Koran created by Noble Drew Ali	Islamic Koran and Christian Bible
God	Allah	Allah in the form of Fard Muhammad
Race	Asiatics	Asiatic Blacks (Tribe of Shabazz)
Place of worship	Temple	Mosque
Heaven	In the mind	On earth
Separation of sexes	Yes	Yes
Names	Bey, El	X (to replace slave name because real name unknown)
Dress	Men: Fez worn during official functions, beards and mustaches allowed, suit and tie optional. Women: Turbans optional, no makeup, pants, long dresses to shoe tops.	Men: Suit and ties, clean shaven. Women: Head covered, no makeup, long dresses to shoe tops.
Citizenship	United States of America	Nation of Islam, Nation within a Nation

Source: Clifton E. Marsh, Figure I.

Noble Drew Ali, intended to change the treatment of Blacks in America by changing their culture and identity. The Moorish Science Temple used religion to change the cultural identity of its members. Table 6.2 illustrates many of the points of commonality between Muhammad's Nation of Islam and the Moorish Science Temple.

But there were important difference between the MST and the Nation of Islam. Drew Ali sought an attached-appendage type of relationship within American culture and society, and citizenship was one of the pillars of membership within the Moorish Science Temple. The MST desired acceptance into the American political, economic, and social structure. The Nation of Islam, on the other hand, offered Blacks a rebirth in another culture—Islam. The NOI rejected the integrationist philosophy of the MST, believing that it amounted to an acceptance of the enslavement of Blacks in America. Drew Ali himself noticed that even the darkest of Africans born outside of the United States received better treatment than Blacks in America.

SOCIAL ORGANIZATION

Use of Religion

Muhammad sought to use religious doctrine to create unity, invite economic prosperity, and incite social, moral, and psychological change among Black America. There are several important reasons the NOI's use of religion was effective among Blacks. First, the NOI helped to halt the diffusion of the sacred and secular aspects of Black culture noted earlier. Consistently, the NOI's popularity among Blacks rested on the organization's adherence to moral principles that are common to all religions and found within the Bible. Second, Elijah Muhammad examined Europeanized Christianity in such a way that forced Blacks to recognize the inherent racism within that strain of the religion. One of the tenets of the Christian religion is that humans are built in the image of God. Elijah Muhammad asked why, given this fact, the Bible does not show a savior in the image of Black people.

Muhammad understood the importance that shared experience plays in the future direction of a people, its sense of identity, and its feeling of mutual trust. Muhammad used the Nation of Islam as a means for expressing the idea that Blacks in America have a common experience. Trust is based on the historical experience of a people. The underlying yield of trust, fostered by knowledge of the historical experience of one's people, is love of that same people. In this systematic manner, Muhammad used religion to counteract a few of the primary methods of American slavery and White subjugation of the Black race, one of which is Black hate.

Muhammad's intentional use of a shared experience among Black people served yet another purpose. By relating the common experience of Blacks in America to an African past, Muhammad countered the stereotypical and, psychological portrayals of Blacks as an innately backward and lazy people. He highlighted the African past of Blacks in America to provide an alternate cultural narrative of success and counter attempts to foist an inferiority complex on Black Americans.

Morality and Whiteness

The Nation of Islam identified the genealogical origins of Blacks with that of Asians. The identification of Black genealogy with Asians allowed the Nation of Islam to declare that Christianity was a religion for whites.

According to the Nation of Islam, history had always shown whites to be of an aggressive nature—inconsistent with those things pertaining to life and harmony. Therefore, white humanity was in its foundation evil. The NOI allegorically employed this perception of white humanity within the Koranic principle of jihad, the battle of good versus evil.

This was in contrast to Martin Luther King Jr.'s views on the humanity of whites. King was of the opinion that the salvation of Blacks, or that of any other people, proportionately depended on the salvation of all other people in the world. Moreover, King insisted that for Blacks not to seek the humanity in any people questioned the humanity of Blacks themselves. There is probably no single factor more influential, in terms of affecting Black consciousness, than the dynamic of culture within the Black community.

POLITICAL ORGANIZATION

Elijah Muhammad's successful rise to power primarily among Blacks with little or no education and labor skills is in keeping with a long line of ancestral precedent set by more than a few Black leaders before him, leaders like Nat Turner, Henry Highland Garnett, and Marcus Garvey. One of the shared philosophies of these Black leaders is that Blacks confer upon themselves their own humanity. Elijah Muhammad talked about Blacks needing to be able to love themselves, the distinct, prideful and rich aspects of Black history, and the beauty of Black physical features.[10]

Besides being psychologically empowering, Muhammad's call for Blacks being able to realize their own humanity was politically strategic. Through his writings, speeches, and interviews, one sees that Muhammad understood the real foundation of Black power as being Black people. It is within and from Black people that Muhammad sought to strengthen the Nation of Islam. Observing the history of this country toward people of color, Muhammad felt that it was unrealistic to petition a violently hostile government and people for concessions of power and the bestowal of humanity on those it had treated badly. He believed that other movements were unrealistic in seeking the assistance of whites. As he wrote,

> You remain as a free slave to your slavemaster. You demand that he recognize you as his equal. . . . If every so-called Negro were fired, what would you do? Would you unite and go to Washington and demand that the government give you a job? . . . You have made yourself his slave.[11]

The Nation of Islam's views on Black morality in America shape and define the organization's political perspective. This becomes crucial when one seeks to link the political ideology of the Nation of Islam to other Black leaders. Martin Luther King addressed the issue of Black humanity through Black morality. He insisted that as long as Blacks were not allowed political equality because of who Blacks are (which includes the system of beliefs held by Blacks), then it would be impossible to begin discussion on the rights of Black Americans as Americans. This was similar to the NOI's belief that white America had to accept Black morality, but the NOI's approach was a strategic refinement of political ideology within Black leadership.

Another point of digression between King's civil rights movement and the ideology of the Nation of Islam centers on the humanity of whites. Basing their beliefs on centuries of racial injustice and race oppression, the Nation of Islam viewed whites as being an innately evil people.

Role of Black Women

The role of Black women in the NOI is essential in understanding the development and maintenance of the organization. While Black women may not control the avenues to status within the NOI and the Black community in general, they undeniably assign the values that people associate with status. Black women have power over priority and measure as they relate to status. Elijah Muhammad explained this phenomenon in terms of two principles: an administrative (male) principle and an organizational (female) principle. Given this analysis, one can conclude that Black women have enormous control over the timing of Black social movements. The periodization of Black social movements might swing on whether material possessions or moralistic principles are the highest measures of self-worth within the Black community.

Fard Muhammad's approach to the members of the Paradise Valley Community certainly reveals his knowledge of the importance of Black women in social struggles. Farad's initial entrance into the homes of Detroit's Blacks came via his peddling of cheap trinkets and goods to Black women. Could he have been as successful in approaching Black men?

ECONOMIC ORGANIZATION

Elijah Muhammad worked several blue-collar jobs from 1923 to 1925 in Detroit, Michigan. Thus, Elijah Muhammad's introduction to the labor force was as a semiskilled worker.[12] Considering the lack of labor unions for Blacks and the caprice of white business owners toward Blacks (especially at the onset of the Great Depression), Muhammad saw the need for Black economic independence as essential to the survival of Blacks within America. As he noted, "The Black man in America faces a serious economic problem today and the white race's Christianity cannot solve it. You, the so-called American Negro, with the help of Allah can solve your own problem."[13] Consequently, his speeches within the Nation of Islam stress the idea that Blacks must do for themselves.[14]

The Nation of Islam encouraged Black economic autonomy through the purchasing of land, the pooling of resources within the Black community, and the aggregation of Blacks with few skills and no skills at all. The NOI owned grocery stores, factories, education centers, and restaurants and gave service contracts to Black entrepreneurs.[15] The idea of a community of autonomous Black merchants parallels the ideas of the Washingtonian school of thought.

CONCLUSION

There is much left to study regarding the similarity between the economic, political, and social ideologies of Elijah Muhammad's Nation of Islam and other Black leaders' movements. To what extent did their various interpretations of white humanity divide them? On what grounds have past Black leaders with equivalent differences agreed to work cooperatively? The various Black movements, even when separated by time, share similarities that constitute a continuum of strategic refinement within Black leadership.

The Nation of Islam came to power during a time when Black identity was in a period of transition. Not surprisingly, Black culture became the foundation of the Nation of Islam's bid for membership from the Black community. The Nation of Islam's strategy for improving the condition of Blacks in America began with addressing cultural awareness among Blacks. The NOI desperately wanted to change the xenophobic behavior that existed throughout Black communities. In attempting to address changes in the behavior of Blacks, a drastic modification of the negative self-images held by Blacks became necessary.

Black fear of Black culture had been deeply and systematically learned by Blacks since the time of enslavement in America. An undoing of this learned process required exposing Blacks to positive images of Black people throughout history. The Nation of Islam, therefore, sought to establish the history of Blacks in America prior to enslavement. This procedure was accomplished through the use of myths. The NOI made the Islamic tradition palatable to Blacks by incorporating aspects of the religion into Black history, partially through the use of these myths.

Elijah Muhammad took the enslavement of Blacks in America and fused the history, mythology, and religion of the NOI. This gave Blacks a sense of nationhood. Clearly, analysis of American slavery and the NOI reveal that humanity is the minimum of all human comforts, for humanity gives any life freedom. In Muhammad's opinion, political assimilation and not theology (in and of itself) had been the opiate of Blacks in America. His life is a testament to the effects of slavery and an understanding of one crucial axiom: Black power resides in Black people.[16]

NOTES

1. This chapter originally appeared in *Engines of the Black Power Movement: Essays on the Influence of Civil Rights Actions, Arts, and Islam*, edited by James L. Conyers, Jr. (Jefferson, NC: McFarland & Company, 2007). Reproduced with permission of McFarland & Company, Inc., Box 611, Jefferson, NC 28640. www.mcfarlandpub.com.

2. Lawrence Levine, *Black Culture and Black Consciousness* (New York: Oxford University Press, 1977).

3. Ibid.

4. Karl Evanzz, *The Messenger* (New York: Pantheon Books, 1999).

5. Clifton E. Marsh, *From Black Muslims to Muslims* (Lanham, MD: Scarecrow Press, 1996).

6. Elijah Muhammad, *Message to the Blackman* (Chicago: Muhammad's Temple No. 2, 1965).

7. Ibid.

8. Evanzz, *The Messenger.*

9. Rachelle Muhammad, *Black Muslim Movement after the Death of Elijah Muhammad* (Ann Arbor, MI: University Microfilms International, 1980).

10. Elijah Muhammad, *Message to the Blackman.*

11. Ibid., 63.

12. Rachelle Muhammad, *Black Muslim Movement after the Death of Elijah Muhammad.*

13. Elijah Muhammad, *Message to the Blackman,* 173.

14. Elijah Muhammad, *An Interview with Elijah Muhammad.* [sound recording] (Los Angeles: Pacifica Tape Library, 1967).

15. Elijah Muhammad, *Message to the Blackman.*

16. For more on the topics in this chapter, see Essien U. Essien-Udom, *Black Nationalism* (Chicago: University Press of Chicago, 1962); Charles E. Lincoln, *The Black Muslims in America* (Boston: Beacon Press, 1973); Richard B. Turner, *Islam in the African-American Experience* (Bloomington: Indiana University Press, 1997).

Chapter Seven

The Peculiar Institution

The Depiction of Slavery in Steven Barnes's
Lion's Blood *and* Zulu Heart

Rebecca Hankins

The term *peculiar institution* was used as a euphemism for slavery in the antebellum South. Legislators and others employed it to highlight the alleged nature of slavery as a feature of Southern culture—and to mask the terrible reality the term *slavery* implied.

Steven Barnes's two novels, *Lion's Blood*[1] and *Zulu Heart*,[2] which comprise his Insha'Allah (If God Wills) series, represent a unique perspective on the *peculiar institution* of slavery written within the genre of science fiction. The stories offer an alternative universe where the Africans and other people of color are the slaveholders and Europeans are the slaves. They are set in the antebellum South, which is now called Bilalistan and mirrors the culture of the books' version of ancient Africa (Ethiopia/Egypt), where the inhabitants are used as pawns in an ongoing succession of battles between Egypt's Pharaoh and Ethiopia's Empress for control of economic wealth. This battle for control emulates the conflict between the Confederate and Union states prior to and during the Civil War.

In the Insha'Allah series, the dominant religion is Islam, and it is primarily Muslims who are the lead characters of the novels. Throughout these narratives the Islamic perspective and tenets of the faith are discussed, questioned, critiqued, and explained as they relate to the system of slavery. In a recent interview posted on the Islam and Science Fiction website, Barnes explained why he set his story within an Islamic framework: "I wanted to explore the nature of slavery, and to create a world in which Africa developed a technological civilization prior to Europe. To do that, I needed a unifying religion, and Islam fit the bill."[3] The story takes pains to paint the Islamic form of slavery as more humane. Barnes notes, "slavery in my world is a mite kinder: the Irish kept their names and were allowed to keep their religions, for instance."

The story focuses on one of the most prosperous plantations within Bilalistan, a place called Dar Kush ruled by a Muslim family; in Arabic, *Dar* means "home," and Kush refers to the kingdom of Kush, an ancient nation in northeastern Africa comprising large areas within present-day Egypt and Sudan. In *Lion's Blood*, the story is centered on the current leader of the family, a senator (*Wakil*) named Abu Ali. Abu Ali has two sons, Ali and Kai, and a daughter, Elenya. The sequel, *Zulu Heart*, follows Kai's tenure as Wakil of Dar Kush. Barnes's other main character is a European slave and childhood friend of Kai, Aidan O'Dere, who functions as a kind of Frederick Douglass character and, along with Babatunde, Dar Kush's resident Sufi, becomes the voice of conscious in the story.

Modeling his stories on slavery in Islam, Barnes attempts to show that Abu Ali and his son Kai, although not color blind, rarely saw the race of the individuals as the reason for their enslavement, nor did they see others as inferior or without humanity, unlike many slaveholders within the Americas who saw the color of black Africans as reasons for enslavement. Historian Michael Gomez, in his book *Reversing Sails,* notes that "Muslim societies made use of slaves from all over the reachable world. Europeans were just as eligible as Africans, and Slavic and Caucasian populations were the largest source of slaves for the Islamic world well into the eighteenth century."[4]

The slaves on Dar Kush are treated well, families remain intact, and not only are they allowed to practice their religion, the plantation maintains a grove that the slaves use as their sacred ground. Barnes advances these so-called humane characteristics throughout the storylines and emphasizes that Islam's view of slavery was not race based nor was it an impediment to advancement within society. Historian Ali Mazrui notes that Islamic forms of slavery permitted the highest degree of upward social mobility historically from serf to sultan."[5] He notes, "the Islamic system was creed-conscious, and the indigenous system was culture-conscious, the Western system was race-conscious in the extreme." Barnes does not attempt to minimize the viciousness of bondage, race, and racism are in the story; the brutality and dehumanizing features are all there. But the framing of the storyline from an Islamic perspective, in which religion impacts your status and station in the world, that dominates the discourse. The stories also relate the Islamic culture's uneasy alliances with the Zulus, Egyptians, Abyssinians, Aztecs, Vikings, and Indians. These alliances have been forged through wars of conquest, marriage, and support for the institution of slavery.

Barnes fashions elements of his story from the historical reality of American slavery, sometimes in stark detail and sometimes in small subtle ways. For example, there is an underground railroad run by Muslims, Jews, and Christians that helps slaves escape to non-slave-holding states in the North.

It is through their interactions that we view slavery and how each group views the other. As Kai and Aidan mature, they discuss the need to abolish slavery, the humanity of whites, and the religions of Islam and Christianity; they speak as equals. Aidan forces Kai to understand what slavery does to people who are enslaved and to the slave owners—speeches that could have come from the mouth of Frederick Douglass or any real-life antislavery advocate. His views on Islam mirror Douglass's statements on the Christianity of slave traders. Aidan, Kai, and Babatunde's characters recreate many of the discussions and debates regarding the ethical and moral aspects of slavery and the slave trade that were ongoing in the United States during slavery. Their discussions channel the words of many of the very arguments spoken by abolitionists, pro-slavery figures, and former slaves. A vivid example is when Aidan challenges Kai on what Islam teaches about the humanity of all people, justice, and equality. He constantly challenges Kai's belief in God: "I can understand how you can believe in God. After all, His light shines upon you and all your people as well. But fate has brought me little save misery." For Aidan there are no benefits of religion, even after he and many of his fellow slaves have won their freedom. The people of Aidan's village continue to struggle to find their place in this world and ponder how or if they will ever recover their culture and establish communities that can prosper in a black-dominated world. These are questions that are left unanswered in Barnes's stories and that leave one anticipating the next chapter in this series.

Barnes's novels demonstrate why science fiction, fantasy, and speculative fiction are rich areas of study for the new approaches to African American Islam. Speculative fiction offers opportunities for exploring themes within the human condition that allows others to "walk a mile in my shoes" without judgment. Science fiction provides for the telling of stories from perspectives that confront our assumptions, stereotypes, and push for a new dialogue about race, privilege, and power. Fantasy literature, similar to its sister genre of science fiction, can engage an audience with its use of imagination, nightmares, and dreams as its foundation. The unexplainable and the impossible are the devices of fantasy literature. Barnes's stories straddle science fiction and fantasy, employing them in ways that force us to rethink commonly held beliefs, to think critically about slavery in ways that make us uncomfortable, and to question the long-term impact of the slavery, the systemic effects of the *peculiar institution*.

In the film *A Time to Kill*, based on the novel by John Grisham, Samuel Jackson's character, Carl Lee Hailey, has killed the men who brutally raped his daughter. As his trial proceeds, he talks to his white lawyer, Jake Brigance, about the impact of race on his situation: "See Jake? You're one of them, don't you see? My life in white hands . . . jury and judge. . . . What would it take to convince YOU to set me free?" This conversation echoes in Brigance's mind as the trial draws near its close. In Brigance's summation to the jury he tells them to close their eyes as he narrates the horrific details of the rape of Hailey's daughter. At the end, he says, "Now, imagine she's white." The verdict comes back not guilty. It is that reversal of roles that makes the jury understand and empathize with the black defendant.

Barnes similarly recognizes the power of role reversal, and in *Lion's Blood* and *Zulu Heart* he forces the reader to imagine the alternative world, these role reversals, and how our twenty-first-century notions of slavery are challenged. Grisham's words could have been spoken by Aidan in Barnes's novels as we read about Kai and Aidan's lives and their growing friendship that forces them to confront and challenge the reader's assumptions about the system of slavery.

Another feature of Barnes's novels is his depiction of gender issues through the use of female secondary characters, both Muslim and non-Muslim. For example, Kai's wives represent composites of the wives of the Prophet (*peace be upon him*) and are used to explore the role of marriage in bridging differences and creating filial bonds. Kai has two wives: One is Lamiya, an Abyssinian princess originally destined to marry Kai's brother; when Kai's brother is killed, Lamiya refuses to accept a life of solitude, rebels against the Empress, and marries Kai. The other is Nandi, a Zulu princess who was destined to be his first wife and resents having to marry him as his second. Their marriage unites the Muslims and the Zulus in alliance to the Wakil. The Zulus' hatred toward the Muslims, however, is not eliminated but is forced underground, and they work to undermine the Wakil with the hopes of removing him, nearly causing the death of Nandi in the process.

Yet another type of gender issue is represented by Kai's younger sister Elenya, who is depicted as an independent and strong woman capable of speaking her mind and using her intellect. Her story is left unfinished at the end of *Zulu Heart* after she was taken hostage by the Pharaoh. Sofia, the wife of Aidan, is representative of the precarious condition of women in the slave-holding society. She was originally just a sexual companion for Kai without any status as a slave or wife, but she eventually chooses to become a slave in order to marry Aidan. When Sofia is taken from him and repeatedly raped by her owner, the emotions are similar to the reality of slave women in the United States.

A third gender issue is represented by Aidan's sister Nessa. As was common in American slavery, in Dar Kush some slaveholders develop an attachment to their female slaves, having children with them and providing them the status of wives without the legal and formal recognition. These tragic figures will have you rooting for the death of the black slave masters and for the success of the white slave uprising, eliciting a powerful emotional reaction to the corrupting role that power and privilege play in any society. For the people of Aidan's tribe, these are the two elements that must be examined and changed before progress toward true equality is achieved.

The most interesting female character is introduced in the second novel, *Zulu Heart*. Chifi Kokossa (based on the historical figure of Sumiya, the first martyr in Islam) is the daughter of a respected friend and companion of Kai's who is murdered by his enemies. Chifi's father had begun the development of what is described as a submarine, and we soon find out that it is Chifi who conceived of the invention. After the death of her father, she tries to get support for building the model herself but runs up against male chauvinism in the Senate. Kai decides to support her work, and it is her submarine along with the help of two Dahomey women and Aidan that saves Bilalistan from an attack by the Pharaoh's fleet. Chifi's arguments with Kai are classic feminist discussions, and she too pushes him to expand his ideas on the status of women and religion. After being turned down and ridiculed by the Senate, she says to Kai, "I came here not for myself, but for you. For you to see the reality I have faced every day of my life. You operate under the illusion that men hold the power for the protection of women. As you probably were raised thinking that slavery was good for the slaves." Chifi's fate is undecided at the end of *Zulu Heart*, and hopefully readers will have the opportunity to follow her story in the next volume of the series. These women show the diversity of women within the Islamic tradition and how the peculiar institution of slavery impacts all within that society.

The diversity of women that Barnes portrays is true of all his characters. Barnes doesn't idealize Islam and Muslims. Some Muslims are portrayed as thoughtful, some as brutal and filled with hate and disdain for the slaves. Kai's father was considered a just master, but his brother Ali and his uncle Malik are more typical slaveholders, with very little concern for their slaves, and often cruel, thinking nothing of selling away a loved one or beating slaves for small or minor offenses.

Steven Barnes's two novels show the complexities of slavery. The enduring struggle of two peoples—black and white—to chart their own destiny while attempting to answer the questions that are always beneath the surface: Will Dar Kush and Bilalistan continue as slaveholding lands? Will the whites continue to be used as slaves and soldiers in never-ending wars? And finally what will happen to Kai and Aidan in their fight for the abolition of slavery? We know that Kai is leaning toward fighting for abolition, and we know that he seeks to prevent more wars. But he also knows that to achieve these goals will require that he fight traditions that are institutionalized and systemic.

The novels emphasize the institution of slavery but one cannot separate the theory of oppression from race and racism. The novels ask, How do we respond to the argument about equality and the fate of an enslaved people when the victims are European? Is our response similar when the dominant culture is black and the dominant ideology is Islamic? Why do we root for the death of the black slave masters and for the success of the white slave uprising? Is it only a matter of the powerless versus the powerful? What contributes to our reaction? The inhumanity of watching women being ripped from their husbands, raped, and prostituted and men being beaten for speaking, touching, or just looking at a slave master or a black woman—these things produce the same horrified reactions that we experience when contemplating the reality of the historical transatlantic slave trade. Barnes uses all of these elements to frame his story and forces us to react in ways that are difficult and foreign.

The genius of Barnes's novels is that for readers ignorant of the long-term impact of slavery, the stories open a vivid window into the struggles, pain, and suffering that enslaved Africans endured. The stories provide insight into the vestiges of slavery and the inequality that becomes systemic. The stories force you to confront the notion of rooting for these enslaved and brutalized people without regard to their race. These are difficult and often jarring emotions that the reader will constantly experience reading these two novels.

The novels also present an Islam that is nuanced and not monolithic, a faith that is told from an African perspective, a viewpoint that many will find revelatory and remarkable for the accuracy and effort that Barnes sought to portray. Finally, as we read these stories by Steven Barnes, he repeatedly challenges us to think about these issues that make us uncomfortable and question deeply held beliefs, stereotypes, and prejudices.

NOTES

1. Steven Barnes, *Lion's Blood: A Novel of Slavery and Freedom in an Alternate America* (New York: Aspect/Warner Books, 2002).

2. Steven Barnes, *Zulu Heart* (New York: Warner Books, 2003).

3. Steven Barnes, Interview by Muhammad Aurangzeb Ahmad, *Islam and Science Fiction*, November 17, 2010, www.islamscifi.com/islam-sci-fi-interview-of-steven-barnes/.

4. Michael Gomez, *Reversing Sail: A History of the African Diaspora* (Cambridge: Cambridge University Press, 2005).

5. Ali A. Mazrui, *Euro-Jews and Afro-Arabs: The Great Semitic Divergence in World History* (Lanham, MD: University Press of America, 2008), 265.

Chapter Eight

Islam in the
Africana Literary Tradition

Christel N. Temple

The institutionalization of the discipline of Africana studies began in the United States, and its U.S. origins complicate the assessment of the Islamic presence in the Africana literary tradition. The extent to which Islam is recognized depends on many factors, including how this area of study should be categorized: whether it includes domestic and international writers, leans more toward traditional "Black studies" (preinstitutionalization) or contemporary Africana studies (based on diverse Diasporic curricula), and focuses on the Islamic element, the African element, or both equally. One observation is clear—that whether or not literature reflecting this content, culture, and experience has been *categorized* and *labeled* as Islamic (or Muslim), it has been represented heartily in the Africana literary tradition.[1]

The issues Africana studies literary scholars must address are wide-ranging: Does literature reflecting a religious or spirit-based culture (e.g., Christianity, Islam, Yoruba, Hausa, Dogon, Voudoun, Santeria) require a separate course, a separate unit, or other characterization that ensures pedagogically measured student competency? Do post–September 11 politics represent a paradigm shift that requires a moment of concentration on the Islamic experience aimed at educating society about the specificities of Islam since it has emerged as a global knowledge requirement? Are the politics and activity of domestic or global Islamic cultural histories significant enough to require literary canonization (in the way the Harlem Renaissance, Black Arts movement, and the Negritude movement are regular topics covered in Africana literary history)? Broad research on the extent to which scholars are publishing on Islamic literatures reveals not only the variable of categorization but also matters of familiarity with the names of key writers who address

Islam in their texts, disagreement on whether Islamic literature is defined as writing by a practicing Muslim or writing that merely addresses Islam as a topic, distinguishing or not between Islamic writers of Arab-African and African-African descent, and challenges of multilingualism, translation, and critics' embarrassing interpretation errors that reveal a lack of familiarity with the Quran and with Islamic custom.

The diverse conversations related to the presence of Islam in the broad Africana literary tradition have not yet been attended to in a linear fashion, even though the continental African segment has been covered to an extent. For example, in his summary of the authors studied in the University of Yaoundé's Department of Sub-Saharan Literature, which is virtually a Diaspora Studies literary curriculum, André Ntonfo listed writers by name in national/regional categories—Senegalese, Nigerian, Ivorian, Congolese, and South African, North African, and Diaspora writers.[2] Ntonfo listed many writers who treat Islam in their texts without emphasis on their unique religious-cultural orientation. Several key works on Islam in the continental African experience appeared in the nineties, namely *Faces of Islam in African Literature* (1991),[3] *The Marabout and the Muse: New Approaches to Islam in African Literature* (1996),[4] *Islam and Postcolonial Narrative* (1998),[5] *Islam and the West African Novel: The Politics of Representation* (2000),[6] and Alamin Mazrui's essay "Islam and Identity in the African Imagination" (1993), which critiques Harrow's 1991 volume.[7] The topic of Islam in African literature is due for an update from an Africana studies literary perspective. In response, I present my findings as a conversational essay with restrained bibliographical intent (with respect to the criticism rather than to the hefty body of work by mainly continental African writers) that aims to be informative and logical in the presentation of ideas and evidence.

INCORPORATING ISLAM INTO THE STUDY OF THE AFRICANA LITERARY TRADITION

There are many writers in the Africana literary tradition who have produced Islamic literature,[8] and from an Africana literary studies point of view, those writers whose works indicate an African-African cultural identity as well as those writers of Arab descent who prioritize Africanness over Arabness are priorities in the curriculum. Continental African writers comprise the largest group, which includes Camara Laye (Guinea), Cheikh Hamidou Kane (Senegal), Yambo Ouologuem (Mali), Zaynab Alkali (Nigeria), Aminata Sow Fall (Senegal), Ibrahim Tahir (Nigeria), Jamal Mahjoub (England and Sudan), Ousmane Sembene (Senegal), Calixthe Beyala (Cameroon), Mariama Ba (Senegal), Ahmadou Kourouma (Ivory Coast), Amadou Hampate Ba (Mali), Leila Aboulela (Egypt and Sudan), Ken Bugul (Senegal), Balaraba Ramat Yakubu (Nigeria),[9] Abdulrazak Gurnah (Tanzania), Nawal El Saadawi (Egypt), and Tayeb Salih (Sudan). In addition, there are many North African writers, such as Tahar ben Jalloun (Morocco), and a large group of Algerian writers—Tahar Djaout, Assia Djebar, Leila Sebbar (Algeria and France), Rachid Boudjedro, Nina Bouraoui (Algeria and France), Rachid Mimouni, Amin Zaoui, Kateb Yacine, Malika Mokeddem, and Aicha Lemsine. Finally, there is a smaller group of Muslim writers of mostly Indian descent from South Africa—Achmat Dangor, Ahmed Essop, Aziz Hassim, and Rayda Jacobs. This list is lengthy, but not conclusive.

Detailing the individual works and background of such a lengthy list of writers is beyond the overview objective of this essay. Critiques of most of these writers' works appear liberally in the journal *Research in African Literatures*, which is the journal associated with the discipline of Africana studies that most frequently publishes scholarship on Islamic literature. The above writers come from a host of African countries, and the most recent criticism presents them less in a literary tradition of Islamic literature and more as representatives of a religious-cultural perspective that is so pervasive (like Christianity has been in the African American literary tradition) that categorization would be anomalous.[10] This does not reduce the value of the dynamic trends, scenarios, speculations, and sociopolitical art whose continuum instigates conversations reflective of the Islamic past, present, and future. Leila Aboulela articulates the complexity of the literary perspectives well, saying she wants to "pass [on] knowledge about Islam," "the psychology, the state of mind, and the emotions of a person who has faith," as well as "Islamic logic."[11] In the case of Tanzanian writer Abdulrazak Gurnah, critic Felicity Hand observes that his work "is written *through* but is not *about* Islam."[12] The categorization is even more revealing in studies such as Jack Kearney's survey of the fictional work of South African Islamic writers—Ahmed Essop, Aziz Hassim, Achmat Dangor, and Rayda Jacobs—who hail primarily from Indian-Muslim, not African, backgrounds.[13]

The diversity of approaches to Islamic literature in the Africana literary tradition becomes even more pronounced with the addition of Marvin X's interpretation of the tradition from an African-centered and Diaspora perspective. Marvin X, sometimes called "the father of Muslim American literature,"[14] writes:

I would like to delineate my lineage. As a spiritual descendant of West African Muslims, I begin my literary biography in the Mali Empire, among those scholar/poet/social activists of Timbuktu: Ahmed Baba, Muhammad El-Mrili,

Ahmed Ibn Said, Muhammad Al Wangari, and the later Sufi poet/warriors of Senegal and Hausaland, Ahmedu Bamba and Uthman dan Fodio.

In America this tradition continued under the wretched conditions of slavery with the English/Arabic narratives of Ayub Suleimon Diallo, Ibrahima Abdulrahman Jallo, Bilali Mohammad, Salih Bilali, Umar Ibn Said and others who told how they got ovah. . . . Their narratives are thus the origin of Muslim literature in America, an integral part of the beginning of American and African American literature in general.[15]

Marvin X continues this lineage with reference to Edward Wilmot Blyden, Marcus Garvey's mentor Duse Muhammad Ali, Noble Drew Ali, Master Fard Muhammad, and the Honorable Elijah Muhammad before resuming the literary history with Malcolm X.[16] He adds:

The next major work is Malcolm X's *Autobiography*, with the assistance of Alex Haley. This neo-enslavement narrative bridged ancient and modern Islamic literature in America. Let us also include Louis Farrakhan's off Broadway drama *Organa* and his classic song A White Man's Heaven is a Black Man's Hell, anthem of the Black revolution of the 60s. Amiri Baraka utilized the Muslim myth of Yacub in his play *A Black Mass*, one of his most powerful works. . . . Askia Muhammad Toure must be credited with his Islamic writings, along with poetess Sonia Sanchez (Laila Mannan) who served a brief tenure in the Nation of Islam. Yusef Rahman and Yusef Iman created powerful Islamic poetry as well.

Marvin X gives the best itemized description of an African American–based Islamic tradition, and he has been the most ardent pioneer of the Islamic tradition in African American arts and letters. Scholars have noticed that the Islamic enslavement narratives are not frequently taught in the curriculum. Florence Marfo's essay "African Muslims in American Literature" seeks to explain the alleged exclusion of these narratives from an over-one-hundred-year tradition of African American literary anthologies.[17] Her work in literary criticism responds to an observation initially made in a work in the discipline of history—Allan D. Austin's *African Muslims in Antebellum America* (1984).[18]

Austin's and Marfo's studies are responses to the decisions made by anthologists, and they reiterate the role of anthologies and literary encyclopedias. *The Oxford Companion to African American Literature* has significant entries and indexes on Islam in the realm of the literary enterprise, and it covers topics of black nationalism, literary usage, names, and the NOI with even more fine-tuned entries on the NOI as it relates to Black Arts, Claude Brown, the critique of Christianity, dress, literary portrayals, Malcolm X, its publishing department, and writer Sonia Sanchez. A more recent critical anthology,

Literary Spaces: Introduction to Comparative Black Literature (2007) is also a good example.[19] It includes sources from nine African countries, eight regions of the Caribbean, the United States, Brazil, England, and Russia. In particular, it is valuable for its overview of Islam represented in works from the United States (a speech by Malcolm X delivered while in the NOI and Laina Mataka's poem about Malcolm titled "Were U There When They Crucified My Lord"); from Nigeria (Chudi Uwazurike's short story "A Song for the Parade" assessing the cultural, political, social, and religious transmutations of recent generations of immigrants); from Senegal (Ousmane Sembene's novella *Xala* exposing exploitation of Islamic law regarding polygyny); and from Egypt (Nawal El Saadawi's *Woman at Point Zero* dramatizing the negative predicaments of a society that limits opportunities for women). These selections appear in five of the eight literature chapters that are organized topically, which means most of the guided comparative exercises give readers an opportunity to evaluate the role of Islam in Africana world literature.

Acknowledging Marvin X's status as a pioneer of "Muslim American Literature (MAL)" scholar Mohja Kahf advances this as a subfield of Africana literature, offers criteria for inclusion of writers, and states an interest in "literary Muslimness."[20] He defines the origins of MAL with the grouping "Prophets of Dissent" to represent that "Muslim works in the Black Arts Movement (BAM) are the first set of writings in American literature to voice a cultural position identifiable as Muslim."[21] Kahf conceptualizes a multicultural MAL, writing "something is gained in reading them together as part of an American Muslim landscape." But the formative literary model of the Prophets of Dissent is based on its "'outsider' status, moral critique of mainstream American values, and often prophetic, visionary tone."[22] While he also lists Marvin X, Sonia Sanchez, and Amiri Baraka as key figures of the tradition, he adds (as "Later Prophets of Dissent") a Muslim spoken-word group from California called Generation M as well as Suheir Hammad (Palestine), who was featured on *Def Poetry Jam* and who claims poet June Jordan as a literary foremother.[23] Inevitably, Kahf declares Muslim American literature to be a regular field of study.[24]

OTHER RESEARCH AVENUES

Recent studies have posed other possibilities for the study of Islamic literature in the Africana literary tradition. Kahf poses the possibility of expanding studies of Muslim American literature to Muslim American culture, which would include "Motown, rap, and hip-hop lyrics by Muslim artists, screenplays such as the Muslim American classic *The Message* by the late Syrian producer Mustapha Aqqad, books written for children, sermons, essays, and other genres."[25] Yusuf Nuruddin's article "Ancient Black Astronauts and Extraterrestrial Jihads: Islamic Fiction as Urban Mythology" carries the literature into science/speculative fiction possibilities.[26] Marvin X's interpretation of the traditions holds promise for a unit study of Africana Islamic thought that would be ideal for a course on black sociopolitical thought or philosophy. Majda Ramadan Atieh examines the trope of the Islamic harem in a Toni Morrison novel.[27] And there are other African/Pan-African Islamic filmmakers in addition to Ousmane Sembene, such as Djibril Diop Mambety (Senegal), Mansour Sora Wade (Senegal), Merzak Allouache (Algeria), and Gaston Kabore (Burkina Faso). These cinema perspectives expand the scope of the study of Islam in the Africana literary tradition.

Filmmaker Julie Dash, in her film-turned-novel *Daughters of the Dust*, has a memorable Islamic character among the mostly Christian, Gullah Sea Island community. Bilal is among the most spiritual and devoted members of the community, as he reads the Quran and makes prayer in most of his scenes. The latter examples suggest that there is an additional category of Africana literature wherein contributions to Islamic *characterization* emerge as noteworthy. Future research would do well to yield a bibliographic essay that captures the presence of similar Islamic characterizations that go largely unanalyzed in the literature. Just as Toni Morrison in her discussion of "whiteness and the literary imagination" suggests that the brief appearances of African Americans in white American literature are symbolic with meaning beyond their brief appearances, the brief appearances of Islam in Africana culture may have an import that is disproportional to its sometimes meager presence.[28]

Islam's geographical statistics lead us to focus on literature emerging from regions with high populations of practicing Muslims. However, in an expanded pursuit to more fully address the phenomenon of Islam in the Africana literary tradition, surveys of African Islamic literary productivity would expand to include the Caribbean, Brazil, Canada, and Europe. Literary awards, regardless of scale, can also contribute to the future of the Africana Islamic literary tradition. Of note is the Muslim Writers Awards sponsored by the Birmingham (England) City Council since 2006. The award hopes to "get more writers from a black and minority ethnic background published by mainstream publishers."[29]

A SAMPLE SYLLABUS

The ideal syllabus for a course on Islam in the Africana literary tradition would cover four themes: traditions, pioneers, contemporary African continental experience, and diaspora and migration. A fifth theme could be a comparativist study that includes Arab and Indian writers from Algeria, Morocco, South Africa, and elsewhere. The paragraphs that follow provide some possibilities for a syllabus arranged along these themes.

Traditions: The syllabus for the section on traditions would provide historical and geographical context. It could include sociopolitical and philosophical writings such as Edward Wilmot Blyden's *Christianity, Islam, and the Negro Race* (1887), writings from the Islamic Hausa literary tradition,[30] the classic epic *Sundiata*,[31] and Elias N. Saad's *The History of Timbuktu: The Role of Muslim Scholars and Notables, 1400–1900* (1983).[32] These writings could be layered with excerpts from Marvin X's list of the West African Muslim tradition and the early Muslim American tradition and with a sample of the enslavement narratives that Marfo discusses: *Some Memoirs of the Life of Job* (1734), "Autobiography of Omar Ibn Said, Slave in North Carolina" (1831), *An Interesting Narrative: Biography of Mahommah G. Baquaqua* (1854), and *The Autobiography of Nicholas Said* (1873).[33] The tradition unit should also reflect an awareness of the Pan-African world and the vast geographic scope of the tradition that spans the continent of Africa and the Diaspora.

Pioneers: The syllabus for the section on pioneers would include early writers from continental Africa whose texts were groundbreaking and definitive. Camara Laye's autobiography *The Dark Child* (1954)[34] and Cheikh Amadou Kane's *Ambiguous Adventure* (1961)[35] are considered two of the classics. Other important texts are Aminata Sow Fall's first novel *Le Revenant* (1976),[36] which addresses the bourgeoisie, and her better known work *The Beggars' Strike* (1979), which was translated from the French.[37] The latter would compare well with Ousmane Sembene's *Xala* (1974) because both are about beggars, local politics, and the potential of the supernatural.[38] Yambo Ouologuem's controversial *Bound to Violence*[39] creatively chronicles almost eight centuries of Mali's history using a fabricated nation-state as a counternarrative to trends of early African novels. Ibrahim Tahir's *Last Imam*[40] is considered one of the most orthodox African-Muslim novels, and Bangura says it best when he notes that Tahir "thematizes the intractable conflict between Islam and the pre-Islamic Fulani-Hausa cultures of Northern Nigeria."[41] These texts are seminal works of the early tradition.

The Contemporary African Continental Experience: The third syllabus section on the contemporary African continental experience would be comprised of texts that are not necessarily "firsts" and that address African Islamic societies at home but not abroad. Mariama Ba's *So Long a Letter* (1981),[42] which is about a Senegalese woman's reflections after learning her husband is taking on a new wife in Islamic tradition, and Nawal El Saadawi's

Woman at Point Zero, which tells of an Egyptian woman's gendered quest for education and respectability, are widely taught in the Africana literary curriculum. Other works would include Ken Bugul's striking autobiography *The Abandoned Baobab*[43] and any one of Balaraba Ramat Yakubu's novels on the experience of Hausa women such as *Who Will Marry An Ignoramus?* (1990)[44] or *I Love Him All the Same* (2001).[45] Zaynab Alkali's novels *The Stillborn* (1984)[46] and *Cobwebs and Other Stories* (1995),[47] both of which address the experience of women in Northern Nigeria, are also vital texts for this category. Finally, Ahmadou Kourouma's *Allah Is Not Obliged* (2007), which chronicles a child soldier's view that life is not fair, rounds out this section as a more contemporary text.[48]

Diaspora and Migration: The fourth unit on diaspora and migration would be the most eclectic. It engages African American writers and the Muslim American tradition outlined earlier by Marvin X that includes Malcolm X, Sonia Sanchez (from her Nation of Islam period), and others. It is also the ideal unit for texts that blend geographical experience based on migration, travel, and returns such as Talib Saleh's *Season of Migration to the North*, a Nubian novel about two lives of migration to and from England. Jamal Mahjoub can be considered an African-European writer with his survey of tradition and modernity in *Navigation of a Rainmaker: An Apocalyptic Vision of War-Torn Africa* (1989), which could also appear in the previous unit.[49] Myriam Warner-Vieyra's *Juletane* is one of a small number of Caribbean novels treating Islam.[50] In *Juletane*, a West Indian woman records her marriage to a Senegalese man and the surprises of her relocation to his Muslim compound in Africa. Sefi Atta's *Every Good Thing Will Come* (2005) can be included in this section because the protagonist goes to England for her education then returns to Nigeria.[51] From Cameroon and now France, Calixthe Beyala's *Loukoum: The Little Prince of Belleville* (1992) is about an immigrant family from Mali that lives in the Paris suburbs.[52] The sequel, *Maman a un amant (Mother Has a Lover)* (1993) is also relevant.[53] Leila Aboulela's *Minaret* (2005), about a well-to-do Sudanese woman who finds herself in exile and poverty in London, would also be included here.[54] The unit on diaspora and migration is also the unit that is most in need of definition. Students will have greater research opportunities to define the Diaspora tradition in search of morsels of African American, Canadian, Caribbean, Brazilian, and African-European literatures that emphasize migration, immigration, translation, and literary movements related to Islam.

The above list and configuration is one possible approach among many and aims to find a balance between traditional/contemporary and African/Diasporic texts in the best model of the diverse experiences and knowledge bases managed in the discipline of Africana studies.

CONCLUSION

Offering an overview of Islam in the Africana literary tradition is an enormous task. However, the material can be managed by approaching it in several waves: familiarizing readers with authors, origins, and contexts; posing key questions about the meaning, implications, and role of the topic; exploring the cultural, geographical, and linguistic demarcations of the global dimensions of Islam in the Africana literary tradition; and clarifying lines of demarcation between approaches to Islamic literature within and beyond the discipline of Africana studies.

This essay has aimed to engage the progress the discipline of Africana studies has made in being a clearinghouse for knowledge of the global African experience. It has proceeded from the foundational point of view that Islamic literature has appeared steadily in the Africana literary tradition through the teaching of texts that reference the Nation of Islam (Malcolm X, Baraka, etc.), West African writers (Sembene, Mariama Ba, Laye, Sow Fall, etc.), and North African writers (El Saadawi and even Albert Memmi). The criticism reinforces the possibility that writers such as Chris Abani (Nigeria), Sefi Atta (Nigeria), Ama Ata Aidoo (Ghana), and others who treat Islam in the social and religious contexts of their writing can also be included in categorizations of Islamic literature. In Aidoo's *Changes* (1991), the protagonist's second husband is Muslim.[55] In Abani's novella *Song for Night* (2007), the young protagonist's father is a Muslim convert.[56] In Sefi Atta's *Everything Good Will Come*, the protagonist's youthful best friend is defined by her in part by her Muslim father and English mother.

An important warning is that scholars in the discipline should be extremely familiar with the origins of Islamic writers addressed, particularly in any *comparative* criticism on texts used in class, which have been selected based on their identifications in the *African*-African (versus the *Arab*-African) worldview. Criticism not based in the discipline of Africana studies does not use an ethnic-racial-cultural filter in its comparisons, and the untrained reader may be unknowingly integrating Arab worldviews with the African worldviews that are the primary focus of the discipline's literary courses. Sudanese writer Tayeb Salih comes to mind with his *Season of Migration to the North* (1966), which was hailed by the Arab Literary Academy as "the most important Arab novel of the twentieth century" and whose categorization has eluded writers searching for African (non-Arab) texts from North Africa. Arab and Islamic identification often trump ethnic-racial identification in the marketing and descriptions of both writers and their literatures, which can also be a challenge.[57]

The field of postcolonial studies produces criticism on Islamic literature that uses its own, as well as cultural studies' theories and contexts for reference;

in comparison Africana studies literary scholars credit African-centered and/ or Afrocentric orientations for certain literary trends. For example, a reviewer of Stephanie Newel's *West African Literature: Ways of Reading* (2006) attributes what he observes in Newell's work as "an African commitment to social change and humanism" to Gayatri Spivak and Homi Bhaba when, in comparison, a critic from Africana studies would attribute that perspective to a more African-centered or Afrocentric approach to literature.[58] Part of the task that lies ahead in managing the role of Islam in the Africana literary tradition involves increasing the visibility of Islam by teaching more contemporary and traditional texts in a more well-defined category, increasing the numbers of publications on the subject by Africana studies scholars in Africana literary and cultural journals, accepting the challenge of multilingualism, and rescuing texts from the obscurity inherent in the publishing industry.[59]

The task that lies ahead also includes locating the discipline's interests in specificity, ethos, and application of knowledge from among criticism generated from other disciplines and areas (such as literature, English, and cultural studies) that contribute regular and significant scholarship to the topic of African/black Islamic literature. Much of the criticism is comparative and merges collective Islamic experience in contexts of immigration and multiculturalism, as in the case of British Muslim literature, where Sabine Klinck suggests "faith is a more stable factor than ethnicity."[60] This is debatable in a modern experience where race, ethnicity, and culture are robust signifiers of experience.

Inevitably, this is one of the most important clarifications as we sift through the global Islamic literary tradition to locate and study those appropriate for the Africana studies. The discipline of Africana studies is a synthesis of academic and practical enterprises that prioritize knowledge related to, and that has the capacity to expand, the quality of life and the cultural stability of people of African descent, and the Islamic literary tradition is pursued along these lines within the discipline's literary approaches.

NOTES

1. Most literature offerings in Africana studies cover texts that introduce aspect of Islam primarily from the United States and African regions.

2. André Ntonfo, "Comparative Literature at the University of Yaoundé," *Yearbook of Comparative and General Literature* 43 (1995): 134.

3. Kenneth W. Harrow, ed., *Faces of Islam in African Literature* (Portsmouth, NH: Heinemann, 1991).

4. Kenneth W. Harrow, ed., *The Marabout and the Muse: New Approaches to Islam in African Literature* (Portsmouth, NH: Heinemann, 1993).

5. John Erickson, *Islam and Postcolonial Narrative* (Cambridge: Cambridge University Press, 1998).

6. Ahmed Bangura, *Islam and the West African Novel* (Boulder, CO: Lynne Reiner Publishers, 2000).

7. Al' Amin Mazrui, "Islam and Identity in the African Imagination," *Literary Griot: International Journal of Black Expressive Cultural Studies* 5 (1993): 58–64.

8. This list is culled primarily from articles referencing Islam published since 1999 in the journal *Research in African Literatures*. This journal, published by the African and Afro-American Research Institute at the University of Texas at Austin, has made an excellent case for its role as an Africana studies journal that liberally publishes on the topic of Islam. While this essay will not focus on the individual works of each writer, it is of note that the journal, of course, included research on the oral performance narrative of Sundiata based on several perspectives.

9. Balaraba is responsible for contemporary Hausa-Islamic feminism.

10. Hausa literature of northern Nigeria is more frequently categorized with the unity and continuum that of a "tradition."

11. Charles R. Larson, "Halal Novelist—Western and Islamic Civilizations Dialogue in Sudanese writer Leila Aboulela's Fiction," *World and I* (2002): 250. *Academic One File.* July 20, 2012.

12. Felicity Hand, "Untangling Stories and Healing Rifts: Abdulrazak Gurnah's *By the Sea*," *Research in African Literatures* 41 (2010): 74.

13. Jack Kearney, "Representations of Islamic Belief and Practice in a South African Context: Reflections on the Fictional Work of Ahmed Essop, Aziz Hassim, Achmat Dangor, and Rayda Jacobs," *Journal of Literary Studies* 22 (2006): 138–57.

14. Nefertiti El Muhajir had a volume in preparation as late as 2007 with Black Bird Press entitled *Marvin X: A Critical Look at the Father of Muslim American Literature*, www.marvinxwrites.blogspot.com/search?q=black+muslim+writers, accessed July 23, 2012.

15. Marvin X, "The Best of Dr. Marvin," blog, www.marvinxwrites.blogspot.com, accessed July 23, 2012.

16. Manning Marable's *Malcolm X: A Life of Re-Invention* (New York: Penguin, 2011), is likely to become a canonical source on Malcolm X in the genre of critical biography.

17. Florence Marfo, "African Muslims in African American Literature," *Callaloo* 32 (2009): 1213–22, 1391.

18. Allan D. Austin, ed., *African Muslims in Antebellum America: A Sourcebook* (New York: Garland, 1984).

19. Christel N. Temple, *Literary Spaces: Introduction to Comparative Black Literature* (Durham, NC: Carolina Academic Press, 2007).

20. Mohja Kahf, "Teaching Diaspora Literature: Muslim American Literature as an Emerging Field," *Journal of Pan African Studies* 4, no. 2 (December 2010): 163–67.

21. Ibid., 164.

22. Ibid.

23. Ibid., 165.

128   *Chapter Eight*

24. Mohja Kahf, preface for unpublished manuscript, "Marvin X: A Critical Look at the Father of Muslim American Literature," marvinxwrites.blogspot.com/2007/05/marvin-x-critical-look-at-father-of.html, accessed April 23, 2015.

25. Kahf, "Teaching Diaspora Literature," 167.

26. Yusuf Nuruddin, "Ancient Black Astronauts and Extraterrestrial Jihads: Islamic Science Fiction as Urban Mythology," *Socialism and Democracy* 20 (2006): 127–65.

27. Majda Ramadan Atieh, *The African American Tafsir Interpretation of the Islamic Harem: Female Resistance in Toni Morrison's* Paradise, Ph.D. Dissertation, Howard University, 2007.

28. Toni Morrison, *Playing in the Dark: Whiteness and the Literary Imagination* (Cambridge: Harvard University Press, 1992).

29. "Muslim Writers–Birmingham City Council," www.birmingham.gov.uk/cs/Sa tellite?c=Page&childpagename=Lib_Children_Accessibility%2FCFPageLayout&ci d=1223092732170&packedargs=website%3D4&pagename=BCC%2FCommon%2F Wrapper%2FCFWrapper&rendermode=live accessed April 23, 2015.

30. See Rotimi Omoyele Fasan, "Mapping Nigerian Literature," http://nobleworld.biz/images/AF_Fasan.pdf, July 31, 2011, where he describes the depth of the Hausa tradition: "The earliest literature in Hausa written in Arabic and Ajami, mostly poetry, was according to Yahaya written right about the seventeenth century by Islamic scholars such as Abdullahi Suka who wrote *Riwayar Annabi Musa* in Ajami, and Wali Danmasani Abdulajalil who wrote the Hausa poem *Wakir Yakin Badar* also in Ajami, etc. Literary writing in Hausaland would come to its height in the nineteenth century during the period of the Islamic Jihadist, Shehu Usman dan Fodio, who wrote hundreds of poems in Arabic, Fulfude, and Hausa. Hausa literature in Boko script were mostly novels that have since become classics, published from the winning entries of a writing competition in the 1930s. These include *Ruwan Bagaja* (Abubakar Imam), *Shehu Umar* (Abubakar Tafawa Balewa), *Gandoki* (Bello Kagara), *Idon Matambayi* (Mohammadu Gwarzo), and *Jiki Magayi* (M. Tafida and Dr. R. M. East). *Six Hausa Plays*, edited by Dr. R. M. East and published in 1930, were the first plays to appear in Hausa. *Kidan Ruwa, Yawon Magi*, and *Kalankuwa* are traditional forms of drama among the Hausa (Kofoworola 1981). After the pioneering efforts of these writers, Hausa literature has continued to flourish becoming one of the most vibrant strands of Nigerian literature in the indigenous languages."

31. Djibril Tamsir Niane, *Sundiata: An Epic of Old Mali* (New York: Longman, 1983). Many versions of the Sundiata epic would satisfy syllabus content.

32. Elias N. Saad, *Social History of Timbuktu: Role of Moslem Scholars and Notables, 1400–1900* (Cambridge: Cambridge University Press, 1983).

33. Marfo, "African Muslims in African American Literature," 1213.

34. Camara Laye, *The Dark Child: The Autobiography of an African Child* (New York: Farrar, Straus, & Giroux, 1994).

35. Amadou Hampata Kane, *Ambiguous Adventure* (Brooklyn: Melville House, 2012).

36. Aminata Sow Fall, *Le Revenant* (Dakar: Nouvelles Editions Africaines, 1976).

37. Aminata Sow Fall, *The Beggars Strike* (New York: Longman, 1986).

38. Ousmane Sembene, *Xala* (Chicago: Lawrence Hill, 1976).

39. Yambo Oulougem, *Le Devoir de Violence (Bound to Violence)* (Portsmouth, NH: Heinemann, 1983).

40. Ibrahim Tahir, *The Last Imam* (London: Kegan Paul International, 1985).

41. Bangura, *Islam and the West African Novel*, 107.

42. Mariama Ba, *So Long A Letter* (Portsmouth, NH: Heinemann, 2008).

43. Ken Bugul, *The Abandoned Baobab* (Charlottesville: University of Virginia Press, 2008).

44. Balaraba Ramat Yakubu, *Who Will Marry an Ignoramus* (Zaria, Nigeria: Gaskia Corporation, 1990).

45. Balaraba Ramat Yakubu, *I Love Him All the Same* (Kano, Nigeria: privately published, 2001).

46. Zaynab Alkali, *The Stillborn* (New York: Longman, 1984).

47. Zaynab Alkali, *Cobwebs and Other Stories* (New York: Longman, 1995).

48. Ahmadou Kourouma, *Allah Is Not Obliged* (New York: Anchor Books, 2007).

49. Jamal Mahjoub, *Navigation of a Rainmaker: An Apocalyptic Vision of War-Torn Africa* (New York: Oxford University Press, 1989).

50. Myriam Warner-Vieyra, *Juletane* (Paris: Presence Africaine, 1982).

51. Sefi Atta, *Every Good Thing Will Come* (Northampton, MA: Interlink Books, 2005).

52. Calixthe Beyala, *Loukoum: The Little Prince of Belleville* (Portsmouth, NH: Heinemann, 1995).

53. Calixthe Beyala, *Maman a un amant* (Paris: Editions 84, 1993).

54. Leila Aboulela, *Minaret* (London: Bloomsbury, 2005).

55. Ama Ata Aidoo, *Changes* (New York: Feminist Press, 1993).

56. Chris Abani, *Song for Night* (Brooklyn: Akashic Books, 2007).

57. Scholar Nzinga Virgilette Gaffin has lectured widely on this challenge and on her pursuit of locating writers in the Nubian literature tradition in which Salih's *Season of Migration to the North* plays a part.

58. K. W. Harrow, Review of *West African Literatures: Ways of Reading* by Stephanie Newell, *African Studies Review* 50 (2007): 209–210.

59. I include as a note, rather than as the dismal introduction seen far too frequently in surveys of African literature, that the lack of multilingualism (that includes Arabic and other African languages), translation, and publication/distribution are still barriers that block the tradition and that need to be addressed.

60. Sabine Klinck, "Asserting the Self: The Importance of Religion for Migrant Women," www.inter-disciplinary.net/wp-content/uploads/2012/02/klinckipaper.pdf, p. 5, accessed August 8, 2012.

Chapter Nine

Martin L. King Jr. and Malcolm X

Charles Allen

Years after the deaths of Martin Luther King Jr. and Malcolm X, the two men still remain fixed images in the American consciousness: Martin Luther King Jr., an advocate of nonviolence, delivering his *I Have a Dream* speech from the steps of the Lincoln Memorial; and Malcolm X, the black nationalist, encouraging African Americans to fight racial oppression "by any means necessary."[1] Martin Luther King is often highlighted in American history. He is one of the few African Americans that young people will discuss in school. Malcolm X is often viewed as his antithesis: a violent racist filled with hate. Malcolm X is ultimately removed from mainstream history because of this, and many people have a false perception of him due to misinterpretation of his messages. These two men who lived at the same time, fighting a similar fight with different tactics are a large contribution to African American, and American, history.

Mainstream media and the white press are culpable in the elevation of Martin Luther King Jr. and the burying of Malcolm X. But even Dr. King's followers frequently misrepresent Malcolm X's views, referring to him as a "messiah of hate" and as a leader of a "black Ku Klux Klan of racial extremists"; in turn, Malcolm X's followers view Dr. King and his followers as "twentieth century Uncle Tom pacifists" used by whites to brutalize black people.[2]

In the following pages, I will discuss the significant differences and similarities between Martin Luther King and Malcolm X. I will also look at their stances on religion and human rights. Lastly, I'll cite the very different approaches in each man's most famous speech—*I Have a Dream* by Martin Luther King Jr.[3] and *Message to the Grassroots* by Malcolm X.[4]

MARTIN LUTHER KING JR.

Martin Luther King Jr. was born in Atlanta, Georgia, as the son and grandson of Baptist preachers. He was a pastor and a very distinguished theologian. He was *Time*'s Man of the Year in 1963 and a Nobel Peace Prize winner in 1964. It is suspected that many whites prefer that African American males identify with Martin Luther King Jr. rather that Malcolm X precisely because the former is likely to be perceived as more socially acceptable insofar as his message of nonviolence can be construed to mean nonaction (ironically, it is assumed that alienated African American males have seen through this cynical ironic use of Martin Luther King Jr. and have identified more with Malcolm X, the African American leader largely ignored by the white press).[5]

Dr. King believed there was no other way to social justice than nonviolence; to him there was no other option for the oppressed peoples of the day. He felt that to stand in the face of tyranny without responding in a likewise manner was the only way for justice anywhere in the world. He felt there was no better way to resolve differences between nations. This began through his upbringing. As a young Christian raised by two Baptist preachers in his father and grandfather, he was taught that he should share the love that Jesus showed to all people no matter what.

This, however, was not always an easy task. As a young boy he was greatly disturbed by a white father who told his son that he could no longer play with King because he was black. This made him want to hate whites at an early age. However, his time in college afforded him opportunities to meet liberal whites who advocated social change. He also read about the nonviolent movements and civil disobedience of others, which reinforced his propensity for love.

Dr. King's intentions were to simply be a preacher at Dexter Avenue Baptist Church in Montgomery, Alabama. He was not seeking to become a leader of the civil rights movement. But after the refusal of Rosa Parks to give up her seat at the front of the bus, Dr. King found himself at the forefront of the movement. Through his faith, he found the strength to lead and to face the verbal threats and acts of violence that resulted from his leadership. He also founded a national organization, the Southern Christian Leadership Conference, in order to demonstrate the power of nonviolence to achieve justice in every segment of American life.[6] Dr. King believed that the only way to reach a moral end was through moral means.

His adherence to nonviolence was received differently in the broader American culture depending on whom his message was directed to. His stature in the white community grew as he encouraged blacks to hold firmly to nonviolence. But he was rejected when he advocated nonviolence for the

United States as a nation.[7] To Malcolm X, this was proof that the nonviolence movement was not effective. If the group you are fighting against is content with your actions, Malcolm X believed that the actions weren't strong enough. Dr. King combatted this criticism often, citing not only his beliefs but also the lack of contribution by Malcolm X and his followers to the civil rights movement or any other actions.

One common contrasting point made in reference to Dr. King and Malcolm X is the radicalness of Malcolm X. He is viewed as one taking the nonfundamental approach to attacking racism. However, both men were radical in their thinking. Dr. King's belief that a black man could be treated in the same way as whites was just as radical of an idea as those of Malcolm X.

MALCOLM X

Malcolm X was a black nationalist. Unlike King, he believed that the best outcome for black people was to have their own land and ultimately their own nation. His ideas of separatism and disdain for Caucasians were seen as racist and hateful, and his views are still omitted from classroom, textbooks, and the mainstream media today. There is no national holiday for him, no parades in his honor, often no streets named after him. He is viewed as someone who opposed the American dream, and this has caused his message to become erased from our history books.

Malcolm X often focused his criticism on the failure of white people to accept black people as human beings and treat them as such. He expressed himself very directly and felt no need to sugarcoat his messages. His absolute refusal to acknowledge any scenario in which blacks and whites could coexist in the United States was viewed as discriminatory. Malcolm X would argue that he was only responding to the historical options that had been given to him.

Malcolm Little was the son of a Baptist preacher as well, but he lived a much different life. His father was a follower of Marcus Garvey and a leader of the movement in his relocated home of Lansing, Michigan. Malcolm's home was burned down at the age of four and his father was murdered at the age of six. Malcolm attributes both incidents to the hate group the Black Legionnaires.[8] His mother failed to cope with the rough times and was eventually admitted to a mental hospital, causing young Malcolm and his siblings to be separated and scattered among different foster families. Malcolm eventually dropped out of school, moved to Boston and then New York, and lived a life of crime that ultimately landed him in prison.

Malcolm's time in prison prompted the development of his faith in Islam, and he became a follower of Elijah Muhammad and the Nation of Islam

(NOI). Malcolm was able to increase his knowledge of the black nationalist movement and an ideology of white evildoing. He became a national spokesperson of the NOI speaking around the country and was particularly critical of white liberals who he felt were acting as double agents toward blacks. He was exceptionally concerned about the desire of whites to embrace Dr. King's nonviolent approach. He felt this was their way to continue to manipulate blacks and keep them under their thumb.

Malcolm X is often seen as an advocate for violence, but he was actually an advocate of self-defense. He believed that it was nonsensical to take beatings without defending yourself. This caused him to be viewed as promoter of hate and violence, which was the exact opposite of Dr. King's love and peace approach. In time Malcolm rejected the racist views of Elijah Muhammad, but he never wavered from his belief in black self-defense.

While Malcolm X is not nearly esteemed in the way that Dr. King is, his legacy lives on in both open and covert ways. In 1992 Spike Lee released the motion picture *Malcolm X*, which detailed the life of the iconic figure. Alienated lower-class African American males have shifted away from the acceptance of Dr. King to a focus upon Malcolm X.[9] This is visible, for example, among hip hop artists, who have paid respect to Malcolm X for years, praising his commitment to self-sufficiency and black power.

I believe we also see the remnants of Malcolm X's legacy through activists fighting for our communities and our schools. Malcolm believed that we could educate ourselves effectively and that our communities were falsely advertised as crime-infested areas. Today our neighborhoods are still viewed in this manner and are often targets of the police. Our children struggle in schools that are often underfunded and understaffed by underqualified teachers. As Michelle Alexander points out in her book *The New Jim Crow*, the image of black neighborhoods as crime hubs, the reality of poor schools, and Reagan's war on drugs colluded to incarcerate multitudes of black men.[10] Malcolm X foresaw just this type of future if blacks didn't take control of their neighborhoods.

Malcolm X's contributions are also seen in black businesses today. Malcolm was a proponent of black people owning and supporting their own businesses in order to gain economic freedom. This was a key component of Marcus Garvey's movement and Malcolm advocated self-reliance as well. This part of his legacy continues to be an important part of the economic landscape for black Americans.

RELIGION

Malcolm X was a Muslim, and most of his learning of the religion largely took place in a prison cell. His initial contact with the religion was though the

Nation of Islam. Malcolm's siblings had become followers of Elijah Muhammad while he was imprisoned. This, along with his relationship with another inmate, gave Malcolm the confidence to make the life change and become a Muslim. While Malcolm's father was a Baptist preacher, he never had any faith that whites and blacks could live harmoniously in America. In fact, he was the president of the local UNIA organization founded by Marcus Garvey. Malcolm X carried that same sentiment with him during his adult life and was a black nationalist because of this.

Martin Luther King Jr. was a Christian, Southern Baptist to be exact, raised by his pastor father in Ebenezer Baptist Church. His grandfather and slave great-grandfather were preachers as well. His parents taught him to love and to restrain from aggression, which he struggled with in his younger years. However, this belief was the foundation of his nonviolent approach and was strengthened through his studies of Gandhi and others. Dr. King held strong to his faith during some of the most tumultuous times. He was a highly educated preacher trained in elite college classrooms.

Both men were advocates of peace. Malcolm X talks of how the Quran teaches peace but also self-defense whereas Dr. King preached that one should turn the other cheek. This difference is often exaggerated to present Malcolm X as an advocate for violence. His often quoted statement "by any means necessary" is grossly misunderstood. He was not an initiator of conflict but was willing to take any means to protect himself if attacked. Both men also believed that their faith would be factor in their redemption.

As a member of the Black Baptist church that had always opposed slavery and the mistreatment of black people, Dr. King believed that God was the God of the oppressed. He believed that through nonviolence God would save black people from the tyranny it faced in America. Dr. King sometimes likened himself to Moses leading the God's people out of Egypt. Malcolm, on the other hand, felt that God would involve himself in the struggle by different means. He believed that God's intervention would be to punish the oppressor as opposed to simply freeing the oppressed.

HUMAN RIGHTS

Malcolm X was keenly aware from the very beginning that human rights were the most important issue facing Black America. He was never in favor of simply improving life through integration. Malcolm felt that it didn't matter if schools and places of business were integrated if black people weren't treated as human beings. After years of focusing on gaining civil liberties that were guaranteed in the Constitution, Dr. King began to focus on human rights as well. He became frustrated with the system over time, especially after laws were enacted with the intent to improve the lives of African Americans in America. Dr. King saw that this was all irrelevant if people weren't able to have opportunities to get themselves out of poverty first.

Both Dr. King and Malcolm X attacked the United States's involvement in Vietnam. Malcolm X stressed that there was no reason for a black man to bleed for America when America doesn't treat him as a human. Dr. King felt the same and emphasized the financial and social costs of war as well. He cited that the resources spent to send troops to fight were taking away from the programs in place to help those in America. Opposing the war was not a popular stance in the eyes of the U.S. government.

Both men desired to work together on human rights issues but failed to do so before the untimely death of Malcolm in 1965. In *Message to the Grassroots*, Malcolm X discussed how if leaders were able to unify and forget differences, greater change could take place. Perhaps if they were able to have this opportunity, the legacies of both men would be forever changed. It appears, however, that Dr. King avoided this possibility. This is likely attributed to him not wanting the association with a man that many saw as racist and an advocate for violence.

I HAVE A DREAM AND *MESSAGE TO THE GRASSROOTS*

In 1963, Dr. King delivered his most famous speech: *I Have a Dream.* The speech was delivered on the steps of the Lincoln Memorial, and over 250,000 white and black Americans gathered in person to hear it; it was televised as well. The speech's popularity and continued use marks it as the peak of the civil rights movement and one of the most famous speeches in American history. Dr. King utilized metaphors, similes, religious references, and repetition to craft an extremely evocative and persuasive speech.

Dr. King described the racial inequality in America as the Negro "languishing in the corners of American society" and living as "an exile in his own land." He stressed how black Americans had not been receiving the protection of life, liberty, and pursuit of happiness that the U.S. Constitution promises. He saw these promises as a blank check that was never intended to be cashed. He quoted from scripture to emphasize his belief that the treatment of black people in American was not only immoral but also unspiritual.

Dr. King emphasized the importance of justice but he saw justice as a possibility only if everyone involved themselves in the process, both blacks and whites. This was very different from what Malcolm X believed: He felt that blacks could never trust the white man for anything. Dr. King also used images of children and how their innocence is stolen from them through senseless racism. He discussed the American dream and how it should be accessible to all children.

Dr. King ended the speech with his vision that one day all will be free. He shared that children of all religions, race, color, and creed will be able to engage with one another to pursue the American dream. This is the underlying basis of what Dr. King desired. He believed he was an American and therefore should be treated as such. He saw the opportunities that were available in this country and felt that all people should have access to those opportunities. Throughout all the turmoil, Martin Luther King Jr. always believed in America.

Malcolm X did not have the same level belief or trust in the American way of life. In his most famous speech, *Message to the Grassroots*, Malcolm offered a very different vision of what needed to be done for black people to feel comfortable in America. The first theme is stressed early on in the speech. Malcolm begins with stating America has a problem and that is the black man. He stresses that black people are not wanted in the United States and must understand and address this. What Malcolm attempted to emphasize was the need to unify: "We must forget our differences and unite," he said. "We must unite against the enemy, which is the White man." He provides the example of the Bandung conference where even those of different religious beliefs were able to stand up to their oppressor. He stressed that the differences should be handled behind close doors, not in the streets where their opponents would frame their disagreements as uncouth. Despite this assertion, elsewhere in the speech he vehemently attacks civil rights leaders, including Martin Luther King Jr.

The second theme of the speech involved Malcolm's definition of a revolution. He cited the differences between the black revolutions that were happening elsewhere in the world and the Negro revolution in the United States. He contended that the term *revolution* was used too loosely. He stressed the historic characteristics of true revolution—motive, objective, result, and methods—and stated that if we truly understood the meaning of a revolution, we might stop using the word. The American, French, Chinese, and Russian revolutions were all based on land and the pursuit of independence through bloodshed, whereas the African American revolution was nonviolent. He stated that black people were often willing to bleed for white people's wars but not for their own revolution right here in America. If given the opportunity to respond on the spot, Dr. King would argue that such a revolution would involve bloodshed and that Malcolm would not be out there with them fighting in the streets.

Malcolm attacked the nonviolent movement because violence was being brought to black folks in the South. He believed we should look at the historic examples from all over the world to determine how we can bring about change here in America. He believed there is no such thing as a nonviolent revolution and that the Negro revolution could not succeed through nonviolence. Also land is the basis all other revolutions and should become the basis of the Negro revolution. Ultimately, his message was that the grassroots has the greatest potential power to make things happen. Malcolm X believed that the power was within the people and as they went, so would a movement toward a true revolution and change.

CONCLUSION

Although Martin Luther King Jr. has been ensconced in American history as the leader of change during the civil rights era and Malcolm X has been largely erased from history books, both men played key roles in changing American society.[11] Dr. King believed in the American dream and in the effectiveness of nonviolence, and Malcolm believed in self-sufficiency and self-defense. However, they used these different tactics to pursue one goal: the well-being of black people in America.

NOTES

1. Robert Kelly and Erin Cook, "Martin Luther King, Jr., and Malcolm X: A Common Solution," *OAH Magazine of History* 19, no. 1 (2005): 37–40.
2. James H. Cone, "Martin and Malcolm on Nonviolence and Violence," *Phylon 1960* 49, no. 3–4 (2001): 173–83.
3. M. L. King Jr., *I Have a Dream*, 1963, www.archives.gov/press/exhibits/dreamspeech.pdf, accessed December 8, 2015. For more of King's writings, see M. L. King Jr., *The Autobiography of Martin Luther King, Jr.* (New York: Warner Books, 1998).
4. Malcolm X, *Message to the Grassroots*, 1963, http://www.historyisaweapon. com/defcon1/malcgrass.html. See also Alex Haley, *The Autobiography of Malcolm X, as told to Alex Haley* (New York: Ballantine Books, 1965); J. L. Conyers and A. P. Smallwood, *Malcolm X: A Historical Reader* (Durham, NC: Carolina Academic Press, 2008).
5. Ralph W. Hood Jr., Ronald J. Morris, Susan E. Hickman, and P. J. Watson, "Martin and Malcolm as Cultural Icons: An Empirical Study Comparing Lower Class African American and White Males," *Review of Religious Research* 36, no. 4 (1995): 382–88.
6. Cone, "Martin and Malcolm on Nonviolence and Violence."
7. Ibid.
8. Ibid.
9. Hood et al., "Martin and Malcolm as Cultural Icons."

10. M. Alexander, *The New Jim Crow: Mass Incarceration in the Age of Color-blindness* (New York: New Press, 2010).

11. Britta Waldschmidt-Nelson, *Dreams and Nightmares: Martin Luther King, Jr., Malcolm X, and the Struggle for Black Equality in America* (Gainesville: University Press of Florida, 2012).

Chapter Ten

Elijah Muhammad's Nation of Islam

Separatism, Regendering, and a Secular Approach to Black Power after Malcolm X (1965–1975)[1]

Ula Taylor

Why would anyone become a member of the Nation of Islam after the assassination of Malcolm X (El-Hajj Malik El-Shabazz) on February 21, 1965, in New York's Audubon Ballroom? More than any other leader, he represented black liberation. His fiercely smart rhetoric helped to shift the dominant political struggle from a strategy of civil rights liberalism to eclectic expressions of black nationalism. As the most charismatic and visible spokesperson for the Nation of Islam, Malcolm moved beyond the Honorable Elijah Muhammad's (the Nation of Islam's undisputed leader from 1934 to 1975) call for economic self-sufficiency nationalism. Combining an application of armed self-defense "by any means necessary" along with a lethal critique of white folks as "devils," Malcolm appealed to the most socially isolated, politically dispossessed, and economically desperate members of the black proletariat. It was Malcolm's undivided commitment to create a powerful group of "believers" in the Nation of Islam that resulted in a substantial membership increase. In 1955, there were only sixteen temples, largely located in the urban North. But by 1960 over fifty temples were sprinkled throughout the United States with registered membership estimated between 50,000 and 250,000.[2]

Malcolm has become a militant martyr for the Nation of Islam and a "Black Power paradigm—the archetype, reference point, and spiritual adviser in absentia for a generation of Afro-American activists."[3] This chapter explores a number of issues, including the Nation of Islam's views of Africa, reparations, land as well as poverty and progress, issues of separatism, and the redefinition of gender roles, specifically the creation of two allegedly complementary subjects, a masculine man and a feminine woman.[4] Clearly, Black Power advocates had multiple visions, but the Nation of Islam provides one of the most imaginative sites to explore their concerns about intimate gender relations, or what Paulette Pierce insight fully calls "boudoir politics," and the creation of a "black nation." This article is an effort to flesh out understanding of African American identity, political subjectivity, gender prescriptions, and nation building during the peak of the modern Black Power movement. Furthermore, I suggest that in the post–Malcolm X period, the religious nature of the Nation of Islam was not major impetus for new membership. Above all, the Nation of Islam's secular programs, promising power and wealth, were the key to its expansion.

A NATION WITHIN A NATION

It is through a consideration of historical shifts in the Nation of Islam that one can locate key transformations and continuities in the meaning of Black Power. The formative years of the Nation of Islam (1930s) developed within a milieu of restrictive, second-class citizenship for African Americans. W. D. Fard Muhammad, the founder and self-proclaimed prophet of the Nation of Islam, was known by his followers as a divine black messiah (Allah in the flesh), and he designated Elijah Muhammad as his last "Messenger."[5] An unorthodox version of Islam, the Nation of Islam is usually studied outside the general scope of Muslim life despite the efforts of followers to draw on orthodox Islam and Islamic cultural representations such as symbolism, extensive numerology, and codes of appropriate living. Similar to devout Muslims, Nation of Islam members conducted all daily activates with reference to religion. Although their faith was not anchored in the recitation of Arabic prayers, Islam became an organizing force that produced a community of "believers" determined to resist the bulwarks of Jim Crow (economic repression, political disenfranchisement, and social ostracism) by building an empowered independent nation within the United States.

Black people, Fard Muhammad explained, were the "original" people on the planet who ruled from "Asia." Historian Claude Clegg underscores that Fard Muhammad believed "the use of the word Africa to denote what he called East Asia" was a ploy by "whites to divide people of color who were, in his view, all Asiatic."[6] The "so-called American Negro" was in fact an "Asiatic Blackman, the maker, the owner, the cream of the planet earth, God or the universe."[7] Fard Muhammad invented a history that disconnected black people in the United States from Africa and Africans, thereby detaching them from the Western imagination of blackness, which was loaded with demeaning stereotypes of African "savagery" and dehumanizing slavery.[8] At the same time, this narrative failed to critique colonialist descriptions of black Africans as "uncivilized"; rather, Fard Muhammad's rhetoric often accentuated negative myths. In effect, early Nation of Islam members wanted to build a modern black nation from a glorification of "Asiatic blackness" and a rejection of sub-Saharan African. This ideological structure expresses not only the internalization of black Africa as "backward," but also the very real alienation that Nation of Islam members felt as a result of colonialism, slavery, and Jim Crow. Thus, as Robert Reid Pharr avers, the Nation of Islam's history produced an identity for black Americans that was "imagined as larger than blackness," even though "very few others are allowed to share this identity."[9]

The elevation of black Americans, most notably above black Africans, paralleled the collective gouging of Caucasians as "white, blue-eyed devils" who were grafted out of black people specifically to bedevil the planet.[10] Fard Muhammad advocated a separate nation from Caucasians, a place where its members were protected from a Jim Crow government and all of the "sins" of the "devil." After he mysteriously disappeared in 1934 from Detroit (the Nation of Islam's center), Elijah Muhammad continued this millennialistic mission to reject the devil's institutions. A complete withdrawal from American society was presumed to be the key to the resurrection of black people. So when President Franklin D. Roosevelt instituted Social Security in the late 1930s, the "Messenger" told his members to refuse the identification numbers since they were the mark of the beast. For Fard Muhammad, Social Security numbers not only kept individuals under surveillance but were also no different from the surnames black folks had inherited from slavery; both systems of identification represented white domination. The federal government became redefined as white domination.

Given that there was no area of policies, economic, or social life where legal segregation did not intrude, scholar Ernest Allen concludes that converts to the Nation of Islam viewed "federal and state agencies as uninstalled repositories of satanic influence.[11] The rejection of such institutions was a critique of both white supremacy and modernity. Nation of Islam leaders had responded to colonial notions that black people were outside of Western modernity and reacted with a general repugnance toward their modern structures. Moreover, Elijah Muhammad's incessant emphasis on a particular brand of Islam—a religion that allegedly accorded black people respect and worth because men were successful patriarchal heads of their homes and women were the epitome of feminine modesty—distinguished and ultimately severed his subjects from an ostensibly corrupt nation of hypocritical white Christians.[12] Nation of Islam followers clearly defined their enemy in both racial and religious terms.

After Malcolm's 1952 prison parole, his talent was used specifically to start new temples in Boston and Philadelphia as well as bolster membership in sagging ones. Within two years, Elijah Muhammad rewarded Malcolm's efforts by assigning him the most coveted temple outside of Chicago, Temple No. 7 in Harlem. It was in New York City that Malcolm's influence reached new heights. As the Nation of Islam's most public minister, Malcolm proselytized not only among the hustlers, pimps, prostitutes, drug dealers, and thieves but also in churches and at political debates. He contended that the teaching of Elijah Muhammad explained that black folks were impoverished and ethically lacking because white racists conscientiously withheld their access to "self" and neglected their most fundamental needs. After vividly detailing the failures of white America, Malcolm provided the foundation for the so-called Negroes to understand that they were indeed the chosen, the supreme of humankind, and that the key to their resurrection could be found in the Nation of Islam. He used his own wayward life history as a powerful example. Malcolm had sold drugs, stolen, and ended up in jail; but after he converted to the Nation of Islam while in prison (1946–1952), his whole attitude and outlook on life changed. Hearing his emotionally stirring and candid testimony, Malcolm's listeners were able to recognize aspects of themselves, which pulled them closer to him and his black nationalist revelation. John Edgar Wideman argued that Malcolm delivered a message during the sixties that was "as absolute as the message runaway slaves delivered to Ole Massa." Malcolm, however, "wasn't running and his direction was not away but toward a future, a center we're still struggling to glimpse."[13]

Prior to his brutal death (Black Muslims who had been implicated in the killing were quickly dismissed by the Nation of Islam leadership as FBI infiltrators and hypocrites), Malcolm wrote in his 1964 autobiography that he knew, "[as] any official in the Nation of Islam would instantly have known, any death talk could have been approved of if not actually initiated by only one man," Elijah Muhammad. No doubt, Malcolm was a loyal convert, and prior to being ousted (in November 1963 after the assassination of President John F. Kennedy) from the Nation of Islam, his deepest personal relief was that Elijah Muhammad was a symbol of moral, mental, and spiritual reform among the American black people.[14] In hindsight, Malcolm told photographer Gordon Parks that as a messenger's national minister and most visible spokesperson, he had done many things he regretted because he had been like a zombie when he followed Elijah Muhammad and, like all Muslims, he was hypnotized, pointed in a certain direction, and told to march.[15] By 1964, Malcolm and others had critiqued Elijah Muhammad as an adulterer who betrayed his followers in the Nation of Islam by moving too slowly and remaining too inactive.[16] Despite this public controversy, a steady stream of women and men continued to be drawn into the Nation of Islam's fold.[17] Refugees from a variety of political groups who sought a structured black political organization swelled the ranks of the Nation of Islam, as the call for black power resonated throughout the United States.

By 1965, the Nation of Islam represented not only a religious answer to problems of poverty and racial discrimination but increasingly a conservative capitalist solution to these difficult circumstances. Under Elijah Muhammad's leadership the Nation of Islam principles and demands had crystallized. "If you want money, good homes, and friendships in all walks of life, come and follow me," said the Messenger.[18] His call yielded a favorable response among black folks who had been disappointed in the reality of the supposed Promised Land of the North. They lived in dilapidated housing projects infested with drugs and hopelessness, representing generations of economically depressed people. The Nation of Islam's platform offered a life chord for black people who were untouched by civil rights victories.

The Messenger cultivated an atmosphere of support and caring for his followers, and numerous testimonies by members suggest that he made good on his promise to improve the conditions of those who believe. The Nation on Islam converts explain that their lives were plagued by drugs, alcohol, and lack of discipline and morals but the Messenger had extended kindness to them when others only condemned their behavior. Inside the prisons, Elijah Muhammad would make sure that jailed converts received encouraging letters, and Malcolm X recalled how he sent money all over the country to prison inmates who write to him.[19] Brother Thomas 18X of Chicago explained that, "For many years, the Messenger has provided us with jobs" and he "taught us how to have peace of mind, friendship, money and decent homes."[20] Members remarked that they had become successful in terms of employment and had progressed in terms of knowing "self." Sister Joan X remembered that the first time that she visited the Nation of Islam's Chicago headquarters in 1972, "it was indeed heaven on earth; all of your needs were met by sophisticated people who looked like you."[21]

BLACK POWER

Even though activists had battled to give substance to the newly acquitted social and political rights of citizenship (represented by the Civil Rights Act of 1964 and the Voting Rights Act of 1965, respectively), many of the younger freedom fighters attended college and were experiencing an increasing sense of disillusionment within the movement. Only a small percentage of middle-class black people had reaped the benefits of legal change while the predicament of the masses seemed to worsen. Occupying a precarious class position, most college students were financially strapped, but a middle-class status was within their grasp via their degrees. As a blossoming middle stratum, student activists struggled to transform institutions that produced inequalities, but at the same time they recognized that their higher degrees would position them to seize certain elite advantages. Constructing an identity within a caldron of inequalities is difficult; this is why Sister Joan 4X spoke for many when she said, "Many of us wonder what we'll do with our education when we leave college."[22] They were not alone in terms of feeling ambivalent about their future. The urban rebellions that spread throughout the country, beginning with the Watts uprising around the time of the passage of the August 1965 Voting Rights Act, was evidence of the demoralization and alienation that Northern black people felt in America as a result of poverty and Gestapo-style policing.

The Student Nonviolent Coordinating Committee (SNCC) members certainly understood the frustrations of black urbanites. Beginning in 1960, they had courageously put their bodies on the line at sit-in demonstrations and on freedom ride treks, but by 1965 many of them were pessimistic and felt influential black leaders were willing to settle for tokens of racial progress. After electing Stokely Carmichael chairman in 1966, SNCC workers, especially the newly formed Atlanta Project staff, began to insist that black people think in terms of black power in order to squash white power. An observer recalled that SNCC members in good standing during this period had digested Frantz Fanon's *The Wretched of the Earth*, which detailed how the "Western man [is] decadent and therefore not to be emulated by colonized peoples" and they could quote at length from *Malcolm X Speaks*.[23] "In the tense aftermath of Malcolm's death in 1965, other political organizations also began to reshape themselves, in the case of the Congress of Racial Equality (CORE), and new organizations were created, most notably the Black Panther Party, the Republic of New Africa, Revolutionary Action Movement, and the League of Revolutionary Black Workers. Black nationalist and separatist ideas, as well as armed self-defense, were designed to give real meaning to Malcolm's legacy and black power.

While these groups argued bitterly over the most effective way to destroy white hegemony, the Nation of Islam hunkered down and simply pushed to further implement its insular nationhood goals. With a long history of racial self determination, cultural autonomy, and black capitalism, the Nation of Islam was able to quickly rebound from the taint of Malcolm's death to rebrand itself as a separatist vanguard. Given that activists were looking to identify the fundamental elements of black power, it is not surprising that in the post-1965 period, they searched for an organization that at its core celebrated a black identity and empowered black people on their own terms.

Anna Karriem's political activism illustrates how the problematic dynamics within the Black Power movement could initiate a conversion to the Nation of Islam. She had been a devoted member of SNCC between 1964 and 1967 and worked to bring political power to black people in Alabama and Mississippi counties. On election day in 1967, however, she witnessed how local registrars held loaded guns to drive SNCC members away from polls and how black sharecroppers were driven off their land and forbidden to take anything with them because they had voted for a black candidate. Karriem found herself, along with other SNCC workers, working with members of the homeless families, driving stakes into the ground and building a wooden floor, so that they could set up tents to get them out to the cold. After 1966, under the leadership of Carmichael, SNCC worked to obtain political and economic freedom for black people. Teaching that "freedom comes from the barrel of a gun," SNCC leaders, Karriem argued, did not teach the outcome of armed revolution by Black people: They did not teach Black people in Los Angeles in 1965 how to restore their burned homes and businesses in Watts; They did not teach the people in Detroit and Newark in 1967 who revolted against slum living and unemployment how to do for self in the way of rebuilding their burned communities. Black power too often led to black deaths, she concluded.

Karriem accepted Islam as taught by Elijah Muhammad because she was tired of the destruction caused by so-called Black leaders who expounded on ideas that had no foundation in reality. The Messenger taught converts that ideology is the science of ideas, and we have had four hundred years to come up with ideas.[24] Karriem summarized that the Nation of Islam had moved beyond ideological rhetoric and call for revolution; their efforts had yielded small businesses, schools, and farmland, and no one had been displaced in the process. Karriem convinced other women activists to pledge loyalty to the Nation of Islam. Sister Marguerite X met Karriem while a student activist at Tuskegee. Before attending the mosque, Marguerite X was in a radical group of college students.[25] Marguerite and Karriem's conversion helps us to understand how the Nation of Islam's conservative vision of action took on revolutionary meaning within a context of effete political resistance and racist violence.

Brother Preston (X) Dixon's experience also sheds additional light on an activist's conversion to the Nation of Islam. He had become involved with the Black Student Union (BSU) in Los Angeles, and the first inkling that something was amiss came when the BSU central committee established a constitution and philosophy that were based on the program of the Most Honorable Elijah Muhammad, known as "Wants and Beliefs."[26] The Black Panther Party for Self-Defense, organized in Oakland, California, in October

1966, had also replicated the Nation of Islam's "Wants and Beliefs" platform in its "Ten-Point Program."[27] Huey Newton had attended mosques in both San Francisco and Oakland, spoke fairly often to a number of members, and regularly read the Nation of Islam's popular weekly newspaper, *Muhammad Speaks.* Newton would have joined them, but he could not deal with their religion. He had been raised in a fairly strict Christian home and had had enough of religion and could not bring himself to adopt another one.[28]

Dixon was not turned off by the religious aspect of the Nation of Islam, but he admits that the changeover "was not immediate," for there was still considerable doubt within him. The turning point came when his local BSU organized a program and only brothers from the Nation of Islam would travel and speak to his group for free. Well-known BSU leaders, to Dixon's disgust, usually required local chapters to pay for airfare, lodging, and an honorarium. Spreading the message of black power soon became a fund-raising tactic for some of its leadership. After 1966, Carmichael took to the speaking circuit and in most un-SNCC-like fashion, insisted on traveling first class on airplanes and receiving a $1,000 honorarium for a lecture. His popularity and his appearance as a gadfly in public debates about civil rights soon earned him the nickname by friends and foes of Stokely of "Star Michael."[29] Brother Minister Billy X, on the other hand, was willing to travel some two hundred miles, and his requirements were just a chance to speak and teach Islam. In turn, Dixon began attending the local Nation of Islam mosques and reading Muslim literature. He wrote, "almost from the start I found myself searching for answers, and simultaneously, becoming aware of how foolish I had acted and sounded when I demanded the same person who had robbed me of the knowledge of myself, teach me back into the knowledge of myself."[30] Disgusted with displays of selfishness and ignorance, Dixon severed his relation with the BSU and "stood up under the banner of Islam."[31]

Other converts recall how, following the 1965 "summer of discontent," their Nation of Islam membership was directly linked to disappointment in other political organizations, but particularly the newly formed BSU, which had spread like wildfire and therefore was the least structurally organized. Sister Lindsay Bryant remembered how she was initially involved in the BSU at the University of California, Santa Barbara, because she sought an organization that would give her an identity as a black woman. Working diligently to obtain a better education system and a better world in which to live, Bryant soon understood that the slogan "by any means necessity" to achieve the BSU goals ironically translated into "sleeping with whites and allowing them to integrate into our ranks."[32] Bryant began attending the local mosque and became more disillusioned with the BSU. She became convinced that the BSU did not have the solution to the blacks' problems "so she decided to unite behind one leader and the only man qualified to lead the so called American Negro was the Honorable Elijah Muhammad."[33]

Sister Joan 4X also came to the Nation of Islam after membership in the BSU because she was constantly in search of the qualities embodied in the Nation. Growing up in the South made her aware of the evils and atrocities that white men enact upon the people every day of their waking lives. Joan 4X readily admits that she was not quite ready for the Caucasians on the West Coast "for they have placed a mental fog over the minds of our people that is much worse that any physical danger." This crisis pushed Joan 4X to become part of the new wave of black students trying desperately to rid themselves of the devil's influence. She and others began to analyze how whites used the media to choose our leaders and then brainwash them and the students who followed them. After becoming a member of the Nation of Islam, Joan 4X argued that the white press served as a decoy to keep black folks from the only true leader in America, the Messenger. For Joan 4X, *The Autobiography of Malcolm X* (1964) was the most "obvious sign" to her that "the devil knows Islam is the only salvation for black people and the only vehicle that really unites us." She pointed out that when Malcolm X was alive and teaching Islam, "devils couldn't do enough to blaspheme him and the whole program of the Messenger; but when the man turned from the light of Islam, and especially now that he is dead, the white press can't put enough copies of his autobiography in the hands of our peoples."[34]

It is somewhat ironic that the Nation of Islam's platform was interpreted as a black power blueprint and that the waves of new members were former student activists, considering the fact that Elijah Muhammad never wavered from his conservative position that his followers eschew mainstream politics. Searching for answers to complicated, multilayered questions produced a longing to be a part of something meaningful. Black power activists were able to fill this lacuna by pushing the idea that black people at home and throughout the Diaspora shared a collective identity and origins rooted in Africa. But Elijah Muhammad taught that Africans were a backward and uncivilized people and that the so-called negro in the United States was in fact the most civilized and superior member of the human race. The diatribe against Africa at times sounded like racist, colonial gibberish, but believers who may have disagreed with him were afraid to speak out against their leader. One Pan-African leader, Queen Mother Moore of Harlem, recalled how Malcolm X told her that before he could say the word *Africa* it would have to come from Elijah."[35] This was a highly unlikely possibility since, as Malcolm X put it, Elijah Muhammad "was as anti African as he was anti white." In fact, Malcolm X adds, he never had one statement that was pro-African.[36] Moore concluded that when she spent three days at the home [she heard] nothing about Africa."[37]

The Nation of Islam's assessment of Africa is confusing since historically and during the modern Black Power movement, Africa was always imagined as home. The Messenger justified his position with the following analysis:

> Many of my people, the so-called Negroes, say we should help the nations of Africa which are wakening. This has been said as if we owned America. We are so foolish! What part of America do you have that you can offer toward helping Africa? Who is independent, the nations of Africa or we? The best act would be to request the independent governments of Africa and Asia to help us. We are the ones who need help. We have little or nothing to offer as help to others. We should begin to help at home first.[38]

Locating a home would provide a wellspring of unity, strength, and cultural meaning in the midst of the revolutionary chaos.

Converts believed that the Nation of Islam, at the very least, offered a path to solving both personal and societal problems in that it linked black nationalist thought with politically transformative action. Black businesses, schools, temples, and black families were very real, tangible examples of successful nation building. At the same time, followers were encouraged to assertively critique the United States using activist language. For example, Sister Christie Deloris X of Birmingham, Alabama, explained that the white man's civilization "can offer us nothing in the way of security, education, and spirituality. In other words these capitalist fascist racist men colonized society [that] as a whole is fallen as our Beloved Leader and Teacher has taught for more that 40 years."[39] Writer James Baldwin was never a member of the Nation of Islam, yet he was also drawn to Elijah Muhammad's peculiar authority. Slender and small in stature, Muhammad had a smile, Baldwin remembered, that "promised to take the burden of my life off my shoulders."[40]

SEPARATE TERRITORY AND INSTITUTIONS

Black Power advocates who shouted the slogan the loudest, Alvin F. Poussaint argued, "were those with the oldest battle scars from the terror, demoralization and castration which they experienced through continual direct confrontation" with white racism. In addition, these activists also recognized that "racial pride and self love alone do not fill the bellies of starving black children in Mississippi."[41] Convinced that white people would never properly share resources nor concede full equality, those in attendance at the 1967 Black Power conference in Newark, New Jersey, called for partitioning of the United States into two separate territories. To shame the government into a concession, Muhammad preached that former slave masters were obligated to maintain and supply their needs in a separate territory for the next twenty to twenty-five years, given that their ancestors had earned it. Long before reparations became a popular plank among black nationalist groups, Muhammad and his ministers had demanded compensation for the generations of enslaved labor. Similarly, at the April 1969 national Black Economic Development Conference in Detroit under the leadership of James Forman, a manifesto was issued that called upon white Christian churches and Jewish synagogues in the United States "and all other Racist Institutions" to give $500 million in reparations and to surrender 60 percent of their assets to the conference "to be used for the economic, social, and cultural rehabilitation of the black community."[42]

By 1965, the Nation of Islam had moved beyond secession rhetoric, buying farmland in three states as well as an abundance of property and small businesses near each of its temples (grocery stores, restaurants, and dry cleaning shops), valued in the millions.[43] The pursuit of economic power through the creation of separate communal institutions was an important element of late 1960s black capitalism.[44] Already acting like people with power and control over their own destiny, members of the Nation of Islam saw these institutions as clear evidence of their material achievements. *Muhammad Speaks* published countless accounts of people who were in the grave of ignorance and poverty before their conversions and how they had made real progress with the Nation of Islam. For example, Brother Charles JX of Detroit says he became inspired to do something for himself after reading Muhammad's *Message to the Blackman* (1965): "Finally the solutions to all of my problems," Brothers Charles recalled, "which had heretofore escape me, became crystal clear." He decided to start a construction business, and he trained his son to become proficient in the field. Until he heard the teaching of Muhammad he never thought he could have a successful and profitable business in his lifetime.[45]

Much of the follower's individual success was connected to the Messenger's "Economic Freedom" plan, which he had introduced in 1964. Members were taught how to economize and save. Followers were told to just save five cents a day or twenty-five cents a week and this would mean millions of dollars per year. At the annual Saviour's Day convention, Muhammad would spell out the distance in dollars and cents that had been accumulated as well as future financial expectations. The relationship between economic success and acquiring a sense of independence and power also had the result of transforming the mindset of members.

One of the main handicaps identified by the Messenger that prevented so-called Negroes from achieving success was the lack of knowledge of self. Members have given countless testimonies on how they had been formerly brainwashed. Elijah Muhammad gave them a new sense of self by explaining their history. Sister Beverly Maurad, national director of education for the Nation of Islam in 1971, in a speech to the graduates of Muhammad Universities of Islam (secondary schools), stated that even though students study some of the same subjects and read from the same books as their peers, their education is "better—more comprehensive" because "once you have been awakened it is easy to understand." The Messenger taught that black people are "the original man, the maker, and the owner of the planet earth. This one fact gives the true student, the true believer, a desire to retain his lost heritage" and "once again become members of a great civilization and Nation." Knowledge of self allows one to "see that you (Blackman) are the ones alluded to in your History Text books as having created wonderful civilizations with marvelous structures and using technological skills." As Black Muslim students, Maurad concludes, they have the advantage because they "know who they are," and thus they are "able to perceive and weigh and balance more clearly the curriculum presented."[46]

Black Power advocates, many of whom were enrolled in or had recently attended college, also insisted on an academic curriculum that reflected the history and culture of black people. The Nation of Islam was already light-years ahead of the activists on this front. For years they had taught members' children in separate schools that were usually located near the temples. The schools, in many ways, were the glue that held the Nation of Islam together. Sonsyrea Tate discusses how her mother stayed in the Nation of Islam so that she and her siblings would be eligible for the schools.[47] Some college students were drawn to the Nation of Islam largely because of its curriculum. Sister Joan 4X argued that black student demands for black studies departments would never be recognized but the Messenger already boldly taught people "Black history."[48] The Nation of Islam's schools also became an important alternative for parents who did not want to have their children vaccinated, a requirement for public education. And, after the Tuskegee Study, based on medical experimentation conducted on African American men between 1932 and 1972 that was authorized by the Centers for Disease Control, became public knowledge in 1932, more African Americans feared the entire vaccination process; thus, the Nation of Islam schools were an important option.

Clearly, the religious Islamic nature of the Nation of Islam was not the major impetus for membership in the post-1965 period. Instead, the Nation of Islam's secular programs and exclusive black membership reinforced the new members' agenda to build a separate black nation. Essentially, Muhammad promised to provide material symbols of power and wealth for people who had been discarded from the American populace and disinherited from the American dream. By offering black Americans a vanguard lifestyle, Muhammad not only trumped the political struggle to extend rights of citizenship but, as T. H. Marshall would argue, couched his call in an ideal expression of the modern citizenship, "against which achievements can be measured and toward which aspirations can be directed."⁴⁹ Thus, nationhood success was predicated upon establishing a separate existence and presenting Islam as a materially empowering religion; one simply had to become a "Black Muslim" to receive the benefits.

REGENDERING

The making of the Black Muslim subject involved a complicated set of social relationships and obligations to the Nation of Islam. Whereas there are always rules for belonging, Roger Smith's concept of "civil myths" explains how guildlines of eligibility and exclusion are used to create political communities and thereby reflect their contested inner workings. In the case of the Nation of Islam, membership was rooted in gendered prescriptions. That is, men's and women's roles had to be reconfigured based on gendered stereotypes and hierarchies, and regulated differently in order to achieve black redemption—political emancipation, economic self-sufficiency, and social isolation from whites.

Nationalist precepts of gender promoted a conservative agenda where patriarchy took center stage. A separatist, masculine nation and the representation of a responsible, disciplined, dignified, and defiant manhood would give black men rights and privileges denied them in white America. The centering of black men, however, pushed black women to the margins of nation-building. Placing black women on the periphery served to counter/ resist the master narrative of slavery that stereotypically portrays black women as jezebels, matriarchs, and mannish, roles that were used to both shame and usurp black manhood. Essentially, for the Nation of Islam, the emasculation of black men and their lack of masculine agency were dialectically connected to a hypersexualized, out-of-control, defiled black woman. According to Elijah Muhammad, "There is no nation on earth that has less respect for and as little control of their women as we so called Negroes here in America."⁵⁰

The building of a nation required public displays of symbols that often occurred at the site of the body. Representations of difference (men and women were considered essentially different by "nature") were accompanied by a prescription of particular relationships between men and women. North American slavery had created two types of victims: women who were raped and not allowed a feminine presence under the burdens of capitalism, and men who were emasculated and rendered powerless. The Nation of Islam returned members to a particular sense of self that was "natural" and denied under slavery. While a real Nation of Islam man was a masculine breadwinner and a good Nation of Islam woman was a feminine housewife, it was also believed that traditional roles would bring a form of emotional intimacy between men and women. Boudoir politics recognizes the human need for love, and "any movement that hopes to empower" women and men "as opposed to just mobilize them" must deal with the issue.[51]

The unreal "matriarchal" legacy of slavery endured during the post-1965 Black Power movement largely because of distorted images of black female identity, for instance the fable that black women were already liberated. Barbara Smith critiqued the myth that black women were emancipated in advance of black men because the women shouldered the responsibilities of heading families and working outside the home. Above all, "an ability to cope under the worst conditions is not liberation. Underlying this myth is the assumption that black women are towers of strength who neither felt nor need what other human beings do, either emotionally or materially." This widespread myth, codified in the 1965 Secretary of Labor Daniel Patrick Moynihan Report, insisted that black women had damned themselves and rendered black men "impotent."[52]

Black male nationalists, within and outside of the Nation of Islam, presumed that women had to be controlled and assume a passive role in order for men to rise up and be "real men" in the United States. Maulana Ron Karenga led the cultural nationalists with perceptions such as "what make women appealing is femininity and she can't be feminine without being submissive."[53] Moreover, as Akiba ya Elimu stated, "The man" should be "the leader of the house/nation because his knowledge of the world is broader, his awareness is greater, his understanding is fuller and his application of this information is wiser."[54] Nation of Islam male leaders added white women into this garbled misrepresentation. In fact, they accused black women of mimicking the immoral habits of white women. Utilizing racial pride rhetoric as a form of control, Elijah Muhammad told black men to "stop our women from trying to look like them [white women]. By bleaching, powdering, ironing and coloring their hair, painting their lips, cheeks, and eyebrows; wearing shorts; going half-nude in public places. Stop women from using unclean language in public (and at home), from smoking and drug addiction habits."[55] In sum, slavery as well as the behavior of aggressive Western women had brought destruction to Allah's social order, generating renegade black women.

Restraining women, also an obsession among Middle Eastern Islamic fundamentalists, positioned the Nation of Islam squarely in line with the patriarchal climate of Black Power. Muhammad, however, helped to camouflage the gender inequalities in the Nation of Islam with the affectionate rhetoric of love, protection, and respect for black womanhood. This is an important point, especially considering the scathing, sexual criticism of black women at the time. One simply has to recall Stokely Carmichael's response to a question concerning the "proper position of women in SNCC." He jokingly replied, "prone." The views uttered by Eldridge Cleaver, leader of the BPP, are without a doubt the most misogynistic. He wrote that "the white man made the black woman the symbol of slavery," which explained his lack of attraction and respect for black women. He gloated, "The only way that I can bust my nuts with a black bitch is to close my eyes and pretend that she is Jezebel. If I was to look down and see a black bitch underneath me or if my hand happened to feel her nappy hair, that would be the end, it would be all over."[56] Paulette Pierce notes that such were the most influential musings of the fertile imagination of Black Nationalist during the sixties as they "labored to birth a free nation or die in the process."[57]

Within this climate, according to *Muhammad Speaks*, some women viewed the Nation of Islam as a safe, loving "home." Sister Charles Ann X said that "Islam elevates that so-called Negro woman by giving her wisdom, knowledge, culture and refinement."[58] No longer did Sandra JX consider herself "just a simple, southern girl," but in the Nation of Islam she was "the queen of the entire planet earth and the mother of all civilizations."[59] Sister Vera X Lewis testified that Muhammad was "not afraid to point out how the black woman has been abused for some 400 years." She was thankful that her leader "instills in black men a rebirth to their natural urge to protect black women." White men "or even misguided black men can no longer use black women for ill purposes," remarked Lewis. Historically, black women's bodies have been commoditized as legal property and their sexuality exploited to justify capitalism and the perverse desires of men. Sister Mable X recalled how her body, now that she was a member of the Nation of Islam, "was overtaken with warmth and beauty." She became very proud, resourceful, and thankful."[60] It seems that it did not matter (or matter enough to prevent membership) to these women that under the conditions of the Nation of Islam (as well as other black nationalist organizations) respect for their personhood and protection from seething forces hinged on their complete obedience to all paternal figures.

There are indeed complicated reasons why Nation of Islam women accepted what appears to be a second-class status. Aaronetta X Anderson remembered that when she was on the outside looking in before joining in 1966, she had many misconceptions concerning the role of women. As "quite an assertive person, and seeing how aggressive the brothers were, I assumed women had to take a back seat." After attending the Muslim's Girls Training and General Civilization Classes (M.G.T.-G.C.C.), it became apparent to her that it was "not so much a back seat as the proper seat."[61] The fact that the back seat had to be addressed indicated that women had to be convinced that they were not being subjugated, and that most efficient way to rationalize limiting the participation of women was thought an ideology that connected their marginalized role to the greater good of black people. It was both their racial and religious duty to sacrifice self for the liberation project.

Sister Melba J. X. Walker of Oklahoma City said it best. Prior to becoming a Muslim in 1971, she always wanted to be famous and beautiful. Her goal was to be a career woman, "successful, progressive and productive." Determined to finish college, she wanted to find her place and "really contribute something valuable to this existing system." After receiving her "X" she understood "exactly that to progress is not just climbing to the top to the devil society, but it means helping her people." The most efficient way to help was to know her place and that place is not on some stage displaying herself, or having her name up in lights, and neither was that place any one of the many careers which she considered from ambassador to Africa to *Playboy* bunny, but rather "it is a place where she wanted to spend her life, Being a Woman, a Natural Black Woman in the Nation of Islam."[62]

Women like Sister Melba J. X. Walker must have faced a major struggle as they transferred their allegiance from organizations that thrived on elevating links with Africa to one that viewed Africa as backward. Most of the post-1965 Nation of Islam converts attended the mosque, which usually had pews as opposed to prayer rugs, and wore African apparel and Afro hairstyles. Elijah Muhammad did not approve of this. He concluded that "if men and women are not satisfied with the styles I give them then I am not satisfied with you being my follower."[63] Islam is a very public and visible religion, and Muhammad was clear about his role as regulator of the material culture and demeanor of his followers. There was little room within the Nation of Islam to challenge prescribed practice or act as a critical citizen.

Clothing was marked as a particularly important sign of Nation of Islam identity and a means for the control over bodies and body image. Like colonial images of Africa, many Nation of Islam converts viewed Africans as a population in need of civilization and lacking in respectability. Elijah Muhammad urged Nation of Islam men and women to be respectable and civilized through the adoption of a strict dress code. Men were expected to wear dark-colored suits, usually adorned with Elijah Muhammad's signature bowtie. Long hair was seen as a woman's style, and he would not tolerate his followers wearing such germ-catchers as beards. "Stop imitating the non modern man," said Muhammad. "Cut off that pillow of hair behind your head, at the nape of your neck and trim your hair line around the back of your neck like modern man."[64] Women were required to wear long gowns and matching head wraps. This uniform was reminiscent of the Black Cross Nurses of the Garvey movement. Although an expression of their link to black nationalism, this attire also kept women within the appropriate Muslim style, covering them from wrist to ankle. It was only a matter of time before members who initially wore colorful dashikis came to accept the Messenger's stringent dress code as appropriate. Sister Marguerite X testified that she was one of those Afro-wearers and was of the opinion that Africans or so-called Negroes imitating Africans was the only beautiful way of life. "I was wrong."[65] Sister Evelyn X stated, "If you see a women dressed as a Muslim sister, you will think that she is a Muslim and treat her with the respect due a Muslim woman. By the same token, if you see a woman dressed in hot pants, halter top, afro puff wigs on her head, and mud packed on her face, you will think that she must be a loose woman and will treat her as one."[66] The clothing was intended not only to combat the sexually deviant myths associated with black people but also to give the appearance of a civilized community with outward forms of religiosity.

Islamic law, as taught by Elijah Muhammad, rested upon the most conservative verses in the Qur'an, which dictated that wives should be obedient to their husbands. Muslims scholars debate the meaning of obedience and whether it is a requirement of good behavior rather than submission. Scholar Haleh Afshar states that in practice, a "Muslim woman must accept many of the dictates of patriarchy if they are to accept Islam and its teachings."[67] In 1965, Elijah Muhammad admitted that in some cities the conversation ratio was as high as five men to one woman. But he reasoned that low female support was due to the destruction of the black woman by "the serpent, the devil, dragon, Satan," the forces of white manipulation, and not the male-centered perspective of the Nation of Islam.

CONCLUSION

The Nation of Islam was so attractive to men because no one articulated the aspirations of the so-called Negros better that Malcolm X. The need to create a new political source of black personhood and solidarity propelled activists to transform the liberation movement after his assassination. Unfortunately, a host of Black Power organizations, fraught with neophyte leadership, nepotism, and a crippling conception of masculinity, rapidly surfaced during the post–Malcolm X period.

Disappointment and contention within the Black Power ranks ironically gave way to an enhanced sense of the Nation of Islam as a radical political alternative. Elijah Muhammad and his ministers weathered the tense aftermath of Malcolm's death by capitalizing on activists' disillusionment. Cultivating a constellation of theory (the original "Asiatic Blackman" and the black woman as a "queen of the Universe") and practice (small businesses and schools), Elijah Muhammad was able to shift the focus away from Malcolm's demise and onto tangible evidence of nation-building. The Nation of Islam became a complicated expression of black power, and it enables us to consider the intricate production and manifestation of political subjectivity vis-à-vis gender, race, class, and nation. In the end, the Nation of Islam offered young people who were constructing a political identity and searching for a stable political home a structured, separatist organization committed to a distinctive moral and religious sensibility. Civil agitation assumed the form of Malcolm's legacy made black folks aware of the Nation of Islam, but it was his teacher's vision that brought activists into its fold during the post-1965 period.

NOTES

1. This chapter originally appeared in *Freedom North*, edited by Jeanne F. Theoharis and Komozi Woodard (ISBN 9780312294670), New York: Palgrave Macmillan, 2003. Reproduced with permission of Palgrave Macmillian.

2. Essien U. Essien-Udon, *Black Nationalism: The Search for Identity in America* (Chicago: University of Chicago Press, 1962), 37–83.

3. Claude Andrew Clegg III, *An Original Man: The Life and Times of Elijah Muhammad* (New York: St. Martin Press, 1998), 239; William L. Van Debug, *New Day in Babylon: The Black Power Movement and American Culture, 1965–1975* (Chicago: The University of Chicago Press, 1992), 2.

4. For the most part, my sources on the reasons why women and men joined the Nation of Islam in the post–Malcolm X period are limited to an analysis of those who joined the organization; the members' testimonies are open to a number or interpretations, some of which I have not yet had the opportunity to explore.

5. The Nation of Islam had been founded in 1930 in Detroit under W. D. Fard. See Erdmann Doane Beynon, "The Voodoo Cult among Negro Migrants in Detroit," *American Journal of Sociology* 63 (1938). For a discussion of the early years and Elijah Muhammad's meteoric rise, see Claude Andrew Clegg III, *An Original Man*.

6. Clegg, *An Original Man*, 48

7. Ibid., 42

8. For example, see Winthrop Jordan, *White over Black: American Attitudes toward the Negro, 1550–1812* (Baltimore: Penguin Books, 1969).

9. Robert Reid-Pharr, "Speaking through Anti-Semitism: The Nation of Islam and the Poetics of Black (Counter) Modernity," *Social Text* 14, no. 4 (Winter 1996): 140.

10. Salem Mauwakkil, "The Nation of Islam and Me," in *The Farrakhan Factor: African American Writers on Leadership, Nationhood, and Minister Louis Farrakhan*, ed. Amy Alexander (New York: Grove Press, 1998), 296.

11. Ernest Allen, "Minister Louis Farrakhan and the Continuing Evolution of the Nation of Islam in Alexander, in *The Farrakhan Factor*, 78.

12. An important millennial ideal is that a devil stands between God's people and the heavenly kingdom. See Perry E. Giannakos, "The Black Muslims: An American Millennialistic Response to Racism and Cultural Denigrations," *The Centennial Review 23*, no. 4 (Fall 1979): 439.

13. John Edgar Wideman, "Malcolm X: The Art of Autobiography," in *Malcolm X: In Our Image*, ed. Joe Wood (New York: Grove Press, 1964), 113.

14. Gordon Parks, "The Violent End of the Man Called Malcolm X," *Life,* March 5, 1965, 29.

15. Parks, "The Violent End of the Man Called Malcolm X."

16. Malcolm X, *The Autobiography of Malcolm X* (New York: Ballantine Books, 1992), 294–95, 316.

17. It is extremely difficult to document the numbers of people who left the Nation of Islam, as well as new members, during the post-1965 period. What is evident is that the Nation of Islam continued to be a thriving, separatist organization.

18. Elijah Muhammad, "Mr. Muhammad Calls for Unified Front of Black Men at New York City Rally," *Pittsburgh Courier*, July 19, 1958, 6.

19. Malcolm X, *The Autobiography of Malcolm X*, 169.

20. Brother Tomas 18X, "United Under Light of Islam," *Muhammad Speaks*, December 29, 1967, 25.

21. Interview of Joan X by Ula Taylor, October 21, 1999, Oakland, CA.

22. Joan 4X, "What Islam Has Done for Me," *Muhammad Speaks*, October 24, 1969, 13.

23. Gene Roberts, "The Story of Snick: From Freedom High to Black Power," *New York Times Magazine*, September 25, 1966, reprinted in *Black Protest in the Sixties: Essays from the* New York Times Magazine, ed. August Meier, John Bracey Jr., and Elliott Rudwick (New York: Markus Wierner Publications, 1991), 140–41; Frantz Fanon, *The Wretched of the Earth* (New York: Grove Press, 1967).

24. Anna Karriem, "The Preacher of Pan-Africanism," *Muhammad Speaks*, April 16, 1971, 15.

25. Sister Marguerite X, "Has Found Path to True Liberation, Righteousness in the Nation of Islam," *Muhammad Speaks*, August 29, 1969, 17.

26. Brother Preston X. Dixon, "Says Black Students Union Is Ersatz; the Nation of Islam Is the Real Thing," *Muhammad Speaks*, July 25, 1969, 17.

27. Ula Y. Taylor, J. Tarika Lewis, and Marion Van Peebles, *Panther: A Pictorial History of the Black Panther Party and the Story behind the Film* (New York: New Market Press, 1955)

28. Huey Newton, *Revolutionary Suicide* (New York: New Market Press).

29. Charles Marsh, *God's Long Summer: Stories of Faith and Civil Rights* (Princeton, NJ: Princeton University Press, 1977), 181.

30. Brother Preston X (Dixon), "Say Black Students Union is Erastz," 17.

31. Ibid.

32. Joan 4X, "What Islam Has Done for Me," 13.

33. Ibid.

34. Ibid.

35. Audrey Moore interview, June 6 and 8, 1978, in *Black Women Oral History Project*, eds. Ruth Edmonds Hill, Arthur and Elizabeth Schlesinger Library on the History of Women in America (Cambridge, MA: Raddiffe College, 1989). (KG Saur Verlag, 1991).

36. Malcolm X, *February 1965: The Final Speeches*, ed. Steve Clark (New York: Pathfinder, 1992), 205.

37. Moore interview, 151.

38. Elijah Muhammad, *Message to the Blackman in America* (Philadelphia: Hakim Publishing, 1965), 35.

39. Sister Christine Delois X, "Dope, Alcohol and Devil's Tricks Strip Blacks of Human Dignity," *Muhammad Speaks*, January 29, 1971, 18.

40. James Baldwin, *The Price of the Ticket: Collected Nonfiction 1948–1985* (New York: St. martin Press, 1985), 360.

41. Alvin F. Poussaint, "A Negro Psychiatrist Explains the Negro Psyche," *New York Times Magazine*, August 20, 1967, reprinted in Meier et al., *Black Protest in the Sixties*.

42. John Hope Franklin and Alfred A. Moss Jr., *From Slavery to Freedom: A History of African Americans* (Boston: McGraw Hill, 2000), 138.

43. David Jackson and William Gains, "Nation of Islam: Power of Money," *Chicago Tribune,* March 12, 1995, 16.

44. Brother Herbert X, "Explains How Messenger Laid Out Plan for Economic Freedom in Slave Land," *Muhammad Speaks,* April 21, 1967, 25.

45. Brother Charles JX, "Found Solutions to All My Problems Lay with Islam," *Muhammad Speaks,* August 29, 1969, 17.

46. Sister Beverly Maurad, "Sister Beverley Addresses All Islam Grads," *Muhammad Speaks*, March 19, 1971.

47. Sonsyrea Tate, *Little X: Growing Up in the Nation of Islam* (San Francisco: Harper Collins, 1997), 84.

48. Joan 4X, "What Islam Has Done For Me."

49. T. H. Marshall, *Citizenship and Social Class* (Cambridge: Cambridge University Press, 1950), 29.

50. Muhammad, *Message to the Blackman*, 59.

51. Paulette Pierce, "Boudoir Politics and the Birthing of the Nation," in *Women Out of Place: The Gender of Agency and the Race of Nationality*, ed. Brackette F. Williams (New York: Roulade, 1966).

52. Barbara Smith, "Some Home Truths on the Contemporary Black Feminist Movement," in *Words of Fire: An Anthology of African American Feminist Thought*, ed. Beverly Guy-Sheftall (New York: The New Press, 1995).

53. Imamu Amiri Baraka, and the Congress of African Peoples, eds., *African Congress: A Documentary of the First Modern Pan African Congress* (New York: William Morrow, 1972).

54. Baraka et al., eds., *African Congress*, 177, 179.

55. Muhammad, *Message to the Blackman*, 60.

56. Eldridge Cleaver, *Soul on Ice* (New York: McGraw-Hill, 1968).

57. Pierce, *Boudoir Politics*.

58. Sister Charles Ann X, "Says Islam Lifts up the Black Woman, Giving Her Wisdom Knowledge, Strength," *Muhammad Speaks*.

59. Sandra JX, "Black Women Find Peace, Freedom in Folds in Islam," *Muhammad Speaks*.

60. Sister Mabel X, "Greatest Gift She Has Ever Known," *Muhammad Speaks*.

61. Melva J. X. (Walker), "Muslim Sister Finds Real Meaning of Black Beauty," *Muhammad Speaks*, July 16, 1971, 18.

62. Ibid.

63. Muhammad, "Warning to the M.G.T. and G.C.C.," *Muhammad Speaks*.

64. Elijah Muhammad, "Beards," *Muhammad Speaks*, July, 4, 1965.

65. Marguerite X, What Islam Has Done for Me."

66. Sister Evelyn, "Modest Muslim Dress Dignifies Black Women," *Muhammad Speaks*.

67. Hale After, "Why Fundamentalism? Iranian Women and Their Support of Islam," *Women: A Cultural Review* 6, no. 4.

Chapter Eleven

"My Malcolm"

Self-Reliance and African American Cultural Expression

Toya Conston and Emile Koenig

Since the establishment of the Nation of Islam in the United States, its various leaders have strived to instill the central tenets of the Islamic ideologies into its members. One of those central ideologies is the concept of self-reliance. Although a number of scholars have attempted to define self-reliance, the most consistent definition states that self-reliance is the ability for an individual, community, or group of people to have economic independence regardless of the dominant structure guiding the nation where they reside.[1] Additionally, self-reliance has been translated into African American daily life and cultural expression. In this sense, the term can be defined as the ability of an individual or group to independently produce creative work that is aimed at an audience within their same community—the "for us, by us" concept. In short, African Americans who were associated with the Nation of Islam—and even those who were not—were introduced to the concept of self-reliance, and that concept was consequently embedded in the psyches of the most disparate black communities across the United States. Because self-reliance is a central ideology of the Nation of Islam (NOI), this examination aims to explore the relationship that exists between self-reliance and the educational elements and creative entities that were created in response to it.

Any discussion of the tenets of self-reliance—especially in relationship to the NOI—must acknowledge the enormous impact of Malcolm X. Through his leadership over the NOI, Malcolm became a symbol of hope for many African Americans who were dealing with societal injustices. Yet for all of his efforts at reinvention, Malcolm X remained at his core "a black man, a person of African descent who happened to be a United States citizen."[2]

While a minister in the Nation, Malcolm encouraged African Americans to know and take pride in their history, to believe in their abilities, and to become self-sufficient.[3] He further posited that through education, African Americans could enable themselves to control their economic, social, and political circumstances. Additionally, amid his many calls to action, Malcolm X rallied for an entire "cultural revolution" that would shift the focus among African Americans to Africana art and culture. Thus, Malcolm advocated for a twofold movement toward self-reliance in the Black community—one that would make them (1) economically independent as well as (2) creatively and culturally connected to their African heritage.

MALCOLM X AND EDUCATION

Malcolm believed that education should be practical and useful for African Americans—particularly as it related to their liberation from the sociocultural norms of the dominant culture. He further theorized that through education, African Americans would gain awareness of the social, political, economic, educational, and psychological challenges that impacted their everyday experiences in the United States.[4] Lastly, he held a high regard for African Americans who had obtained graduate and professional degrees, stating that graduates should be more vigilant in educating the masses with a sense of responsibility and duty to the collective.

Akin to his predecessor Elijah Mohammed, Malcolm also preached a strong message regarding self-reliance in African American communities. He believed that it was not enough for African Americans to seek employment; they needed to create the businesses to employ other African Americans. The economic philosophy of Malcolm X was a simple one. He felt that African Americans, through education, could empower themselves to take care of their communities. By owning and operating businesses in their communities, African Americans would create job opportunities for one another.[5] In this context, self-reliance became a vehicle to open economic doors and to bolster the idea that African American communities could successfully exist in a nation that deliberately oppressed them.

The ideals of self-reliance were clearly illustrated through the various views and opinions of the leaders of the Nation of Islam. Some business models were even implemented but unfortunately failed over time. Although Malcolm's message of self-reliance is the most apparent in the extant literature, other NOI leaders still stand by this message. The goal for African Americans to create their own businesses and spend money in African American communities is a message that is still advocated today.

Although Malcolm X was ultimately assassinated, his message of self-reliance can be translated in a modern postsecondary context. One of the questions that guided this investigation was, Which majors are available to African American students that encourage self-reliance? One major, as illustrated by Louis Farrakhan, an NOI leader, is agribusiness. Ideally, agriculture-related majors can provide the training that African American students need to cultivate and produce food. Subsequently, the ability to produce food can lead to great self-sufficiency and economic independence. Because there remain institutions that provide an agriculture-centered curriculum, examination into the connections between them and self-reliance are warranted.

Agriculture always has been a core curriculum in the land grant colleges. These schools traditionally emphasized the practical side of education and—more than many other courses of study—agriculture curriculums forge a closer link between educational means and occupational ends. Recently, a social trend emphasizing the usefulness and relevance of a college degree has been reflected in rising undergraduate enrollments at land grant schools in general and in colleges of agriculture in particular. Although these changes have been noted for several years, little systematic attention has been given to the composition and aspirations of student bodies that are interested in agriculture or to the new directions being taken in agricultural training and placement.[6]

African Americans have been particularly hard hit by the decline in farm tenancy and trends toward consolidation into larger farm units. Since the sons and daughters of many African American farmers have migrated out of the South, the death of the landowner often results in the sale of the land in order to settle the estate.[7] In addition, traditional farming skills and a willingness to work are now rivaled by managerial expertise, access to capital, and ownership of heavy equipment as key elements in successful farm operations. Many institutional and social restraints limit the access of small farm operators to those elements.[8]

The capital demands of modern agriculture often discourage the entry of individuals into farming, and their interests and aspirations frequently are deflected into farm-related occupations in the broad area of agriculture. Farming and agriculture in general are viewed less as a way of life than as growing sources of jobs and occupational advancement.

As the spectrum of agricultural occupations has broadened, so has the range of people seeking agricultural careers. Traditionally, an agriculture student has been the son of a farmer, and therefore he has generally possessed practical farm experience. Eventually the face of agriculture changed as more nontraditional students began to enroll in the major; however, African Americans were not among these groups who accessed this type of career.

Although recent generations of African Americans often have strayed from fields related to farm work and agriculture, experiential programs may take on increasing importance as more nonfarm students seek agriculturally related careers.[9]

Given changes in the economic climate, agriculture-related industries may provide opportunities for employment and the space for African Americans to practice the concepts of self-reliance. In a postsecondary context, efforts should be made to widen student and faculty perspectives on the purpose of agriculture education and the kinds of occupations that are available. A broader understanding of agricultural careers is a central concern for minorities, particularly African Americans who are entering what has been a traditionally male, white occupational structure.

AGRICULTURE AND MECHANICAL INSTITUTION IN TEXAS

Prairie View A&M University is the second oldest public institution of higher education in Texas. It was established as a "separate but equal" institution created by the Agricultural and Mechanical College of Texas in 1871. In 1945, the name of the institution was changed from Prairie View Normal and Industrial College to Prairie View University. The courses that would be offered include agriculture, the mechanical arts, engineering, and the natural sciences.

Although the institution was established to provide opportunities for African Americans in agriculture-related fields, the major has gained little popularity through the years. According to 2006–2010 data, the College of Agriculture and Human Sciences graduated a relatively small number of students per program. For the 2005–2006 academic year, only 53 undergraduate and 53 master's degrees were awarded. More specifically, 29 students majored in agriculture, 18 in family and community services, and 6 in human nutrition and food. With regard to master's degree attainment, only 1 graduate student completed an MS in agricultural economics, 5 in animal science, and 47 in human sciences. For 2006–2007, only 23 undergraduate degrees were awarded in agriculture, 1 graduate student in agricultural economics, 2 graduate students in animal science, 3 graduate students in soil science, and 24 graduate students in human sciences. For the remaining academic years 2007–2008, 2008–2009, and 2009–2010, there were no graduate degrees awarded in agricultural economics, animal science, or soil science. As far as undergraduate degrees for the aforementioned years, only a total of 63 degrees were awarded in agriculture.

As indicated above, agriculture-related majors are not enrolling or graduating a substantive amount of students. This can be detrimental to African

American communities because agriculture plays a huge role in the United States. Agriculture is the principal source of food for Americans. Moreover, the United States is the largest food-producing nation in the world. The capital gains and economic independence that agribusiness can produce may positively impact African Americans, especially those who seek to be self-reliant.

Currently, agriculture is the largest economic sector in the United States. Oftentimes, agriculture is viewed as farmers who produce the crops or raise livestock. However, the field presents many other economic opportunities outside of the perceived norm. The fact that agriculture has such a practically, and theoretically, important role in the U.S. economy, coupled with the fact that it is an essentially untapped resource by some African American communities, positions postsecondary education in the field of agriculture in a uniquely valuable role. Because African Americans can be self-employed, self-promoted, and self-sustained as the result of such a postsecondary education, careers in agriculture directly speak to the notions of self-reliance that were so actively propagated by Malcolm X and the NOI.

Malcolm believed that every church, civic organization, and fraternal order should help their community by teaching and encouraging entrepreneurship.[10] Malcolm even went as far as to say that if "Blacks weren't going to be allowed out of the ghettos, they ought to run them."[11] Malcolm X's message about self-reliance and entrepreneurship is as relevant today as it was when it was spoken, particularly as it relates to postsecondary educational endeavors and choices. People gain freedom by controlling their destinies, and in order to control their destinies, they must control their community.

THE ART OF SELF-RELIANCE

The generations that have succeeded Malcolm X have been unquestionably influenced by his beliefs, rhetoric, and social commentary. His emphasis on self-reliance and relentless activism influenced numerous groups to follow him, particularly the artists and poets of the Black Arts movement. As opposed to economic self-reliance, which focused primarily on fiscal independence, the artists of the Black Arts movement interpreted Malcolm's pleas for self-reliance as a call for black artists to express their African roots to a specifically African American audience.

As Andrew P. Smallwood writes in the article "The Legacy of Malcolm X's Leadership: In the Tradition of Africana Social Movements," "Malcolm X laid a foundation of uncompromising Black cultural expression for Black people to follow."[12] This became a significant influence on the Black Arts

Movement of the late 1960s. It was Malcolm's charge that inspired a generation of Black artists to examine African American life. Poets and writers, such
as Amiri Baraka, thematically and topically engaged the ideas of Malcolm X,
and after his assassination a poetic eulogy—entitled *For Malcolm*—was composed by these Black Arts movement writers, celebrating his life and work.

In addition to inspiring artists to confidently address their African heritage,
Malcolm X's own life became a source of confidence and motivation. James
Smethurst notes that Malcolm

> drew many of the young black artists to him because he provided a model of
> how one might be a black man and artist-intellectual and still be grounded in the
> African American community. Like many artists and intellectuals in the United
> States, many of these artists felt isolated from the people among whom they had
> grown up, often living in bohemian communities of similarly alienated white,
> Latina/o, and Asian American artists. . . . As a result, Malcolm X's stance as a
> radical leader whose mass appeal and masculinity were uncompromised by his
> emphasis on the intellect and education and his deep interest in culture (and
> without macho posturing) was even more attractive to young people who would
> form the Black Arts Movement than to the general black population.[13]

Thus, not only did Malcolm X refer to the power and "appeal" of a "cultural
revolution," but he also existed as a living example of the immense power
of the "artist-intellectual." Young artists of the time witnessed a powerful
rhetorician, who was uncompromising in his support of African culture, who
desired *global* pan-Africanism, and who was himself an "artist-intellectual."
By Malcolm X opening up the purview of African culture on a global scale,
artists were given a theoretical—and physical—stage to present their ideas to
an international audience.

THE ART OF SELF-RELIANT EXPRESSION

When asked about African American artistic expression, Malcolm X asserted
that "Afro-Americans will be free to create only when they can depend on
the Afro-American community for support, and Afro-American artists must
realize that they depend on the Afro-American community for inspiration."[14]
Malcolm's desire for a "community" of black artists reflects the segregation
and oppression that artists faced in the pre–civil rights era. Before the civil
rights movement, African American performing artists had been forced to
exist as a subset within white entertainment. Whereas white artists were the
"stars" and patrons, their African American counterparts were included only
in brief snippets.

For instance, the acclaimed Nicholas Brothers began their career performing before white audiences at the Cotton Club, and they continued throughout the 1930s and 1940s to be included in three-minute segments of Hollywood films such as *Stormy Weather*. Despite the fact that moviegoers regarded the brothers as huge stars, they were never allowed even a fraction of the respect that was unquestionably lauded to their white colleagues. "Both brothers resent[ed] the fact that they were never allowed to do anything else [other than tap dance in such brief segments]. 'All we did was dance in the old movies just like Lena (Horne) always sang,' Harold [Nicholas] recalls. 'They never thought about giving us other things to do.'"[15]

Similarly, despite Lena Horne's prominence and fame, she was denied the leading female role in the film *Show Boat* due to Hollywood's historic prohibition on interracial relationships on film, and she had to continue doing bit parts solely because of her ethnicity. Generally, black actors, musicians, and dancers were the last names to be listed in an all-white cast—figuratively, and actually—or their immense talent was manipulated and suppressed in order to bolster white profits. Recognizing that the perceived secondary status and the oppression of African Americans was sustained even in the realm of the arts, Malcolm X envisioned a space of cultural expression that would be performed for black audiences and would be composed in an effort to validate and to represent Africana culture. In this way, black artists could participate in the pan-Africanist movement that Malcolm X advocated so strongly by presenting African culture on the world stage.

In his essay "Malcolm X and the Black Arts Movement," James Smethurst affirms,

> Malcolm X saw this [African American] culture as African at base and advocated a reclamation and renewal of this base through a migration back to Africa "culturally, philosophically, and psychologically, while remaining here physically, the spiritual bond that would develop between us and Africa through this cultural, philosophical and psychological migration would enhance our position here, because we would have our contacts with them acting as roots or foundations between us."[16]

By focusing on issues that affected people of African descent, and by using African cultural tenants thematically in their art, African American artists would become vital components and preservers of African identity and culture in the United States Smethurst continues, "While he [Malcolm X] did not outline what a new (or recovered) liberated black culture would look like in any detail, he issued a call for a movement to develop such a culture, one that at base was closely tied to African culture and modes of thought."[17]

Again, Malcolm X's death prevented him personally from pursuing this cultural revolution to any great extent. This "cultural revolution" would be in and of itself a liberation from white oppression and subordination. Instead of abandoning their cultural heritage—and thus, either assimilating into white culture, or living without recognition of any cultural heritage—Malcolm X advocated for a conscious validation and embodiment of African culture and ideas. This rallying cry reverberated throughout the African American community, and Malcolm's charge was taken up by the artists whose work would later come to be termed the Black Arts Movement.

TOWARD AN EMPOWERED COMMUNITY

The "empowerment" that Malcolm X advocated for was the result of self-reliance and confidence in one's own African heritage. A community of African Americans, coming together to perform before a black audience, while simultaneously presenting African themes and culture, results in a validating experience for the artists, the audience members, and the entire community. With this in mind, African American dance companies and artists have moved away from the "secondary" positioning imposed upon them by white agents and audiences and have created their own companies and productions.

In her essay "Awkward Moves: Dance Lessons from the 1940s," Marya McQuirter posits that the performing arts empower African Americans because they excel artistically and physically in those areas. She mentions, "The innate superiority that blacks had over whites in dancing fit into Malcolm X's ideology of racial difference."[18] When white supremacists were busy fabricating ways in which African Americans were "naturally subordinate" to whites, dance became an arena where blacks clearly excelled. In the years following Malcolm X's assassination, artists began to embody the cultural revolution that he had envisioned.

Among them, Alvin Ailey established the Alvin Ailey American Dance Theater in New York City in 1958, which revolutionized modern dance, black dance companies, and African American involvement in concert dance at large. Today, the company remains one of the most acclaimed and celebrated dance companies in the world. Arguably, Ailey's best-known production, *Revelations*, serves as a representative of the cultural revolution and of the pan-Africanist ideas propagated by Malcolm X. In the essay "Toward a Theory of Diaspora Aesthetics," Samuel A. Floyd notes, "The entire suite—with its African-like incremental repetition and development, call-and-response figures, West Indian-like rhythms and gestures in the processional and 'Honor'—confirms and stresses the grounding of *Revelations* in African-Diaspora aesthetics."[19] In addition to presenting themes of African culture in the work, Alvin Ailey himself confirmed and confessed that the entire inspiration for the work came from a desire to present African Americans in a celebratory light. In a

1986 interview he said that the piece was "about the beauty of black people, about their intelligence, their spirituality, their elegance, their ability to entertain, their love of self, their wanting to transmit through discipline their feelings to the audience."[20] Ailey's inspiration for *Revelations*, and his creation of the Alvin Ailey American Dance Theater and their entire repertoire, responds directly to Malcolm X's call for "Afro-American artists [to] realize that they depend on the Afro-American community for inspiration."[21]

In 1996, Savion Glover's *Bring in Da' Noise, Bring in Da' Funk,* the Tony-nominated off-Broadway show, presented similar themes. Through tap dance, the show chronicles the African American story—from the involuntary migration on the slave ships, through the minstrel show era, and into the hip-hopping community of today. Author Ben Brantley applauded the production, asserting that it "found choreographic equivalents for the black experience in the days of plantations, urban industrialization, the Harlem Renaissance and latter-day race riots. . . . This sense of flaming individuality is finally what the evening is about: not just the collective history of a race but the diverse and specific forms of expression that one tradition embraces."[22] *Bring in Da' Noise, Bring in Da' Funk* toured throughout the United States and thus brought the ideas of pan-Africanism and the narrative of the Afro-American community onto the global stage, as Malcolm X had worked for.

These are just some of the numerous examples of the new generation of performing artists who have been directly influenced and inspired by Malcolm X's advocacy of a cultural revolution. As Spike Lee commented, dancers and artists of today pick and choose from Malcolm X's ideologies, presenting what resonates in their own lives on the stage, and essentially create their own Malcolm that fits their own personal and political agenda.[23] Despite the variety of representations and dance styles, one thing remains clear: Performing artists are interested in propagating black issues, African culture, and celebrating African heritage throughout the Diaspora.

CONCLUSION: SELF-RELIANCE, EDUCATION, AND EXPRESSION IN A GLOBAL SENSE

Despite Malcolm X's adamant pleas for the African American community to become self-reliant and self-sustaining, the statistics remain harrowing. Making more students, particularly African American students, aware of the myriad of options available in the field of agriculture is the challenge faced by educators in the nation's 136 colleges of agriculture. Enrollment numbers in programs across the country indicate that as a major, agriculture does not have the appeal of other professions. In the fall of 1999, there were 4,209 African American students studying in agriculture-related fields according to preliminary data from the Food and Agricultural Education Information System, a database to which the nation's colleges of agriculture report. This number is minuscule when compared with just about any other major or discipline.

Educators say it is crucial for the number of African Americans in agriculture to increase. The demographics of a recent poultry science class at the University of Tennessee illustrate the severity of the problem. Out of about thirty students, only two were minorities and only one was African American. Research has found that if the situation doesn't change, African Americans may miss out on an epochal change taking place in agriculture and the opportunity to participate in careers that will have a huge impact on the twenty-first century. Educators say a big part of the problem is that the professions of agricultural education and food production often are stigmatized in the minds of students, particularly African American students.

Similar to African American college-goers, today's African American artists and dancers have faced a myriad of social and economical challenges. Moreover, contemporary African American artists and dancers have had to repeatedly fight to remain economically stable in a market that has been historically dominated by whites. Amid the struggles, African Americans still seek to hold true to Malcolm X's ideologies regarding self-reliance. This notion lends support to the conception that Malcolm's legacy still greatly impacts African American communities today.

In addition to being recognized by today's generation as one of the most prominent African Americans in history, Malcolm X's image has been displayed on the covers of various hip hop albums and flaunted across numerous music videos. In response to this, Smallwood continues, "Then, after the civil rights era, the legacy of the Black liberation struggle found its way in the creative self-expression of urban social commentary in the hip-hop culture of the 1980s and 1990s."[24] Hip hop artists such as Public Enemy and Talib Kweli have continued to explore Malcolm's philosophies, and they have contributed to making "Malcolm" a household name today.

As Spike Lee posited, each one of us has "[his/her] Malcolm" who is dear to them. He has risen as a symbol of empowerment and of self-reliance in all aspects of African American life. His position on social injustices and self-empowerment will forever impact the psyche and ideologies of people around the world for many, many years to come.[25]

NOTES

1. C. Ross, "Your Personal Finance: The Economic Philosophy of Malcolm X," *The Tennessee Tribune*, February 22, 1966, 13.

2. P. E. Joseph, "Still Reinventing Malcolm," *Chronicle of Higher Education* 57, no. 35 (2011): B6–B9.

3. A. Lichtenstein, "Elijah Muhammad and the Nation of Islam," *Footsteps* 8, no. 2 (2006): 11.

4. J. Morgan, "African Americans and Agriculture," *Black Issues in Higher Education* 17, no. 8 (2000): 20.

5. Ross, "Your Personal Finance."

6. J. J. Molnar, J. E. Dunkelberger, and D. A. Salter, "Agricultural Education in the South: A Comparison of Student Characteristics at Land Grant Institutions," *The Journal of Negro Education* 50, no. 1 (1981): 26–40.

7. Morgan, "African Americans and Agriculture."

8. Molnar et al., "Agricultural Education in the South."

9. Ibid.

10. A. Lichtenstein, "Elijah Muhammad and the Nation of Islam."

11. Ross, "Your Personal Finance," 84.

12. A. P. Smallwood, "The Intellectual Creativity and Public Discourse of Malcolm X: A Precursor to the Modern Black Studies Movement," *Journal of Black Studies* 36, no. 2 (2005): 248–63.

13. James Smethurst, "Malcolm X and the Black Arts Movement," in *The Cambridge Companion to Malcolm X*, ed. Robert Terrill (Cambridge: Cambridge University Press, 2010), 81.

14. Smallwood, "The Intellectual Creativity and Public Discourse of Malcolm X."

15. Aldore Collier, "The Nicholas Brothers: Still Kicking after 62 Years," *Ebony Magazine*, May 1991.

16. Smethurst, "Malcolm X and the Black Arts Movement," 85.

17. Ibid.

18. Marya McQuirter, "Awkward Moves: Dance Lessons from the 1940s," in *Dancing Many Drums: Excavations in African American Dance*, ed. Thomas DeFrantz (Madison: University of Wisconsin Press, 2002), 90.

19. Samuel A. Floyd Jr., "Toward a Theory of Diaspora Aesthetics," *Lenox Avenue: A Journal of Interarts Inquiry* 4 (1998), 60.

20. Ibid., 61.

21. Ibid.

22. B. Brantley, "Theater Review: Story of Tap as the Story of Blacks," *New York Times*, November 16, 1995, 1A.

23. S. Lee and H. L. Gates, "Generation X," *Transition* 56 (1992): 176–90.

24. Smallwood, "The Intellectual Creativity and Public Discourse of Malcolm X."

25. For more on the topics in this chapter, see J. L. Conyers and A. P. Smallwood, *Malcolm X: A Historical Reader* (Durham, NC: Carolina Academic Press, 2008); T. DeFrantz, *Dancing Many Drums: Excavations in African American Dance* (Madison: University of Wisconsin Press, 2002); A. T. Franklin, "Schoolin': Critical Consciousness, Black Consciousness, and the Pedagogies of Transformation," *International Journal of Learning* 17, no. 8 (2010): 493–502; L. Lum, "Working Outside the System," *Diverse: Issues in Higher Education* 22, no. 26 (2006): 26–27; J. E. Morris,

"Malcolm X's Critique of the Education of Black People," *Western Journal of Black Studies* 25, no. 2 (2001): 126–35; R. Terrill, *The Cambridge Companion to Malcolm X* (Cambridge: Cambridge University Press, 2010); I. P. Ukpokodu, "African American Males in Dance, Music, Theater, and Film," *Annals of the American Academy of Political and Social Science* 569 (The African American Male in American Life and Thought) (2000): 71–85.

Chapter Twelve

Dr. Martin Luther King Jr. the Modernist and Minister Malcolm X the Postmodernist?

An Analysis of Perspectives and Justice

Kelly Jacobs

Black identity has not only survived its challenges, it has become a vital and codominant element in American and global society. This is largely because it is a social entity that has accumulated power through overcoming insurmountable odds—a matter of the most tenacious facets of agency overwhelming immutable structure. The incalculable wisdom and unbending fortitude of Black identity would not be possible without the contributions of both Dr. Martin Luther King Jr. and Minister Malcolm X. The contributions made by these leaders to Black identity created an antecedent resistance of a dualistic nature in response to the ensuing strikes at its essence posed by the challenges of gratuitous paternalism, which permeates post–civil rights America. Analyzing the vital contributions of Dr. King and Minister X through modernist/postmodernist juxtaposition reveals a powerful dualism in the means and ends sought by Black identity advocates.

In terms of epistemological and political perspectives, this chapter presents the idea that Dr. Martin Luther King Jr. was largely modernist in outlook and approach while Minister Malcolm X's views and actions stood much more within postmodernism. Demonstrating the respective natures of these leaders in such terms leads to the establishment of three key points. First, Black identity bears a highly unique essence that is marked by agency supplanting structure, as evidenced by tangible progress toward justice and equality. The second point is that the results of the leaders' gravitations toward modernism and postmodernism yielded different outcomes that were necessary to the vitality of Black identity. Third, Dr. King and Minister X played equally vital roles in the construction of Black identity as it stands today despite their methodological differences. These accomplishments speak to the capability of Black identity to harness social and political power to the betterment of all human interests despite ongoing challenges.

METHODOLOGY

This chapter combines historical and philosophical analysis to demonstrate the modernist tendencies of Dr. Martin Luther King Jr. and the postmodernist tendencies of Minister Malcolm X. After establishing a common understanding of the modern-postmodern divide, eight of the most significant contributions of each leader are analyzed and applied to the dichotomy. Although both leaders achieved countless vital steps toward fairness and human rights, each leaves a legacy defined by a number of key events or attributes.

Dr. Martin Luther King's legacy is perhaps best defined by the following characteristics:

- Civil rights legislation
- Civil disobedience
- The four steps to peaceful action
- Vision of racial unity
- Support of labor strikes
- The dynamic between the SCLC and the SNCC
- Protest of the Vietnam War
- An optimistic belief that society can improve itself

The legacy of Minister Malcolm X is most accurately defined by the following characteristics:

- The establishment of Pan-Africanism
- His metamorphosis from Malcolm X to El Hajj Malik El Shabazz, which signified a profound change in perspective, which led to
- His views, while with the Nation of Islam, that held that Islamic values engendered black liberation
- His shift from separatism to racial unity
- Attempts to make the United Nations acknowledge human rights abuses suffered by African Americans at the hands of the United States of America
- The concept of black liberation
- Justification of self-defense "by any means necessary"
- Rejection of European surnames and identity

Analysis of the most notable characteristics of each leaders' legacy reveals their tendencies toward modernism and postmodernism.

MODERNISM AND POSTMODERNISM

There is much debate on the exact meaning of modernism and postmodernism, but both are perspectives on the nature of knowledge, truth, and human interaction. Central to the dichotomy of modernism and postmodernism is epistemology, the philosophy of knowledge. In general terms, modernism holds that objective knowledge is attainable whereas there is a strong reluctance in postmodernism to acknowledge objective truth that is not tainted by the subjectivity of the observer. The implications of adhering to either epistemological viewpoint are far-reaching.

The modernist perspective acknowledges universality in social structures and ethical values. Thus, politics from the modernist perspective is more commonly understood through the observation of elite institutions and codes of values. It is through these commonly acknowledged institutions—such as legislatures, religious institutions, socioeconomic classes, and historical metanarratives—that the modernist seeks to affect change. Postmodernism is somewhat more difficult to elucidate than modernism. To understand postmodernism, one must understand the theory of poststructuralism a significant contribution made by the German philosopher Friedrich Nietzsche. Poststructuralism holds that metanarratives—used to describe the world and to formulate universal codes of justice—are inherently false. Metanarratives, like the realm of Forms posited by Plato, are nothing more than imaginations that ultimately cannot escape the subjectivity of the individual in understanding and application.

Poststructuralism paved the way for postmodernism, which views politics in terms of identity. The majority of the most influential modernists—many of whom even came long after Nietzsche and were contemporaries of King and Malcolm X (e.g., John Rawls and Jürgen Habermas)—saw a certain universalism in ethics and politics and therefore believed that the social structures affected should be artificially arranged to accommodate its individual agents in the most efficient and equitable manner. For the postmodernists, however, it is the individual agents and their identities that continually arrange the social structures themselves in an ever-evolving environment in which power flows disjointedly among the multitude of society's agent actors. Political theorist Leslie Paul Theile provides insight into politics in this light: "Politics is not only a question of actions that serve particular interests but also a question of identities."[1] Therefore, politics is not solely contained within a small body of actors such as corporations, socio-economic-political elites, or the local, federal and state governments that set barriers on action and choice; it is in constant flux within the plethora of society's identities, harnessed at different times by different identities.

Conversely, these identities are constructed by the very social structures whose power they often wield. Theile elaborates on the poststructuralist construction of identity in *Thinking Politics*:

> Poststructuralist theory is not only or even primarily concerned with the capacity of power to constrain action and desire. It focuses on the capacity of power to construct identity, and by doing so, induce action and desire. Identities become constructed within hierarchically organized categories of experience and social structure.[2]

Therefore, all individuals both consider themselves and are considered as parts of particular identities. In turn, it is through these identities that individuals control social structures and are simultaneously controlled by them.

The question of the primacy of structure over agency embodies the modern-postmodern divide. It is in this context that Black identity emerges. Black identity is an embodiment of experience within varying social structures, the majority of which were and continue to be oppressive. Rising up to the challenges posed to it by oppressive social structures like slavery, interrupted cultural history, and racism, Black identity has constantly responded with wit, tenacity, and dignity. It transcends race and history; it is a collection of connected identities through time. Black identity is not exclusively African American, although African Americans arguably play the most influential role in its construction. This is because Black identity—always having a vital part of American identity—gradually coupled successfully with American economic and cultural influences.

All peoples of the African Diaspora are among Black identity's vastly diverse ranks. It is the collective experience of all of those people as it interacts today. Black identity might be regarded as "Pan-Africanism" moving through time. Although Black identity bears countless attributes, it can be largely defined by its moral eloquence in response to oppressive social structures. It is because Black identity has had to contend with imperialistic and racially dominant social structures wherever it is—be it in North America, Africa, or elsewhere—that it should be regarded as sovereign. Thus, Black identity deserves its capitalization.

DR. KING THE MODERNIST
AND MALCOLM X THE POSTMODERNIST?

Whereas both Dr. Martin Luther King Jr. and Minister Malcolm X acted from religious foundations, both leaders dealt with societal struggles through both modernist and postmodernist avenues. It is the leaders' individual perspectives on social structures and the ability of society to change that define their modernist and postmodernist tendencies and outcomes. Dr. Martin Luther King sought to change the hierarchy of society as a whole. Malcolm X sought to break away from American society and form a new Black identity through Pan-Africanism.

Dr. King's victories were largely legislative, while Malcolm X's victories were largely within the Black identity, although it must not be overlooked that Malcolm X was attempting to have the United Nations adopt a resolution charging the United States with human rights abuses for the slavery and countless aggressions it had allowed on African Americans throughout its history. Even with Malcolm X's attempts at affecting change in the global political structure, his focus was on identity. Minister X wanted the global political structures to acknowledge the injustices suffered by the African Americans as part of humanity. If Malcolm X's life had not been tragically cut short, and if his attempts at the adoption of the UN resolution had been successful, perhaps the next step would have been a massive empowerment of the Black identity through formal acknowledgement by the global community at large of the abuses it has suffered.

The modernist-to-postmodernist departure drawn by Leslie Paul Theile can certainly be applied to the different views and approaches toward liberation taken by Dr. King and Minister X:

> Postmodernists do not assume the unchanging nature of the individual who willfully wields power in pursuit of chosen interests, as modern individualists do. Nor do postmodernists take for granted the unchanging nature of the social structures that shape individual human behavior, as structuralists do. Instead, postmodern theorists insist that human identities are continually being constructed and contested within protean social environments owing to the interactions of specific forms of power.[3]

To apply the modern-postmodern divide to the phenomena of Dr. Martin Luther King and Minister Malcolm X, the key characteristics of their legacies must be called into observation.

Table 12.1 lists the notable characteristics of the legacies left by Martin Luther King Jr. and Malcolm X in their lifelong quests for equality, justice, and human rights. Characteristics in table 12.1 that acknowledge formal structural power and universal codes of ethics are regarded to be of a modernist approach. Acts or views that consider identity to be the means to empowerment and liberation are regarded to be postmodernist. Further distinction between the two approaches is characterized by modernism's assertion that the nature of the individual is unchanging, whereas postmodernism acknowledges the tendency of individual nature to continuously change over time.

Table 12.1.   Dr. King and Minister X Modernist/Postmodernist Approaches to Justice

MLK: Modernist Approaches	*Malcolm X: Modernist Approaches*
Civil rights legislation	Attempts at UN resolution condemning
Vision of racial unity	US human rights abuses
Civil disobedience	Considering Islamic values as foundation
Four steps to action	for liberation during NOI years
Reluctance toward SNCC autonomy	(Sociology of Malcolm X)
Supporting strikes	
MLK: Postmodernist Approaches	*Malcolm X: Postmodernist Approaches*
Protest of Vietnam War	Black liberation
Not taking for granted that society can	Pan-Africanism
change	Self-defense "by any means necessary"
	Rejection of Anglo-European surnames
	Departure from NOI
	Separatism and eventual equality

DR. MARTIN LUTHER KING, THE MODERNIST

Dr. King was much more of a modernist than Malcolm X because of his views on the unchanging nature of the individual. This is not to say that Dr. King did not successfully seek to change the perspectives of racists. Dr. King adhered to the modernist notion of an unchanging human nature in that he saw racism as something taught to otherwise good human beings. It was through numerous attempts at undoing racism through peaceful action and civil discourse in the public realm that Dr. King sought to unearth the true human nature in all people.

Dr. King was not without some postmodernist tendencies. He was a post-modernist in the sense that he saw the potential for change in social structures. Seeing the potential for change in social structures was postmodernist in nature, but the route King took to affect that change was almost exclusively modernist. He did not seek to reconstruct American society or to form a new one as Malcolm X did through Pan-Africanism. He sought to change the American social structure through its own institutional mechanisms—the legislative process.

The Civil Rights Act of 1964 made racial discrimination illegal and established the Equal Employment Opportunity Commission to enforce that prohibition. The Voting Rights Act of 1965 eliminated poll tests and various other state tactics to disenfranchise black as well as poor voters. The Fair Housing Act of 1968 made substantial progress toward eliminating racial discrimination in American real estate markets. Each of these acts of legislation owes its passage to Dr. King who personally lobbied Congress and President Johnson on their behalf.

Modernism is also embodied in Dr. King's vision of equality, his attempts at fostering racial unity through peaceful action and civil disobedience. To strive for racial unity is to acknowledge universal qualities in all individuals. To attain such a vision through peaceful action and civil disobedience is to address the formal power structures that perpetuate racial oppression. Dr. King even created a universal model for incorporating such means.

In his famous *Letter from Birmingham Jail*,[4] Dr. King offers a universal model for accomplishing his particular method of peaceful action. This model is comprised of four steps. First, a collection of facts must be conducted. Second, attempts at negotiation with the offender(s) must be made. Third, the individuals who are to take action must undertake the process of self-purification, in which they release any anger, hate, or negativity that might cloud their judgment. Finally, direct peaceful action may be taken in the various forms of protests, sit-ins, and civil disobedience.

An additional indicator of Dr. King's tendency toward modernism is his attempt to control the Student Nonviolent Coordinating Committee (SNCC) and to keep it under the umbrella of Southern Christian Leadership Conference (SCLC). When black students across America began to grow wary of Dr. King's method of nonviolent action after suffering intense abuses at the hands of racist whites, they sought to break from the SCLC. Dr. King resisted the break, led by Ella Baker, which sought to redirect the quest for equality and justice by young African Americans.[5]

On Dr. King's postmodernist side, he protested the Vietnam War. In doing so, he seemed to no longer recognize the optimism he once had in the American social structure's ability to change for the better.[6] Dr. King's protest of the Vietnam War also speaks to the notion that he did not take for granted that society can change. After analysis of the key characteristics of Dr. King's legacy, it is clear that his views and approach gravitated much more toward modernism than postmodernism.

MALCOLM X, THE POSTMODERNIST

Minister Malcolm X was more of a postmodernist than Dr. Martin Luther King Jr., although he did adhere to some modernist views and approaches throughout his life. The postmodernist tendencies of Malcolm X do not come as a surprise, as he had concrete firsthand experiences of changing human nature. At least two epiphanies can be marked on the timeline of Malcolm X's life experience. First, while in jail his inward view of human nature shifted.

Second, his metamorphosis from Malcolm X to El Hajj Malik El-Shabazz represented a shift in his outward view of human nature.[7] Despite the fact that Malcolm X came from a religious viewpoint and that even his later views still acknowledged universality, his acknowledgment of human nature as being in a state of flux and change steered him toward a largely postmodern approach to liberation.

In his famous lecture *A Message to the Grassroots*, Malcolm X presents the idea of black liberation as a struggle existing in a state of authentic revolution.[8] Black liberation, according to Malcolm X, justified reactive violent action as a valid form of self-defense, thus departing from adherence to a universal concept of civility. What is demonstrated is that Minister X countered injustice from a religious—and modernist—position, but the injustices he confronted subverted universality in the most negative ways and did not allow for the ethical rigidity religious dogma prescribed to counter such injustices. Furthermore, Minister X praises Islam for allowing self-defense. Therefore, it appears that Malcolm X may not have actively sought a perspective of the postmodernist variety but rather was thrust into it.

Minister X further cast off the modernist perspective in his approach to form a new Black identity. He is well-recognized for his rejection of his birth name, Malcolm Little. Joining in the rejection of European surnames with the Nation of Islam, Malcolm X eventually sought to create Pan-Africanism as a new Black identity construct. The goal was the formation of an entirely new identity for those who shared his struggle and circumstances: Black identity.

Malcolm X's departure from the Nation of Islam signified a profound change in his tendencies. After experiences abroad in Africa and in the Middle East, he underwent the transformation from Malcolm X to El Hajj Malik El Shabazz. His transformation either coincided with, or was correlated to, his departure from the Nation of Islam. Shedding his previous views of separatism, Malik El Shabazz began to acknowledge a universal quality in people of all races that was visible in certain identities that encompassed more than one race while under a uniform tent of interests, such as Muslims or revolutionaries.[9]

However, it is questionable that Malcolm X entirely rejected the notion that social structures change. His emphasis on black liberation may have demonstrated that he did not believe that social structures like American society *could* change and therefore that new social constructs like Pan-Africanism must be formed. Furthermore, in *A Message to the Grassroots*, Malcolm X contended that America saw African Americans ("us") as a problem of which it sought to rid itself and that acceptance of this notion was necessary for African Americans to appear intelligent in American society.[10] Again, Malcolm X appears to have been thrust into a postmodernist perspective.

Thus far, this analysis presents a largely postmodernist, liberation-oriented Malcolm X with views that still acknowledge some modernism, and a largely modernist, equality-oriented Dr. Martin Luther King Jr. with views that ultimately reject the immutability of social structures. Dr. King's attempts were more focused on structure—through legislation, civil disobedience, and peaceful action—while Malcolm X's attempts focused more on agency—attempting to form a new society with the establishment of Pan-Africanism.

PROCEDURAL AND SUBSTANTIVE JUSTICE SOUGHT BY DR. KING AND MALCOLM X

The focus on structure and agency found within Dr. King and Minister X are synonymous with their focus on procedural and substantive justice. Procedural justice is the establishment of equality within the law while substantive justice establishes equality of opportunity within society. Table 12.2 lists the modernist and postmodernist attributes of the two leaders' legacies with regard to procedural and substantive justice.

Through his successful attempts at lobbying the passage of civil rights legislation, Dr. Martin Luther King Jr. saw that procedural justice was served. In strengthening African American and Black identity, Minister Malcolm X

Table 12.2.   Dr. King and Minister X Modernist/Postmodernist Approaches to Procedural and Substantive Justice

MLK: Modernist Approaches	Malcolm X: Modernist Approaches
Civil rights legislation +	Attempts at UN resolution condemning
Progress toward racial unity –	United States human rights abuses +
Civil disobedience +	Considering Islamic values as foundation
Four steps to action +	for liberation during NOI years
Reluctance toward SNCC autonomy –	(Sociology of Malcolm X) –
Supporting strikes –	
MLK: Postmodernist Approaches	**Malcolm X: Postmodernist Approaches**
Protest of Vietnam War –/+	*Black liberation –/+*
Not taking for granted that society can	*Pan-Africanism –*
change –/+	*Self-defense "by any means necessary" +*
	Rejection of Anglo-European surnames –
	Departure from NOI –/+
	Separatism and eventual equality –

+ An approach to procedural justice.
– An approach to substantive justice.

Chapter Twelve

saw that substantive justice was served (through empowering his brothers and sisters to forge greater opportunities for themselves within their own collective identity).

CONCLUSION

The assessment of Black identity being heavily influenced and affected by a modernist Dr. King who sought procedural justice coupled with a postmodernist Malcolm X who made achievements in substantive justice brings three key conclusions about Black identity:

1. Black identity bears a highly unique essence that is marked by agency supplanting structure, as evidenced by tangible progress toward justice and equality in American society and political culture.
2. The philosophies and actions of both Dr. King and Minister X resulted in concrete progress toward justice and equality in America that originated from each leaders' gravitations toward modernism and postmodernism in approach and perspective. This was a vital component in civil rights and is now part of Black identity. This is also seen in the observation of the focuses of Dr. King and Minister X on procedural and substantive justice, respectively.
3. Addressing the goals, methods, and outcomes of both leaders through abstract modernist-postmodernist juxtaposition while also accounting for their nascent accomplishments in justice reveals that both Dr. King and Minister X played equally vital roles in the construction of Black identity as it stands today, despite their methodological differences. These accomplishments speak to the capability of Black identity to harness social and political power to the betterment of all human interests despite ongoing challenges.

These conclusions point to the joint contributions of both men in making tangible progress toward justice and equality in American society and political culture—progress that now resonates globally. They also reveal both leaders' lasting contributions to Black identity and the interconnectedness of the two men within the civil rights struggle. Their methodological differences speak to the capability of Black identity to harness all relevant resources to improve the social and political standing of all people.

Whereas Dr. Martin Luther King Jr. and Minister Malcolm X eventually arrived at the same philosophical conclusions of universalism in varying shades, they took different approaches with both modernist and postmodernist tendencies. While their end goals were ultimately similar, the different paths and means they prescribed equipped the Black identity with the tools that enable it to endure and flourish in the noblest fashion.

NOTES

1. Leslie Paul Thiele, *Thinking Politics: Perspectives in Ancient, Modern, and Postmodern Political Theory* (New York: Seven Bridges Press, 2003), 72.
2. Ibid., 78.
3. Ibid., 80.
4. Martin Luther King Jr., "Letter from Birmingham Jail" (1963). www.archives.gov/press/exhibit/dream-speech.pdf.
5. Britta Waldschmidt-Nelson, *Dreams and Nightmares: Martin Luther King, Jr., Malcolm X, and the Struggle for Black Equality in America* (Gainesville: University Press of Florida, 2012), 75.
6. Rare video of Martin Luther King Jr. on civil rights and peace.
7. Britta Waldschmidt-Nelson, *Dreams and Nightmares*, 29–44.
8. Malcolm X, "Message to the Grassroots" (1963). www.blackpast.org/1963-malcolm-x-message-grassroots.
9. Rett Jones, "Methodology and Meaning: The Sociology of Malcolm X," in *Malcolm X: A Historical Reader*, ed. James L. Conyers Jr. and Andrew P. Smallwood (Durham, NC: Carolina Academic Press, 2008).
10. Malcolm X, *Message to the Grassroots*, 1963.

Bibliography

18X, Brother Tomas. "United Under Light of Islam." *Muhammad Speaks*, December 29, 1967.

3X, Ann. "Kitchen Is Our Medicine Cabinet." *Muhammad Speaks*, May 1962.

3X, Audrey. "Our Children among Most Beautiful." *Muhammad Speaks*, April 1962.

3X, Sister Audrey. "Dr. Thomas Patrick Warns against Television Slavery." *Muhammad Speaks*, February 1962.

4X, Joan. "What Islam Has Done for Me." *Muhammad Speaks*, October 24, 1969.

67X, Charles, and Alonzo 4X. "Jamaica Government Hosts Muslim Delegation." *Accomplishment of the Muslims* (1975): 24.

9X, Sister Lt. Deborah. "Our Divine Garment." *M.G.T. Bulletin*, September 1974.

Abani, Chris. *Song for Night*. Brooklyn: Akashic Books, 2007.

Abilla, Walter Dan. "A Study of Black Muslims: An Analysis of Commitment." Ph.D. dissertation, Case Western Reserve University, January 1972.

Aboulela, Leila. *Minaret*. London: Bloomsbury, 2005.

Acevedo, G. A., J. Ordner, and N. Thompson. "Narrative Inversion as a Tactical Framing Device: The Ideological Origins of the Nation of Islam." *Narrative Inquiry* 20, no. 1 (2010): 124–52. doi: 10.1075/ni.20.1.07ace.

"African Nation Names Woman to Cabinet Post." *Muhammad Speaks*, July 1962.

"Africans Stop Praising Wise Bossism of British Masters!" *Muhammad Speaks*, February 1962.

"Afro-Asian Women in UN 'Language, Custom Not a Barrier to Understanding One Another.'" *Muhammad Speaks*, December 30, 1962.

After, Hale. *Why Fundamentalism? Iranian Women and Their Support of Islam*. York: University of York, 1994.

Aidoo, Ama Ata. *Changes*. New York: Feminist Press, 1993.

Akbar, N. *Akbar Papers in Black Psychology*. Tallahassee, FL: Mind Production, 2003.

Alexander, M. *The New Jim Crow: Mass Incarceration in the Age of Colorblindness*. New York: New Press, 2010.

Alkali, Zaynab. *Cobwebs and Other Stories*. New York: Longman, 1995.
———. *The Stillborn*. New York: Longman, 1984.
Allen, Ernest. "Minister Louis Farrakhan and the Continuing Evolution of the Nation of Islam." In *The Farrakhan Factor: African-American Writers on Leadership, Nationhood, and Minister Louis Farrakhan*, edited by Amy Alexander. New York: Grove Press, 1998.
Al-Mansour, Khalid Abdullah Tariq. *Betrayal by Any Other Name*. San Francisco: First African Arabian Press, 1993.
Ansari, Zafar Ishaq. "W. D. Mohammed: The Making of a Black Muslim Leader, 1933–1961." *The American Journal of Islamic Social Sciences* 2 (1985): 245–62.
"Are Fashion and Beauty the Same? Fashion is Seasonal but Beauty is Eternal." *Muhammad Speaks*, April 1962.
Asante, Molefi Kete. "The Afrocentric Idea in Education." *Journal of Negro Education* 60, no. 2 (1991): 170–80.
———. *Race, Rhetoric, and Identity: The Architecton of Soul*. Amherst, NY: Humanity Books, 2005.
Atieh, Majda Ramadan. *The African American Tafsir. Interpretation of the Islamic Harem: Female Resistance in Toni Morrison's* Paradise. Ph.D. dissertation, Howard University, 2007.
Atta, Sefi. *Every Good Thing Will Come*. Northampton, MA: Interlink Books, 2005.
Austin, Allan D., ed. *African Muslims in Antebellum America: A Sourcebook*. New York: Garland, 1984.
Axelrod, Stanley. "The Treatment of the Negro in American History School Textbooks." *The Negro History Bulletin* 29, no. 6 (1966): 135–44.
Ba, Mariama. *So Long a Letter*. Portsmouth, NH: Heinemann, 2008.
Bagdadi, Ali. "Saviour's Day." Savior's Day Address, the Nation of Islam. DVD, February 1975.
Baldwin, James. *The Price of the Ticket: Collected Nonfiction 1948–1985*. New York: St. Martin's Press, 1985.
Bambara, Toni Cade, ed. *The Black Woman: An Anthology*. New York: Washington Square Press, 1970.
Bangura, Ahmed. *Islam and the West African Novel*. Boulder, CO: Lynne Reiner Publishers, 2000.
Banks, J. A. *An Introduction to Multicultural Education*, 5th edition. Boston: Pearson Education, 2014.
Banks Jr., William H. *The Black Muslims*. Philadelphia: Chelsea House Publishers, 1997.
Baraka, Imamu Amiri, and the Congress of African Peoples, eds. *African Congress: A Documentary of the First Modern Pan African Congress*. New York: Morrow, 1972.
Barnes, Steven. Interview by Muhammad Aurangzeb Ahmad. *Islam and Science Fiction*, November 17, 2010. Accessed December 8, 2015. http://islamscifi.com/islam-sci-fi-interview-of-steven-barnes/.
———. *Lion's Blood: A Novel of Slavery and Freedom in an Alternate America*. New York: Aspect/Warner Books, 2002.

————. *Zulu Heart*. New York: Warner Books, 2003.

Basit Naeem, Abdul. "Sees Divine Purpose in the Trials, Humiliation, Suffering of Muslims." *Muhammad Speaks*, July 7, 1967.

Beals, Melba Patillo. *Warriors Don't Cry: A Searing Memoir to Integrate Little Rock's Central High School*. New York: Pocket Books, 1994.

"Beauty of a Black Woman." *Muhammad Speaks*, July 1963.

"Beauty of Being Black." *Muhammad Speaks*, July 1962.

Bell, D. *Faces at the Bottom of the Well: The Permanence of Racism*. New York: Basic Books, 1992.

Berg, Herbert. *Elijah Muhammad and Islam*. New York: NYU Press, 2009.

Beyala, Calixthe. *Loukoum: The Little Prince of Belleville*. Portsmouth, NH: Heinemann, 1995.

————. *Maman a un amant*. Paris: Editions 84, 1993.

Beynon, Erdmann Doane. "The Voodoo Cult among Negro Migrants in Detroit." *American Journal of Sociology* 63 (1938).

Blackmon, Douglas A. *Slavery by Another Name: The Re-enslavement of Black Americans from the Civil War to World War II*. New York: Anchor, 2009.

Blake, J. Herman. "Black Nationalism." *Annals of the American Academy of Political and Social Science* 382 (1969): 15–25. Accessed December 8, 2015. www.jstor.org/stable/1037110.

Brantley, B. "Theater Review: Story of Tap as the Story of Blacks." *New York Times*, November 16, 1995, 1A.

Britannica Encyclopedia of Black Profiles. *For the People, By the People*. Encarta Encyclopedia CD-ROM. Paterson, NJ: The People's Publishing Group, 1998.

Brooks, Roy L. *Integration or Separation: A Strategy for Racial Equality*. Cambridge: Harvard University Press, 1996.

Brother Lovell. Interview by author. Philadelphia, PA, December 2007.

Bugul, Ken. *The Abandoned Baobab*. Charlottesville: University of Virginia Press, 2008.

Bundles, A'Lelia Perry. *Madam C. J. Walker*. New York: Chelsea House, 1990.

Cade, Toni. "The Pill: Genocide or Liberation?" In *The Black Woman: An Anthology*, edited by Toni Cade Bambara, 203–12. New York: Washington Square Press, 1970.

Cleaver, Eldridge. *Soul on Ice*. New York: McGraw-Hill, 1968.

Clegg III, Claude Andrew. *An Original Man: The Life and Times of Elijah Muhammad*. New York: St. Martin's Press, 1998.

Cole, J. Betsch, and B. Guy-Sheftall. *Gender Talk: The Struggle for Women's Equality in African American Communities*. New York: Ballantine Books, 2003.

Collier, Aldore. "The Nicholas Brothers: Still Kicking after 62 Years." *Ebony Magazine*, May 1991.

Cone, James H. "Martin and Malcolm on Nonviolence and Violence." *Phylon 1960* 49, nos. 3–4 (2001): 173–83.

Conyers, J. L., and A. P. Smallwood. *Malcolm X: A Historical Reader*. Durham, NC: Carolina Academic Press, 2008.

Conyers Jr., James L., and Alva Barnett, eds. *African American Sociology*. Chicago: Nelson Hall, 1999.

Bibliography

Cunningham, George E. "Derogatory Images of the Negro and Negro History." *The Negro History Bulletin* 27, no. 6 (1965): 126–42.

Curtis, E. *Islam in Black America: Identity, Liberation, and Difference in African American Islamic Thought.* Albany: SUNY Press, 2002.

Curtis IV, Edward E. *Black Muslim Religion in the Nation of Islam, 1960–1975.* Chapel Hill: The University of North Carolina Press, 2006.

Deanar, Tynnetta. "Muslim Woman Is Model Personality." *Muhammad Speaks*, January 1962.

———. "Why No Makeup? Cosmetics Produce Two People in One: Not for Our Women." *Muhammad Speaks*, January 1962.

DeFrantz, T. *Dancing Many Drums: Excavations in African American Dance.* Madison: University of Wisconsin Press, 2002.

Delgado, R., and J. Stefancic. *Critical Race Theory: An Introduction*, 2nd edition. New York: NYU Press, 2012.

Denear, Tynnetta. "Family Most Powerful Unit in Islam." *Muhammad Speaks*, May 1962.

———. "Women in Islam." *Muhammad Speaks*, February 4, 1963.

Divine, Robert, T. H. Breen, George M. Fredrickson, and R. Hal Williams. *America Past and Present*, 2nd edition. Glenview, IL: Foresman, 1987.

El Muhajir, Nefertiti. *Marvin X: A Critical Look at the Father of Muslim American Literature.* Accessed July 23, 2012. www.marvinxwrites.blogspot.com/search?q=black+muslim+writers.

Elliott, David L., and Arthur Woodward, eds. *Textbooks and Schooling in the United States.* Chicago: The University of Chicago Press, 1990.

Erickson, John. *Islam and Postcolonial Narrative.* Cambridge: Cambridge University Press, 1998.

Essien-Udom, Essien U. *Black Nationalism: The Search for an Identity in America.* Chicago: University of Chicago Press, 1962.

Evanzz, Karl. *The Messenger: The Rise and Fall of Elijah Muhammad.* New York: Pantheon Books, 1999.

Fall, Aminata Sow. *The Beggars' Strike.* New York: Longman, 1986.

———. *Le Revenant.* Dakar: Nouvelles Editions Africaines, 1976.

Fanon, Frantz. *The Wretched on Earth.* New York: Grove Press, 1967.

Farrakhan, L. *What a Friend We Have in Jesus.* VHS. Chicago: Final Call, 1996.

Fasan, Rotimi Omoyele. "Mapping Nigerian Literature." Accessed December 8, 2015. www.nobleworld.biz/images/AF_Fasan.pdf.

Floyd Jr., Samuel A. "Toward a Theory of Diaspora Aesthetics." *Lenox Avenue: A Journal of Interarts Inquiry* 4 (1998): 25–67.

Former NOI members. Group interview by author. Philadelphia, PA, January 2008.

Foucault, M. "Right of Death and Power over Life." In *The Foucault Reader*, edited by P. Rabinow, 258–72. New York: Random House, 1984.

Franklin, A. T. "Schoolin': Critical Consciousness, Black Consciousness, and the Pedagogies of Transformation." *International Journal of Learning* 17, no. 8 (2010): 493–502.

Franklin, Donna. *What's Love Got to Do with It: Understanding and Healing the Rift between Black Men and Women.* New York: Touchstone, 2000.

Franklin, John Hope, and Alfred A. Moss Jr. *From Slavery to Freedom: A History of African Americans*. Boston: McGraw-Hill, 2000.

Freire, P. *Pedagogy of the Oppressed*. New York: Continuum, 2000.

Fuller Jr., Neely. *The United Independent Compensatory Code/System/Concept*. Author, 1971.

Giannakos, Perry E. "The Black Muslims: An American Millennialistic Response to Racism and Cultural Denigrations." *The Centennial Review* 23, no. 4 (Fall 1979): 439.

Gomez, Michael. *Reversing Sail: A History of the African Diaspora*. Cambridge: Cambridge University Press, 2005.

Goodwin, Michele. *Black Markets: The Supply and Demand of Body Parts*. New York: Cambridge University Press, 2006.

Griffin, Farah Jasmine. "Ironies of the Saint: Malcolm X, Black Women, and the Price of Protection." In *Sisters in the Struggle: African American Women in the Civil Rights–Black Power Movements*, edited by Betty Collier-Thomas and V. P. Franklin. New York: NYU Press, 2001.

Guy-Sheftall, Beverly, ed. *Words of Fire: An Anthology of African American Feminist Thought*. New York: The New Press, 1995.

Hacker, Andrew. *Two Nations, Black and White, Separate, Hostile, Unequal*. New York: Scribner, 2003.

Hakim, N. *The Black Stone: The True History of Elijah Muhammad, Messenger of Allah*. Atlanta: M.E.M.P.S. Publications, 1997.

———, ed. *The Theology of Time*, 3rd eds. Atlanta: M.E.M.P.S. Publication, 1997.

Halasa, M. *Elijah Muhammad: Religious Leader*. New York: Chelsea House Publishers, 1990.

Haley, A., and A. Balk. "The Black Merchants of Hate." *Saturday Evening Post*, January 26, 1963. Accessed December 8, 2015. www.alex-haley.com/alex_haley_black_merchants_of_hate.htm.

Haley, Alex. *The Autobiography of Malcolm X, as Told to Alex Haley*. New York: Ballantine Books, 1965.

Hand, Felicity. "Untangling Stories and Healing Rifts: Abdulrazak Gurnah's *By the Sea*." *Research in African Literatures* 41 (2010): 74.

Harrow, Kenneth W., ed. *Faces of Islam in African Literature*. Portsmouth, NH: Heinemann, 1991.

———, ed. *The Marabout and the Muse: New Approaches to Islam in African Literature*. Portsmouth, NH: Heinemann, 1993.

———. "Review of *West African Literatures: Ways of Reading*, by Stephanie Newell." *African Studies Review* 50 (2007): 209–10.

Heller, Jean. "Syphilis Victims in U.S. Study Went Untreated for 40 Years." In *Tuskegee's Truth: Rethinking the Tuskegee Syphilis Study*, edited by Susan M. Reverby, 116–18. Chapel Hill: University of North Carolina Press, 2000.

Higginbotham, Evelyn Brooks. "African-American Women's History and the Metalanguage of Race." In *We Specialize in the Wholly Impossible: A Reader in Black Women's History*, edited by Darlene Clark Hine, Wilma King, and Linda Reed. Brooklyn, NY: Carlson Publishing, 1995.

Hilliard, A. "Race, Identity, Hegemony, and Education: What Do We Need to Know Now?" In *Race and Education: The Role of History and Society in Educating African American Students*, edited by W. H. Watkins, J. Lewis, and V. Chou, 7–33. Needham Heights, MA: Allyn and Bacon, 2001.

Hood Jr., Ralph W., Ronald J. Morris, Susan E. Hickman, and P. J. Watson. "Martin and Malcolm as Cultural Icons: An Empirical Study Comparing Lower Class African American and White Males." *Review of Religious Research* 36, no. 4 (1995): 382–88.

"How Well Do You Know Africa?" *Muhammad Speaks*, July 1962.

Howard, G. *We Can't Teach What We Don't Know: White Teachers in Multiracial Schools*, 2nd edition. New York: Teachers College Press, 2006.

Irons, Peter H. *Jim Crow's Children: The Broken Promise of the Brown Decision*. New York: Penguin Group, 2002.

Islam, T. *Master Fard Muhammad: Who Is He? Who He Is Not?* Atlanta: All in All, 2007.

"Islam School's Expanding Role: Announcing New Adults' Program." *Muhammad Speaks*, April 1964.

Jackson, David, and William Gains. "Nation of Islam: Power of Money." *Chicago Tribune*, March 12, 1995, 16.

Jefferson, T. "Thomas Jefferson's Thoughts on the Negro, Part 1." *Journal of Negro History* 3, no. 1 (1918): 55–89.

Jones, Rhett. "Methodology and Meaning: The Sociology of Malcolm X." In *Malcolm X: A Historical Reader*, edited by James L. Conyers Jr. and Andrew P. Smallwood. Durham, NC: Carolina Academic Press, 2008.

Jordan, Winthrop. *White over Black: American Attitudes toward the Negro, 1550–1812*. Baltimore: Penguin Books, 1969.

Joseph, P. E. "Still Reinventing Malcolm." *Chronicle of Higher Education* 57, no. 35 (2011): B6–B9.

JX, Brother Charles. "Found Solutions to All My Problems Lay with Islam." *Muhammad Speaks*, August 29, 1969.

JX (Walker), Melva. "Muslim Sister Finds Real Meaning of Black Beauty," *Muhammad Speaks*, July 16, 1971, 18.

JX, Sandra. "Black Women Find Peace, Freedom in Folds in Islam." *Muhammad Speaks*.

Kahf, Mohja. Preface for "Marvin X: A Critical Look at the Father of Muslim American Literature." Unpublished manuscript. Accessed April 23, 2015. www.marvinxwrites.blogspot.com/2007/05/marvin-x-critical-look-at-father-of.html.

———. "Teaching Diaspora Literature: Muslim American Literature as an Emerging Field." *Journal of Pan African Studies* 4, no. 2 (December 2010): 163–67.

Kane, Amadou Hampata. *Ambiguous Adventure*. Brooklyn: Melville House, 2012.

Karriem, Anna. "The Preacher of Pan-Africanism." *Muhammad Speaks*, April 16, 1971.

Kearney, Jack. "Representations of Islamic Belief and Practice in a South African Context: Reflections on the Fictional Work of Ahmed Essop, Aziz Hassim, Achmat Dangor, and Rayda Jacobs." *Journal of Literary Studies* 22 (2006): 138–57.

Kelley, Robin D. G., and Earl Lewis, eds. *To Make Our World Anew*. New York: Oxford University Press, 2000.

Kelly, Robert, and Erin Cook. "Martin Luther King, Jr., and Malcolm X: A Common Solution." *OAH Magazine of History* 19, no. 1 (2005): 37–40.

Kincheloe, J., and S. Steinberg. *Changing Multiculturalism*. Buckingham, PA: Open University Press, 1997.

King Jr., Martin Luther. *The Autobiography of Martin Luther King, Jr.* New York: Warner Books, 1998.

———. *I Have a Dream*. Speech, 1963. Accessed December 8, 2015. www.archives. gov/press/exhibits/dream-speech.pdf.

———. "Letter from Birmingham Jail." 1963. Accessed December 8, 2015. www. africa.upenn.edu/Articles_Gen/Letter_Birmingham.html.

Klinck, Sabine. "Asserting the Self: The Importance of Religion for Migrant Women." Accessed August 8, 2012. www.inter-disciplinary.net/wp-content/up-loads/2012/02/klinckipaper.pdf.

Kourouma, Ahmadou. *Allah Is Not Obliged*. New York: Anchor Books, 2007.

Ladner, Joyce A. *Tomorrow's Tomorrow: The Black Woman*. Garden City, NY: Doubleday & Company, 1971.

Larson, Charles R. "Halal Novelist—Western and Islamic Civilizations Dialogue in Sudanese Writer Leila Aboulela's Fiction." *World and I* (2002): 250.

Laye, Camara. *The Dark Child: The Autobiography of an African Child*. New York: Farrar, Straus, & Giroux, 1994.

Leaks, Sylvester. "The Natural Look Is Reborn in Brilliant New Show Beauty of Negro Womanhood Theme of Naturally '63' Hair Fashion Revue." *Muhammad Speaks*, February 1963.

Lee, Martha. *The Nation of Islam: An American Millenarian Movement*. Syracuse, NY: Syracuse University Press, 1996.

Lee, S., and H. L. Gates. "Generation X." *Transition* 56 (1992): 176–90.

Levine, Lawrence. *Black Culture and Black Consciousness*. New York: Oxford University Press, 1977.

Levtzion, Nehemia, and Randall L. Pouwels, eds. *The History of Islam in Africa*. Athens: Ohio University Press, 2000.

Lichtenstein, A. "Elijah Muhammad and the Nation of Islam." *Footsteps* 8, no. 2 (2006): 11.

Lincoln, C. Eric. *The Black Muslims in America*. Boston: Beacon Press, 1961.

Lincoln, E. *Black Muslims in the United States*. Ph.D. dissertation, Boston University, 1960.

Livingston, Samuel T. "NOI: Divided We Stand." *International Journal of Africana Studies* 5 (December 1999): 50–51.

Lum, L. "Working Outside the System." *Diverse: Issues in Higher Education* 22, no. 26 (2006): 26–27.

Mahjoub, Jamal. *Navigation of a Rainmaker: An Apocalyptic Vision of War-Torn Africa*. New York: Oxford University Press, 1989.

Marable, Manning. *Malcolm X: A Life of Re-invention*. New York: Penguin, 2011.

Marfo, Florence. "African Muslims in African American Literature." *Callaloo* 32 (2009): 1213–22.

Marsh, Charles. *Gods Long Summer: Stories of Faith and Civil Rights*. Princeton, NJ: Princeton University Press, 1977.

Marsh, Clifton E. *From Black Muslims to Muslims: The Resurrection, Transformation, and Change of the Lost–Found Nation of Islam in America, 1930–1995*. Lanham, MD: Scarecrow Press, 1996.

———. *From Black Muslims to Muslims: The Transition from Separatism to Islam, 1930–1980*. Metuchen, NJ: Scarecrow Press, 1984.

Marshall, T. H. *Citizenship and Social Class*. Cambridge: Cambridge University Press, 1950.

Martin, Tony. *Race First: The Ideological and Organizational Struggles of Marcus Garvey and the Universal Negro Improvement Association*. Dover, MA: The Majority Press, 1976.

Maurad, Sister Beverly. "Sister Beverley Addresses All Islam Grads." *Muhammad Speaks*, March 19, 1971.

Mauwakkil, Salem. "Nation of Islam and Me." In *The Farrakhan Factor: African American Writers on Leadership, Nationhood, and Minister Louis Farrakhan*, edited by Amy Alexander, 296. New York: Grove Press, 1998.

Mazrui, Al' Amin. "Islam and Identity in the African Imagination." *Literary Griot: International Journal of Black Expressive Cultural Studies* 5 (1993): 58–64.

Mazrui, Ali A. *Euro-Jews and Afro-Arabs: The Great Semitic Divergence in World History*. Lanham, MD: University Press of America, 2008.

McCloud, Aminah Beverly. *African American Islam*. New York: Routledge, 1995.

McLaren, P. *Life in Schools: An Introduction to Critical Pedagogy in the Foundations of Education*, 6th edition. Boulder, CO: Paradigm, 2015.

McQuirter, Marya. "Awkward Moves: Dance Lessons from the 1940s." In *Dancing Many Drums: Excavations in African American Dance*, edited by Thomas DeFrantz. Madison: University of Wisconsin Press, 2002.

Meier, August, John Bracey Jr., and Elliott Rudwick, eds. *Black Protest in the Sixties: Essays from the* New York Times Magazine. New York: Markus Wierner Publications, 1991.

Mohammed, W. D. *Al-Islam Unity and Leadership*. Chicago: The Sense Maker, 1991.

Molnar, J. J., J. E. Dunkelberger, and D. A. Salter. "Agricultural Education in the South: A Comparison of Student Characteristics at Land Grant Institutions." *The Journal of Negro Education* 50, no. 1 (1981): 26–40.

Moore, Audrey. Interview, June 6 and 8, 1978. In *Black Women Oral History Project*, edited by Ruth Edmonds Hill and Arthur and Elizabeth Schlesinger Library on the History of Women in America. Cambridge, MA: Radcliffe College, 1989.

Morgan, J. "African Americans and Agriculture." *Black Issues in Higher Education* 17, no. 8 (2000): 20.

Morris, J. E. "Malcolm X's Critique of the Education of Black People." *Western Journal of Black Studies* 25, no. 2 (2001): 126–35.

Morrison, Toni. *Playing in the Dark: Whiteness and the Literary Imagination*. Cambridge: Harvard University Press, 1992.

Moses, Wilson Jeremiah. "From Booker T. to Malcolm X: Black Political Thought, 1895–1965." In *Upon These Shores: Themes in the African American Experience*

1600–Present, edited by William R. Scott and William G. Shade. New York: Routledge, 2000.

Moss, Edwin. "Wallace Muhammad Says Women Not Forbidden to Make Up." Mr. *Muhammad Speaks*, September 1960.

Muhammad University of Islam Yearbook, 1968.

Muhammad, Amir Nashid Ali. *Muslims in America: Seven Centuries of History, 1312–1998*. Beltsville, MD: Amana Publications, 1998.

Muhammad, Askia. *Black Muslim Millennium: A Brief History of the Nation of Islam*. Drewryville, VA: Kha Books, 2002.

———. "*Muhammad Speaks*: A Trailblazer in the Newspaper Industry." *Final Call*, March 10, 2000.

Muhammad, Christine. *Muhammad's Children: A First Grade Reader*. Chicago: University of Islam Press, 1963.

———. "We Need Our Textbooks." *Muhammad Speaks*, April 1962.

Muhammad, D. "Scholar C. Eric Lincoln Dies at 75." *Final Call,* May 30, 2000.

Muhammad, Elijah. "Beards." *Muhammad Speaks*, July, 4, 1965.

———. *How to Eat to Live, Book 1.* Phoenix, AZ: M.E.M.P.S., 1967.

———. *An Interview with Elijah Muhammad*. Sound recording. Los Angeles: Pacifica Tape Library, 1967.

———. *Message to the Blackman in America*. Chicago: Muhammad Mosque of Islam, 1965.

———. "Mr. Muhammad Calls for Unified Front of Black Men at New York City Rally." *Pittsburg Courier*, July 19, 1958, 6.

———. *The Supreme Wisdom*, volume 1. Atlanta: M.E.M.P.S., 1957.

———. Videotape from the biography series African American Achievers.

———. "Warning to the M.G.T. and G.C.C. class." *Muhammad Speaks*.

Muhammad, Harriett. "Children Now, Black Self-Determination Committee Brings African History to L.A. Schools." *Muhammad Speaks*, May 1965.

———. "Men of Africa Pledge Aid in Negro's Fight for Freedom." *Muhammad Speaks*, April 24, 1964.

———. "Tanganyika Talks of Fossil Fuels." *Muhammad Speaks*, May 8, 1964.

Muhammad, J. *This Is the One: The Most Honored Elijah Muhammad, We Need Not Look for Another*, 3rd edition. Phoenix, AZ: Book Company, 1996.

Muhammad, Minister Tynnetta. "A Brief History on the Origin of the Nation of Islam in America: A Nation of Peace and Beauty." *Nation of Islam*. Accessed December 8, 2015. www.noi.org/noi-history.

———. *The Million Man March: Women in Support of the Million Man March*. Chicago: Final Call, 1995.

———. "The Cultural Revolution Begins: In Search of the Messiah." *Final Call,* June 14, 2011.

Muhammad, Rachelle. *Black Muslim Movement after the Death of Elijah Muhammad*. Ann Arbor, MI: University Microfilms International, 1980.

Muhammad's Mosque of Islam. "The *Muhammad Speaks* Newspaper." In *M.G.T. & G.C.C.: Your Orientation Brochure*.

"Muslim Writers–Birmingham City Council." Accessed April 23, 2015. www.birmingham.gov.uk/cs/Satellite?c=Page&childpagename=Lib_Children_Accessibili

ty%2FCFPageLayout&cid=1223092732170&packedargs=website%3D4&pagena
me=BCC%2FCommon%2FWrapper%2FCFWrapper&rendermode=live.

"Nasser's Advocacy of More Freedom for Egypt Women Opposes Old Time." *Muhammad Speaks*, September 15, 1962.

"Nation Mourns Muslim Leader." *Jet Magazine*, March 13, 1975, 14–15.

Nation of Islam. *Accomplishments of the Muslims*. 1975.

"Nation of Islam Mourns Elijah Muhammad." *Ebony Magazine*, March 1975, 79.

Nelson, Jennifer. *Women of Color and the Reproductive Rights Movement*. New York: NYU Press, 2003.

Newton, Huey. *Revolutionary Suicide.* New York: Harcourt Brace Jovanovich, 1973.

Niane, Djibril Tamsir. *Sundiata: An Epic of Old Mali*. New York: Longman, 1983.

Nieto, S., and P. Bode. *Affirming Diversity: The Socio-Political Context of Multicultural Education*, 6th edition. New York: Longman, 2012.

Noel, J. *Notable Selections in Multicultural Education*, 2nd edition. New York: McGraw-Hill, 2008.

"Northern Leaders Verify Mississippi Genocide against Blacks." *Muhammad Speaks*, July 21, 1967.

Ntonfo, André. "Comparative Literature at the University of Yaoundé." *Yearbook of Comparative and General Literature* 43 (1995): 134.

Nuruddin, Yusuf. "Ancient Black Astronauts and Extraterrestrial Jihads: Islamic Science Fiction as Urban Mythology." *Socialism and Democracy* 20, no. 3 (2006): 127–65.

Nyang, Sulayman. "A New Beginning for the Black Muslims." *Arabia* (1985): 50–51.

Ogbar, Jeffrey Ogbonna Green. *Black Power: Radical Politics and African American Identity* (Reconfiguring American Political History). Baltimore: John Hopkins University Press, 2005.

Onwuachi, P. Chike. *Black Ideology in African Diaspora*. Chicago: Third World Press, 1973.

Oulougem, Yambo. *Le Devoir de Violence/Bound to Violence*. Portsmouth, NH: Heinemann, 1983.

"Pan Africanism." In *The Oxford Companion to African American Literature*, edited by William L. Andrews, Frances Smith Foster, and Trudier Harris, 558–59. New York: Oxford University Press, 1997.

Parks, Gordon. "The Violent End of the Man Called Malcolm X." *Life* 58, no. 9 (March 5, 1965).

"Pawns in a Pattern That Points toward Genocide." *Muhammad Speaks*, September 30, 1962.

Perry, Bruce, ed. *Malcolm X: The Last Speeches*. New York: Pathfinder Press, 1989.

Perry, T. *Teaching Malcolm X*. New York: Routledge, 1996.

Pierce, Paulette. "Boudoir Politics and the Birthing of the Nation." In *Women Out of Place: The Gender of Agency and the Race of Nationality*, edited by Brackette F. Williams. New York: Roulade, 1966.

Pipes, Daniel. "How Elijah Muhammad Won." *Middle East Forum*, June 2000. Accessed December 8, 2015. www.danielpipes.org/341/how-elijah-muhammad-won.

Pitre, Abul. *The Educational Philosophy of Elijah Muhammad: Education for a New World*, 2nd edition. Lanham, MD: University Press of America, 2008.

———. *An Introduction to Elijah Muhammad Studies: The New Educational Paradigm.* Lanham, MD: University Press of America, 2009.

Poussaint, Alvin F. "A Negro Psychiatrist Explains the Negro Psyche." *New York Times Magazine*, August 20, 1967.

Pride, Armstead Scott. "The Names of Negro Newspapers." *American Speech* 29, no. 2 (May 1954): 118. Accessed April 3, 2009. www.jstor.org/stable/453331.

Pride, Armstead S., and Clint C. Wilson II. *A History of the Black Press.* Washington, DC: Howard University Press, 1997.

Rashad, Adib. *Elijah Muhammad and the Ideological Foundation of the Nation of Islam.* Hampton, VA: U.B. and U.S. Communications Systems, June 1994.

———. *The History of Islam and Black Nationalism in the Americas.* Beltsville, MD: Writers' Incorporated, 1991.

Rassoull, A., ed. *The Theology of Time.* Charlotte, NC: Conquering Books, 1992.

Reid-Pharr, Robert. "Speaking through Anti-Semitism: The Nation of Islam and the Poetics of Black (Counter) Modernity." *Social Text* 14, no. 4 (Winter 1996): 140.

Reverby, Susan M., ed. *Tuskegee's Truth: Rethinking the Tuskeegee Syphilis Study.* Chapel Hill: University of North Carolina Press, 2000.

Roberts, Gene. "The Story of Snick: From Freedom High to Black Power." *New York Times Magazine*, September 25, 1966.

Rodgers-Rose, La Frances, ed. *The Black Woman.* Beverly Hill, CAs: Sage, 1980.

Ross, C. "Your Personal Finance: The Economic Philosophy of Malcolm X." *The Tennessee Tribune*, February 22, 1966, 13.

Saad, Elias N. *Social History of Timbuktu: Role of Moslem Scholars and Notables, 1400–1900.* Cambridge: Cambridge University Press, 1983.

Schiff, Martin. "Community Control of Inner-City Schools and Educational Achievement." *Urban Education* 11, no. 4 (1976): 415–28.

Schomburg Center for Research in Black Life and Culture, New York Public Library. *African American Desk Reference.* New York: Wiley, 1999.

Scott, William R., and William G. Shade, eds. *Upon These Shores: Themes in the African American Experience 1600–Present.* New York: Routledge, 2000.

Sembene, Ousmane. *Xala.* Chicago: Lawrence Hill, 1976.

Shor, I., and P. Freire. *A Pedagogy for Liberation: Dialogues on Transforming Education.* Westport, CT: Bergin and Garvey, 1987.

Shujaa, M. J., ed. *Too Much Schooling, Too Little Education: A Paradox of Black Life in White Societies.* Trenton, NJ: Africa World Press, 1994.

Simmons, Charles A. *The African American Press, with Special References to Four Special Newspapers, 1827–1965.* Jefferson, NC: McFarland & Company, 1998.

Sister Christine. "Education of Relief Clients: Why Is Chicago Afraid?" *Muhammad Speaks*, May 1962.

———. "Self Help or Oblivion for the Negro." *Muhammad Speaks*, February 1962.

———. "We Need Our Textbooks." *Muhammad Speaks*, April 1962.

Sister Claretha. "Graduation Address, Whoever Controls School, Controls Future." *Muhammad Speaks*, April 1962.

Sister Dela. Interview by author. Atlanta, GA, March 2008.

Sister Evelyn. "Modest Muslim Dress Dignifies Black Women."

Sister Wilma Ann. "What Have You Taught Your Child Today?" *Muhammad Speaks*, 1962.

Smallwood, A. P. "The Intellectual Creativity and Public Discourse of Malcolm X: A Precursor to the Modern Black Studies Movement." *Journal of Black Studies* 36, no. 2 (2005): 248–63.

Smethurst, James. "Malcolm X and the Black Arts Movement." In *The Cambridge Companion to Malcolm X*, edited by Robert Terrill. Cambridge: Cambridge University Press, 2010.

Smith, Barbara. "Some Home Truths on the Contemporary Black Feminist Movement." In *Words of Fire: An Anthology of African American Feminist Thought*, edited by Beverly Guy-Sheftall. New York: The New Press, 1995.

Sokolowski, Robert. *Introduction to Phenomenology*. New York: Cambridge University Press, 2000.

Spivey, D. *Schooling for the New Slavery: Black Industrial Education 1868–1915*. Trenton, NJ: Africa World Press, 2006.

Staples, Robert. *Introduction to Black Sociology*. New York: Oxford University Press, 1988.

Streitmatter, Rodger. *Raising Her Voice: African-American Women Journalists Who Changed History*. Lexington: University Press of Kentucky, 1994.

Sugrue, Thomas J. *The Origins of the Urban Crisis: Race and Inequality in Postwar Detroit*. Princeton, NJ: Princeton University Press, 1996.

Swan, Quinto. *Black Power in Bermuda: The Struggle for Decolonization*. New York: Palgrave Macmillan, 2009.

Tahir, Ibrahim. *The Last Imam*. London: Kegan Paul International, 1985.

Tate, Sonsyrea. *Little X: Growing Up in the Nation of Islam*. Knoxville: Tennessee University Press, 2005.

Taylor, Ula Y., J. Tarika Lewis, and Marion Van Peebles, *Panther: A Pictorial History of the Black Panther Party and the Story Behind the Film*. New York: New Market Press, 1955.

Taylor, Ula Yvette. "As-Salaam Alaikum, My Sister, Peace Be Unto You: The Honorable Elijah Muhammad and the Women Who Followed Him." *Race & Society* 1, no. 2 (1998): 177–96.

Temple, Christel N. *Literary Spaces: Introduction to Comparative Black Literature*. Durham, NC: Carolina Academic Press, 2007.

Terrill, R. *The Cambridge Companion to Malcolm X*. Cambridge: Cambridge University Press, 2010.

Thiele, Leslie Paul. *Thinking Politics: Perspectives in Ancient, Modern, and Postmodern Political Theory*. New York: Seven Bridges Press, 2003.

Tsoukalas, Steven. *The Nation of Islam: Understanding the Black Muslims*. Phillipsburg, NJ: P & R Publishing, 2001.

Turner, Richard Brent. "The Ahmadiyya Mission to Blacks in the United States in the 1920s." *The Journal of Religious Thought* 44, no. 2 (Winter–Spring 1988): 59–60.

———. "Islam and Black Nationalism." In *Microsoft Encarta Africana 2000*, edited by Henry Louis Gates and Anthony Appiah. Redmond, WA: Microsoft, 1999.

———. *Islam in the African American Experience*. Bloomington: Indiana University Press, 1997.

———. *Islam in the African-American Experience*, 2nd edition. Bloomington: Indiana University Press, 2003.

Ukpokodu, I. P. "African American Males in Dance, Music, Theater, and Film." *Annals of the American Academy of Political and Social Science* 569 (The African American Male in American Life and Thought) (2000): 71–85.

"University of Islam Graduates Tomorrow Leaders." *Muhammad Speaks*, April 1962.

Van Debug, William L. *New Day in Babylon: The Black Power Movement and American Culture, 1965–1975.* Chicago: The University of Chicago Press, 1992.

Vorenberg, M. "Abraham Lincoln and the Politics of Black Colonization." *Journal of the Abraham Lincoln Association* 14, no. 2 (1993): 22–45. Accessed December 8, 2015. www.jstor.org/stable/20148897.

Waldschmidt-Nelson, Britta. *Dreams and Nightmares: Martin Luther King, Jr., Malcolm X, and the Struggle for Black Equality in America.* Gainesville: University Press of Florida, 2012.

Walker, Louis. "Packaging." *Muhammad Speaks*, October 1962.

Walters, Ronald W. *Pan Africanism in the African Diaspora: An Analysis of Modern Afrocentric Political Movements.* Detroit: Wayne State University Press, 1993.

Warner-Vieyra, Myriam. *Juletane*. Paris: Presence Africaine, 1982.

Watkins, W. "Black Curriculum Orientations: A Preliminary Inquiry." *Harvard Educational Review* 63, no. 3 (1993): 321–38.

———. *The White Architects of Black Education: Ideology and Power in America 1865–1954.* New York: Teachers College Press, 2001.

Watkins, W., J. Lewis, and V. Chou. *Race and Education: The Roles of History and Society in Educating African American Students.* Boston: Allyn and Bacon, 2001.

"We Charge Genocide." *Muhammad Speaks*, June 1962.

Weisbord, Robert G. "Birth Control and the Black American: A Matter of Genocide." *Demography* 10, no. 4 (1973): 571–90.

Welsing, Frances Cress. *The Isis Papers: The Keys to the Colors.* Chicago: Third World Press, 1999.

Wesley, Charles H. "The Concept of Negro Inferiority in American Thought." *Journal of Negro History* 25 (1940): 540–41.

West, Cynthia S'thembile. "Nation Builders: Female Activism in the Nation of Islam, 1960–1970." Ph.D. dissertation, Temple University, 1994.

———. "Revisiting Female Activism in the 1960s: The Newark Branch Nation of Islam." *The Black Scholar* 26, nos. 3–4 (Fall–Winter 1996): 41–48.

———. *Veiled Thoughts.* Unpublished manuscript.

Whitford, D. "A Calvinist Heritage to the 'Curse of Ham': Assessing the Accuracy of a Claim about Racial Subordination." *Church History and Religious Culture* 90, no. 1 (2010): 25–45. doi:10.1163/187124110X506509.

Wicker, Tom. *Tragic Failure: Racial Integration in America.* New York: William Morrow, 1996.

Wideman, John Edgar. "Malcolm X: The Art of Autobiography." In *Malcolm X: In Our Image*, edited by Joe Wood. New York: Grove Press, 1964.

Wilson, A. *Blueprint for Black Power: A Moral, Political, and Economic Imperative for the Twenty-First Century.* New York: Afrikan World Infosystems, 1998.

Winters, Clyde-Ahmad. "Afro-American Muslims—From Slavery to Freedom." *Islamic Studies* 17, no. 4 (Winter 1978): 187–203.

"Women of Africa in America." *Muhammad Speaks*, March 27, 1964.

"Women of Africa in U.S.—Part II." *Muhammad Speaks*, April 10, 1964.

Woodson, C. G. *The Mis-education of the Negro*, 11th edition. Trenton, NJ: First Africa World Press, 1999.

Woodward, Van. *The Strange Career of Jim Crow*, 3rd edition. New York: Oxford University Press, 1974.

X, Brother Herbert. "Explains How Messenger Laid Out Plan for Economic Freemdom Slave Land." *Muhammad Speaks*, April 21, 1967.

X, Joan. Interview by Ula Taylor. October 21, 1999, Oakland, CA.

X, Malcolm. *The Autobiography of Malcolm X*. New York: Ballantine Books, 1992.

———. *February 1965: The Final Speeches*. Edited by Steve Clark. New York: Pathfinder, 1992.

———. "Message to the Grassroots." *BlackPast.org*, 1963. Accessed December 8, 2015. www.blackpast.org/1963-malcolm-x-message-grassroots.

X, Marguerite. "What Islam Has Done for Me." *Muhammad Speaks*, August, 2 1968.

X, Marvin. "The Best of Dr. Marvin." Blog. Accessed July 23, 2012. www.marvinxwrites.blogspot.com.

X, Sister Charles Ann. "Says Islam Lifts up the Black Woman, Giving Her Wisdom Knowledge, Strength." *Muhammad Speaks*.

X, Sister Christine Delois. "Dope, Alcohol and Devil's Tricks Strip Blacks of Human Dignity." *Muhammad Speaks*, January 29, 1971.

X, Sister Mabel. "Greatest Gift She Has Ever Known." *Muhammad Speaks.*

X, Sister Marguerite. "Has Found Path to True Liberation, Righteousness in the Nation of Islam." *Muhammad Speaks*, August 29, 1969, 17.

X, Sister Mary McCalm. "Through Islam Confidence Replaces Her Uncertainty." *Muhammad Speaks*, July 1964.

X, Velma. "Education or Indoctrination." *Muhammad Speaks*, July 1962.

X. Dixon, Brother Preston. "Says Black Students Union Is Ersatz; the Nation of Islam Is the Real Thing." *Muhammad Speaks*, July 25, 1969, 17.

X. McCalm, Sister Mary.

X. Walker, Melba H. "Muslim Sister Finds Real Meaning of Black Beauty."

Yakubu, Balaraba Ramat. *I Love Him All the Same*. Kano, Nigeria: Privately published, 2001.

———. *Who Will Marry an Ignoramus?* Zaria, Nigeria: Gaskia Corporation, 1990.

Yancy, G. "A Foucauldian, Genealogical Reading of Whiteness: The Production of the Black Body/Self and the Racial Deformation of Pecola Breedlove in Tony Morrison's *The Bluest Eye*." In *What White Looks Like: African American Philosophers on the Whiteness Question*, edited by G. Yancy, 107–42. New York: Routledge, 2004.

Index

About the Contributors

Jinaki Muslimah Abdullah, is a writing instructor at Winston-Salem State University. She received her undergraduate degree from the University of North Carolina Pembroke and her master of education from North Carolina A&T State University. For thirty-four years she has been a practicing Muslim under the leadership of Imam W. D. Mohammed.

Charles E. Allen, Jr. is an administrator in a Houston Area School District. He is also a doctoral candidate at University of Houston.

Toya Conston, Ph.D., is a visiting assistant professor in the Department of Psychological, Health, and Learning Sciences at the University of Houston College of Education. Her most recent publication entitled "Perspectives and Experiences of Financial Aid Counselors on Community College Students Who Borrow," where she is the coauthor along with Lyle McKinney and Pamelyn Shefman, is featured in the 2013 *Journal of Student Financial Aid*.

James L. Conyers Jr., Ph.D., is the director of the African American Studies Program, director of the Center for the Study of African American Culture, and University Professor of African American Studies at the University of Houston. His most recent published work is an edited volume titled, *The Black Family and Society*, published in 2015 by Transaction Publishers.

Malachi D. Crawford, Ph.D., is the assistant director of the African American Studies Program and adjunct instructor at the University of Houston. His most recent publication is, *Black Muslims and the Law*, published in 2015 by Rowman & Littlefield.

Rebecca Hankins is an associate professor at Texas A&M University. Her book chapter was featured in the two-volume series *Muslims and American Popular Culture* edited by Kennesaw State University profsessors Iraj Omidvar and Anne R. Richards, entitled *The Influence of Muslims and Islam in Science Fiction, Fantasy, and Comics.* Professor Hankins is an MLIS, Certified Archivist.

Kelly O. Jacobs is an associate professor of political science at Lone Star College. She is a graduate of the African American Studies Graduate Certificate program at the University of Houston. Professor Jacobs is currently doctoral candidate in Educational Leadership at Sam Houston State University.

Bayyinah S. Jeffries, Ph.D., is an assistant professor in the Department of African American Studies at Ohio University. Her most recent publication, published in 2014, is entitled *A Nation Can Rise No Higher Than Its Women: African-American Muslim Women in the Struggle for Black Self-Determination.*

Emilie Koenig is a teaching fellow at the University of Houston, where she is also a Ph.D. candidate in English with a concentration in Rhetoric, Composition, and Pedagogy. Her most recent publication is a forthcoming book chapter entitled "'A Soldier Till the War Is Won': Black (DeHUMANizing) Iconography As Critiqued in The Boondocks."

Abul Pitre, Ph.D., is professor and department head of Educational Leadership and Counseling at Prairie View A&M University, where he teaches Multicultural Education for Educational Leaders, and Leadership. He is the author and editor of several scholarly books and articles.

Ula Taylor, Ph.D., is an associate professor of African American Studies at the University of California at Berkeley. She is the author of several books and scholarly articles in the field of African American history and culture.

Christel N. Temple is an associate professor of Africana Studies at the University of Pittsburgh. She is also the author of *Literary Pan-Africanism: History, Contexts, and Criticism* (2005), *Literary Spaces: Introduction to Comparative Black Literature* (2007), and a forthcoming book, *Black Cultural Mythology.* Her research and essays on global Afrocentric cultural theory and practice appear in *Journal of Black Studies*, *Western Journal of Black Studies*, *International Journal of Black Studies*, *Journal of Pan African Studies*, and *Africalogical Perspectives* as well as in a host of edited collections. Professor

Temple earned a Ph. D. from Temple University's African American Studies Department.

C. S'thembile West is Professor Emerita at Western Illinois University. Her *Journal of Dance Education* article, "Black Bodies in Dance Education: Charting a New Pedagogical Paradigm to Eliminate Gendered and Hypersexualized Assumptions" [2004; 5(2): 64-69], has been reprinted in the book *Sexuality, Gender and Identity: Critical Issues in Dance Education* (Routledge, 2015). Professor West holds a Ph.D. from Temple University and an M.A. and B.S. from Columbia University in New York City.

HIT THE DECK!
Memoirs of an Apprentice Boy

To Jim, wishing you smooth Sailing

By
Capt. Gaither Stevens

Presented and edited by Terrie Biggs

Blue Mountain Publishing
1105 N Avenue
La Grande, OR 97850

ISBN 10: 1982079886
ISBN 13: 978-1982079888
First Printing: February 8, 2018
Updated April 11, 2018, June 10, 2018, & March 8, 2020

Cover design by my talented son Daniel Biggs, Jr.

TABLE OF CONTENTS

i

DEDICATION

To my family, and especially to my grandson Johnny who has made a career out of the Navy, and to the men and women of the United States Navy who honorably serve our country.

Senior Chief Petty Officer Johnny Luzitano

And, finally, to my little sailorman brother Richard Lee "Dickie" Bennett, who died of leukemia during WWII at age four.

SPECIAL THANKS

To my two cousins, Nan Bullough and Wendy Sarrett who trusted me with our grandfather's precious, original, typed manuscript which they kept safe for many years. They allowed me to re-type, to edit it as needed, and to publish this most wonderful memoir.

To Retired Captain Nick Richards and his wife Retired Commander Christy Wheeler. Thank you for your encouragement.

Finally, to my son Daniel who created this glorious book cover along with four other book covers for my books to date.

INTRODUCTION

How many times have you said to yourself or heard from a friend or family member, "I wish I had recorded my (*fill the blank with*) grandfather/grandmother, aunt/uncle, friend or any relative's story? Many people have said the same thing to me when I told them about this book. That is why I feel so fortunate that my grandfather wrote his manuscript about a time in his life that defined his character, even though I was not privileged to listen to his stories while he was living.

I   vaguely remember my maternal grandfather, Gaither "Steve" Stevens. I recall seeing him when I was about six because I have a photo with him and my front teeth were missing. A family photo album of his early life was given to his step-son, Tom, and lost track of.

Cropped family photo: Terrie's mom Myra,
Grandfather Gaither Stevens, Terrie, Aunt Frances, Uncle Hod
(Horace) and cousin Wendy (Sarrett)

He became blind at some point from glaucoma which may have been later than this photograph. I recalled he was kind and sweet. Grandpa Stevens and my Uncle Gene and his family stayed in the Pacific Northwest whereas my father was in the Air Force and we traveled, so I did not grow up around aunts, uncles, cousins, grandparents, etc.

My cousin Nan and her sister Wendy protected his unpublished manuscript until 2017 when they handed it to me to publish. My cousins provided me with genealogical records of the Stevens (researched before the internet) going back to 1605. Therefore, when I joined Ancestry.com I was able to find more family names and records.

I edited my grandfather's manuscript leaving out sentences that repeated, some phrases, added descriptions of nautical terms and expressions in the book without changing his intent. I broke up his sections into chapters. Photos of Navy ships I found on-line at www.history.navy.mil which offered downloads of photos of ships in alphabetical order and gave in-service dates for most of the vessels. Since my grandfather gave no time-lines I researched dates of events he mentioned. More nautical terms, brief family history, and names of sails are in References.

He referred to "in those days" and he described how things had changed when he wrote his memoirs. Of course, there would have been giant changes in the Navy and places he visited from the time he re-enlisted and wrote his memoirs as a Captain, many years ago. I found a service record (Headstone Request) which showed the following:

Enlisted USN (Apprentice Boys) December 16, 1899
Discharged August 1, 1905
Enlisted USNRF (Navy Reserves) July 22, 1918;
discharged August 18, 1919, as Lieutenant

So far, I find no record of him re-enlisting in the regular Navy after the Apprentice Boy Program. There are records of passenger lists of ships he boarded as Lt. JG in the Naval Reserves in 1919. My cousin Nan knew he joined the Merchant Marines and was commissioned as the rank of Captain. I am still researching military records and will update when possible.

What incredible adventures he had! What great stories of places and people! I didn't read ahead as I typed into my word processor and every turn of the page I was captivated by his stories and looked forward to how his situations unfolded. To me, he wrote his memoirs from the innocence and naivety of a young man as though he was experiencing the world for the first time.

Note regarding ships: the ships referenced in this book amount most Navy ships, were commissioned and recommissioned several times, some even changing names.

FORWARD

Between the years of 1900 and 1915, very little was recorded about the United States Navy. First of all, many national events over-shadowed the part the U.S. Navy played in the history of these years. Secondly, the Navy, as a career, was not an attractive one and was often castigated for many reasons. This Navy—which had to fight and win two wars if our country was to continue to exist—was formed during the lifetime of officers trained under the apprentice-boy system. It was the training and austere life of the apprentice boys which laid the foundation for this great Navy.

The daily life aboard the old training ships--such as the USS *Adams*, which was propelled by both sail and steam— changed drastically by the end of the transition period between the old Civil War Navy and what is now known as our modern Navy. The men who served as youngsters during this period observed gigantic changes in ship propulsion, armament, etc. They saw ships propelled first by sail and steam, then diesel, and finally nuclear power. These men had to be made of stern stuff if they were to survive these confusing changes and technical improvements.

The many amusing incidents and often strange life of the apprentice boy in the U.S. Navy during this period offer a rare insight into the proud heritage of our country

This story endeavors to present the activities which molded many of the Naval leaders of today. This life was a combination of hard tasks and a healthy existence. It often had

its comical side. Many mothers of today would shudder to think of their children experiencing the life which is set forth in the following pages. These stories will give the reader pictorial knowledge of our Navy during those years.

By Captain Gaither "Steve" Stevens
{date unknown when he finished his manuscript}

Commissioned 1861 to 1911

LIFE ABOARD THE *PENSACOLA*

Reporting for Duty

We were living in San Francisco at the start of the Spanish-American War and every day we saw soldiers marching in the streets and sailors everywhere we turned. The port was full of ships--merchant and Navy. I used to go down to the waterfront every chance I got, and oh, the thrill to see those boys in blue going aboard their ships and off to far-away places to fight those Spaniards! If only I could go along! The bands would play. The boys would march. And my heart pounded harder than ever! Finally, I had a birthday on August 2 and was fifteen in 1899.

At that time, the American Navy had the apprentice system. In other words, a boy, if he could pass the physical and mental tests, could go in the Navy at the age of fifteen. I begged my father to go with me to enlist, but he was reluctant to give permission which would expose me to the rigors of naval life and war at such an early age. I talked, and I pleaded and finally wore him down, and he went to Goat Island with me and signed the necessary papers. (Yerba Buena Island was always referred to as "Goat Island" in those days).

What a thrill! What excitement! I was sworn in immediately after passing the examinations and I was in the Navy. I was an apprentice boy!

While the doctors were giving me the examination, father walked from the *Pensacola* which would become my training ship, onto the dock where a bunch of the boys were boxing in a ring they had rigged there. Two evenly-matched boys were putting on a fine show and Dad was thoroughly interested. After the bout ended father went up and talked to the boys and he questioned them about their weight and experience. He told

them that he belonged to the Olympic Club in San Francisco where Jim Corbett first learned to box and later became a boxing instructor during his hours away from the bank where he worked, and finally up the ladder of success to the World's Championship. Of course, the boys were all interested in everything he said about Corbett and were somewhat awed to meet a man who had boxed with him and knew him. Father had a good time for himself in the limelight of the admiration of these boys.

When I was through my examination and came out to join him, telling him that I had just scrooched through on the weight and height requirements, he was still talking to some of these boys. He introduced me to them with a great deal of paternal pride, and this did me more good than anything he could have done for me as they all seemed to make it their business to see that nobody knocked me around because I was just a little fellow.

I had a difficult time getting in because I just squeezed in by the skin of my teeth, you might say. I weighed only ninety-seven pounds and I don't know whether the doctors fudged a quarter of an inch or so on my height because they saw how much I really wanted to get in — but I just scrooched in. When it came to issuing me clothes, they had no clothes on the old *Pensacola* that would fit me, so they had to have them made by the ship's tailors. Consequently, I was a dude! My clothes fit me nicely and some of those boys looked like they were wearing gunnysacks. It was that way in those days. After a boy could afford it, he always had tailor-made clothes so that they would fit him.

Typical Apprentice Boy Uniform

We went into training on the *Pensacola*, an old wooden, full-rigged ship. The class stayed there until a wooden frigate—in our case, it was the old frigate *Adams*, made over and modernized—returned from a cruise and graduated her class to be officially apprentice boys.

She had an engine to enable her to get in and out of the port. When she was ready to put into port she would furl her sails and put the smokestack up and steam into port. She was, at that time, out on a cruise which lasted six months, and had one hundred and twenty apprentice boys in the class. When she returned the boys would be put through inspection—an admiral's inspection—and would be given their examination, part of which was a verbal examination and another in which they would be required to perform their different duties. If they passed, they would be made second class boys. We enlisted as

third-class apprentice boys. That system has been done away with.

We had to wait until the *Adams* got in and after the formalities of induction were completed, I was allowed to go home with my father to get my personal belongings and was instructed to report for duty the following morning.

The Dirty Shea Brothers

Accordingly, I got the early boat over to the *Pensacola*, and as I came aboard, my heart was thumping. Then a couple of long, lanky boys who were standing there (I later learned that they were the Shea brothers) took all the joy out of me, sneering, "What the hell is this man's Navy coming to? Sure must be getting to the bottom of the barrel when they have to take kids like that. He'll never be any good to the Navy. What can he do? Why, he won't even be able to keep himself clean!"

Well, you can just imagine how I felt and I couldn't say anything. They were too big to tackle, and I couldn't say too much because they might land on me, so I just had to swallow it. But that made me boil. After they were gone I stood there thinking about it and I said to myself, *I'll make you fellows eat those words before I'm through.* I resolved then and there that I would keep as clean as any man on the ship—that I would strive to be the cleanest apprentice boy aboard.

I reported to the officer of the deck who gave me a slip from the ship's writer bearing the number which was called my billet number, or ship's number, and he told me to give that to the master-at-arms and to report to him at once. In the Navy, a ship's writer described and assigned all the positions on our ship and had nothing to do with being an author or journalist.

Too *Little* for My Britches

On reporting to the master-at-arms, he took my billet slip and took me first to the sailmaker where I was given a hammock with my ship's number on it, and a bag bearing the same number, a ditty-box. This was my gear, which we took up to the Jack-of-the-Dust who issued the clothes and uniforms that the government fitted the boys with. The Jack-of-the-dust was another name for the storekeeper, just like the carpenter's mate was called "Chips" and so on. I was given the smallest underwear they had, and it went around my waist twice. The Jack-of-the-dust suggested that I put pleats in them, so they wouldn't fall down. When it came fitting me for my white clothes, they hung on me like a gunnysack, but the master-at-arms told me he would show me how to take them in.

Fortunately, years before, my mother had taught me how to sew fairly well, so I did not have too much trouble fixing them. But when it came to the blue clothes, they were hopeless! The master-at-arms took the clothes and took me back to the quarterdeck and asked for the first lieutenant. When he came out he was shown how those clothes fitted me.

"I didn't know that we had no clothes smaller than that!" he exclaimed in astonishment. "Why, he would disgrace the ship if he went ashore in clothes like that. Take him up to the tailor and tell the tailor that I want him measured up and two new suits of blues made for him in the proper size."

As we went up to see the tailor—or sheeny as the master-at-arms called him—he said, "You're a lucky kid. I wasn't going to see you going around like that and I knew that if we went about it right we'd get you some decent clothes."

This master-at-arms was a great big fellow who had been in the ring at one time and he always refereed the fights on the ship. He was a pretty good fellow to have for a friend and he

7

gave me the needed feeling of security I had lost after hearing those remarks by the Shea brothers.

Well, right away, as soon as I began to get my bearings and get squared away, I mapped out my campaign. I went to those friends I already had, and some of them had been on the ship for quite a while and got all the information I could. I asked them to show me how to go about doing daily tasks correctly. We had a men's crew who were the regular crew members, and I had some friends among them, too, who helped me.

I learned how to wash my clothes in a bucket and every spare minute that I had I was out on the dock, scrubbing and washing these clothes. In the mornings after we washed our faces and washed the ship down, we would wash our clothes, and out I'd be with these clothes of mine, scrubbing them. How white they got! They were originally unbleached drill {a course linen} but with the saltwater and lots of sun, they would turn white. I hung them on the line to dry in the sun and every time I washed them they got that much whiter.

All the time this was going on I kept my eye on those two tall, gangling fellows who had insulted me, and I watched their performance with their clothes. Every day they got dirtier and dirtier. They seemed to believe that they should wash their clothes only when they got so dirty that they wouldn't dare wear them anymore. That's just what they did. Of course, when you are washing clothes with salt water, with muscle, hand, and brush, you can't let them get very dirty and then get them clean again for a long time. Dirt stains are hard to get out. This went on for quite a while and they were about the dirtiest looking fellows that we had on the ship among the apprentice boys, and they were in my company, too.

We had inspection every morning at nine o'clock. The clothes that we were wearing and our underclothes were

inspected to see how clean they were for the day. My division officer would look harder and harder at the Shea brothers every morning but never said a word. This went on for about a week and finally, he asked them to step out. I don't remember if they were twins or just brothers, anyway, they stepped out of ranks before him.

"Look at them!" the division officer shouted. "Just look at those slobs! Did you ever see anything like that? Great big guys like them and as dirty as they are!" Then he called my name and he asked me to step out.

Oh, my laws, I thought, *what have I done? I'm sure I'm not as dirty as those fellows.* I had that squeamish feeling in my stomach when I stepped out.

"Now there is that youngest and smallest boy on the ship," he said. "Look at him." And he put me up against those fellows and said, "Look at the difference. This boy is the smallest boy on the ship and look how clean he is. Now, look at these dirty slobs. Now," he said to the Shea brothers, "that's all I have to say, and you know the rest! If you big slobs appear at quarters again in that condition, it's going to be serious with you. Get yourselves cleaned up, and fast!"

I heaved a big sigh of relief. That was the first time that I had any encouragement—the first ray of encouragement that had come my way since I came on the ship. I had been homesick and lonesome, and it was hard work, and the food was government-issued allowing nine dollars a month to feed us. There were all kinds of stories about what became of the food. I don't know whether they were true or not, but we didn't seem to get much of it but beans. So, when I got that attention it did me a lot of good. My morale was raised to the best in the world. When I met those guys the next time, I had the courage to say, "Hello there you dirty slobs," and they didn't even go after me.

This apprentice system, I think was the finest training they ever had in the Navy. It was the next thing to going to Annapolis. I was too young to go to Annapolis then, but in the Navy apprentice system, they made it so tough for those boys that if they pulled through and did well, they could stand anything. It seemed to me that was the main idea of that kind of training.

Apprentice training was a good deal like Annapolis used to be. Everything was made hard for those boys and if they could stand up under it, they made wonderful officers. With few exceptions, those apprentice boys who stayed with the Navy were outstanding. They all made warrant officers and during the first world war, were commissioned and some of them went clear on up to be rear admirals. They did away with the system about 1904 as nearly as I can remember, and I never could figure out why they did it because those boys, if they could go through that training, could stand anything.

The Golden Gate

All the talk of the ship centered about the anticipation of the *Adams* coming in, and the time when we would be going out to sea. We were very disillusioned later, but at that time it seemed about the last word and that we could wish for nothing more.

All the apprentice boys were designated as "boy" on the ship. A day or so after I enlisted I heard the boatswain's pipe and a call go through the ship, "Boy Stevens!"

"Who would Boy Stevens be?" I asked as I looked around for someone to respond.

"Somebody by the name of Stevens," I was told.

"Well, Stevens is my name, but I'm no boy," I said.

"That is the way you are designated. An apprentice boy third class is "boy" until he gets to be a second class apprentice boy, then he is a second class boy. But you're designated as 'boy.' You better answer that call quick."

A petty officer was in charge of our parties when we went across the island to the opposite side where we could see the Golden Gate {the strait that connected San Francisco to the Pacific Ocean}. Goat Island {Yerba Buena} was a small island then. It wasn't like it is now, all filled in and built up and civilized. We used to have a nice walk and good exercise out of these jaunts and enjoyed the hike. On that particular day, we were sitting there resting. We had walked from the ship across the island to a spot where we were looking right through the Golden Gate. As I sat there musing, I unthinkingly spoke up, saying, "You know what I think, fellows? What I'm pretty sure we're going to see?"

And some of them chorused, "No."

"Someday," I said, "there is going to be a bridge across there—across the Gate, and we'll live to see it if we live a normal span of life."

There was a burst of laughter and they started kidding me and razzing me saying that such a thing was impossible and couldn't be done; that the water was too deep; that the distance was too great, etc., but having a stubborn streak in me, I stuck to it and insisted that we were going to see it! Well, we argued and talked, and I had no backing at all. I stood alone. All the way back to the ship they teased me and called me the Old Prophet.

"The only way you, or anyone else, will ever get across there without going in a boat, will be to swim it or fly across when you are dead and get to be an angel," they laughed.

When we got back to the ship it wasn't long before it was all over the ship that I had made this rash prediction and that I seriously stuck to it. My shipmates just came down and razzed me, and while we were eating supper they kept right on poking fun at me and didn't let up until taps were sounded and we had to turn in. Even the next day, and for days afterward, I was ridiculed about the bridge that was going to be built across the Golden Gate.

But I did live to see the day when they started to build the bridge and to see it completed, too. I lived in Southern California where I was in the shipping business when the bridge was started. By the time I got up to San Francisco the bridge was across the Golden Gate and practically finished. The construction began in 1932 to its completion in 1937. There was still some work to be done on it, and the ferry boats continued to run over to Sausalito and San Rafael. My wife and I were going to Oregon by the coast route and I suggested that we take the ferry boat to San Rafael so that we could take a good look at the bridge. I couldn't keep my eyes off of it, and of course, the time I was just telling about, all came back to me,

about getting razzed making that prediction. I told my wife about it and she was amused and very interested. We took the ferry and on the way over I had to get out and walk up and down the deck and feast my eyes on that bridge. I thought it was the most wonderful thing I had ever seen. To me, it is one of the wonders of the world. But it just goes to show you that predictions do come true!

Tough Fighting Boys

Looking back on all this I can't help but marvel at the way that the apprentice boys grew closer together when they got to sea and had to help one another. It was a good thing to behold.

While on the *Pensacola*, we had drafts of men and boys come in, all perfect strangers. Anyone west of Chicago came to our station. Those east of there went to Newport, Rhode Island, to do their training. Consequently, we had boys from Chicago, westward across the continent. Southern boys, western boys, boys from all over the country westward from the Mississippi. Those from Chicago were tough. They were mostly from the stockyards, and, boy, when they spit, they spit a stone, they were so tough. And of course, we had boys on our ship from San Francisco that weren't any little Lord Fauntleroys. We had a boy by the name Tony Merino who became quite famous afterward. He was a fighter and at that time he was about a lightweight. We had another boy by the name of Bill Darby who was verging on the heavyweight. Then Jimmy Breen from Chicago was as good as any of them. Jimmy was a lightweight-class also. Those boys, of course, had all their spare time interests centered in boxing. I used to take advantage of their friendship and every time they wanted someone to box with them, I would volunteer, but they didn't hit me as hard as they did the bigger boys. I know they didn't. But I got to be very fast and it did me a lot of good. It helped me many a time in bad corners because I could hold my own with a large boy through the knowledge gained in workouts with these boys. They were good! One of them named Darby went into the professional ring after his apprenticeship was up. He made quite a name for himself.

It was a funny thing that when a draft was received on the *Pensacola* there were always one or two boys who thought they could fight, and some of them could, too, especially if they were from the Chicago stockyards. Jimmy Breen was as good as anyone his weight class and in the amateur line, and, also our boy Tony Merino was just about on equal terms. As soon as the draft got straightened out the first thing that evening we would put them through their paces. We'd have to haze them-- kangaroo court, we called it. Some of them resented it very much and showed it and acted accordingly. But they never got out of it. We would run them up to the yardarm, out the yardarm, and lower them into the water two or three times, bring them in, and bump the south end of them against the hard, belaying bit {moveable bars around which ropes of the rigging are coiled} which was made of lignum vitae. We would put them through various other maneuvers and finally, we would all form a double line and as they passed between the two lines, we would swat them with our white hats. That was supposed to be the height of fun, but the newcomers didn't enjoy it at the time. Afterward, they were just as much for it as anyone else when it came to their turn to haze a new group of recruits. It was like all initiations; it was hazing, and very rough.

When the Chicago draft arrived, Jimmy Breen was with them. He had boxed in the clubs in Chicago to pick up a little money. His folks were hard-working people, but they enjoyed sports. Then it came Jimmy's turn to go through the mill. He refused and said, "I can whip any kid on this ship and I'll do it. If you don't gang up on me, I'll whip two or three of them in their turn." Well, of course, that was quite an order.

As soon as a fight would start, one of the biggest boys or a petty officer would step in as a referee. The rest of the boys would then form a hymen ring {a ring of men that expanded and contracted} and what the referee said, went. At a knockdown,

15

the one combatant had to stand away until the other fellow got up. They were not allowed to hit while one of them was down, but there were no rounds. It was a continuous fight.

Our best man from Telegraph Hill stepped forward to challenge Breen. That was Tony Merino. They began to fight—bare fits, shirtless, wearing only a pair of white pants. It was a serious business and they really went to it. I'll tell you, it was the old stuff in the raw. It seemed to me that it lasted over an hour. Blood! Oh, I never saw such a bloody fight in my life, and I've seen some fierce ones. They were both covered with blood! I liked both of those boys and it just made me almost cry to see them taking that punishment. Neither one of them would holler. Neither one of them would quit. Finally, they noticed that Tony couldn't hit with one hand, and the referee stopped the fight and examined him, and he found that Tony had a broken wrist. Tony had been fighting that way for fifteen or twenty minutes, so it showed the remarkable intestinal fortitude that those boys had. Of course, that ended the fight. The referee wouldn't allow it to go on any longer. But, boy! I never will forget that fight as long as I live. After we got to sea, and during the whole cruise, both of them would fight just as hard for the other one if he was in trouble. That fight cemented a close and lasting friendship between Breen and Marino.

The Barbary Coast

I was allowed to remain all night when I went ashore because my folks lived in San Francisco. I had a great desire to see Chinatown and the Barbary Coast. Of course, I had never been there because I was so young, and then, too, my relatives didn't hang out there. Things were rip-roaring there at that time. Throngs of soldiers came to San Francisco en route to Manila, as this was during the Spanish American War. A great many of them found their way to that part of town to have a last fling before going on their way. It was wickedly hot there! Now that I was in the Navy, I wanted to see it all, too. So, one night I joined a liberty party going ashore to see the sights. They got a big kick out of taking me along. In some of the places where we went, they wanted to put me out because I looked so young. They would ask, "How old is that boy?" And I would say that I wasn't a boy and that I was in the United States Navy. Some of them would quiet down and say nothing more about it, and some of them would make quite a fuss about it. They wouldn't serve me any liquor, but that was alright with me because I wouldn't have taken any, anyway. I was just a curious kid and wanted to see the sights and to know what the boys were talking about when they came back from shore leave. It was rough on the Barbary Coast, there was no doubt about it. In those days, you could get into a fight on the least provocation. I remember that there was one place called Cowboy Mag's and it was on Pacific Street. Her place was known as the toughest place on the Pacific coast. I guess it ranked with any of those kinds of places, and it was run by a woman. She was a large, muscular gal, and fundamentally, I guess, she had a fine heart. She was the kind who would get all the sailors money, but she would always see that they had enough for a bed, and in the morning, she would

17

give them breakfast and carfare to the docks, so they could get to their ship. There were mostly two-story buildings where her place of business was located, and they presumably had lodging rooms upstairs.

There were lots of stories about Cowboy. The boys would rather have a run-in with any man than with her. She spent most of her time circulating greeting her customers, taking care of her trade, and keeping an eye on her girls, some of whom would be out in the larger hall where they danced.

One of the stories which impressed me the most about Cowboy's tenacity was concerning the time when a colored regiment was in town. They had come in from the South and they had been issued ground corn—cornmeal, it was—and it wasn't long before they were making corn whiskey right out there at the Presidio where they were waiting until a transport arrived to take them to the Philippines. A lot of them were going around seeing the sights, going through the town, and two of these colored boys came into Cowboys. They were great big fellows. I think one of them was a sergeant who thought he was pretty tough. They ordered drinks. The man behind the bar said, "We don't serve colored people in here."

The soldier said, "You better serve it to me! We got a lot of our boys down here, downtown, that will see that you do."

Well, they argued back and forth, and somebody went for Cowboy. She was there in a minute and when she slipped behind the bar she reached down and pulled out two large .45 Navy colts and put them right on the bar in front of her.

"Now," she said, "make tracks colored boys, make tracks!" There was no more argument. They got right out. And what is more, they didn't come back. She would have used those shootin' irons, too! Thank goodness, times have changed for the colored folk.

On another night, I went ashore with some of the boys. We went to a place called The Thalia. I guess the old-timers in San Francisco remember The Thalia. It was a beer hall. Downstairs they served drinks and they had a stage where dubious talent cavorted. You were welcome there if you bought a drink of beer once in a while. It also had a balcony around it on which there were small compartments or booths where a guy could take a girlfriend for a beer; it was less conspicuous up there. So, we wandered around and saw everything downstairs and then went upstairs and sat down in a booth. I don't remember whether the other two boys bought a beer or not, but they probably did. Nobody would have sold me one, anyway, and I never did have any desire for it. I was sitting there looking down at the crowd below, very interested in the activity. I had never seen sights like that before. A shadow fell across me and when I looked up, one of the "girls" that worked in the place was standing there, all painted up like a Christmas tree, and she looked right at me.

"Hello, beautiful big brown eyes!" and she winked at the boys. I was so embarrassed that I wanted to jump right off the balcony. Of course, my two friends just roared, and my face got redder and redder. Well, when we got back to the ship they recounted all over the ship word-for-word just what she said to me. The boys thought that it was such a good joke that it just had to be told which added to my embarrassment. So, for days after I was the butt of their jibes about Great Big Brown Eyes!

Finally, we got word through the grapevine that the *Adams* had left San Diego and was sailing up to Goat Island. Of course, the excitement was great. One morning two or three days

later, when we turned out at five o'clock, there she was, anchored off our port side! Oh my, didn't she look wonderful to us!

Captain Glass, the commander of Goat Island, and his staff went aboard for admiral's inspection and the class started right in to go through their drills which were part of their examination. We could see it all from the *Pensacola*, and, of course, it was very wonderful to us. We just wondered if we would ever be that good. The way they would make sail, and swing those yards around, wear ship {turn it away from the wind}, get up anchor, let to anchor—every imaginable drill that is done on a sailing ship was done by them and done smartly. It was very, very wonderful! The drill lasted about a week and then the boys put on their go-ashore clothes and all received furloughs according to the distance they lived from San Francisco. Those who lived the furthest away got the longest time for traveling. They were given all the money they had saved.

When we were on the ship we got only a dollar-and-a-half of our nine dollars and were told not to spend all of it in one place. Of course, that was a joke because it just barely bought us toothpaste. We were not allowed to smoke until we became second class boys.

1874 to 1919

LIFE ABOARD THE USS *ADAMS*

Scuttlebutt

After all the boys of the *Adams* got away on their furloughs, we moved aboard. Boy! That was a thrill! The ship had all been cleaned up for admiral's inspection and you could lie on her decks with a white suit on and not get dirty. She was so clean you could eat off her decks, as the saying goes. What a beautiful ship she was with all the rigging tarred, the masts and spars varnished, and her brightwork shining!

They moved us aboard and gave us our billets and about a week was spent getting accustomed to the vessel and doing simple drills required at sea. Then one morning we got underway and, leaving San Francisco behind us, proceeded out of port through the Golden Gate and we were at sea! We were not told officially where we were bound but the grapevine said it was the Hawaiian Islands, which proved to be true.

Fortunately, all the men in the ship's crew were experienced sailors picked for that work, and they were good, too. They knew their stuff and they were going to teach it to us. We steamed out past the Farallon Islands, clear of all land, then we set sail, established the watches and got the ship on her course. When I look back on it now, I can easily see why so many of the men of the regular crew had a frown on their faces when the job was done. It looked alright to me, but I guess we made every mistake that it was possible to make while we were undergoing this maneuver. It was in the fall of the year and, although the weather was clear, a stiff Norwest breeze was blowing off our starboard beam, causing the ship to roll, and man oh man, how she could roll! They say that if the ship rolls over fifty degrees, she capsizes but I swear I watched that roll-meter go to fifty-four degrees many times, and then roll back.

By that time everybody I looked at was getting greener and greener. They looked like frogmen in the face. Whether it was from my experience on the *Cupid* or just because I didn't know any better, I didn't get seasick, and I never was seasick in my whole life. But oh, how sick some of the boys were! Some of them—two, in fact—never did get over being seasick and they had to be discharged because of chronic seasickness. Watches were then set for the night. Half of the apprentices were starboard watch and half port, and we stood what they called watch and watch. That meant four hours on and four hours off, all the time we were at sea.

Sometime after we went aboard I noticed the boys going over to a fine, large oak barrel amidships, just abaft the foremast on the gundeck. The barrel had been skillfully made by a fine craftsman and it had brass hoops and was clean and bright looking. Those brass hoops were polished every morning. The small top could be lifted off the hole which was large enough to dip into with a cup. Chains were fastened into the barrel at regular intervals and drinking cups were secured to the other end of the chains.

"Just what is that barrel?" I asked one of the men of the crew.

"That, my son, is the famous scuttlebutt," he answered. "It has two important functions. It furnishes the water for the boys to drink and, from its dark insides, it dispenses all the rumors which are going around the ship. If you want any information on any subject or happening aboard the ship, you just go and lift that little hatch off the top and dip your cup in the water for a drink, then you ask the scuttlebutt about it. It always has the answer. You've heard one of the boys say to another, 'Who told you that?' and the other boy reply, 'I got it from the scuttlebutt.'" I nodded assent. I had noticed that but

didn't know what they meant. So that important point was cleared up for me before we were out of sight of land.

I had also noticed a brass lamp abaft the scuttlebutt amidships. I wondered why a little brass lamp was hanging there. Sometimes it burned, sometimes it was out. I was interested in it, too, so while I was asking questions I asked, "What is that little lamp hanging there for? It doesn't seem to be for any special purpose that I have noticed."

With a broad smile on his face, he replied, "That just goes to show how ignorant you are about a sailing ship. That is one of the most important things we have, at least from the crew's point of view!"

"How could such a little old brass lamp be so important?" I asked.

Just at that moment the boatswain's mate of the watch stuck his head down the hatch and tooted that thing he called a "pip" and sang out, "The smoking lamp is lit!"

Immediately the master-at-arms of that deck got up off his sea chest and struck a match and lit the lamp. Right away the whole string of the crew lined up and in turn, lit their pipes from the lamp. My friend turned to me and said, "You couldn't have any better demonstration than that, now could you?" and I agreed.

All Hands on Deck

While we were on the *Pensacola* we practiced going aloft to get the boys accustomed to height and climbing the rigging. The *Pensacola* didn't have any sails bent on her yards, but she had practically everything else up there, and we always had a petty officer along with us to instruct us in the proper way of going out on the footrope and doing the things that we had the gear to do up there. Of course, this training helped a lot when we got to sea. Still, when we put to sea in the *Adams*, we were green as grass. Naturally, the Old Man didn't want us going aloft to shorten sail at night in the dark, with half of us seasick, so excitement ran high when he gave orders to the officer of the deck to take off the light sail before it got dark. The light sails in our case were the royals, the topgallant, and the flying jib. Was it any wonder that the heart of every apprentice boy thrilled as the officer of the deck started right in, in a man-of-war and seaman-like manner, to get these operations done?

The bo's'n's {boatswain's} mate is always within calling distance of the officer of the deck and is ready at all times with his bo's'n's pipe— the instrument with which he makes all those funny noises. We heard the officer of the deck sing out,

"Bo's'n's Mate!"

And the boatswain's mate answered, "Sir!"

Then the officer of the deck sang out, "Pass the word for all hands on deck to shorten sail."

At this command, the boatswain's mate went forward and, as was customary whenever operations required the services of all hands, gave seven or eight short peep peeps with his pipe to alert the other boatswains' mates and the crew to there being an "all hands" operation. Then the boatswain's mate gave one long, loud blast on his pipe and sang out, "Alllllllll

haaaaaaaaaaaands on deck! Shorten sail!" He then followed this with, "Bear a hand! Bear a hand! Bear a hand!" This last call was to hurry them up.

The chief boatswain's mate who was hanging out on the forecastle (which he usually did when he wasn't in his hammock) got up and went to the hatch of the companionway and blew the same call down to the gun deck which was the next deck below. The man on the gundeck gave the call plainly on his deck and then stuck his head down the hatch of the companionway and made the same call to the berth deck. By that time the ship was thoroughly conversant with what was going to happen. The men all came up from below and took their stations for going aloft to take in light sails. Those who weren't to go aloft, lined up along the rail to heave on the lines that were necessary for performing the operation.

Then the officer of the deck took over and sang out, "Royal yardmen in the rigging!" The four men who belonged to both the royal yards got in the rigging of their respective yard. Then he sang out, "Topgallant men on the sheer-pole!" Next, he sang out, "Aloft, royal yardmen!" And they went aloft and when they got up there stretched out on the footrope, two men on each side of the yard, the fore and mainmast men threw the bottom sheets off the belaying pin. Of course, that allowed the bottom of the sail to balloon out to the wind. Then they hauled away down on deck on the buntline—one of the lines used to haul the sail up to the yard for furling—pulling the corner of the sail down toward the center of the sail, spilling a lot of wind out of it, then they hauled away at the clewlines. The clewlines run from the center of the sail out to the leech and that spilled the air out of the middle of the sail, and by a couple of the boys hanging onto the jackstay and throwing their weight out, they could pull the sail up on the yardarm with no wind in it. Then the man out on each end of the yardarm started winding the

messenger line around the sail toward the mast. When they got the sail well secured on the yardarm with the messenger line, they called for the men below to haul away on the bunt-whip. That caused a sizeable piece of canvass to pull the sail up forward of the mast and protect it from the weather and wind.

When this operation is done properly, it is really a nice-looking job. As each man finished his work, he was instructed to go below, down the rigging to the deck. The instructors were the last men to come down. Sometimes the boatswain's mate sends some of them up again to reconstruct the job because it is not done neat enough, but in this case, it came off in nice shape and no one was sent aloft again. Every boy just busted himself to do the job right.

I was very lucky to have a fine lad whose name was Webber, with me on the starboard watch, which was my billet. My position in sail while taking in or making sail was the fore royal yard. He was large and was practically a full-grown man, and strong as an ox. He helped me all that he could, as he seemed to know more about taking in sail than I did, and I think that he might have been to sea at some time before joining the Navy. The *Adams* was bar-rigged, and the royal yard is the top yard, so I was most fortunate to have such a boy with me. I don't know what I would have done without him because when we went aloft to shorten sail, I just hung on with one hand and tried to smother after they clewed up the sail which was to draw the sail's lower ends up to the mast to furl it. It was our place to furl the sail on the yard and I was so small and light and inexperienced that I needed someone like Webber with me. I tried hard, and between us, we did a pretty good job, but I was glad when we went down the rigging and had the solid deck under our feet again.

Shooting Charlie Noble

About a week out, after leaving San Francisco, I was sitting close to the wheel. The officer of the deck was walking up and down when the second-class gunner's mate came up and asked his permission to shoot Charlie Noble. He had in his hand a large pistol, the like of which I had never seen. It was about two feet long and the caliber appeared to be about that of a ten-gauge shotgun. The officer of the deck asked him if the chief cook was ready and he replied that the fire was cooled down in the galley to the required temperature. I knew that my eyes were getting as big as saucers and I said to myself, *I knew they didn't practice capital punishment and that they had cut out using the cat-o'nine-tails, but I had no idea that they still shot them—and it began to sound as if they cooked them!*

"Very well, Johnson," said the officer of the deck. "If they are ready down there, go ahead and do the job."

"Aye, aye, sir," replied the gunner's mate, saluting.

I followed him down, saying to myself, *I just have to see this, if I can never see anything else.*

We walked to the forward companion hatch and he turned down and I followed him as close as I dared. The cooks were there with the lids off all the galley stoves and the gunner's mate put a great big shell of about number ten gauge, in this awful looking pistol. Then he covered his arm with a sack to protect it from the heat, after which he ran it in the stove and up the galley stovepipe and shot the thing off. I knew there was something foolery going on, as it didn't look like they were shooting men. He went right down the line and shot three of those stovepipes on the starboard side, and then shot three of them on the port side, and every time he would look at me with a kind of a funny grin on his face. When he was through, I asked

28

him what kind of a maneuver that was called. "That's what we call shooting Charlie Noble," he answered me. "Didn't you ever hear about shooting Charlie Noble?"

I told him no, I had never heard of it. He was very surprised, and he shook his head and said, "My! You really must be a landlubber if you have never heard of that before." He was quite amused when I told him that I was scared almost to death because I thought he was going to shoot a man, and he laughed, and after a while, I saw the joke, too.

Finally, I realized that this operation was all done to clear the soot out of the galley smokestacks so that they would draw properly.

As we went up the forward companionway we found a tarpaulin thrown over the brass railing and the galley hatch closed. The deck was black with soot although the ship's hoses were running full stream to wash it off. It was but a little while until they had it all washed off and the decks were clean again. Johnson asked me if I knew what that pistol was for and I said that from the size and looks of it, it must be used to repel boarders. Then he had another good laugh about that. He said that that was not the function of these pistols. He told me that there were a number of them down in the armory and that they were used to fire red, white, and green stars as signal flares for use at night. He also said that there were rockets for use at night, too. In the operation of signaling, the signal might call for a rocket, two red stars, and two green stars. Such a signal would convey a whole sentence. There were no electric lights on the *Adams* and all signaling had to be done in this way at night.

Hawaii and The Abels

It took us thirty-two days to reach Diamond Head. For about ten days that heavy wind held off our starboard beam, then gradually it began to pull further aft and ease up a bit. Then it seemed that life was getting worth living and it wasn't quite so bad, but we had a lot of the romance knocked out of us by that time. We found that it wasn't such a great thing, after all, this sailing ship. But we began to like certain things. A healthy body overlooks a lot. We were always hungry, but my goodness, I could see me taking on weight and growing, and all the rest of the boys were getting husky, too.

Having to turn out at four o'clock in the morning when we had that watch was pretty tough at first. We got up and had to get under a shower on deck, right under the bridge with saltwater and it was cold! And just in case anyone tried to evade it, the officer of the deck was on hand to see that everybody got under it. Then we got into our white pants and undershirts as soon as we possibly could, and we lined up for a cup of hot coffee. Did that ever taste good! As soon as our coffee was finished we turned to and washed down and holystoned decks {a large piece of sandstone used to scour wooden decks}. This seemed rugged, especially while we were still close to San Francisco and the mainland. However, as soon as we drew near the Islands, the water was warmer, and we were toughened up some by that time, and it didn't seem quite so bad. Anyway, we gradually got used to it and undoubtedly felt better for it. None of us were hurt by this regime but between you and me, we would have much rather dispensed with this part of the training.

Finally, after thirty-two days, the lookout reported land and the officer of the deck sang out the usual, "Where away?"

and the reply was, "Dead ahead, Sir," and of course we were all up craning our necks. We could just make out what looked like a small green cloud on the horizon, which proved to be Diamond Head. We were all thrilled and it looked mighty good to us.

When we were about ten miles from Diamond Head we took in sail, raised our smokestack, got underway by steam, and sailed into the harbor. In those days, they had no Naval Pearl Harbor and we had to moor across from the place where the steamers docked at the center of Honolulu. There was a wooden English ship—a frigate of war—which looked quite a bit like the *Adams*, only she didn't carry as much sail and she wasn't a training ship. Her name was The *Shearwater*. She was immediately dubbed the "Bilge-water" by our crew, but her name really was The *Shearwater*. We were moored next to her with about a hundred feet between the two vessels. We were there! Honolulu! We had arrived.

Shortly after we were moored, a gentleman came aboard the ship to see the commanding officer. I was surprised when I was called down to his cabin and learned that this man was inquiring for me. He introduced himself as Lem Abels. At one time, he was engaged to marry my aunt, but the engagement was broken, and he had come over to Honolulu to go into business. At the time that we took our training cruise, the Islands had been in the possession of the United States only a short time. But, as I was saying, Mr. Abels came over to the Islands and his business expanded and he became quite influential in the business of Honolulu. Being such a substantial citizen of that city, he secured permission for me to go ashore and stay all night at their home, which was a grand thing for me and I knew that I was a very lucky boy. It was wholly unexpected, and I could hardly believe that it was happening to me.

The Abel home was a beautiful place only a block from the Queen's palace. Their home was built near the center of a

large plot of land, approximately an acre, and was beautifully landscaped. Mrs. Abels had just returned from the mainland. She was a very lovely, gracious person with lots of warmth and understanding, and she did a great deal toward making my stay in Honolulu pleasant. I went ashore many times while we were there. They would come down to the dock and send over to the ship for me and would take me riding in their carriage. They had a nice two-horse, smart carriage, and they would drive out nearly every afternoon and take me to hear the Royal Hawaiian band which played at the grounds of the Queen's palace. I was too young to appreciate all of that at that time, but the memory has meant a great deal to me in the years since. My whole stay in the Islands was made more enjoyable through this contact and I have always been grateful to the Abels for their wonderful hospitality, and the way they took me around the country and to meet their friends.

However, I think one of the nicest things that I remember was the way Mrs. Abels got up that first morning I stayed there and cooked my breakfast herself. I had to get back to the ship by seven o'clock, so instead of waking the servants, she got up and personally saw to it that I had all I could eat before leaving. She certainly knew all about boys! I remember especially, the fried bananas. She just stepped out the back door and came back with bananas, fresh from the stock. I had never heard of fried bananas and thought it was awfully funny to fry them, but when I tried them, they sure tasted better than I imagined. Boy! Were they good!

We had been thirty-two days on ship's food; thirty-two days on government-issued food! If it hadn't been for the lowly bean I would not have been able to survive. We had salt horse, and it really was salt horse. There it was, burned right into the barrel, "Salt Horse. U.S. Government Inspected 1862." When that was opened the whole deck smelled like a morgue and we

had to get out of there. The cook cooked it for three days and at the end of that time, the chief tried to stick his fork into it and it just bounced back. Well, of course, we couldn't eat it. They just simply couldn't get it tender enough to cut a piece off. That whole barrel of salt horse was condemned.

We had lots of that kind of stuff. The old corn wooly, or corned beef, was almost as bad. That which was canned wasn't so bad. The cooks couldn't do much on nine dollars a month, even then, and they had no cold storage. A few days after we would leave port, we would have to go to hardtack. The hardtack had "chafing gear" on it—it had cobwebs and we called it chafing gear, and some of it was moldy but we had to eat it just the same. We had to put *something* into us. Some of the mush had worms in it. We had dried fruit that had the same affliction, but we had to eat it, and eat it we did! But we got awfully hungry.

Our idea of heaven was "all night in, and beans for breakfast." That meant that we could get to sleep all night and then have beans—real, good slow-baked beans—for breakfast. We had Navy cooks who knew how to cook those beans. They would put them on a slow fire in the afternoon and those beans would simmer all night. The watchman on that deck would keep just enough coal in the firebox to keep them baking; the fire would be banked and then in the morning the beans would be ready to eat. Every morning we turned out at five, got under a cold shower, turned to and scrubbed down the decks with holystone and sand, sand and canvas on the other stuff, and then, just before seven o'clock, we would have to go over the masthead and down. By that time, we were so hungry we could go down to the gundeck where we ate, and you could hear the first spoonful of beans hit the bench. I don't know how we were able to hold so much food. I just wish I could do it now. I used to eat two heaping plates full. Of course, baked beans were special.

We usually had them on Sunday morning. There was always plenty and any that were leftover we'd eat cold through the week. But it didn't make any difference how we had them, they were good.

The chief petty officers and warrant officers were served in their quarters, but we were served and ate on the gundeck. The oak tables, when not in use, were put overhead and secured by a steel bar at each end. The seats were folded and put on top of the table overhead, but when in use, the tables were hung by steel cables from the beams. The seats were collapsible benches which were as long as the table, and there was one on each side of the table with sufficient places to accommodate the men assigned to eat there. Each man was assigned a place as part of his billet.

Once a month the ship's writer assigned a mess cook for each table. When mess call was sounded by the boatswain's mate on his pipe, every mess cook let down his table and hooked it to the cables; set up the benches and took the gear (knives, forks, etc.,) from the steel lockers on either outboard side of the ship and set the tables. After the tables were set, the mess cooks lined up at the galley. As each mess cook came up to get the food for his table, he told the cook how many men were to be served there and was given the quantity needed, accordingly. This was carried to the tables, ready for the men when they were "piped" to dinner by the boatswain's mate.

After a month of this life at sea, is it any wonder I looked forward to every visit at the Abels? I think they took me every place and showed me everything and they wouldn't let me spend a cent of my money.

The weather was fine and so warm we had our gun-ports open all the time. The old muzzle-loading guns had been replaced by the new four-inch breech-loading rifles and they were placed so that there were three on each side of the deck. I

slept on the gundeck, right over the gun, so I could look right out into the water below me from my hammock. Even life aboard ship was a pleasant experience in Honolulu.

The Hawaiian people were wonderful, soft-spoken, gentle, and big-hearted. The nights I stayed aboard the ship I enjoyed their music when they came out to the ship to entertain us, which was almost every night. Their big, flat-bottomed boat had enough beam to permit them to stand with quite a bit of freedom while they played and sang. They would come alongside the ship and stop under the various gun ports and they would play their stringed instruments and sing. It was pleasant to lie there in my hammock and look down on those happy, peaceful natives playing their guitars and ukuleles and maybe mandolins, and listen to their soft, sweet voices singing their native songs.

The Hawaiian girls were beautiful. Some were clothed only in grass skirts and others who had come under the influence of the missionaries, wore wrappers or Mother Hubbards {probably muu muus}. They all wore their hair down around their shoulders, entwined with flowers. Both the men and women wore leis of fragrant blossoms around their necks.

In those days, all the man-of-war ships in the anchorage opposite the docks in Honolulu Harbor put out booms on either side of the ship where they would tie up the boats in use instead of hoisting them into their davits. Any visiting boats would be tied up to these booms while their crew was aboard. Each boom had a boat tender whose duty it was to look out for the boats tied up and to keep them from bumping and damaging one another.

Well, one day shortly before we left Honolulu, a boat came alongside, bringing one of the men from the *Shearwater*. He was invited to pull out to the boom and leave his boat. He brought an invitation to our boys to attend an entertainment on

his ship that he called a "singsong." It seemed that they had quite a lot of talent on their ship and they wanted to give us a singsong, which was very nice of them and we appreciated it. He went to the captain, who accepted the invitation on behalf of the crew, and the messenger then went back, got in his boat, and returned to the *Shearwater*.

Our boat-tender was very excited about the whole thing. He had never met an Englishman before and he could hardly wait until the chap got away before calling to some of his shipmates, "Hey fellows! Did you hear that fellow from the *Shearwater*? Why, he can talk English as good as I can!"

On the given night, all who could be spared from the *Adams* went over to the singsong. They had a lot of talent aboard the *Shearwater* and they also had brought in some outside talent. One or two groups of the Hawaiian singers and musicians volunteered to come over and help entertain. It was, all in all, a very successful evening. There were many beautiful songs sung, both by the Hawaiians and the various quartets and choruses of the ship. We enjoyed listening to lots of the songs they had brought from England and joined in on the chorus of many of them. One song seemed to label the crew as women-haters. It went something like this:

Oh, boys keep away from the girls, I say
And give them lots of room
For when you are wed
They'll band you on the head
With the baldheaded end of a broom.
So, keep away from the girls I say,
For I'll tell you it's no fun
When the butcher comes around to
collect his bill
With a dog, and a double-barreled gun.

36

When I mentioned to one of the boys that they seemed to be a bunch of woman-haters he responded, "Blimey, it's not that, you know. They are just too homely and salty to catch a girl."

Aloha Hawaii

It wasn't long after the sing-song that we began to prepare for sea again. I paid my last visit to the Abels and you may be sure that I was sorry that we were going to leave. I had been telling Mr. Abels that I was messenger boy for the first lieutenant who was known throughout the Navy as "Red Mike." He was extremely interested, and he asked me if I could introduce him when I had to go back to the ship. I was pretty sure that Red Mike would be aboard, so when I went back to the ship, Mr. Abels went aboard with me and I took him to the first lieutenant's quarters and told the first lieutenant that Mr. Abels wished to meet him. When they were introduced, Mr. Abels shook hands with a great deal of vigor and told Red Mike, "I've heard about you and I have always wanted to shake your hand and tell you how much I admired you. You, Sir, are a fine gentleman and officer. Would that the Navy had more of your caliber!"

That struck me as being a peculiar speech and right there I knew that there was something about Red Mike that I didn't know, and I determined that at the earliest possible moment I would find out what it was. I was sure that Jimmy Patterson could tell me. But right then we were so busy preparing for our cruise among the Islands, that it was several days before I got around to asking him about the story behind Red Mike.

Shortly after the *Shearwater* gave us our sing-song and thoroughly impressed upon us that we should never get married, it came our day to leave. And, of course, it was a big day for us. Everyone was up at four o'clock with everything ready by daylight to back out of our mooring. We got up our mooring anchors and steamed out slowly. In fact, we couldn't steam any other way than slowly because we didn't have the power.

Leaving was a very beautiful and impressive ceremony. We never knew nor realized that there would be other people around to see us go, but we were mistaken. Everybody's friends that they had made while in Honolulu seemed to be down there to see us off. The natives in canoes and a few of the white people living shore came alongside in boats and threw us leis, and, of course, we were supposed to put a flower behind our ear and throw the leis back, and that meant that we would be back again. It was quite touching, and we had a surprise there that made us have a wonderful feeling for Honolulu. They followed us out into the channel, waving, some throwing kisses. As we sailed slowly away from them and Honolulu, their voices came over the water to us, growing fainter and fainter, singing their songs of the Islands, *Aloha Oe* {"Aloha ʻOe" is Liliʻuokalani's most famous song and a common cultural symbol for Hawaii}, until we could no longer hear them. A ceremony of this kind is worth seeing. Nowadays it is all done at the docks with steamships. The docks are lined up from one end to the other, but in those days, there were not many docks, so lots of ships left in the way that we did.

A full-rigged ship with her sails all set and drawing nicely is a beautiful sight. The weather was good, and after cruising among the Islands, we headed for San Diego by the southern route. We went south where we could have plenty of good weather to drill including sail drill-boat drill, gunnery, and everything we needed to know without rough weather bothering us much. We had very little rough weather and it was a very pleasant trip, although we were twenty-eight days getting to San Diego from Honolulu. That wasn't considered so bad,

considering that we had spent a lot of time drilling and going out of our way, and so on, but we didn't try to hurry.

It was on pleasant evenings after we had left Honolulu behind and were cruising among the Islands, that we would congregate on the fo'c's'le {forecastle}. That was Jimmy Patterson's domain where we lived, had his boatswain's chest, and that's where he used to tell his stories. Jimmy really cared a lot for us boys. We didn't realize how much until we started back from Honolulu, but Jimmy was the best friend we had on the ship. He'd tell us things that we should know, gave us advice, and he had a nice, pleasant way of doing it. He was not a foul-mouthed man. He wasn't a preacher either, but he was very fine with the boys. I can see why Red Mike picked him to go on his ship. And Jimmy knew his stuff. I don't think there was anything on a sailing ship that Jimmy couldn't make or do when it came to managing a ship under sail, I don't believe he had an equal in those days. When the weather was calm and not too much rolling, we would have boxing in the evening after supper. That meant a lot to me. I learned how to box and that meant that I didn't get picked on.

In the evenings, we would all sit around, some of us on deck, some against Jimmy, and others on the chests, and on his sea-chest, and listen to Jimmy spin yarns. Of course, Jimmy's favorite character was always Jack Weir, about whom I will tell you later because I was fortunate enough to be shipmates with him. But that night, we were all around, snugged down, talking, when Jimmy gave me recognition. My shipmates used to call me everything from 'kid" to "old lady," and about everything in the world except my real name. So, when one of the boys called to

me saying, "Say, Old Lady," Jimmy took issue with him and said, "Why don't you call him by his right name? That doesn't sound decent." Then he turned to me and asked,

"What is your name, son?"

"Gaither Stevens," I replied.

"Well, then," said Jimmy, "why don't you call him Steve if you want to call him by a nickname? Don't call him "Old Lady." He's not an old lady. He'll fight any one of you if you get too damn smart. That kid's got a lot of guts. I've watched him plenty and he tries to hold his end up. He pulls as much on a line when we're hoisting a sail as any of the rest of you. He keeps himself clean," he said, "and I don't want to hear you call him Old Lady anymore."

Well, of course, that made me feel pretty good, so from then on, I was called Steve, which made me happy.

As I have said, Jimmy Patterson was chief boatswain's mate and was in charge of all apprentice boys in charge of drill and anything connected with the working of the ship. We were told Jimmy was originally an apprentice boy in the English Navy, but when he got over to the United States, he absented himself without leave and stayed in the United States. He later enlisted in our Navy. At any rate, he sure knew his stuff! Of course, as almost every old-timer knows, our Navy is modeled after the British Navy in sail, and when Jimmy put us through our drills and our work, there was no fooling about it. But there wasn't any apprentice boy who wouldn't have given his all for Jimmy.

Red Mike & Murder in Hong Kong

It was one evening after we had left Honolulu behind that we got Jimmy in a talkative mood. He had been talking to me and had asked me what I had been doing the past week as he hadn't seen me on deck. I told him that I had been detailed as night messenger boy for the first lieutenant.

"Oh," he said, "so you're Red's messenger boy. How do you like Red?"

"He sure knows his stuff," I replied. "but I can't figure him out. He seems so nervous and impatient and very high-strung. He acts like he's mad all the time. He frowns at me even though I haven't done anything."

"Don't let that bother you, Steve," Jimmy told me. "If you had gone through what he has gone through, you'd frown, too."

"Well," I said, thinking the time had come to learn about Red Mike, "I don't know, but I kind of like him and he seems to like me at times. There are times he can be awfully nice and then other times he flies off the handle and starts cussin' somebody and I don't know how to take him. I have been wondering what is wrong with him."

"Don't take him seriously," said Jimmy. "He went through a terrible experience in Hong Kong. Didn't you know that he's the famous Red Mike?"

"But who is Red Mike?" I queried. "He's not famous to me."

"I guess you were pretty young to know about what happened out in the Orient a few years ago or you would know all about him. The story was in every newspaper in the country."

"What did he do in the Orient?" I asked.

42

The boys who had been listening with one ear started moving closer to us, sensing that a story was in the making, and boys who were out of earshot, noticing the movement, began drawing closer.

"Well," drawled Jimmy, "he went over there under sail as the executive officer on a ship larger than the *Adams*. It was sent to the Asiatic Station with Hong Kong as its base. He had just been married to a beautiful young girl whose folks had all the money they could ever use in this world, and of course, she was spoiled. Men had made over her because she was such a beauty." Warming to his story, Jimmy went on, "Because Red Mike hardly noticed her and didn't pet her particularly, nor make a fuss over her, she fell for him and they were married. He went out to Hong Kong on his ship and she went over on one of the passenger boats, probably a Pacific mail boat. She had class! Beauty, culture, clothes, education, charm—everything. Her "coming out" after she had completed finishing school was one of the swankiest events of the season. Oh, I'll tell you boys, she was tops.

"Over in Hong Kong, there was an Englishman purported to be of noble birth, who was a banker. That is, he worked in the bank when he worked. He didn't work much because he was a society butterfly. He was God's answer to a maiden's prayer, as they say. He had a reputation that a woman only had to look at him and she would start trembling and just be powerless to resist him. Consequently, as far as the men were concerned, especially husbands, he wasn't very popular, but with the women, he was a go-getter. That was his game in life. Some men play tennis, but he played the women when he wasn't in the bank.

"Well, Mike's wife went over by steamer. Naturally, she got over there quite a while before her husband did. She secured the nicest quarters she could get in Hong Kong and launched

into a social whirl where she did lots of entertaining. The minute this bank chap got his 'blims' on her, he said she was just his dish, and by golly, he got her. He went through his regular routine and it wasn't long before she fell for him.

"All the Americans, the English, the French, and all the white people used to congregate together. They didn't mix with the Orientals in those days. So, by the time Mike got there on his slow old sailboat, all this thing was going at its top speed. It wasn't long until some had told him the whole story.

"There was, and still is, a large English population in Hong Kong. There were not many troops nor military units, but lots of people making a living in Hong Kong; lots of people of English birth, because it is an English colony. There are some Americans out there, many of them executives in large firms.

"Well, when Red Mike found out what was going on, he came back aboard ship and went to the armory and got a .38 Navy revolver, maybe two—I don't know—but anyway, he had one. He went ashore again in Hong Kong and walked right into the bank where that guy worked. Mike looked on the doors until he saw the man's name. The bank guard started to stop him, but Red Mike said, 'I have a long-standing engagement with him,' and he was so sure of himself that the guard stepped back and let him go in.

"Mike went into the office and this fellow was sitting at his desk, smoking a pipe. Red Mike asked him if he was so-and-so, and the man said, 'Oh, I say now!' and he began to get a little nervous, of course, but he was very polite and asked, 'What can I do for you?'

"Red Mike said, 'You can get your gun out, that's what you can do. That's the thing that will suit me.'

"The fellow opened his drawer in front of him, where he evidently kept his gun, and he started to reach for it. When he got it just about out so that Red Mike could get a good look at

44

it, Red Mike shot him right straight through the heart. That was the end of that Lochinvar.

"Red Mike went down to the police station before it was all over Hong Kong. Hong Kong was ruled by a governor who was the representative of the English government at that time. Nobody knew what would be done. The ordinary working Englishman didn't think it was right for a Yankee to walk in and shoot an Englishman in the bank, so they started to congregate with the idea of taking Red Mike away from the police department and they were going to string him up. That word was taken over to the ship immediately, and the call for all hands went up—not officially—but all hands were called and every enlisted man on the ship that could be spared went ashore armed. Only the merest skeleton of a crew and the officers remained, and maybe one or two of the boys who were too sick to go ashore.

"Red Mike was very popular in those days. He wasn't cross and nervous then. Anyway, that crew wasn't going to let any Limey hang a Yank. This ship, in addition to the sailors, had a company or two of Marines. The boys formed in battalion formation off the ship. The drums came up along with the bugle corps and they marched right up to the jail. The English tried to stop them at the jail and the boys just pushed on them like chaff and went right in. They found the cell that Red Mike was in and they just simply tore it to pieces and took him out. Then they marched back to the ship, still playing Yankee Doodle Dandy, and they deposited him in his quarters aboard ship.

"Later the case came up before the officials. I do not know the rank or status of these officials, but the case was argued for a long time and was finally dismissed. Red Mike was absolved. There was a tremendous amount of evidence given and

it might be said that feeling ran high on Red Mike's side and many felt the banker got just what he deserved.

"Naturally Red Mike felt pretty bad about all this. His spirit was at a low ebb and he was pretty shaken about the whole thing. The whole crew was on Mike's side and they wanted to let him know how much they thought of him. They wanted to show their feelings in some concrete way, so they got up a subscription and with the money thus obtained, they bought a fine solid-gold watch engraved with his name and stating that it was from the crew of his vessel. The day came when it came back from the engravers it was a lovely thing. Presentation ceremonies were arranged, and the presentation was made by one of the chief petty officers of the crew. Of course, the commissioned officers had nothing to do with this. They couldn't get into this thing. So, at the designated time, all hands were called, and they marched aft on the quarterdeck. Red Mike was there, all dressed up and trying to smile. The chief petty officer made his speech and gave Red Mike the watch. He said that everyone admired his principles and courage and then he presented the watch."

Then Jimmy made a wry face and went on, "You know, I just happened to glance back toward the officers' quarters and darned if I didn't see that wife of his sticking her face out of the door to his stateroom, listening to all that was going on. I don't see how she had the gall to even come aboard. I felt mad enough to go back there and throw her overboard, but I didn't."

As Jimmy finished I thought to myself that it was no wonder that Lem Abels wanted to go back and shake Red Mike's hand when he found out who the first lieutenant was. And I had a better understanding of the officer who wanted me as his messenger.

And, so it was, with the good weather all the way to San Diego, the pow-wows around Jimmy's domain were frequent and

interesting. He was full of good stories, but I think the best one was about Jack Weir. The gem of them all was the story of Jack and the Chinamen. This story has been told and re-told in the Navy, but it is worth repeating.

Jack Weir & the Capsized Junk

Sometime after the battle of Manila Bay, Admiral Dewey took the Olympia, his flagship, to Hong Kong. They had no means of quick communication with Washington at Manila. Communication was only through the dispatch boats, so going to Hong Kong would give them the crucial link of communication. Then, they had to resupply coal for the ship and I guess the officers didn't mind stretching their legs in the evening, so they pulled into Hong Kong.

The ship had been there about a week when one evening just about dusk there was a great deal of excitement. The Olympia was anchored far out in the bay and the junks were serenely sailing by with their old sails made of matting and whatever they could get to hold the wind, when all at once the quartermaster on watch dimly saw what appeared to be a junk, capsize. In those latitudes, the darkness comes fast and at certain times of the year, the tide runs very swiftly. However, in the light of the falling darkness, the object looked to be a capsizing junk.

Immediately the quartermaster reported it to the officer of the deck, telling him what he had seen, and the officer of the deck reported it to the first lieutenant, who happened to be on deck at the time, along with the admiral and the skipper. The first lieutenant started to call away a boat, but the captain spoke up and said, "Call away all boats and we'll make a competition of it. Pass the word that anybody who saves any men from the capsized junk, gets forty-eight hours liberty and a month's pay. Let's make a sporting event out of it and give the men something to keep them occupied."

This was done. The call went all over the ship and all the boatswains took it up. A little excitement! Not only did they

48

pipe the boats away, but they gave the general call to the buglers for abandoning ship, but of course, only the boats' crews went.

Now, up to this time, Jack had held about every rate in the Navy. He even, at one time falsely enlisted in the Marines because he couldn't get on a ship any other way. But he got it straightened up and got back into his new clothes. Jack had been everything from an ordinary seaman to a chief boatswain's mate. He would get busted for pranks and his devilment, but that would never deter him from the next one. He just couldn't help himself. He was a born comedian and he just had to do these things, that was all there was to it. Everybody expected it of him, too, which made it worse, and he just couldn't disappoint them. His name was famous (or maybe infamous) throughout the Navy. I heard about him the day I enlisted.

At the time of this story, Jack had been reduced to coxswain and was in command of a rowing cutter and always had a good crew. Somehow or another Jack was always able to get the best men. I guess they liked his stories. Therefore, his boat was one of the first to hit the water and get started out toward the spot indicated by the quartermaster as the place he had seen the junk go down.

Of course, the tide was running rather swiftly and by that time it was getting dark, and it was hard to see what was going on over where the junk had capsized. It wasn't long until Jack pulled over there. If there had been a junk capsize, Jack and his crew couldn't find it, nor did anyone else ever find it. But Jack kept his boat going towards the shore until he was sure he was out of sight of the ship and that the night glasses couldn't pick him up. He waited there until another junk came sailing along, its crew smoking their opium, dreaming of their favorite gods, and Jack boarded her.

The boat stretcher is the board against which the oarsman braces his feet, and every man had a boat stretcher in his hand

when the junk was boarded by Jack and his men. They threw all the poor men overboard and then proceeded to rescue them. The Chinese of those days believed that whatever happened to him was his fate and very few of them could swim. They believed that if it was their fate to drown, why then, drown they would. These Chinese men held to that creed and they didn't make any effort to save themselves. Jack and his crew threw them all overboard and then went around fore and aft with boathooks and pulled them all out of the water. They were thoroughly soaked and chattering like magpies, and Jack shoved them down in the stern-sheets, right by him, aft. When they started remonstrating, Jack simply tapped them on the bun with the tiller and they kept still. Jack with his chattering cargo turned back toward the ship and the junk drifted away into the night.

The other cutters and small boats of the ship had gone around in all directions and scoured the bay, but they didn't see any sign of a capsized junk, so they pulled back to the ship. Jack didn't show up! Even the admiral and the captain came on deck and began watching and waiting for him with interest. The first lieutenant was up there with them, and all the boys began to line up along the rail towards the shore, straining for a sight of Jack. Then the betting began. Sailors always gambled on events, and the betting was getting spirited. They laid wagers on whether Jack would get any Chinese men; how many he would bring back; and they even laid bets on whether he would come back that night or not. But the first lieutenant was Jack's strongest supporter.

"Jack gets into a lot of trouble and has to be dis-rated, but, by George, when it comes to a pinch or crisis, Jack is always there! I'll bet he comes in with some Chinamen."

Excitement was very high when the dip of the oars was heard, and everyone rushed to the rail. The quartermaster challenged the boat that was approaching, and sure enough, it

was Weir. He was standing up in the stern-sheets of his boat and his crew was given a race-stroke. Jack stood there giving them the stroke with his hands as though the fate of the ship depended on him getting back there quickly. The men from the "capsized" boat huddled down and were very quiet in the stern-sheets. Jack made an admiral's turn and brought his boat alongside, sensing the drama of it all. The first lieutenant rushed over to the gangway and asked, "Did you get any, Weir?"

"Yessss Sir! I got six."

"Ah, that's it. Did you lose any?"

"Got 'em all, Sir!"

"That's a sailorman! He gets drunk once in a while and gets in trouble, but he goes out and gets 'em. Come right on up and go down and change your clothes and get into your shore clothes. Go to the paymaster and draw your month's pay and get forty-eight hours liberty," he said. "You've earned it."

So, the boys didn't lose any time. All the rest of the boys on the ship volunteered to jump in and handle the boat while she was being hoisted. All that Jack's crew had to do was to boat their oars and get up the gangway. The drenched men didn't appear to be very happy about the rescue. They acted awfully funny and apparently were not a bit grateful. They began yapping and yapping and they couldn't speak a word of English. There was no one aboard that could talk Chinese--which was something in Jack's favor. These weary men made some very questionable moves and actions that appeared as though they were complaining.

In the meantime, Jack and his crew hurriedly got into their clothes. The officer of the day called away a special boat—probably the admiral's barge or the captain's gig—and sent them ashore. Away they went with forty-eight hours of liberty! Up to that time they had no liberty because only officers were allowed to go ashore, and they, presumably, only on business.

The mailman or the ship's steward was about the only enlisted men who got ashore. So, Jack got away with his whole crew in the special boat, in a blaze of glory, and those soaked men were still going around in circles on the quarterdeck, pouring out Chinese.

The first lieutenant couldn't get anyone who understood what they were saying so he turned to the captain and said, "I don't know what's the matter with those fellows, they act as if they are sore because we didn't save their boat."

'Oh," the captain replied, "get them off the ship! Call away a boat and get them off the ship!"

This was done and the poor men, who had been so woefully wronged, were taken ashore. I think the officers probably intended to give them some dry clothes, but I think they yapped so much that the officers got disgusted and just sent them ashore the way they were— without any hot tea or dry clothes. Be that as it may, Jack and his boys were ashore a long time before that with their forty-eight hours leave and a month's pay, so we didn't hear anything of them until the day they were to report back to the ship.

The following day, the captain of the Chinese junk came aboard, bringing an interpreter with him, and told the story to the ship's captain. Of course, it was too late to do anything about Jack and his crew, and they could only wait until they returned to confront them with the story. Despite what had been done, the officers had a good laugh in private over the whole thing, knowing full well that it was one of Jack's pranks.

Well, the boys had their leave and they weren't heard from until the day they were to report back. They began trickling back, one or two at a time. Some of them looked the worse for wear and some of them looked respectable; still, others were in pretty bad shape. They hadn't had any liberty all through

the war while they were waiting to get a whack at that fleet in Manila Bay, so they all made the most of their leave.

About twenty-four hours after the expiration of the leave, a thing arrived at the gangway and by stretching your imagination, you could identify it as Jack Weir. He was in terrible shape! Most of his clothes had been stolen; he had lost a shoe and his shirt—his blue shirt—his neckerchief, and his flat cap, and he was quite woozy, the aftermath of liquor, I suppose.

As soon as he came up to the ship, the officer of the deck notified the first lieutenant. The first lieutenant came to the gangway and met Jack and he just stood there looking at him, speechless. Jack looked back at the first lieutenant and finally got up enough ambition to give him something that looked like a salute, and a sickly grin. If you'd have seen it, you'd probably have laughed, too. Everybody else had to. Well, the first lieutenant looked at him again, and they stood there just looking at each other. The story told by the captain of the junk was going through the lieutenant's head—Jack throwing them all overboard and then fishing them out when they were about half-drowned. He knew the story had gone all over the ship. It was a good story on the first lieutenant and I imagine that secretly he had many a chuckle over it, but not publicly. So, he looked at Jack, and Jack just kept grinning. Finally, the first lieutenant said, "You blankety-blank, blankety blanketly blankety-blank! If that wasn't such a damn good joke on me, I'd court-martial you!" Then he roared, "Go forward!"

Jack saluted the best he could and went forward.

The story of that incident went all over the Navy and was a very famous story at the time.

Walking on Their Faces

There were times on the ship when life was pretty hard. Every ship had its quota of officers who thought they had to be mean and tough, and our ship was no exception. When we would turn out at midnight, we would, of course, be very sleepy. Boys always are. We would muster and then we would lay up alongside the weather rail so that we would be sheltered from the wind. There were several large tarpaulins and we would put these down and get under them and get some rest and keep warm. When we would be wanted by the boatswain's mate of the watch, we would disengage ourselves quickly and report. There was a first-class boatswain's mate on every watch and the chief boatswain's mate came on at the morning watch.

Now it seemed to us that we always had those mean, tough officers on duty during the mid-watch. Some of them would keep us on our feet most of the time. The boatswain's mate of the watch would pipe the watch to what duty was required of it and there would be a great stir as every boy sprang to his station. Pull on this sail! Pull on that sail! Haul away on this sail! Shorten that sail! Order after order just to keep us busy. They seemed afraid that we might get a little sleep. Well, anyway, that was the way it seemed to us.

We had one Limey first-class boatswain's mate who probably deserted from the English Navy. He was a most unpleasant fellow. In fact, we didn't like him one bit. He would sit back, close to where the officer of the deck stood his watch, and when everything would be going along lovely—the sails would be drawing perfectly—we'd just be on a nice breeze, and then all at once he'd say, "Boatswain's mate."

"Sir!"

"Lay aft the watch! Weather main-braces!"

Of course, we would all be sound asleep. He would go forward and start his boatswain's pipe for the watch and if they didn't just jump right out their skin and come to heel immediately, he would start up the deck, walking on their faces. Fortunately, often their faces would be covered up with tarpaulins, but a great many times they wouldn't be, and he would walk right on a fellow's face to wake him up. You can imagine the things we called him! Sometimes he heard us and sometimes he didn't. He never was much of a hand to get far away from the officer of the deck to call us because he was afraid that some of the boys would take a crack at him or hit him with a belaying pin and he wanted the protection of the officer of the deck.

This practice went on all the time during the whole cruise—for the whole six months. This boatswain's mate never lost an opportunity to wake us up at night and mostly without reason, except that he wanted to keep us on our feet. And he was generally with this officer I speak about. They were kindred souls.

After we left the Islands the food got worse and worse. In those days, it was hard to get fresh vegetables in Honolulu at the price we paid for them. Nine dollars a month wasn't very much—it didn't go far, even then. The boys were vegetable hungry. We loved the beans and we'd eat two great big plates of beans—the finest beans in the world because those old Navy cooks could sure cook them. But, we lacked vegetables and enough fruit. We were hungry for those foods and we would buy fruit for ourselves if we had the money. We had some bananas, coconuts, and fruits, but vegetables were very, very scarce.

The officers had two or three slatted lockers out on the midships—about midway between the foremast and the mainmast, right abaft the navigator's house. There were onions,

potatoes, and I don't know what all in these lockers and the boys on watch at night would lean up against them they would take their knives—regulation ship knives—and would cut slices off some of those vegetables and slip the slices through the slats and eat them. They even ate raw potatoes. The officers finally put a guard on those lockers, so we wouldn't eat up all their vegetables.

One night this Limey caught one of the boys with a half a slice of onion, or an onion sliced in half, in his possession, which he had just gotten out of the locker, and he ran the poor kid up to this mean officer that he always liked so well—to whom he was always so ingratiating— the one who allowed him to walk on our faces. Well, the boy was put on report and when we got to San Diego they held a summary court-martial and found him guilty for stealing this half an onion. He lost some of his pay and had fifteen days of confinement.

All the boys were particularly enraged over this and every chance we got we let this Limey know that there would come a day of reckoning. You know how youngsters like to talk big once in a while. Of course, it didn't seem to make any difference to this fellow at all, but I knew from the way the feeling was running, that something was going to come out of this incident.

After we got to San Diego and after the court-martial, when this officer (we'll call him "Mr. Barney" for the sake of giving him a name) would have the deck, some boy would get up forward and when he and the Limey weren't looking, the boy would heave an onion down the deck past Barney, and all the other apprentices would be on the other side and would yell, "Look out for the court-martial! Here comes the court-martial! Look out for the court-martial!"

I guess that didn't make those men feel so good about that onion incident, but youngsters don't always take things lying down.

But to go back to our voyage from the Island to San Diego, one night on the midwatch we were startled to have the lookout on the starboard cathead sing out, "Light-O!"

The officer of the deck answered, "Where away?"

The lookout came back with the "Broad off the starboard beam, sir!"

He had no more than finished than the man on the port cathead watch sang out, "Light-O!"

Again, the officer of the deck responded with the, "Where away?"

"Broad off the port beam, sir!"

The officer of the deck came forward about midships and then he began to laugh. He was highly amused and had a good laugh about it. It seems that we were looking at what is known as St. Elmo's fire. There was one on each yardarm of the topsail yard of the foremast. They looked just like great big fireballs and gave the appearance of two ships on fire a great distance apart. The sight gave us an uncanny feeling of the supernatural as we gazed at those two things about the size of a cantaloupe or a little bigger, maybe a football, at the end of the yardarm. I have been told that this phenomenon often occurs on sailing ships. This condition is not visible by daylight but at night, when the electricity collects on the yardarm it shows up in the darkness as a ball of light or fire on each end of the yardarm.

The Abduction of Nels Nelson

As we sailed on and on, we drilled and drilled and listened to more of Jimmy's stories when we gathered around his sea chest. One night we were gathered around, just shooting the breeze, and Bill Shaw brought the conversation around to the foremast man.

In those days, they had a man on the foremast and he was called the foremast man. The one on the mainmast was the mainmast man, and on some full-rigged ships, they had the mizenmast man. Those are the men who take care of the gear that is belayed around the mast and out at the tar-rail and keep it in its right position because it is quite a complicated thing to know every line and where it leads unless you have been a sailorman for many years. The reader may notice that I use the "sailorman" because in those days a man took pride in being a sailorman. You could tell him that he was a great fighter or a great wrestler, or a great oarsman, but when you said that he was a great sailorman, you covered it all, and those men took real pride in their work. They had to know their stuff. In years after, when steam came along, it did away with a lot of that feeling. You couldn't go up and take the wheel of a full-rigged ship at sea unless you knew how to steer because you wouldn't be allowed to. It was the same way with other things, too, so the word means just what it says—he is a sailorman!

We were sitting around that evening, talking, having jam sessions, and Bill Shaw spoke up. "Well, you never can tell about people," he said. "Now here's that foremast man. He's the funniest guy I ever saw. I don't really mean funny—I should have said queer. He's so grumpy that when you speak to him he just grunts at you. You can't even tell whether he understands

you or not. I know he's a Scandinavian, a square-head of some kind, but…"

"Oh," Jimmy said, "you mean Nels Nelson?"

"Yes, that's the guy," responded Bill.

Jimmy chuckled way deep down inside himself and said, "You know, Nels is getting along in years. It won't be many years now before he retires. He went to sea when he was just a kid, younger than most of you boys."

Jimmy took a deep breath, and he had a far-away look in his eyes. We began moving in. Here, we knew, was another story!

"When he was about eighteen or nineteen years old," he began, "Nels was on a full-rigged ship in the South Seas and they were getting short of water. Finally, they picked up this island, but the chart didn't show any island there and they didn't know anything about it. They sailed into a little bay on soundings and they found a pretty good channel. They went in as close as it seemed safe and dropped anchor. A party was sent ashore to see if there was any sweet water and they were lucky and found a dandy place where they could fill their casks. So, as the captain wanted to fill all his water casks, a party was sent ashore with them to be filled with fresh water which apparently was fine.

"The island was very thickly wooded and there were lots of coconuts and bananas and other tropical growth. While they were filling their casks, Nels Nelson, who was one of the shore party, spotted some bananas just a little way in from where they were getting the water in the jungle, and he saw an opportunity to get some fresh fruit for himself. That fruit looked mighty good to him because he hadn't had any for such a long time. He shinnied up the tree and got a couple of bunches of bananas and when he came down and turned around, there, right beside the tree, was a great big, black woman over six feet tall! She had a big club in her hand and she just let Nels have it on the head.

Lights out for Nels! That was the last thing he knew for some time. She grabbed him and took him into the jungle along her private path and when the boat was ready stowed, his shipmates looked around and they couldn't find anything of Nels Nelson. He had just vanished. Not one of the boys had seen what had happened to him.

"'Well," they said, 'he can swim well. We'll get along with our work and go aboard and stow this stuff and maybe he'll show up.' But it wasn't as simple as all that. This big amazon picked Nels up and threw him over her shoulder and carried him up to the village. Nels regained consciousness just about the time he got into the village. He found that they were a tribe of amazon women—tall, large, and strong. They allowed only so many male babies to live. All the rest were destroyed at birth. The women ran everything under the leadership of a queen.

"When the queen saw Nels with his lovely red hair and blond complexion, her heart just throbbed! He was bound, so that he could not escape, and was put in a tent. Two stalwart guards were put on watch so there would be no danger of Nels escaping from the tent, which was a crude affair.

"Now every black woman in the village had visions of a red-headed baby. Out in the South Seas, a white or light baby with red hair was the most prized of all. And one by one, they paid Nels a visit. Nels was a busy man for a while. He was a fine specimen of manhood himself, and they had him where he couldn't get away. Well, they held him captive all the next day and the night and the next day. Poor Nels! When he didn't show the proper interest, they would beat him or slap him, and they weren't delicate females, either. Well, this business turned into a serious thing for Nels. He didn't know what was going to happen to him. He was afraid that his ship had gone and left him. Fortunately, the skipper hung on a day or so, thinking that maybe Nels had become lost and that he would come out of the

jungle and find the shoreline and would look around and find where the ship was anchored.

"The next night the guard happened to get drowsy and Nels slipped through the grass and got away. He was bedraggled and weak by the time he got to the shore and slipped into the water. It was tough, but he summoned up all the reserve strength he had and swam to the ship. After they fished him out of the water, he went to the captain and told him what had happened to him. Well, every man on the ship thought it was a great joke but Nels couldn't see anything funny about it. Some of the men even offered to stay there but Nels warned them that it wasn't anywhere near the joke that they thought it was. He assured them that such an experience was a very serious and traumatic matter.

"This adventure, or misadventure, soured Nels. It was probably because he was the butt of his shipmates' humor. Wherever Nels went, the story followed him. When he went ashore he was sure to meet someone who knew about it and told the story with all the sailorman's humor that he could put into it. Enough was enough and finally, Nels became a lonely person because he shunned company to get away from the butts of their jokes. If you want to get him sore, just kid him and see what will happen to you. But you want to be ready to get out of the way!"

This story made quite a sensation among the boys. It seemed to fascinate them. Some of them even wanted to know where the island was—it's longitude and latitude. But, Jimmy said he didn't think that it existed anymore. He thought that probably conditions had changed now.

One day not long after that, one of the boys went by Nels and said to him, "How're your girls over on the island? Have you seen any of them lately?"

Nels bounded up and grabbed a belaying pin and it went whizzing by his head and just missed him by a frog hair. After that, hardly any of the boys bothered Nels, but when they did, they had to look out! Although he was getting along in years, he would hit anybody that would josh him about this amazon experience of his.

The Swallows of Capistrano & San Diego

Day turned into night and night into day and we drew nearer and nearer to San Diego. One day about noon, when we were two or three days away from our destination and still out of sight of land, there was a great living cloud that came over the ship. A nice, gentle breeze was blowing; every sail was set; this cloud bore down upon us and it proved to be swallows— thousands and thousands of them! They lit all over the rigging, all over the sails, the yardarms, every place that there was a space to light. They were so close that we could almost reach out and touch them. It didn't seem like there was room for another bird to light on that ship. I had never seen anything like it in my life, nor had I ever heard of anything like it since then. As they stayed on, the captain came on deck to look at them and then the first lieutenant came up, and they were both very interested in the spectacle. The captain gave orders not to disturb them although they would undoubtedly dirty up the ship a little. He said to let them stay, that they were an omen of good luck. So, they stayed.

After the birds had rested about four hours, suddenly they all flew up and away toward the north. It seemed that one minute the ship was covered with birds and the next, whoosh! They were just a receding cloud disappearing northward. Our birds were gone!

None of the old-timers at sea who were with us at that time could give any reason for this, nor any explanation of where they came from. One or two had seen flocks of birds light on ships before, but no one had ever seen so many, nor in that locality.

Time passed and in later years the Capistrano swallows became very famous, coming in and arriving at Capistrano on St.

63

Joseph's Day. No one knows how long this migration had been going on. They fly into the mission and drive the other birds out of their nests and proceed to rehabilitate their old nests or build new ones, as needed, and set up "housekeeping." People come from all around the country to await their arrival and each year the birds arrive just about the way they arrived on our ship. Since I became a navigator myself, I figured where the ship was at the time the swallows lit on the *Adams*, and as close as I could remember, and the distance that the swallows had to go, I figured that they just stopped on the ship for a rest en route to Capistrano. There was a good place to rest, and they were probably a little ahead of time. They weren't due until early the next morning, so they rested on our ship. I am fully convinced that that is what happened. I've seen no evidence to prove that I am wrong. It is a curious thing. The Capistrano swallows now are famous all over the United States. In those days I had never heard of them, but they were coming to Capistrano even then, as records prove.

A few days after the swallow incident about four o'clock in the morning, we picked up Point Loma lights. We had a very light breeze and when daylight came, we took in sail and raised our smokestack and started our "teapot" going. I really believe that, with everything favorable, and forces draft, we could make four or five knots under steam power. However, it got us clear of land or got us into port. It kept us from taking on pilots everywhere we wanted to go and eliminated the necessity of a tugboat to pull us in. It was a beautiful sight that morning, coming into the Silver Gate, as the entrance to San Diego is called, but of course, it was very different then than it is now. We steamed up the channel and anchored off the heart of the city. As I remember, there was one dock then, and we anchored off that dock.

San Diego was just a sleepy little Spanish village, you might say. Father Horton and his Horton House was the center of activity. He was a very reverend gentleman with a fine, luxurious, white beard and he did many fine things for San Diego. His faith in the city and its future was the rock on which the city was built.

In those days the blue-jacket, as the sailor was called, was rather frowned on in the better circles of society. This was probably because so many of the blue-jackets would be bad boys, not knowing people there. They would drink too much and frequent the section of town known as "stingaree." I guess the name will probably suggest what went on in that section of town. It held the bars, women of easy virtue, and that sort of thing. It wasn't very interesting to me, although I did want to see it, so I would go down occasionally with the gang. My great trouble— or difference—was that I didn't drink, and I didn't have any money to spend on that sort of thing anyway. Carousing was too expensive, but the boys would want to treat me, so I learned to take a cigar instead of a drink, and I would often come back to the ship with the whole front of my blouse sticking out with cigars. Since the apprentices were not allowed to smoke, I would give them away to the regular crew members who were allowed to smoke. Those trips were not very uplifting, but they did me no harm. I could recall old jokes about the place, but I will desist.

As I recall, we lay in San Diego Harbor for about two weeks. We did a lot of cleaning up and painting the ship while we were there, looking smart again when we proceeded on our way, this time to Magdalena Bay, located nearly at the end of the peninsula of Lower California.

The wind prevailing at that time of year in that section between San Diego and Cape San Lucas was always from the

northwest, consequently, we had a fair wind and not too much of it, therefore our trip was just about as perfect a ride on the water as one could have. It was perfect for drills and such things as that and perfect for our purpose. We put floating targets out on the way down and began gunnery instructions. None of those apprentice boys had ever shot a gun of that caliber. We had the old four-inch, breech-loading rifles, which were as modern as any at that time. We played lots of pranks in the evening, did lots of boxing and wrestling, all of which were good for us.

Harpooning for Steak

We were always hungry. Webber and I devised a means of getting a little choice titbit occasionally. The foretop of the foremast was directly over the edge of the captain's galley. The captain had a Chinese cook, and he was good, too. Well, we used to lay over the fiddle of the galley when he'd raise it while cooking meals to let the heat go up, and to keep his working area a little cooler. We would admire his beautiful little steaks and chops that we could see cooking on the top of the stove and it was just too, too much! We used to dream about them. It just hurt to think of them! So, we figured on what we could do about it. Finally, we made a little brass spear—very sharp—and we got a small line that reached from the foretop up above, down to the stove, and when he'd cook his chops and filet of mignons, one of us would get up on the foretop and lower our harpoon. The other one would hang over the edge. We would do this in the evening when there was no one around. Everyone was busy at something else. When the cook would turn his back to go away from the stove for a few minutes, why, we would let go with the harpoon, and you would be surprised how many times we'd hit it—how many times it would stick into the steak or chop. When the cook turned around, magic had happened, and the steak or chop disappeared.

At first, he accused the boys who were sitting close to the galley, then he accused the other cooks—the ones who cooked for the crew—of swiping the food that he was cooking for the officer. Of course, they denied it. The disappearance of those steaks and chops was quite a mystery! In the meantime, we fared on mighty good food. Just one chop or steak was a banquet for us. But, like everything else, a good thing had to end. When they could find no one else to blame, the finger of suspicion was

turned in our direction. Lucky for us that we had good friends who tipped us off that we were being watched, so we quit before we got into trouble. We were careful and when we learned that they were trying to catch the culprit, we did no more spearing, keeping in mind the court-martial of the lad who stole half an onion. I suppose we'd still be in jail if we had been caught eating a filet mignon. The call of the stomach was too great when temptation reared its ugly head, and we were very lucky to get by without being caught. I'm sure some of the boys knew, but none would ever make any trouble for us.

Magdalena Bay

As we sailed on and on, many miles south of Ensenada, some days the waters were quiet and still, and there was practically no wind. It was on those days the turtles came out. Oh, my! Great, big lovely green turtles! We harpooned one occasionally and then there would be turtle soup for all hands. I have never known of any place where there were as many turtles as there were down there in that section, and I have been almost every place from San Diego down to the Horn. But these were the greatest turtle waters in those days.

Magdalena Bay is a large bay, as one can tell from the charts, much larger than it looks from the sea, and that is where we were going. It has a good channel, so we got our "teapot" going and took in sail and steamed into the bay and anchored just off the town, which was just a sleepy little village.

We soon found that this little village had its problems, too. The greatest handicap at that time was that there was no fresh water in the town and they had to go about fifty miles, if I remember right, by boat and burro, to get fresh water and bring it to the town for the people to use for living purposes. There was a crude little dock there, the church and other buildings, and their cemetery which, I would say, was about six hundred yards from the center of the village. I have never seen a cemetery such as this one. They built an open box about three or four feet high, around three sides of the graves. This was to protect the candles and keep the wind from blowing them out on the nights they were burned over the graves of their loved ones. Many villagers would come two or three times during the night to keep the candles burning and say their prayers. No matter how crude and humble the adobe houses were that they lived in, the graves of their departed ones were always well kept. There were no weeds,

and everything looked nice and clean and orderly. They didn't have many flowers there because they had no water, and I think that when we were down there that time, there hadn't rained for forty years! About the only rain they get is when a hurricane swerves in from the southwest and gives them a little flash flood.

Magdalena Bay delighted us fellows because the bathing was just about perfect, and swimming was a most pleasant pastime since the water was so warm. Most of the time we were permitted to wear very little clothing because of the warm climate, and there was not much breeze as the place where we were anchored was sheltered by a little range of mountains or hills between us and the sea. The boys thoroughly enjoyed Magdalena.

Every afternoon we would go fishing. We would get the launch, or rig a sail on the cutters, and we'd troll. We used to catch those lovely, big sea bass and mackerel; the bay also abounded in the finest mullet that I ever saw. When it was discovered that they had all that wonderful mullet so handy in the bay, the petty officers told us about the net aboard the ship— a seine—and said that they would go with us and we could make a cast and see if we could get into the school of mullet so that we would have some delicious fish for all hands. Well, we did. We made a cast not far from the ship and happened to hit the school of fish. My gracious! What a catch! I wasn't ashore at the time. I remained aboard, but I could tell by the activity and what was going on that they had hit the jackpot. They had with them a little Swede coxswain— coxswain of the dinghy—and he came rowing madly over to the ship and the officer of the deck called, "Did you get any, Ole?"

"Oh, my Got," he says, "Chuck full mit the dinghy! Ten t'ousand on der beach!"

So that was the byword around the ship for a while. Everything was, "Chuck-full mit the dinghy und ten t'ousand on

70

der beach." However, we did furnish the town with nice mullet for a long time and they dried some of it to use at a later day. Mullet is a very choice fish, as people on the seacoast know.

We also had the finest variety of sharks anyone would want to see. Tremendous sharks! In later years, I got personally acquainted with a famous shark called Taboga Bill. The legend was that he took liberty parties ashore in Panama Bay and returned them to the ship. Of course, that is hard to believe, but a sailor will believe anything, anyway. But I don't believe he was any bigger than some of the sharks I saw in Magdalena Bay, and they didn't do any ferry business either.

We rigged up a very good range for heavy gunfire and a good course, and, considering the poor training the boys had been given, and the poor method of training in those days, I think we did very well. I look back on it and compare that with what is done today, and I wonder how in the world Dewey ever hit any Spaniards over there in Manila. But I guess the methods were the best known at that time. Then after we finished the heavy gunfire practice, we split up into four divisions—the first, second, third, and fourth division. We sent one division at a time ashore with all the equipment that they would use on a campaign ashore, including camping equipment. This operation was for small arms practice with the rifle. Our division was the second to go ashore. Each division put a week ashore on small arms practice, and everything went along nicely.

The Ghost on Saints Night

The camp was established on the south side of the cemetery and the range was just beyond that, where there was no danger of hitting anybody. When our time came to go ashore in the second week, we were all thrilled at the prospect of using rifles and live ammunition and living under regular military regulations for protecting the camp. We looked forward to sentry duty at night and the watches as we would have to stand them ashore. It was all so different from the life aboard the ship. We had four sentry watches at night and we were on duty for two hours at a time. Sentries were posted on all four sides of the cemetery and I am sure that the rest of the boys felt as uneasy as I did at the beginning. Cemeteries at night are spooky places.

The first night we were ashore I drew the two-a.m. sentry duty—two hours sentry watch. We were supposed to call the corporal of the guard and to use "halt! Who goes there?" and "Advance, friend, and be recognized," and all the military terms that were used at that time. I didn't particularly like the cemetery business. None of the boys said much and no one would admit that they were scared, but I had funny feelings in the pit of my stomach, and I admit to being apprehensive. But I went on my post at two o'clock in the morning and I got out there and tried to keep from shivering and to look as brave as possible. I wasn't cold, I was just scared. The man that I relieved told me that this was some Saint's night and he told me that they were burning candles on the graves. I could see one or two places where there was a faint glow of light, as it was a dark night with no moon.

I started walking bravely up and down. My post was along the east side of the cemetery, from south to north and back again. All was dark and what sounds there I heard, were magnified by the eeriness of the night. I increased my pace and

hoped that I wouldn't encounter anything. After a little while, when everything began to get familiar and nothing happened, I began to breathe easier and was getting braver and braver. I was beginning to feel easier in my mind when my serenity was shattered in an instant! All at once a white thing raised up out of a grave! And it looked twelve feet tall. Boy! When it raised up, my hair raised with it. I threw a shell into the gun (and I must admit to trembling when I did it). I was going to die fighting, anyway. However, I mustered up the courage to challenge this white thing that was approaching, but it wasn't as tall as it first seemed to be. Even if it was a ghost, I challenged it. I challenged it once! I challenged it twice! I was supposed to challenge it three times, but after the second time I heard a soft musical laugh and a sweet feminine voice speaking to me in Spanish, which I couldn't understand, and the white thing kept coming toward me. I realized that she was one of the villagers and I was mighty glad that I had held my fire. However, I called out for the corporal of the guard. I called out again, "Corporal of Guard!" as she came up, and I guess I could have been heard a mile away. She started to explain to me in Spanish why she was there. I know now what she was doing. Even then I got on to the fact that she wanted to take me over and show me the candles she was burning. But I had a good excuse to get out of that because the corporal of the guard came up about that time. He knew a little Spanish, so it was explained away without killing the poor Mexican girl. But she didn't know what a close call she had. I was mighty glad to get off sentry duty that night when my watch was up.

Turtle Races & a "Stingaree"

The ship was anchored in a spot which, I imagine, was about three miles on a direct line to the ocean; perhaps it was a little further walking the crooked path that we had to take to get there. There was always a big party of us going across to the ocean from the ship and we looked forward to going to the beach along the ocean in the afternoon or on Sundays, or whenever we could get away because we liked to do our swimming on the ocean side. There was such a beautiful beach there, and some days there would be nice big breakers coming in and we loved this. The beach along the ocean there was just as fine a beach as you would ever find. The gradual slope of the sand contributed to the easy roll of the surf and there was practically no undertow.

We would carry water to drink while we were at Magdalena Bay as it was warm and there was no fresh water at the beach, but nobody minded that.

We hadn't been anchored long before we learned that the turtles favored that spot, too. We would find them laying their eggs in good old turtle fashion by digging a hole and depositing their eggs in it, and then covering them up with the warm sand to let nature take its course. At that time of the year, the weather was warm, and the eggs would hatch themselves. We used to get the eggs when we could find a nest that had just been laid. They were fine eating if they were fresh, but if they had gotten too old, they weren't any good.

We found lots of turtles asleep on the beach enjoying the beautiful sunshine, and we soon learned about a new sport. We would run along the beach and turn them over on their backs and, because the beach was so smooth and level, they couldn't turn back again. After we had turned over all the turtles we needed, each one of us would grab one, turn him right side up,

74

mount him, and as he tried to get away, we would steer him out to the water. By stretching out flat on his back, we would take hold of the front of his shell with our hands, and every time he would try to go down, we would stop him by pulling up on the shell, and he couldn't dive.

It was great fun having races. First, we would each get a stable of turtles. Then we would all line up with our mounts and we would see who could win the most races. That was really fun! When one turtle would give out, we would let him go and would go back and get a fresh "horse" and go out again. I never ran into anything that was so much fun. By the time we had them all worn out, we would be worn out ourselves.

One day we were all enjoying our favorite sport and we heard one of the boys scream. Two or three of his shipmates ran over to him where he was hopping around on one foot. It seems that he had stepped on a stingaree {stingray}. The stinger is very poisonous, and it had caught him right above the knee. It must have been a big fellow. The bigger they are, the more powerful the poison and the faster it works. It was only a matter of minutes before we were all down to the beach ready to help. We grabbed the boy and laid him down on the beach and cut his pants open down the leg, and we could see that the stinger had gone in deep and his leg was starting to swell. We found a couple of pieces of lumber that had been washed in from some steam schooner or ship and we fashioned a crude litter by putting the two-by-fours through our white jumpers. There were two or three boys on each side to take hold of the litter, and we all started back to the ship on the run carrying this contrivance. When one fellow would give out, there would be a man to take

his place, and we carried him right down to the bay, opposite the ship. A couple of the boys who could run the fastest, went ahead to signal the ship by wigwag and tell them what had happened. By the time we reached the bay shore, there was a boat waiting and a doctor there to take charge. We quickly got him into the boat and took him aboard ship. His leg had swelled so much and had turned so black, that I thought he would surely lose it and so did another boy, too. The doctor saved his leg and it healed well, but for a while, he suffered a great deal of pain and it was quite a tragic accident.

We all learned a lesson and we were mighty careful boys after that so that none of us got near any stingarees. We learned to drag our feet through the sand because the stingarees lie along the beach in the sand where the water washes up on the shore, and they don't make a sound nor give any sign to let you know where they are, but if you step on them, they just flick that tail up and jab it into whatever stepped on or molested them. I suppose they catch their prey that way. But it was a bad ordeal for that boy and for all of us. We didn't go over to the beach for quite a while after that, as this episode made quite an impression on us.

A Dinner Party for the Mayor

The day approached when we were to leave Magdalena and boat up against the northwest wind to San Francisco for admiral's inspection and examination at the end of the cruise and then a furlough! But before we left, there were certain amenities which had to be taken care of, the most important being the entertaining of the chief official of the village.

A day or two before we left Magdalena, the captain gave a dinner for the mayor or alcalde, of Magdalena and his family. We had been used to seeing those ten or twelve children running around in just the skimpiest of clothes. The boys up to eight or ten didn't wear any clothes and the girls were about six years old before they had any kind of covering. So, on that evening the captain sent his gig over for the family, and it was a tight squeeze to get them all in. But, boy, they were cleaned and polished! They just shone. Their mother must have scrubbed them all day, and combed their hair and trimmed it, and put their best clothes on them. They really looked good. The mother was deserving of a lot of credit, with what meager means she had to do with.

They came aboard, and all the children stood about, wide-eyed and excited. Pretty soon Red Mike, who loved children, appeared and took over the brood while the captain took the mother and father below for refreshments. It wasn't long before Mike had a shy little girl in his arms and the rest of the little ones hanging onto him. He took great delight in taking those children over the ship, telling the boys all about the things that boys are interested in and making it a delightful experience for the little girls, too.

It was fortunate, indeed, that he could speak their language, but I guess most of the officers were able to make themselves understood. Finally, they all went to dinner, and the

party was a real success. When they came up on deck to go aboard the gig once more, those children were nothing but smiles and loaded down with goodies to take home with them including candy, cookies, oranges, and everything children liked. I guess the captain's cook must have been kept busy for several days before that dinner. Anyway, we didn't get any of his steaks, nor anything else that his cook was fixing up.

Guadalupe Island and Drills

A few days after the party the old familiar call of two quick beeps on the boatswain's pipe and then a long drawn one sounded at daylight between four and five o'clock and the call went out "All hands! Weigh anchor!" The first time I heard that call I wondered why they had to weigh the anchor. It seemed that every time they put it overboard they had to weigh it when they brought it back. But I was getting to be an old sailor by this time and I knew the answer. At that time, we hoisted the anchor by hand and, as we pushed the capstan bar around, we were entitled to sing "We are Homeward Bound," an old sea chanty. It's a long, long song. I can't remember any of it now because after that cruise I never again had to participate in hoisting the anchor by hand. We got the "tea kettle" going and we got the "old girl" well out of the bay because we had a prevailing northerly wind at that time of the year. It was a northwest wind, and we had to practically beat our way up the coast, so we had to get well offshore to get a little more wind…and lots of drills.

My goodness! I thought we never would get through sail drill. Just about the time, we thought we could sit down or take a nap, sail drill would begin again, and we thought we would wear all the lines out going up that coast. We had every kind of drill, even abandon ship in the boats. Everything that pertained to safety and efficiency on the ship was practiced then, and we were finally doing it well, too, and taking pride in it! We went so far out that we brought the Guadalupe Island close aboard on our starboard side.

Elephants in the Sea?

Guadalupe Island is the home of the sea elephants {elephant seals} and they abound in the waters and on the island. I thought the fellows were kidding me when they told me about there being sea elephants and I said, "Of course I know we have flying fish, but don't tell me there are elephants in the sea! That's a little too much for me." Well, everybody had a good laugh, but they didn't convince me until I saw one. Sure enough, when we were lucky enough to get up there in the daytime and close aboard the Guadalupe Islands, there were sea elephants, alright.

I suppose anybody that's been to the San Diego Zoo or some of the other zoos have seen them. They are very difficult to care for and it is hard to keep them alive in captivity because they require just the right kind of food and it must be given to them, consequently, they do not get the proper exercise in the zoo. They look like an elephant, in a way. They have a decided proboscis which could be said to resemble an elephant's trunk, although it is only about half the length. It undoubtedly assists them in catching fish. If they just had legs they would look quite a lot like an elephant. They weigh two tons and they are tremendous things. These great big, clumsy mammals look so lazy that you wouldn't believe that they could catch a fish until you saw it with your own eyes. But we watched them go down time and time again, and every time they came up eating a fish. They probably stowed another one away in their trunks.

Years afterward I had the pleasure of watching a Navy tug unload several sea elephants that were destined for the San Diego Zoo. Such unloading is quite a technical job and very interesting to watch. They seem to be harmless, but I wouldn't care to go over and swim with them. I don't know of any place else in the world where they exist besides the Guadalupe Islands.

The Admiral's Inspection

The trip north to San Francisco was uneventful. Everybody worked hard, and we were all anxious to get home. The day of our arrival had been set but we hadn't been informed of the date. We probably would have killed time out there on the high seas if it had been necessary, but our officers knew their business and we got into San Francisco Bay on the day scheduled for our arrival.

It was on a Thursday night that we anchored off the old *Pensacola* at Goat Island. Those rookies ashore and on the *Pensacola* were as excited about us as we had been about the previous class of apprentice boys, but we had great contempt for them because they were landlubbers—very ignorant people—and we were now Sailormen!

We had worked very hard while we were going up the coast, making ourselves fit for the examination we would have to take. The sailmaker had classes in sail making; the bo's'n's mate had a class in splicing and in worming {protecting a section of rope from chafing}, in parceling {winding tarred canvas around a rope}, and in everything pertaining to the line gear. We were now able to make any part of the standing gear of the ship such as rattlings {ratlines}, backstays, and we were able to do splicing, even cable. By the time we got to San Francisco, we knew how to follow every line from its place on the sail, down to where it belayed, and there were many of them, I'll tell you! By this time every apprentice had taken his trick at the wheel regularly until he now knew how to steer. Of course, we had been doing all of this during the whole trip, but we were drilled especially hard while going up the coast on this final leg of the cruise. While heading into the wind we were executing all kinds of sail

maneuvers and we were busy getting the ship clean. We were, indeed, a bunch of busy boys.

We were ready for the admiral's inspection by the time we got up to San Francisco, and it came off in fine shape. We all did very well and even got a compliment from the admiral himself. Everyone in our class passed the examination. However, there had been two boys who had been let out because they were considered unsuitable for the service and before that, while we were in Honolulu, there had been a couple of boys let out because of chronic seasickness. They had tried, oh so hard, but they never were able to overcome their seasickness. Therefore, out of nearly one hundred and twenty boys, there were only four who didn't make the grade.

Revenge of the Apprentice Boys

In those days, they gave a medal which was called the Bailey Medal, to the most outstanding boy in graduating apprentice classes, and it was won through examinations. The smartest boy on the west coast was pitted against the smartest boy on the east coast in the final heat to win the medal. Imagine my surprise when I was selected as one of the two boys on the west coast to compete for the honor of representing the west coast in the finals. However, I asked to have my name withdrawn because I knew that the other boy who was picked along with me had the advantage of a better education and the medal didn't interest me much. The other boy was a smart lad and I knew that he could execute any of the other parts of the examination just as well, if not better than I could. When the finals came, the boy from the east coast won the competition and the medal.

As soon as the examinations were over it was customary for us to go ashore and away on furloughs. For several days before we were ready for this, there was an undercurrent running along the grapevine. Two or three fellows with their heads together swabbing down decks were talking in very low in undertones at the scuttlebutt. It was barely noticeable, but it was going on all over the ship. Whispering, whispering, whispering! And all of it had to do with that Lime-juicer who walked on our faces. Word had it that we were to meet at a certain place ashore down in the Barbary Coast region, and await the arrival of that certain guy, even if we had to wait all night.

The examinations being behind us, we were paid what money we had left on the books. Our pay was nine dollars a month to spend, so we had most of that left as there had been no place to spend it. Sometimes an emergency would come up

and in such cases, we could draw against our accounts, but such an operation required an excellent reason.

So, when we were paid and received our furloughs, we were all ready to leave. We were now sailormen. We could smoke or do anything that the regular crew had been doing. Our ditty-bags and boxes and hammocks were ready. These were to be taken to the receiving ship at Mare Island, which was called "the Guardo." I do not know why they called it the Guardo, but it was always referred to in that way. While our gear was to be taken to the receiving ship, we were to be taken ashore to get our trains, boats, rigs, horses, or whatever mode of transportation we were going to use to get home or to get to our furlough destinations. There were no buses in those days, although one could get a horse-drawn stage to destinations that were not served by other modes of transportation. The *Adams* would leave for a cruise to the Puget Sound area for recruiting purposes.

It was about noon when we all went ashore. All the cutters were filled up with boys going ashore and we were towed by the steam launch to the landing in San Francisco. As we poured out of the boats we headed straight for the rendezvous. Our "secret service" had learned that the Lime-juicer was going ashore that afternoon and there wasn't one of us who didn't want to get at least one punch at that fellow who had been so mean to us throughout the cruise and who had consistently made it a point to walk on our faces whenever he could.

Two boys who had come over from Goat Island were selected to await his arrival and to follow him in regular cloak-and-dagger style so that we could keep track of him. When he finally came ashore he headed for a place which was not far from our rendezvous. One of our lookouts came to notify us of his whereabouts, so we all headed there.

It was late afternoon. Some of the boys had been having a few beers, or something stronger, to fortify themselves. Our

actions were not commendable. There was only one poor Lime-juicer and there were a good many of us. But there wasn't a boy among us who didn't want to get one poke at him. Even I, who didn't pose as a tough guy, wanted just one whack at him. Oh, we didn't use any clubs or anything like that. We just used our bare fists.

Some of the boys in the party were husky lads and had been fighting in bouts aboard the ship. They later went into the ring and became outstanding fighters of the time. There were some heavy-weights and light-weights, any one of which could have cleaned him up without any help, and that is just what they had intended to do. They were just going to let one of these men step out and start something. But we couldn't wait. We flocked into this place and surrounded him and gave him a terrible beating. Finally, the police arrived and rescued him, but he was busted up by that time. I am ashamed to say that we were so hard on him that he spent his furlough in the hospital. But, I'll bet he learned his lesson and that he never walked on the face of another apprentice boy while he was in the Navy.

That party was over, and I headed for the depot where I caught the train for San Jose, where I was going to visit with relatives for fifteen days, after which I was to report to the *Independence* at Mare Island. It had been a fine cruise. I weighed only ninety-seven pounds when I started and I came back weighing well over one hundred and twenty pounds. There wasn't an ounce of fat on me. It was all good, hard muscle. I felt wonderful, but I was hungry all the time. My furlough had at last begun. I was looking forward to eating good home-cooked meals where there was always plenty of food and the women just loved to cook for boys who had appetites and appreciation like mine. Fifteen days before I had to report to the Guardo!

Commissioned 1897,
Recommissioned 1903 to 1908 (1914 and 1919)

USS *IOWA* & HOSPITAL AT MARE ISLAND

Gimpy Evans

Robley Dunglison "Fighting Bob" Evans

I had a wonderful time visiting my relatives, but I missed the boys and I was glad to get back with them again at the Guardo. I arrived at Mare Island on the day that I was supposed to be there and, never having been there before, everything was new to me.

The *Independence* was an old-timer. She had cockroaches that I swear were almost as big as jackrabbits. I never saw any cockroaches before nor since that could compare with them. They had quartets and sextets, and I truly believe that at night they would get out and stage an opera. They were the biggest things of their kind I had ever seen and there never

seemed to be any limit to them. Pest control was not known in those days and they didn't know how to cope with cockroaches as they do now. We used to say that they were old boys waiting around until their thirty years were up, like old sailors.

Half or maybe even seventy-five percent of the men in the crew of the *Independence* were waiting and killing time until their thirty years in the Navy were up. Some of them were old men. It was quite amusing to see those old men come down in their tight-fitting sailor suits. They looked like little boys.

Duty was rather boring at the Guardo because there was practically no drill and after our strenuous training on the *Adams*, we had very little to do except swab down decks and take care of ourselves, and we missed all that activity that had kept us jumping on the training ship. It was very slow, just waiting for some ship to call for some of us to complete its crew, and the wait seemed longer than it actually was. It was probably only a few days, maybe a week or ten days at most until drafts began to come in and some of us were called up. I think The *Philadelphia* was the first to draft. They had a good, large draft and took about a third of our class to replace the men whose time was running out; men whose service was getting close to discharge time, and that ship was short of men in its crew anyway. Then it went along for another week or so and there came a draft for the *Boston*, which took almost another third of us. Occasionally there would be requests for one or two boys for special duty or a couple of boys for some small ship in the fleet. That left about a third of us on the *Independence*.

One morning when we got notice, I was called up and told that I was going to the battleship *Iowa*. Well, that pleased me. She had done good work during the Battle of Santiago Bay and I admired the captain of The *Iowa* very much, and to this day, I claim that he was the smartest admiral the Navy ever had. He was only a captain then, but afterward, he led the fleet around

the world, and he was affectionately known as "Gimpy" Evans. He had been wounded during the Civil War and it left him with a limp. But he was a very smart man. There was nothing that a man on a Navy ship knew that Gimpy Evans didn't know, too, and he could tell a man all about it. With this draft, all the rest of us went up to San Francisco on a tug and aboard The *Iowa*. She didn't come up to Mare Island because no drydock would accommodate her there. We went aboard, and oh, I was so proud. She was just about the greatest ship I had even seen— the biggest and the most comfortable thing that I was ever on. She was what was known as a "home," and if the crew did their work, they enjoyed that ship.

We coaled the ship a few days after I got aboard and boy, that was really hard work! Big baskets of coal were passed by hand. We'd get on platforms and pass them right up from the lighters. A lighter was a flat-bottom barge that transported the coal to us. It seemed to me that we took all the coal that there was in the world when we coaled our ship. It was a job! I thought that she must have been about empty when she got to San Francisco. She had just come back from the east coast and the war and didn't know when orders would be received to go again, so she was filled to capacity. I never was so tired in my life as after passing that coal. It was very hard work. The captain put it up to the boys whether they wanted to continue to work late that night, finish up quite early in the morning to clean ourselves up, clean the ship, wash down, and then go ashore on liberty.

Anything that Gimpy wanted, they would agree to. How dirty everything got! Coal dust all over the ship. We put on our old white work pants and an old blouse and tied our necks up and the bottoms of our pants, put on old shoes, and we got out there and worked. We were so covered with coal dust and so black that we looked like a gang of negros. We got so black

89

because that coal dust got into our hides. Well, we worked until ten o'clock and knocked off. Then we had a cup of hot, black coffee. Nobody took his hammock out. Nobody wanted to get his bedding dirty because it had to be washed all over again if he did that. The bedding was all in the hammock nettings, away from the coal dust.

Earlier, during the operations, I had noticed a little fellow running around, up one lighter, down another. I asked one of the other boys who that guy was that kept going around there as if he was running the whole job. He laughed and said, "He is running the job. That's the Old man! That's Captain Evans! That's Gimpy himself."

"My," I said, "he doesn't have to do that, does he?"

"No, he doesn't have to do it but just does it. He's that kind of an officer."

After we had our coffee, we all hunted a warm spot such as some old canvass or anything we could find. I squeezed into a spot on the engine room or the fire room hatch, I forgot which. It was warm, and I dropped off to sleep as soon as my head touched something solid to rest on. During the night, somebody crowded in there with me and got his knee in my stomach. It woke me up. It looked like he was going to take all my place and crowd me out, so I started cussing and shoved his knee down, out of my stomach, and I cussed him out thoroughly. By that time, I knew how to handle cussin' which I had learned from some very good cussin' men. Well, he didn't say a word. He just turned over the other way and we managed to sleep until morning and time to turn to. They called us early at four or five o'clock. We got a cup of black coffee and turned to, in order to

finish the job before breakfast. When the bugle call and bo's'n pipes awakened us, and as I became more conscious, I looked over to see who this guy was that was poking me in the stomach with his knee, and there was that presumptuous guy who was running around and up and down all over the lighters the day before—the Captain! He looked at me and just grinned and went up on to his quarters. There was nobody else who knew anything about that night.

Years afterward I was asked to join the American Legion Post that was named after him. It was called the Fighting Bob Post, and they had nobody joining who had ever served under Bob Evans. Somehow or other they found out that I had served under him for a short time on The *Iowa*, so they came and asked me if I would join. His son was to be the first commander of the Post. So, I joined the Post so that they would have at least one member who had served under Gimpy Evans who they referred to as Fighting Bob. While we were waiting for the ceremonies to begin, I had a nice talk with his son who was a captain in the Navy at that time, and he had never heard anything about the incident when his father had bedded down with me, and he was quite amused by it.

"That was the Old Man!" he said. "That was the old man, alright."

William Goat

Before I go any further, I want to tell about the ship's mascot. This narrative would not be complete without a bit about him. The *Iowa* had a goat which they called William Goat, and he was their mascot. He was in the battle of Santiago with them. This goat was exceptionally well trained, and he was very close to being human.

The boys got him when he was very young, and they fed him on the bottle, I guess. They made a hammock for him and taught him to go up a rope ladder from the deck to the hammock, where there was a nice bed. William fell right into it. It didn't take him long before he got the idea and he wouldn't sleep any other place. Then, in the morning he'd come down, but it was a little harder to teach him how to get out of the hammock. He would struggle down, hang on until he could get down to the deck. His hammock was marked, "Wm. Goat." Since he grew up in the Navy, he had a great antipathy towards civilians and the boys helped this feeling along to make him dislike civilians, but he played with everybody on the ship.

About once a month we had general muster at which time the Articles of War were read. We all lined up on the deck where we belonged in our division, with the first lieutenant of each division standing in front of his division, and right behind this division officer stood the chief master-at-arms. After the reading of the Articles, each man answered "present" as his name was called, and he stepped out, went forward, and he was checked off.

William belonged to the chief master-at-arms on the gundeck, and the goat was combed and brushed, and his horns were polished and shined like a ship's bell, and he was dressed in

his full-dress uniform which was a red felt with his mascot stripes and his war service stripes. He seemed to feel that he had to act more dignified and proud, for William, too, answered muster. The names were arranged in alphabetical order so when the ship's writer came to the "G's" and the mascot's name, he would call out, "William Goat, Mascot First Class," and William would let out a loud bleat and go forward as the men did. This always got a good laugh out of everybody, including the admiral himself, if he was aboard.

The goat went anywhere he wanted to go on the ship. Well, he could climb like a goat! The boys taught him a lot of other tricks. Some of them were in fun, some of them were serious tricks, and always he had that intense dislike for civilians. He would go ashore when the chief master-at-arms went ashore, and when the whole bunch went ashore in San Francisco, William Goat went ashore, too. They checked him off at the gangway. His name was on the liberty party. They'd sing out "William Goat" and he'd let a bleat out of him, step forward, go down the ladder, get in the liberty boat, and he'd stay with the bunch until they came back to the ship. I never went to a hotel with them, so I'm not sure whether he stayed in their room (he probably did) or not. William had very good manners and he was kept very clean. Every morning he had a bath and was washed down. William was one of the few sweet-smelling goats that I ever encountered.

Well, one holiday we had a parade in San Francisco. I don't remember which one it was, but it was a big and important parade and we were to be in it. Every man in the battalion not needed aboard went ashore and paraded, including the ship's band and William Goat. William had a magnificent suit to wear for such occasions. All the tailors had cooperated to make it a fancy thing. It was made of red felt and across the back, in gold letters was "William Goat, Mascot Ist Class, USS *Iowa*." He

always marched in the parades and he always wore this fancy uniform. I think he got more of a hand than any of us. He would walk in a proud and haughty manner with his eyes front. This applause from these mere civilians didn't affect him at all. He just marched on with great dignity.

After the parade was over, a good many of the boys didn't go back to the ship. There wasn't anything special for the boys to do except to make the rounds and spend their money. So, a bunch of the boys, including the chief master-at-arms, who was the custodian of William Goat, went into a saloon on Market Street and William went in with them. The goat put his front feet up on the bar for his glass of beer, and if he didn't get it, he would let them know about it in no uncertain terms. He was in there with us having a good time and he had had a couple of glasses when he stepped outside, and immediately we heard a great commotion out there. One of the boys looked out when William began blatting, and people were beginning to gather and make a lot of noise. Then we all looked out to see what was going on and what we saw was the pound-master with his net, trying to corral our William by putting his net over him. He intended to take him to the pound {animal shelter}. Of course, William yelled for all of us, and he took a stand against that pound-master. We all streamed out of that saloon and when the pound-master looked up and saw a bunch of wild-eyed blue jackets coming for him—some of them husky boys—he changed his mind about catching William Goat and he jumped into his wagon and away he went as hard as he could get his horses to go, cracking the whip all the way. William made a lunge after him, loudly blatting, just as if he were saying, "Come on back and fight like a man!" This little episode gave us something to talk about for a long time afterward.

William took a lot of watching, especially when there were civilians aboard. We generally tied him up with a chain

when one visited the ship because anyone who would bend down to fix his shoelaces was in jeopardy. William would hang around for just such a chance, and he was a good shot, too. He would make right for him and dump him every time, and you may be assured that this action was not appreciated as there wasn't a soft spot on the deck to land. The boys taught him to do that, so you couldn't blame the goat much. The boys who were there at the battle of Santiago said that all during the battle, William ran up and down the ship. They thought they had put him away safely, but as soon as the guns started to fire, he got loose somehow and ran up and down the deck, blatting and giving his private opinion of the Spaniards. I guess he had more fun than the boys did. He thought it was a celebration.

The Realm of King Neptune

One of the things that I remember on The *Iowa* was that there was never anything that went on aboard that ship that Gimpy didn't know about. His eyes were open all the time and he was on the quarterdeck most of the time. He never missed a thing. At that time, all signaling was done by wigwag as the semaphore {an upright post with arms moving vertically used for signaling} had not yet been adopted. It was all wigwag, which was Army and Navy code. Often while he was walking up and down the quarterdeck, getting his ship exercise, some other ship of the fleet would call The *Iowa*. He'd stop and watch the signal, and if the boy didn't catch it, and would make the familiar "C C C," meaning repeat, oh boy! Gimpy would go right up in the air.

"Answer that signal, you dumb-head! Answer that signal!" he would shout. The boy would look back on the quarterdeck to see who was yelling at him.

"Come down here!" Gimpy would call, and the signal boy would go down and he would get a roasting! The captain had caught it all, and oh, he would roast that signal boy. You can just bet that that boy got busy right away and boned up on his wigwag. The old sailors on that ship knew very well that somewhere Gimpy had an eye out when they were signaling.

Captain Evans was known as a sailor's captain. He was a sailor's admiral. If you were right, Gimpy would go to the bat for you. If you were not right, you were done. There was no foolin' about it.

A short time after coaling the ship we left San Francisco and went down the west coast of North and South America to Chili and clear down to the Straits of Magellan, then back up the coast, stopping at Valparaiso and Callao. I don't remember

whether we coaled ship on the trip or not, but when we returned to San Francisco, we coaled ship again.

It was on this trip that I was initiated into the Realm of King Neptune when I crossed the equator. I was shaved with a razor made of tin from the lid of a hardtack can and a shaving brush made of a whitewash brush, and anyone who didn't keep his mouth shut got a mouth full of soap. Everybody who had never crossed the equator had to go through this ceremony and were given a very fancy certificate to be shown if there was ever any question about having gone over the line. Of course, the boys who did the initiating had the most fun, but after it was all over we could laugh and think about what we were going to do when we were a member of an initiating party.

Signal Boy

After coaling again in San Francisco, we put to sea again, this time heading for Bremerton, Washington, where we were going into drydock at the Puget Sound Naval Shipyard. The *Iowa* was just a little too big for the Mare Island drydock.

On the way up, my division officer took the new boys and gave us an examination to see how much we knew. When he came to me and was on signals and wigwag, he sent me a wigwag message and I got it. I sent him one back that was just a little too fast for him to catch, so then he sent me one as fast as he could send it, and I sent him another one back that he couldn't catch. It was too fast for him and he was quite surprised.

"You know that stuff, don't you?" he said.

"Why," I replied, "it comes natural to me. I was signal boy before I went out on the training ship, and all the time I was on the training ship when they needed help, I would fill in."

"Well," he said, "how about the Navy Code of Flags? Do you know the flags?"

"Yes, Sir, I know the flags," I answered. Then he took out the book and he asked me what they meant as he pointed to different flags and covered their names, and I knew them all. I told him what they were for.

"You're really okay," he said. "You're really good at it. How about the merchant code, the international code? Do you know that, too?"

"Yes, Sir," I said. "I know the flags."

"Ah! That's fine. I am glad to hear that." He then gave me one or two more tests in signaling and then he asked me if I could sew flags.

"Well," I answered, "I haven't had an awful lot of practice but I'm pretty sure I could."

When he finished the examination, he gave me a note to give to the chief quartermaster and the navigating officer who oversaw the signal division of the quartermasters and signal boys. That was how I was assigned to the bridge as a signal boy. There was no extra money, of course, because we were not supposed to get any more money for a year after being made a second-class boy, although I was fortunate enough to do so. This assignment was pretty nice and very interesting, giving me contact with the old quartermasters and signalmen. They were a kind of family of their own and it was pleasant to be among them.

A Lovely Lady in Bremerton

Bremerton was, and still is, a beautiful spot. After spending all my time before this in southern waters, the northwest made a tremendous impression on me. At that time, the drydock was made of wood, rather than cement, but it was large enough for our ship. She was such a comfortable ship and so fine at sea, that it was a pleasure to be on her.

After we arrived at Bremerton and were berthed in drydock, we got liberty. The chief quartermaster was especially nice to me but there was a first-class quartermaster who was born in the Puget Sound country who took a shine to me. He was about middle life and seemed pretty old to me. His name was Peter Hansen. I think that he liked me because I did my work well and showed him a great deal of respect. I did like him and I am sure that he felt flattered by this admiration. So, when he was getting ready to go ashore he asked me to go with him. I looked out from the ship at the straggling town and said, "I don't know what you're going to see."

"Oh," he replied. "I've been up here many times before," and he smiled, "I know my way around."

That sounded like kind of a joke to me, but I said, "It looks to me like it's all woods. We might run into bears out there. Hadn't we better take a gun along?"

The town seemed to be about three blocks from east to west and four blocks from north to south beyond the Navy yard. We walked along going north-northeast for two or three blocks on the wooden sidewalks, then we came to the end of them and the town thinned out and we proceeded along a well-worn path. I asked him what we were going to see out there and I said, "You don't think you're going to run into a bear without a gun, do you?"

"No, no," he said, "it's alright. I have a little business to transact out here. After I'm through, then we'll go and see the rest of the town. I want a few drinks, you know." He liked his beer pretty well. So, we went along the path for another block or two and came to a very nice house of about eight or ten rooms. It was painted white and was exceptionally clean and well kept.

The appearance of the place greatly impressed me, and I said, "Oh my, the people who live here must be awfully rich!"

He grinned more to himself than at me, and he replied, "Well, I don't know about that. They do have a nice place out here."

We went to the door, he rang a bell, and a colored girl greeted us wearing a black dress, a stiff white apron, and a little French cap on her head. Pete gave his name and she asked us in and took us into the parlor. It seemed to me that I could see a couple of parlors. The place was well furnished in the style of the era and everything had such a polished, well-kept look. We sat down, and it wasn't long before a very nicely-dressed woman came in and she seemed very glad to see him. They shook hands and she was very cordial to us. She asked him if I was his son.

"No, no. He's just my boy. He's a signal boy," he exclaimed. "I'm showing him the town."

She giggled and they both laughed about that. Then he asked about some girl. I didn't catch her name. "Is she still here?"

His friend answered, "Oh, yes, she's still here."

"Is she busy?" he asked.

"No, I don't think so," she replied. Then our hostess sent the colored maid after the girl and it wasn't more than a few minutes before she came in. She was nicely "gotten up" but I was amazed at how short her skirts were. In those days women didn't wear skirts up above their knees, but she had hers way up and very little coverage on the top. They all laughed and seemed

to enjoy some joke that I wasn't in on, and it made me feel somewhat uncomfortable. It was all over my head.

Finally, Pete said, "Please excuse us. We're going upstairs and see some pictures she wants to show me." Our hostess nodded and said that she would visit with me while they were gone. They all looked amused, and Pete and the other woman went upstairs and left me in the parlor.

I soon found out that Pete's friend who remained with me knew a lot about the Navy and had a lot of friends who were in the Navy, and she seemed to know about all the far-away places where they had been. She asked me about my experiences and all about my cruise. It seemed that there were a lot of boys from around Bremerton and Seattle in our class, and she knew who many of them were, who their parents were, and all about them. It was comforting to me in my embarrassment to find that we had friends in common.

Finally, Pete came back, and the girl came back with him. We all talked for a few minutes longer and then we shook hands and took our leave. They told me to call again, to come around and see them any time, and I said, "Thank you kindly. It's very nice. I don't know anybody up here but it's nice to have a place to go." And that tickled them, too, and seemed to make quite a hit with them.

Then we went back to town and saw Bremerton, such as it was. There was a small department store which sold mostly dry goods and notions, and a grocery store that drew the flies from near and far. I can't remember what else was there besides saloons. In addition to exploring the town, we had a nice walk in the woods. We'd go to the end of a street until it would run into a path to the woods and we would explore a little way along the path and then we'd come back and get into civilization again and walk down another street. We had a dandy time. Pete and

I went into two or three saloons and he renewed old acquaintances and had a beer each time, but they served me a soft drink, being that I was underage and still looked it. We managed to kill an afternoon and evening, then we went back to the ship. That was about all there was in Bremerton. Seattle was the only place one could go for more sightseeing and excitement.

The next day I was talking to the boys aboard and told them I had been walking with Pete and he showed me the town, and they said, "Did he show you everything?"

"I guess so," I answered. "He told me so. There wasn't very much to see except this nice house we went to. It was a nice place where they evidently have lots of money. They have a servant girl that comes to the door. She wears a black dress, a stiff white apron, and has a little white cap on her head. They must have lots of money to run a place like that."

The boys looked kind of funny for just a second and then they busted out laughing. They howled and guffawed and slapped each other on the back, and they just about rolled on the deck, they laughed so hard. It was a couple of days before I learned where I'd been and why the boys had laughed so hard. I always laugh at myself when I look back on it.

I remember afterward that I had heard some women talking and they seemed to be speaking a foreign language or speaking broken English. It seemed that they had a powerful accent which I couldn't quite identify but I imagined it was French, and I found out later that I was right. I look back on those things now and get a terrific kick out of it.

Everett and "Annie's Corsets"

From Bremerton, we went to Seattle where I had some distant relatives. There I enjoyed myself very much. A Seattle doctor had married a lady who was a second or third cousin of mine. They had a nice home and I was invited to visit them and I certainly did enjoy it. It was just like being home. And how I enjoyed the cooking! These people knew about boys and they liked to see me eat with such relish and they filled me up. How good everything tasted! Their little girl was eleven or twelve years old and she made me her idol, which gave quite a boost to my ego.

After spending a few days in Seattle, we pulled up anchor and went to another place called Everett. It appeared to be a new town. Some of the stores were built and a few houses were there, but they were making streets and laying out the town nicely. I remember that I thought it was an especially nice layout because it had such wide streets and I wondered what they were going to do with those great big wide streets. Well, I was up there maybe five or six years ago, and they didn't look so wide anymore. In fact, they didn't look wide enough. But at the time that I was first there, I thought that that was one of the prettiest sites for a town that I had ever seen.

After a day or two at Everett, we were ordered to Anacortes for the Fourth of July. They were to have a big celebration including bicycle races, ball games, contests, and whatnots.

There were one or two big canneries there and the boys were quite delighted that they were going to go there and see all those cannery belles (lots of dates) and that they were going to have such a good time with a big dance and quite a blowout to top it all off. We sure did have a swell time.

104

We lay-to off the cannery wharf and the boats were busy all day taking people back and forth to visit the ship. Nobody seemed to mind the fishy smell and we got used to it after a while. We had a fine time anyway. Of course, we had to give the town a nickname. With a name like that, we couldn't pass up the opportunity, and we were delighted when someone called it "Annie's Corsets," and we all took it up. I've always thought of that town as Annie's Corsets ever since, and I catch myself saying that instead of Anacortes, even now.

While we were at Anacortes there was an incident that irked me to no end. I couldn't get rid of that kid look, and I still looked like a youngster. The older men on the ship had quite a lot of fun showing me off, like I was only ten or twelve years old, and seeing the surprised look on people's faces.

One afternoon I was stretched out on the boatswain mate's chest, just a little way from the number-one companionway to the gundeck. I had not gone ashore with the boys. There was no one in Anacortes that I knew, and I didn't care particularly about being ashore, and our ship was full of visitors anyway. The chief boatswain's mate of our division came down the ladder with several people who had come over from the town, and he was showing them around the ship. There were five or six in the group and it struck me that it was a nice family, there being girls and boys and a couple of older people who I judged to be the father and mother in the party. I was stretched out on the chest, just half dozing, when the boatswain's mate spoke to me, and I raised up. Then I jumped up thinking those people might be his folks or somebody he knew and that he wanted to introduce me to them. But he didn't. If he knew their names, he didn't say a word, but he just had me stand there so they could look at me! Then the lady exclaimed, "Why, he is only a child. Just a child!"

Of course, that made me mad. I was hurt deep down. I had made my cruise, and everything had gone fine. I had gotten good marks and I was doing well on The *Iowa* on the bridge, and I was rather proud of myself. Then to be called "just a child" really stabbed me to the heart. Without thinking, and rather tartly I'm afraid, I said, "I can hold my own and do my work, anyway." The lady looked startled and realized that she had hurt my feelings, but she didn't say anything more.

The chief boatswain's mate said, "Yes, he can hold his own. He's just as good as any man I've got in the division."

That mollified me a little and I chatted with them for a while. They asked me if I missed my mother and I told them of course not (which I wouldn't admit that I did). Then the lady asked me, "How do you get your washing done?"

That also nettled me some, but I answered her, "My mother washed my clothes until I went into the Navy, and," I said, "I ought to be able to wash them now!"

They thought that was pretty good. I'll never forget getting up off that chest, thinking I was going to meet some nice people, and then to be called "just a child!"

Sick Bay for Six Months

From Anacortes, we went over to Port Angeles, a beautiful spot on the Olympic Peninsula. There was a place west of town where wonderful wild strawberries grew. We went over there to shoot small arms (rifles) and we discovered the strawberries. How good they were! They were a sort of a bonus because we put in two or three days there at small arms practice. I never saw such wonderful strawberries in my life, nor hadn't up to that time. After we went back to the ship, vendors would come alongside. We used to call the people who'd come out to sell their stuff the "bumboat." They'd come alongside with delicious strawberries for five cents a box, and a great big Navy cup full of rich milk that was practically cream to go with the berries. Boy, I was busted all the time. I never had anything that tasted so good in my life as those strawberries tasted. I still like them.

Unfortunately, while we were at Port Angeles, I caught something and was very sick. I ran a temperature and had a bad sore throat, and I had to go to sickbay. It developed later into diphtheria. I was given so much calomel when I was first stricken, that I thought that to be the cause of my losing my voice.

When we arrived in San Francisco I was transferred to the hospital at Mare Island. By that time, I was suffering quite a lot of pain, although my throat was getting better. I never did know what it was that I had, but I have an idea that today it would be diagnosed as polio. I lost the use of both legs for six months and I spent that six months at the Mare Island hospital and so lost my fine ship that was such a good home.

Some interesting things happened there. The Naval Hospital was a decent hospital, but there were no women nurses

in those days. That made it unpleasant to me, but outside of that, it was a good hospital.

In the bed next to mine, there was a marine sergeant major who had been in the Boxer mix-up in China, and he had had a stroke which they called a sunstroke, and they were just waiting for him to die. As I look back on it now, it doesn't seem to me that it could have been a sunstroke. A person can get anything in China. Finally, I got better and could get around using crutches, so they had me bring his meals to him and wait on him since he was paralyzed on one side. We became close friends.

He used to go off the beam at times and would try to give his money away. The Navy was still paying him, and he had a stack of twenty-dollar gold pieces. I don't know how many hundred dollars he had there. Ordinarily, he kept them under his pillow, then when he'd get these spells, he'd start giving those gold pieces away. All of us boys knew about him and wouldn't allow it, and when we wouldn't take them from him, he'd throw them at us and we would keep quite busy picking them up and giving them back or taking them away so that he wouldn't lose them.

My bed was alongside his, and when he would get his tongue caught in his throat, I would call the steward on duty who was the nurse, and he would quickly get the doctor. Three different times the doctors pronounced him dead and they covered him up with a sheet and left him there, telling me to get back in bed and go to sleep. They told me they would call me early in the morning if they needed me to help take him down to the morgue. But I was never called on for that duty because each time on the following morning when I awoke, I looked over at him and there was Dick, sitting up smoking a cigarette. I remember that while I was there, he died three different times, and lived to tell about it. Three times! Finally, Dick got well and could walk by using two canes. When he gained enough

strength, he took the train and went back to Boston where his folks lived. I thought his recovery was one of the most marvelous things in medicine and I don't believe the doctors ever knew how it happened because everybody was surprised.

Well, it wasn't long after Dick left that I was able to leave, too. I was sent to the *Independence* to wait for a ship.

Recommissioned 1899 as a survey ship
Decommissioned 1903 to 1905

USS *RANGER*: FIRST VOYAGE

Still Called a Boy

I was finally sent to duty from the hospital and I hated to leave the good friends I had there, but I reported for duty at the *Independence* to await a seagoing ship.

The old *Ranger* was in the Navy yard getting her yearly going-over. She was in survey duty, surveying and making charts for the Gulf of California. At that time the United States had an international agreement with all the countries that could afford it and had the equipment to do surveying all over the world. Those that didn't have the equipment nor the know-how usually paid something to have it done, but some of them contributed nothing. England, the United States, France, and Germany, and a few of the other countries were doing all the work of surveying and marking channels and obstructions to navigation.

We had other regular survey vessels out, but the *Ranger* was well equipped for the work and she wasn't a modern warship, so they put her in that duty, too. She was an iron gunboat and square-rigged on the foremast and fore and aft rigged on the main and mizzen but classed as a steamship with auxiliary sail. The sail was used only in cases of emergency.

One day a fine-looking officer came over to the *Independence* and he had another officer with him. One was a four-striper {captain} and the other officer was a two-striper {lieutenant}. I believe the two-striper was acting as first lieutenant. Of course, we were all curious about them and I asked one of the men at the gangway if he knew who they were.

"Sure, I know who they are. The captain is William P. Potter {promoted to Rear Admiral, Secretary of the Navy in 1909} and the other is Lieutenant Harrison, nephew of the late President Harrison."

"My! Isn't the captain a fine-looking man?" I exclaimed.

"And he is just as good as he looks," was the reply. "He's a regular sailor's captain, a fine man, and he has just recently been assigned to the *Ranger* from duty in Washington, D.C."

I didn't think anything about their being aboard but shortly afterward I got a call to go to the office of the ship's writer and he told me that two or three of us were to go to the *Ranger.* That was why they came aboard, to see if they could use any of the men available on the *Independence.* The next morning, we were taken in the ship's launch and delivered to the *Ranger.* The other two fellows were older men, and there I was, a kid again, the same old trouble as I reported aboard and was assigned to a division.

As we came aboard the *Ranger,* quite a few of the crew lined up at the gangway. They eyed us up and down and sized us up because we were to be new shipmates and they wanted to look us over, a custom on all ships in those days. I reported to the officer of the deck, as did the others, and he gave me a billet showing where I slept and kept my hammock, bag, and ditty-box, and then I was through and I could go down and put all that stuff away. Generally, the master-at-arms on the lower deck would be there to show me all I needed to know and where the different spaces were, which they were usually marked, and as I started to pick up my bag to take it below, the first-class quartermaster, who was quite bald and what little hair he did have was red, came down off the bridge. I noticed, too, that he had a most luxurious flowing mustache. He was a New Zealander by birth and he had come to the United States because he liked to sail out of this country better than New Zealand, and so he had stayed in America and joined the U.S. Navy. His rating was first-class quartermaster, and as he came off the bridge he looked me up and down and said hello to me, and just as I got past him he turned to one of the fellows nearby and said,

"My gosh! Is that what they are sending us now, children? They sure must be getting to the bottom of the barrel."

I dropped my hammock and turned around to him, and I told him, "I can do practically everything you can do as far as my work is concerned. I may not be up on the signals and flags and certain things that you are, but I'm a second-class boy, not a first-class quartermaster. I can do most everything else you can do." He got red in the face as I went on, "If you fellows don't like me, you know what you can do. If I had a few more pounds on me I'd take a pop at you, anyway."

Then he started to laugh and everybody along the gangway had a great laugh about that. There was nothing for me to do but pick up my hammock and go down and get over feeling bad about it. I think that he felt bad about it, too. The fact that I turned on him and said what I did, kind of made him ashamed, I'm sure because afterward, we became the best of friends on the ship. In fact, he was one of the best friends I had while I was in the Navy. I never was shipmates with him after we put the *Ranger* out of commission. His name was Dick Bigby, and he was a lot older than I was. He was a very wonderful character and a very fine fellow. We'd always laugh every time he'd talk about the time when I was going to lick him.

I put my gear away and busied myself around there and felt kind of lonesome, but soon the messenger boy came down and said that the navigator wanted to see me, so I went aft to his room and reported.

"I was looking over your record," he said, "and I see that you have very high marks in signaling and work on the bridge. You have fine marks, but especially fine in signals."

"Yes, Sir," I replied, "I rather like that work. It comes easy to me and I have done it everywhere I have gone, and I really enjoy it."

"We're short a signal boy," he said, "and I just don't know why we should not put you on that bridge. You report to the chief quartermaster and see what he thinks about it."

I went to the chief quartermaster who was a Scandinavian named Johnson. He was a fine man. We sat down and talked, and he asked me questions and quizzed me a while. He had me send him a couple of messages and he couldn't catch them. It impressed him anyway, and I was put on as signal boy, which made it nice for me because I liked the work so much. I would write up the log for the officer of the deck and do a lot of handy things around there, and I could see what was going on. If it had been then like it is today, I'd probably have started learning navigation, but in those days, they wouldn't even let me at a sextant. That was supposed to be terrifically mysterious, celestial navigation, so mysterious that a little youngster like me couldn't even put the sextant away in the box. My name wasn't even dry on the books yet.

Jack Weir's Picture Gallery

The *Ranger* had the old-fashioned open bridge with the wheel right out in the open. One day while I was standing on the bridge a little, chunky fellow went by. He verged on being bald and was not so young, and I noticed that he was a second-class boatswain's mate. I asked the chief quartermaster who he was. He chuckled a little and said, "That's the famous Jack Weir."

As the old maid said, you could have knocked me over with a feather. "Well, for goodness sake," I exclaimed, "that fellow doesn't look like any of the stories I have heard about him."

"Don't take too much for granted," he said. "His looks are very deceiving. You'll get a lot of fun out of him. All the boys do. He wears all their clothes. They'll do his washing for him if he tells them stories, and he's a good storyteller. He's in a class by himself."

"Well," I replied, "according to Jimmy Patterson on the *Adams*, he certainly is!"

"I've been shipmates with both Jimmy Patterson and this old ram's horn down there," he went on, "and you may be sure this fellow will surprise you. Don't ever get into any trouble with him. He can beat any kid over the rigging right now."

"He certainly doesn't look it, does he?" I answered.

"No, but looks don't have anything to do with it. He is the famous Jack Weir, and we're quite proud of him. He gives us a lot of amusement because he's always playing tricks. Don't worry, you won't escape. He'll play some on you."

And, sure enough, the first time I met Jack, he took a good look at me. He knew who I was, so he looked at the fellow I was with and he made a telescope of his hands and started

115

looking up and down and all around on the deck, and around the ship, and the other fellow got interested and asked, "What'cha lookin' for, Jack?"

Then he answered, "I thought I saw a little insect come along here with you that looked very much like a boy. But I can't see him anymore. He must have fallen between the mast and the deck."

Everybody had a laugh out of that. He could think of more original stuff. His stuff wasn't shopworn, it was original. He didn't crack his jokes and play his pranks because he'd heard about them. He made them up as the occasion arose. Naturally, I did all I could to be friends with him because I admired him, having been influenced by what Jimmy Patterson had said about him and the "capsized" boat. As soon as he found out that I was trying to be friends he warmed right up and reciprocated. There wasn't anything mean about him, he just wanted everybody to be laughing, so he made them laugh. I had been on the bridge and had the wheel, and we watched when we were hauling on lines on a cleat just abaft the foremast—that's a little forward of the bridge— and he'd get his fat tummy up against that and take in the slack while the rest of the crew hauled on it. The faces he's making and the way he did it had everybody laughing. The officer of the deck, a little fellow named Williams, looked at me and chuckled. "My gosh, he can't help making people laugh," he said. "It just comes natural to him." And it was true. If I just looked at him I'd begin to laugh, and I couldn't for the life of me tell you why.

About the second or third morning out, coming down the coast to Pichilinque, Mexico, I stepped into the shower area and I thought I had walked into a picture gallery. In those days, they had galleries or arcades where there were machines with pictures in them and when a guy dropped a nickel in the slot he could see pictures of girls with very little or no clothes on. Well, I blinked

my eyes and wondered if we had one aboard and I had gotten into it by mistake. But this one was moving, and it turned around and grinned at me, and when I saw that pug nose, I knew it must be Jack Weir. What a sight he was! Tattooed all over his body. His whole back was covered with a big full-rigged sailing ship. It was beautiful work. He had it done while he was in the Orient where there were some great artists in tattoo work. This had been done in either China or Japan. Even though he had taken on weight since the work was done, it was still beautiful. On his breast was a battleship drawn in as fine detail as the sailing ship. On his arms were dancing girls with some in gay, Spanish costumes; some in grass skirts; and I believe that some hadn't taken time to put a skirt on. He liked to flex his muscles and make them move. Jack was a colorful sight because I'm sure there wasn't a place on his body that had not been tattooed. I could have studied him for an hour or two and not looked at all the different pictures on him.

I became interested because I had never seen anything like that outside of the circus. I had seen tattoos on other men, but nothing like Jack Weir had. On each heel, there was a pig tattooed with the English flag stuck in a certain part of its anatomy above the tattooing which said, "My flag in a pig's valise."

Jack didn't like the Limeys. He was born in Ireland and I guess his folks were very poor and he didn't want to stay at home where there would have been one more mouth to feed, so he went to sea when he was just a child. They took them as young as twelve years old then, as cabin boys. Somehow, Jack made his way to this country, probably on a merchant ship. He jumped ship in the United States when he was old enough to enlist in the Navy and they never could get rid of him. He stayed until his time was out and a lot longer.

As I admired him he grew real friendly and he said, "Oh, you'll get some of this stuff on you before you get out of the Navy, boy. They all do."

I told him that I had promised my mother that I wouldn't ever have any tattooing put on me and that I expected to live up to my promise. He thought that was a real shame and said so.

Shortly after the battle of Manila Bay in May of 1898 during the Spanish-American War, the government issued medals to all those who took part in the battle. The medals looked to be about as large around as a man's hand but probably were not quite that big. They were made of bronze and engraved with a fine picture of Admiral Dewey on one side, and the other side of the medal there was a picture of the battle or the names of the ships that were in that engagement, I have forgotten which. However, there was nothing like them ever worn in the Navy before, and everybody made so much fun of them that the boys who had earned them wouldn't wear them except at general muster where regulations required them to wear all their medals and decorations. As soon as a man got forward, away from the eyes of the officers, he would take his Dewey medal off and put it in his ditty-box.

One morning we had just finished washing down and, as usual, a lot of us were on the fo'c's'le, when one of the boys came running up from the gundeck, wild-eyed, and all excited, and he told us that one of the boys below had his Dewey medal stolen right out of his ditty-box! The boys began to talk about this theft and were greatly excited about it. Everyone was shocked, everyone except Jack. He owned one, having been on the Olympia with Admiral Dewey during the battle, and he wore it

only under compulsion. As the boys were excitedly discussing this terrible crime that had been committed, one of them turned to Jack and queried, "Jack, what do you think should be done to a man who would do a thing like that— swipe a man's Dewey medal?"

Jack looked up with a solemn look on his pug-nosed face and said, "I'd make the darn blankety-blank-blank-blank scoundrel wear it."

Tar Baby: More of Weir's Tomfoolery

On a Sunday afternoon on the trip down I had the wheel. I took a trick at the wheel the same as the seamen and also, stood by signal-boy watch. On that particular Sunday, when I had the wheel, the awning was spread right below me. It was warm and there was just a light following breeze, and everybody was taking his Sunday afternoon nap—"calking off," we called it. "Little Williams," a j. g. lieutenant had the bridge. He was a dandy fellow and had a keen sense of humor. While we were talking there, we noticed Jack Weir come creeping up on the deck to look around.

Next to the foremast was the sailmaker whom we dubbed "our society man." He was sleeping like a baby, stretched out on his back with both arms extended. We knew that he had had an argument with Jack, and he probably thought that he had come out ahead, but nobody ever came out ahead of Jack. Jack spotted him by the foremast and I could just see that Jack felt that he owed the sailmaker something, and he saw his chance to even the score. Jack sized him up from all angles and then turned and went down the companionway to the next deck where the paint locker was located. When he came up again, he had a paddle of runny tar which we used on the ship's riggings that he carried close to the foremast. He picked out a broom-straw from a broom close by, then he squatted down and gently poured some of the tar on the outstretched hand of the sailmaker. He waited for a moment. Nothing happened. He eased himself about, to an advantageous point, then he tickled the poor fellow's nose with the broom straw. The sailmaker stirred and twiched his nose a bit. Jack waited a few seconds and then tickled a little harder. Wham! The sailmaker brought his hand up and slapped the tar all over his face. By the time he could look around to

find the culprit, Jack was up forward, stretched out on his sea chest, innocent as a baby. When the astonished sailmaker realized what had happened to him, he began to look about to see who could have committed such a dastardly deed, but there wasn't a soul around that he could pin the guilt on. Everybody appeared to be innocently sleeping. Even Jack Weir was asleep up forward on his sea chest.

The whole procedure was extremely funny to those watching, and as the poor sailmaker stomped off to repair the damage, the officer of the deck just lay back on the signal-flag chest and laughed until the tears rolled down his face and he was breathless. My sides were splitting, too. Finally, he turned to me, shaking his head and laughed saying, "He just can't help it! The Good Lord made Jack that way and he just can't help it!"

The sailmaker tried to find out who had done this tomfoolery trick but apparently, nobody had seen it. Jack undoubtedly felt that he had evened the score because the sailmaker had a hard job to get the tar off his face.

When I found that Jack was on the *Ranger* it became a more desirable berth to me. I had heard so much and I had always wished I could be shipmates with him, so I was delighted when I learned I was a shipmate of his on the *Ranger*. We were shipmates until we put the *Ranger* out of commission, which was about two or three years later, and I had many enjoyable associations with him. I have always been glad that I had the opportunity to know him and to enjoy his special brand of humor, which was in a class by itself. I have never met a man like him since.

Preparing for Mexico

As I have mentioned before, the chief quartermaster was a Scandinavian named Johnson, and he was one of the finest chief quartermasters I ever sailed with. He and I got very well acquainted and he put me on the bridge as signal boy. While we were still in the Mare Island Navy Yard, and before we were quite ready to leave, he was talking, and he said that there were a couple of signal boys whose time was almost up, and the quartermaster's time would be out by the time we made this first trip. He wished he had a good signalman and a good man to take the quartermaster's place. They always promote a man on their own ship when possible because the chief quartermaster and the navigator then know just what this man can do.

I got to thinking about this and made up my mind to go over to the *Independence* and look around, so shortly after that I went there, and I met another young fellow. Smidders was a little older than I was, and, if I remember correctly, he was an apprentice boy, too, but I think that he was first-class apprentice. We began talking and he said that he was expecting to be shipped out any time, and he asked me about getting on the *Ranger*. He said he had heard that she was a "home."

"Well, that's what I hear," I said. "Every day I hear it more and more and it strikes me that it is exactly what she is. She has a nice crew on her and a wonderful skipper and the first lieutenant of the first luff {the roundest part of the ship's bow} is a nephew of President Harrison. He was gunnery officer for the turret guns on The Oregon during the battle—the twelve or thirteen-inch turret guns—and during the excitement of the battle he got out on deck and got a little too far forward and his eardrums broke. His whole nervous system was upset, so he had a nervous affliction, but he was still a fine officer and all his

122

sensibilities were keen." And so, we chatted on and during our conversation, I asked him how he stood on signals and working on the bridge.

"Oh," he said, "I have always liked working on the bridge and I can send a wigwag message alright. I haven't had any trouble with them."

"Well, send me one. I might get a chance to tell the Chief about it and he'll put in for you because there is going to be an opening on our bridge by the time we get back from this trip."

He sent me a wigwag signal, and he was good at it. It was alright. With a little practice, he would be able to hold his own with the best of them. I found out what I wanted to know, and I liked what I had found, so I went back to the ship and I told Johnson about him. He was interested right away, and he said that he would put in for him. I gave Johnson the boy's name and he sent a request to the *Independence* for him, asking that he be sent over to our ship. It was the navigator's duty to go through the first lieutenant, and this was done. They don't come any finer than Smidders and we were always glad to have him aboard our ship. Considering what happened afterward on the ship, I was always glad that I had a part in getting him from the *Independence*. A little later I shall have an occasion to tell of an incident reflecting on his ability and knowledge.

One morning at daylight we pulled out of Mare Island when we finally got everything done and everybody aboard which included our surveyors and chart makers, our crew, and equipment. We didn't go to San Francisco but put right out to sea and headed down the coast for the Gulf of California. It was the nicest time, in the fall of the year, when the weather was

especially nice down there. Summertime is the hurricane and tropical storm season, and for that reason, there was no survey work done in the Gulf by the United States in that season. As soon as the danger of these tropical storms had passed, work was continued. The weather around La Paz is delightful during the late fall and winter months, and well into the spring of the year. I doubt that finer weather could be found anywhere than is found there during those seasons.

Dick Turpin and the Foo Foo Band

John Henry "Dick" Turpin

Practically every ship has its Foo Foo band and I soon discovered that our ship was no exception. We had a good one which practiced nearly every night. Our bugler, who was a very fine cornet player, was the leader. He came from Chile or Peru and had a fine musical education. He could read music and he could play that coronet so soft and sweet it would lull you to sleep. There was also a Peruvian whose name was Danny Gomera, who played the guitar. Bill Edwards, from Santa Barbara, played the mandolin and several other instruments. Bill's mother was from one of the old California-Mexican families and his father was an American. Bill had the grace and rhythm of the Latins and he had a good musical education, also. These boys formed the nucleus of the band and they drew others into it when they found a boy who could play a musical instrument of any kind.

These boys got in all the musical practice they could on the way down the coast because they were looking forward to fiestas when we reached La Paz, and they knew they would be in demand because they had been there before. Whenever the officers held parties on the quarterdeck, there was usually dancing, and these boys were always called on to play. The boys worked hard at perfecting their band and it was pleasant to listen to them in the cool of the evening's velvet blackness and the smooth sailing on a quiet sea.

One evening while we were on our way down to Pichilinque, the Foo Foo band was practicing, and I joined the boys who began to gather around to listen and to sing. There was one boy in the band who particularly interested me. He didn't play any instrument but because he had such a good voice, he always went along with the band. When the main part of the practice was over, and the band played songs we all knew, this boy's fine voice led our singing. It wasn't because of his voice that I was especially interested, it was because he was such a fine-looking fellow—tall, slender, and upstanding. He was quite a bit older than I was and I noticed that everybody respected him. After the band practice broke up I went to Danny Gomero, the second-class quartermaster, and asked about the singer.

"Who is that tall, fine-looking Negro?" I asked Danny. "Who is he? What is it about him that makes you look at him again and again?"

"That's Dick Turpin. He was blown up on The Maine."

"My," I exclaimed, "you'd never know that to see him now!"

Danny said, "He saved a lot of the boys. The Maine went down fast. He helped pull a lot of them out and to get the boats out. He did fine work on The Maine." Turpin was nominated for the Medal of Honor but never received it. Later I talked to

126

Dick and got well acquainted with him because he was in the deck department.

⚓

In those days, according to regulations, every time a ship came into port there had to be a man in the chains heaving the lead. He was called a leadsman. As the ship approached the channel, the call would go out from the officer of the deck, "Send a leadsman in the chains!" and if it was close and the way hazardous, and if Turpin was a member of that ship's crew, they always sent for Turpin. He was the finest leadsman I ever saw in all my life. He could stretch a twenty-fathom lead-line out without any effort whatsoever, and he was very accurate, which was one of the things that made him such a wonderful leadsman, and I wished that I could heave the lead, too.

The chief quartermaster learned of my desire and he went to Turpin and told him, "Stevens wants to be a leadsman. He should be a leadsman when he is on the bridge, and we may need him anytime to go in the chains. I wish you would take him in hand and teach him to be a leadsman."

The lead weighed fourteen pounds and a person would have to be able to throw it out twenty fathoms to be a good leadsman. A man would help pull the lead-line after it was measured, and the ship was going forward all the time. The leadsman had to practice until he could do it with the ship going full speed ahead.

I learned to be as good a leadsman as was physically possible for me to be, and I wasn't bad. Dick was a good teacher and I always remembered with a glow of pride years later when Dick got quite a lot of publicity and fame in the Navy, that it was he who had taught me to heave the lead.

Arriving at Pichilinque Bay

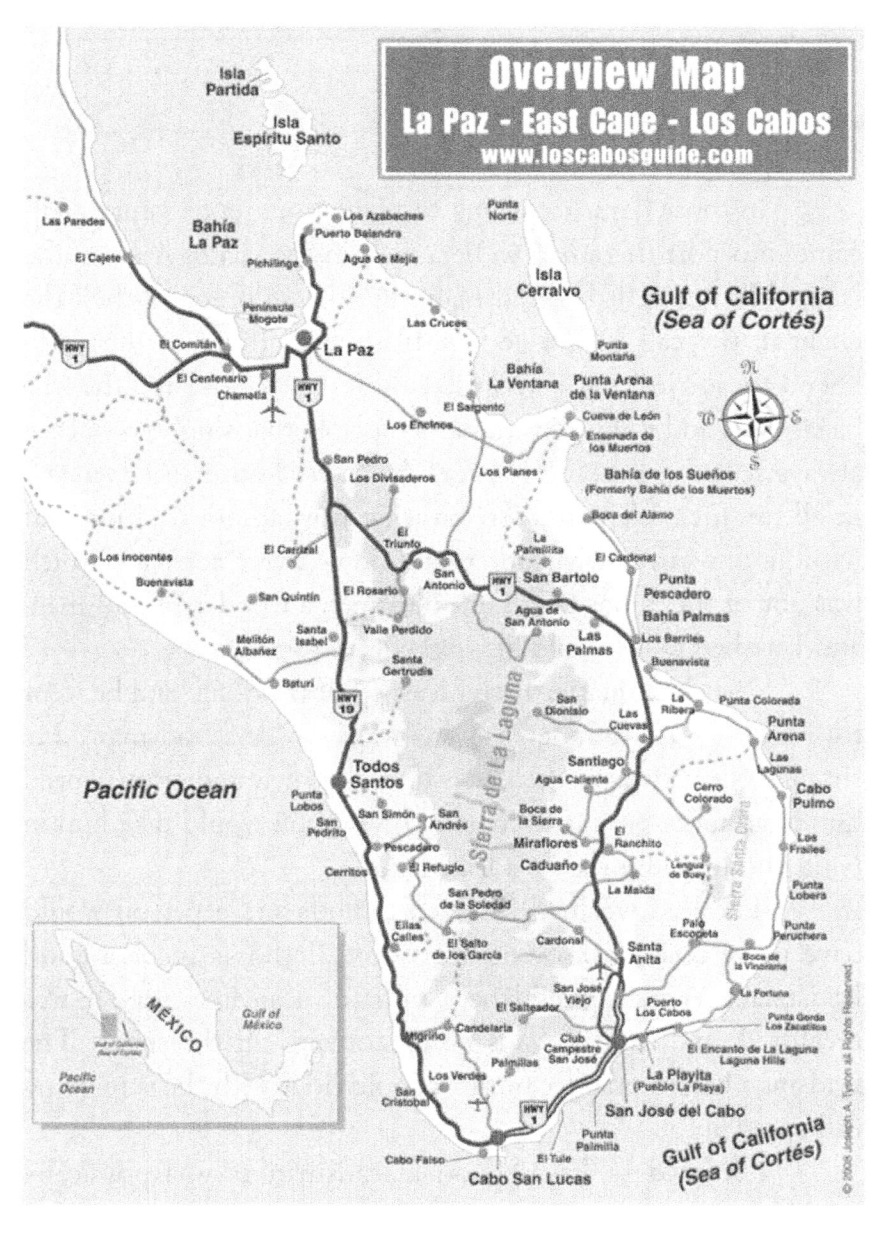

I had never sailed with any of the men in this crew, so they were all new to me. There was a second-class bo's'n mate that I noticed particularly. I learned that his name was Jim

Garrish, that he was a Gloucester, Massachusetts, man and had acquired great skill at fishing and harpooning while on the fishing boats and whalers before he joined the Navy. He was nearly seven feet tall and built accordingly, and he must have had a tremendous strength because there were times when he drove his harpoon through two turtles swimming along, one on top of the other.

As we approached Magdalena Bay and Turtle Bay, which was close by, we began to sight turtles and the call went out for him. Immediately the boys were out with the glasses, scanning the sea for the nearest turtle. As soon as one was spotted that was not too far off course, the ship was hauled over to bring the turtle right under the bow where Jim had taken his place to work on either side of the bowsprit.

Jim had his harpoon ready, and that man's work was something wonderful to behold. He rarely missed one and often harpooned two at once if they were swimming "double-decked." The instant he had his harpoon in one, we were right there to haul it aboard. By the time we had the harpoon out of it, another one would be spotted and away we went after that one. It wasn't long before we had turtles all over the deck. The turtles didn't die when they were harpooned, and they were killed as needed for food. We loved the excitement of getting them and it was a welcome diversion from our everyday routine. Also, the seven different kinds of meat found in a turtle gave a welcome relief to our regular diet and the soup made by our cook was something out of this world. We kept all the turtles we hauled aboard on deck and we still had a lot of them when we reached Pichilinque Bay, which is about five miles east of La Paz, in Lower California, where we anchored and were going to be based.

After rounding Cape San Lucas, our course was practically reversed and as we headed northward, we had the peninsula between us and the ocean. The half-day run took us

close to Cerralvo Islands and when we reached Espiritu Santo, we passed to the south of it, down the narrow channel and into Pichilinque Bay, where there was a fine, deep-water anchorage in a landlocked harbor. Although small, it was ideal for us while we were surveying and putting out some thirty to forty buoys to mark the channels there and all the way to La Paz, which was about five miles further on.

From La Paz, there is a fine view of Pichilinque and a ship of any size is easily seen, so of course, we were observed coming in about noon. Since the *Ranger* had been down there before, it wasn't long before people who were friends of the crew began showing up looking for familiar faces and shouting and waving to those they recognized on board.

Because of the nature of the survey duty, we carried an extra steam-launch and it wasn't long before both launches were in the water. The captain and as many of the other officers as could be spared were taken into La Paz immediately, where they paid their official calls on the *Commandante* and the American Consulate. No one else was allowed to go to La Paz until the captain and his aides had returned from their official visit, so the other launch was tied up to the boom for the time being. We were only a stone's throw from the shore at Pichilinque and we could go ashore there but not to La Paz.

"Please Keek My Ass"

The Yaqui Indians in that area had become great friends of the crews of previous trips and it was amazing how quickly news of our arrival got around, and they began showing up. For the most part, they were the same ones who had been coming down every time the *Ranger* came in, and of course the boys who had been there before knew them. This was my first trip, but the boys told me all about these Yaquis and how they came a great distance in canoes to get to Pichilinque every time the *Ranger* came in. There were no telegraphs into their country and it was a mystery how they knew of our arrival, but I always did believe that they had a lookout on some high mountain which was perhaps their stronghold. At any rate it wasn't long before canoes began showing up, coming from the upper end of the Gulf with two or three Yaquis in each.

It gave us all a lot of pleasure to give turtles to the civilians of La Paz and to our Indian friends near Pichilinque. They were all delighted to get them because they knew from experience just how good turtles are and it was a food that they greatly appreciated.

These Yaquis liked to go with us and they hung around, staying close by. They established their camp at the saltworks on the shore closest to our anchorage. They made a pretense of asking for work, but it was just a gesture, so they could go along and be with us. They liked to ride in the cutter and we would take some of them along when we went fishing. They were a great help when it came to pulling in the net.

The Yaquis collected tin cans. They saved every can we threw away, carefully washing and drying them, and stowing them away. They especially prized the empty hardtack cans. These cans did not have lids but had to be opened on one side

131

to take the hardtack out. They were a square can and they were evidently just suited for some special need of the Yaquis.

We got very well acquainted with the Yaquis who hung around the ship and we found their word to be to absolutely good and reliable with us. We treated them well and they had a lot of fun with us as well as getting a little work now and then and increasing their stock of tin cans.

The story about the Yaquis is an interesting one, although I cannot vouch that it is true. However, rumors were rife down there concerning their stronghold someplace in the mountains. It was said that their country was fabulously rich and that they found almost pure gold up there. This could have very well been true because when they would come down wanting to buy a firearm or something else that they coveted, they would offer solid chunks of gold for it.

The Yaquis are about the bravest of all Indians and it was said that their stronghold had never been penetrated by the soldiers. According to the story, the road which led to the stronghold was a very difficult one, climbing at a steep angle between sheer rock cliffs. It eventually narrowed to a trail where they were obliged to walk in single file. Such a gateway to their stronghold was heavily guarded and defended by a few men who could hold off a whole regiment of soldiers if necessary. At this time, the Yaquis were at peace as they had a treaty with the Mexican government whereby the government agreed that they would never go up there to the Yaquis stronghold and attack if the Yaquis would not attack their military elsewhere.

Many of the Indians worked at the saltworks where they made crystal salt which was shipped out in the small sailing schooners that called there. I don't remember where it was shipped for further refining, but it was probably shipped to the mainland. However, at Pichilinque when the salt was dry and cured, it was sacked and then put in the warehouses.

The Mexicans didn't have any burros or mules to haul the carts, as they do in lots of places. Instead they had Yaquis working there, each carrying a hundred-pound sack of salt on his back. Old or young, they were hard workers while they worked. It seemed that these Yaquis, like old soldiers, never died, they just faded away. There was one old fellow who looked so old that he must have had all he could do to carry himself. But that old fellow took his turn in the line and worked on that salt all day and never faltered.

This old fellow struck up an acquaintance with Jack Weir and became very fond of him, and Jack liked the old man, too, and they got to be real chummy. Jack would often take some little thing from the ship to the old man, and he and Jack would sit and talk and talk and talk. Jack spoke fairly good Mexican Spanish, so he was able to understand them and to make himself understood.

The old man wanted to buy an old white blouse that Jack was wearing. Those white blouses were tough and could stand a lot of wear, and just the fact that Jack had owned it meant a lot to the old Indian. Anyway, when he kept pressing Jack to sell him the blouse he had on, Jack said, "You don't have to buy this blouse. I have an old one over on the ship in my bag and I'll bring it over to you." The old one was greatly pleased and could hardly wait for the next day when Jack would bring it to him.

The next day Jack brought the blouse to the old man and on the back, he had painted in red boot-toppin' "Please kick my ass." The old fellow was just tickled to death with it. He put it right on and wore it, strutting around so that all the rest of the them could admire him. He was the envy of all the other Indian workers because he and he alone had a white jumper. Since Jack didn't have any more that he could give away, this one was very precious.

The Mexicans who could read English translated to the others and they all had a good laugh out of it. However, it was the next day before I learned that our joke was lost in their translation, but it was a joke, just the same. As one of the bosses at the saltworks who could speak good English explained it to me, he thought it was terrific. "Oh, that Jack Weir, he make the funny joke," the boss said. "He say with the paint on the back of the shirt, 'Please keek my ass,' and of course the joke is that the old one has no ass! He has never owned an ass or burro, and when he found out what Jack had put on the blouse, he is so proud to think that Jack believes he owns an ass. All the Indians think it a great joke."

We knew Jack well enough to know that he couldn't help being funny. We all had the laugh our way on the ship and the Indians had it theirs. As it turned out, no one ever did tell the old man what Jack had intended.

The Barefoot Escapee

The ship spent a few days getting established before we started on the job we had come down to do. The surveyors who came down on the ship with us, began to assemble their supplies and organize the survey parties. These men were from the U.S. Geodetic Survey Department and were sent down there to survey the coast and mark the channels and reefs and set out buoys. The Geodetic Department was the branch of government determining the shape of the earth and locating points on the surface. The *Ranger* and her crew were put at their disposal for this work and the work parties were drawn from the members of the crew and each party was led by one or two of the surveyors. The party always included a signalman who could use heliograph for sun signals, as well as wigwam.

A certain area was designated for surveying and the ship took the party there. On the way the Yaquis would hook on back with their canoes and ride down to the campsite and back, trolling and catching fish en route.

When the campsite was reached, the men and supplies were put shore and usually one of the launches was left for their use. Some of the Indians would remain with the party and the rest would return with the launch going back to the ship.

When camp had been set up, the boys turned to carry up the lumber and heavy beams to be used in the construction of large triangles on a prominent high bluff or hill which had previously been selected for the site. All this lumber was carried up on their backs and the help of the Yaquis was indeed welcome. They were strong and agile and loved to work with the boys although they got little or no money for it.

When the triangle was set up, it was painted white with a red flag in the center of the triangle. The supports for these

structures were put deep in the ground for stability. They were built to last. I was down there about ten years ago, and I saw one still standing.

Pichilinque and La Paz have a most beautiful climate—a salubrious climate, I'd call it—in the wintertime. It rarely rains down there except when there is a hurricane. These storms come between April and October. That was the reason that we only surveyed there in the wintertime, thus we missed any hurricanes. Anyway, the climate was just about perfect. However, it was a bleak and bare-looking place. Water was a problem and fresh water was limited, consequently there was little vegetation. It was too hot to grow anything except cacti.

Life was very nice there for us. We got up early, worked until noon and then, in the afternoon was siesta time when we napped until it began to cool off and the sun began to go down. Then we would come to life and go swimming or fishing, and of course, that was duck soup for the Yaquis who always followed us everywhere. They were great fishermen and they taught us boys all the tricks that they knew about catching fish. There was just enough breeze blowing the cool air off the sea to keep us comfortable in our white duck pants and light shirt. That was all we needed to wear during winter there. Oh, occasionally it would be a little cooler and we'd need a light jumper.

One evening we had quite a bit of excitement when we were fishing in Pichilinque Bay. We had made a cast and were pulling in the seine when we heard hollering and shooting, and we looked up and at the brow of the hill which was not far away from us, we saw a man running as fast as he could, considering all the cacti. He appeared to be barefooted and came leaping and jumping, dodging the sharp rocks and cacti as best he could.

At some distance behind him came five or six men who were either Mexican police or soldiers. They were banging away at the poor fellow and every time they would shoot, he would

jump a little higher and come on a little faster. When he spied us, he swerved and came right for our boat, and jumped in. Our coxswain shoved off at once and we pulled for the shore across the bay. The man, a Yaqui Indian, threw himself on the nets and rested while we were rowing for the other shore.

He had escaped from the jail at La Paz where he had been for some time. I don't know what his crime was, but he was plenty scared, and our boyish imaginations worked overtime until we determined that he must have killed somebody. The Mexicans had a way of putting a man in jail and going off and forgetting about him. They never tried their prisoners, it seemed.

The judge would always say, "*mañana*" but *mañana* never came. He was a very thankful Indian to make his escape with our help and it would have taken the police hours to get around the bay where we took him.

There were a couple of Yaquis fishing with us at the time and they spread the story among their friends at the saltworks. You would have thought that we had saved the whole Yaqui tribe, the way those Indians came to thank us. But we learned afterwards that our saving the Yaqui didn't endear us to the police of La Paz.

Shark vs. Whale

One bright moonlight night we were laying in Pichilinque Bay. There was a full moon making the night almost light enough to read a newspaper. The stars and the moon seemed brighter down there because the atmosphere was so clear. This night was calm, clear, and beautiful when suddenly the tranquility was shattered by a terrific slam bang on the water! It was so sharp and loud it sounded like a gun going off. I ran over to the opposite side of the bridge to see what was going on and what I saw was a battle between two denizens of the deep.

It seemed that a whale had tried to elude a thrasher shark by coming into the bay, but the attempt had been unsuccessful, and the thrasher seemed to have the whale cornered. His tail was very thick at the end, and very wide. He would twist and turn and bring it down on the whale's head. When the shark made a hit of any kind, the whale would moan just like a man, and dive deep into that little bay, the shark following him. Then they would come up again, around and around the bay. Sometimes they were so close to the ship I was afraid they were going to bump us. I called the officer of the day to see if there was anything that could be done to get them out of there, so he came up and watched them, too. It was a tough battle and the whale took quite a beating but at last it finally got the advantage when it dived and headed out for the open sea. We never did find out who won the battle. We hoped that it was the whale, but it probably was the thrasher. They are ferocious fighters and they get their food by using that terrible club-like tail.

Christmas Fiesta

As we worked and fished, we became familiar with the country down there. We hiked and went in swimming, and time just flew by and it was Christmas before we realized it. The day before Christmas Eve the ship went to all the camps to pick up the boys and bring them in for Christmas. They could spend the day aboard ship where there would be a good dinner and entertainment, or they could go ashore and to La Paz, whichever they elected to do. The Yaquis had "hooked a ride" on the ship with their canoes and had gathered up their fellow Indians to bring them back to their own fiesta on the salt flats.

I had a shipmate by the name of Edwards who had been down there before on the *Ranger*, and he had friends in La Paz. Edwards came from Santa Barbara. He was the one who played in the band and whose mother was from an old California-Mexican family and his father was American. He spoke Spanish fluently and he always associated with the nice people of La Paz. He had lots of invitations and was always welcome in the best homes.

Among his friends was a family by the name of Silva who had invited him to a Christmas party and asked him to bring a friend along, so he asked me to go with him. He said that he knew that I would enjoy the party and that the Silvas would make me feel welcome even though I didn't speak Spanish. He also arranged for the Foo Foo band to go along to furnish the music for the fandangos. Of course, I was delighted for an opportunity to get away from the ship and go to somebody's nice home. I was still young and homesick, even though I wouldn't admit it.

The Silvas were very nice people. They were not the elite of La Paz, but they were refined and cultured people. They lived in a rather large adobe house which had above-average comforts

in that little Mexican town. I was delighted to go with Edwards. We went early to attend the party which was lots of fun and very interesting to me because I had never been to anything except the American way of celebrating Christmas. There were lots of nice girls and some of them were exceptionally pretty. We had games in which just the young people took part, like bobbing for apples, and then there was one which is a regular Christmas custom in that country. A bag of candy and nuts was suspended from the ceiling and each takes his turn at being blindfolded and tries to hit the bag and break it. When someone broke the bag, what a scramble for the nuts and the candy scattered all over the room! Such shouting and squealing and giggling with everybody trying to get some. It was lots of fun for everybody. {His first exposure to a *piñata*}. After the games the Foo Foo band began to play, and everybody danced, and danced, and danced! After a while a small group of natives with stringed instruments, mandolins, guitars, and so forth, came and they played native songs and danced until it was time to eat.

Like all home parties, there were aunts and uncles and grandmas and grandpas, and goodness know who all. They had been working hard to prepare a sumptuous feast. I can't remember what all we ate, but I do remember the special tortillas with syrup on them, and the Mexican coffee *con leche*, which was their own way of instant coffee with hot milk. The coffee was black and syrupy in one pot, and the hot milk was in another, and both pots were tipped over the cup and the steaming liquids blended in the pouring {an early version of a latte}.

While we were eating I noticed a lot of twittering and giggling going on around the table and in an adjoining room, also. They would look at me and whisper when they thought I wasn't looking at them. Then suddenly someone came up behind me and put his hands over my eyes and held them tight so that I couldn't wiggle out. And then it seemed like I got kissed

by about fifty women. I was only a boy and they could do that and get away with it. I was so embarrassed, and I blushed and the redder my face got, the more they laughed and clapped their hands. I was taken by surprise, but I soon adjusted to the fun and laughed with them. I don't know who it was that kissed me, but I think it must have been every woman at that party.

As evening neared midnight, everybody got ready and we all went to the church for Christmas mass. I had never been to this service before and was impressed with the beauty of the service. Away off in that little corner of the world they were keeping Christmas just the same as they were in San Francisco, New York, or Paris.

After the services we all went back to the Silva home for a while and then we said our thank-yous and goodbyes and returned to the ship. I have never forgotten how kind those people were to me, a kid away from home, away from all my loved ones. It was such a kindness the way they made me feel like one of them. They were wonderful, understanding people.

Sharks and Mantas

With the holidays over, it was back to work for us. There were always four or five camps working at the same time and we would go from camp to camp with supplies or to find out if they needed anything. When their job was finished at one place, we'd move them to another.

So, it was on that day we shifted a camp and took them over to Snake Island, which is one of the islands on the route to Cape San Lucas. There are two islands that might be called a gateway to Pichilinque and the boats sail between them. One is named Cerralvo and the other we called "Snake Island" because it looked like a snake. We anchored close to this island. A triangular range was being established from Snake Island to Cerralvo Island to the main part of the peninsula.

It was Sunday and the engineers, surveyors, and chart-makers were aboard getting their gear and equipment together, making ready to go ashore the next morning. The boys took advantage of this time and were sailing, fishing, and doing whatever they liked to do.

I joined a couple of the boys and we got permission to take the dinghy and go sailing with it. The dinghy was the smallest boat on the ship, used for handy purposes, but it had a mast and sail. We were going to sail around the island and see what it looked like at closer range.

Earlier in the day, Jim Garrish and a couple of his shipmates had been put ashore at a little land-locked bay that ran up into the island. This was a shallow little bay and was about four or five feet at the deepest place at low water, and when the tide was out it left practically a bare bar so that nothing could get in or out. If anything came in on high tide and didn't get out before the tide was low, it was stuck until the next tide. The

ship carried some shotguns for hunting and the boys had brought two of them along. They thought they might run into cottontail or a brace of quail or dove, and they were permitted to take the shotguns and a high-powered rifle with them.

As we approached this little bay or inlet, we heard the darnedest banging away. You've have thought that the war was on again. When we got close enough, we learned that they were shooting at fish. As soon as the men on the bar spied us they signaled us to go back to the ship for some harpoons and then to come right back and bring the harpoons ashore.

Jim Garrish was the man from Gloucester who was so expert with the harpoon, and there wasn't much connected with fishing that Jim couldn't do. As I have mentioned, he was nearly seven feet tall, angular, and muscular and a great sailorman.

We did what we had been asked to do and hurried to reach the ship and get the harpoons, then we hurried back as fast as we could and landed on the bar. They boys saw us and came running to meet us. One of them shouted, "My God! If you want to see a sight just come with us. We'll lift the dinghy over the bar."

We had taken our mast in and stowed it, so we all picked the dinghy up and slid her over the bar into the inlet. Jim then got in the bow with his harpoon. My Lord! The place was crawling with sharks and mantas, otherwise known as stingarees, and about every other kind of thing that lives in the water. The inlet must have been the clubhouse for all those fellows because we saw sharks of every size and breed, and mantas of all sizes.

We put a couple of the boys ashore with a line which we had in the boat, and they kept that line with them and when Jim would catch a shark with a harpoon he would just transfer the line and let the boys haul it ashore. My laws! It wasn't long before we had that smooth, level side of the shore strewn with

sharks and mantas and every other kind of fish. That day I saw fish that I had never seen before nor since.

The boys took their knives and cut the jawbones right out of the sharks. The teeth of the sharks were the things they wanted the most. We could have dried the shark fins and sold them to the Chinese merchants in San Francisco had we known enough to do it. They were considered quite a delicacy and were used for shark-fin soup, and we later learned that they brought a good price. But, the boys just took the teeth. My, they were vicious looking teeth! Make a necklace out of them and you could win the heart of any south sea maiden with it. The ivory part of the tails of the mantas were very nice for making things. If the manta was large enough, its tail made a nice cane. After it was smoothed down and polished, it made a nice curio.

We fooled around there pulling in sharks and mantas all afternoon until the beach was strewn with dead fish from the pool. When the tide began coming in and filling it up again, the fish started to get out into the deep water of the channel. We finally got all the shark jaws and other mementos we wanted, and we got out of there.

⚓

Sunday was always a day for swimming or fishing and Pichilinque was a good spot for such sport, and exciting things seemed to happen on that little land-locked harbor. I remember another time when we had a great deal of excitement and Jim Garrish was right in the middle of it. He and one or two other boys were out in the dinghy and I was aboard the ship, watching them with the glasses. Jim always had a harpoon with him when he went out, so I was sure something exciting was bound to happen. Sure enough, a huge manta came sliding up close to

Jim's boat. It must have been at least twelve feet across. It was huge! Well, it came along so easy and Jim just let go of that harpoon and it went right through the manta's back. There was a good line on that harpoon and that manta started out with Jim in the boat, holding on for all he was worth. The manta towed that dinghy like it was nothing but a match. Jim started yelling and the other boys out in the boats began to rally for the fun. A whaleboat sailed over and the boys in Jim's boat managed to get a line on the whaleboat and hitched the whaleboat on. Soon a cutter came over and it hitched on to the whaleboat. All this time the manta was taking them around and around the bay. They didn't want him to go outside the bay and they were afraid that was what he was going to do unless they got enough power to hold him. Besides the dinghy there were two cutters and a whaleboat. Finally, a sailing launch joined them. They knew Jim had something on that harpoon, but they didn't know what it was.

As soon as the excitement began, I called the others on the ship and officers and men lined the rail and watched the battle. Every pair of glasses on the ship was in use. The captain sent the power launch to see if they were alright or needed more help, but by that time the manta was running out of power and with the harpoon clear through him, he gave up the ghost.

He was such a big catch that when they pulled him ashore on the salt flats we all got into the act and got lines and eased him up on the beach. My goodness! The Yaqui Indians said that they had never in their lives seen one so large. Even the Old One, who wore the decorated blouse, said that he had never seen a manta as big as that one.

When we got him firmly up on the beach, they made certain that he was dead because he was really a bad one. They cut the tail out of him and carefully removed the barbed end which was poison. The remaining part measured over six feet

long and Jim took care of it to cure it and later when things were quiet, he polished it and decorated it, making two beautiful canes out of it. This was indeed quite a prize.

Man the Battle Stations

About a week before the surveying for the season was completed, and we were already preparing for the trip north for overhaul and our yearly repairs, a miner leading his two well-laden burros from far back in the mountains appeared on the salt flats, seeking transportation out to the *Ranger.* He waited until one of our boats went ashore and he asked if our captain was aboard. On being told that the captain was on board, the miner asked to be taken over to the ship to see him, saying that he had some business with him. He was a man of fine physique and appeared to be well educated. His soft southern accent was pleasing to listen to and his every action was that of a gentleman. On the way over to the ship he said that he had a mine back in the hills and that he had been having some trouble with the Mexican government.

It turned out that he and our captain had been schoolmates and they were tickled to death to see each other. Many years had passed since they last met so there was plenty of reminiscing to be done. But, that had to wait for a better time as the business at hand was urgent.

The miner's son was being held in jail in La Paz. The Mexicans had worked the old stunt of putting him in jail without a trial and had forgotten about him. Two or three months earlier there had been some trouble at the mine with one of the Mexican workmen and the son had been obliged to get tough with him. He fired the workman, who immediately headed for La Paz where he told the authorities some cock-and-bull story and the authorities sent some officers out to the mine and arrested the boy and left him there. His son was a young fellow in his twenties. They wouldn't bring him to trial, and they wouldn't let him out. The father had been to the American

consul, who was not an American at all, but a Mexican. The United States hired him to represent them. This was done in those days. This consul probably represented several other countries, also. He wasn't interested in doing any work, just drawing his salary. He didn't want to stir up anything that would get him involved in such a way that he might lose his job and lose favor with his country, so he did nothing.

In those days when a person went down to Mexico he was always told to be exceedingly careful and to avoid any trouble, and for goodness sake, to keep out of jail because God only knew when he would ever get out. Americans were warned and told that the Mexican police wouldn't bring a case to trial even if they just picked someone up for questioning, they would throw him in jail and wouldn't try him or let him out of jail. They just went away and forgot about him.

Everybody knew that they were giving this young fellow the same treatment, so when the miner heard that we were in Pichilinque, he came right down with the hope of getting some assistance. He had exhausted all his own sources of help and he knew that our captain would know whose hands to put it in and he hoped to get help though him. The boy's father had written to everyone he knew in the States who might have any influence and they wrote him back that they would do something about it, but there was never anything done—the authorities were always waiting for *mañana*. When he heard that the captain on the *Ranger* was named Potter, he decided to see if it could possibly be his old schoolmate whom he remembered had an appointment to Annapolis.

A launch was dispatched to La Paz with instructions to bring the consul back to the ship with them. When the consul arrived, the stage was all set. Our captain showed his disapproval of what was going on without beating around the bush, and his tirade so cowed the consul that he shrank back, fearing the

captain was going to attack him. I'll tell you, that consul had never had the riot act read to him like our captain read it! The captain demanded that the Mexicans release the man at once, that there was not going to be any more diplomatic writing of letters, and he ended the session by giving the consul an ultimatum that he would give him until eleven o'clock the next morning to release the miner's son. He further stated that if they didn't bring the man down to the ship and deliver him to us by eleven, that we would be up there with the ship stripped for action, cleared for action, and that we would come and get him.

The captain was true to his word. In the morning the ship's crew was bustling with activity. When we got underway the old *Ranger* was rigged for action. Ordinarily the guns were pulled in the ports and turned fore and aft and the ports closed, and then the large guns on her could not be seen. However, she did have six modern four-inch rifles on her, anyone of which could have blown about everything to pieces there. In addition, she also had several six-pounders. She was well armed with modern guns for her size.

It was ten o'clock when we got up anchor and hoisted both our battle flags. In fact, we hoisted three flags. We had a battle flag at each masthead and she was rigged with three masts. We headed toward La Paz with our battle flags flying and the ship bristling with guns. The Mexicans had never seen her with her guns out and she must have looked warlike and awe-inspiring. We had a company of marines aboard and they were all lined up fore and aft in full battle dress.

We were getting up plenty of steam and making quite a display and as soon as people saw us coming, they began to move out of La Paz. I looked off toward the hills which sloped gently away from the town and I saw people leaving, using any available means of transportation. Some of them were carrying their bedsprings and bedding on their backs. The women and

children were all carrying whatever they could, too. Some were leading burros and mules, but the whole town was getting out of there because the captain had told the consul that we would blow the town off the face of the earth if we came there and they didn't have the young man released by eleven o'clock.

The ship's writer had been sent ashore early in the morning in case the Mexicans decided to convene court and try the prisoner. Our ship's writer was a well-educated man and he could read and write Spanish as well as speak it fluently. He was to take down the proceedings and to attest to the fact that the trial had been conducted fairly and in a manner acceptable to us.

If any town was ever evacuated quickly, that town was it. They just melted away. Even those who were too old to walk, or who were crippled, were being carried away from there on quickly improvised litters. Everyone was getting out of town as fast as they could.

We sailed right up to the dock and dropped anchor. When we got there, the chief of police and the mayor of the town were at the end of the little pier, and they had the miner's son with them. They had seen to it that he was washed, shaved, and had a haircut. They made him look as good as they could, but that wasn't saying much as he had been a prisoner for a long time. The consul was there too, and he sang out that they had the boy and that he had been cleared in court, and that if we wanted him, he could go with us. We sent a boat over to the pier to pick up the boy and the ship's writer, and there was no reluctance on the part of the boy to get in the boat and get away from there. He was mighty glad to get into the boat.

As soon as everyone was back aboard, and the ship's boat was stowed on deck, the order was given to get out of there, and as we backed and filled and turned and pulled up the mudhook to get out of there, we pulled our battle flags down. On the way

back to our anchorage at Pichilinque we ran our guns in and closed the ports again.

The father and son being reunited, decided that Mexican mining was not for them so when the *Ranger* pulled up anchor and headed for home, we had two more aboard than when we entered the bay. There were no regular merchant-men calling down there so the captain provided accommodations for them as far as San Diego.

The Imaginary Furloughs

Shortly after the incident of the miner and his son, our survey work was finished, and we pulled up anchor and headed for home. Home meant San Diego where the *Ranger* would spend a month or six weeks before going to Mare Island for overhaul. The officers usually took their yearly furlough while the ship was in San Diego and the same privilege was offered to as many enlisted men as could be spared. San Diego was considered home to the *Ranger* and San Diego felt that the *Ranger* was their ship. The city was good to the crew of the *Ranger.*

I was very fortunate to have relatives who lived in San Diego. I had a place to go and was always welcome in nice homes there and could go with a crowd my own age. My uncle, the county auditor, had three boys, one a little older than I was, one boy was my age, and other about a year younger. I brought civilian clothes and kept them at their house so that I could put them on when I was ashore. In those days the poor blue-jacket was looked down on and the mammas wouldn't let their daughters be seen with a man in uniform. And it was no wonder, because the sailors of old were lusty fellows. But the ones who had friends there were always considerate and wore civilian clothes while visiting. The lusty boys didn't care, and they moved in circles that nice girls didn't even know about.

On the first Saturday afternoon after we arrived in San Diego, I went ashore with a liberty party. I had forty-eight hours leave, so I headed for the home of my uncle. Dick Bigby, the first-class quartermaster, was on the same launch, so when we got ashore we started to walk up Broadway together. After we had walked three or four blocks, Dick stopped at a popular saloon and he drew me inside the door as he said, "Wait in here a minute

for me, will you? I'll walk the rest of the way up Broadway with you to get your car {maybe street car}, but I have an errand in here first."

He went over to the barkeeper who seemed to be the proprietor as well, and they shook hands. I couldn't hear what was said but the proprietor seemed glad to see Dick and they chatted for a few minutes and then I heard Dick ask him if he had seen O'Leary who had come ashore on liberty a couple of days before. The proprietor laughed and said that O'Leary was in a little room there, stretched out on a cot, and that he was on one of his famous furloughs, and they both laughed. He told Dick that O'Leary had not sobered up enough to go back to the ship. Bigby looked into the room and O'Leary was sound asleep, so he came out and we continued on our way up Broadway. I asked if O'Leary was sick or if there was something wrong with him, at which Bigby laughed and said, "I forgot that you don't know about O'Leary!"

I said, "No, I don't know anything about him except that he is a darn nice old man and seems to be about the most wonderful gunner's mate that I have ever been shipmates with. His knowledge and care of guns seems to be tops." He agreed with me and said that there was no better in the Navy.

O'Leary's thirty years in the Navy would soon be up and everybody hoped he wouldn't get a general court-martial before he could get out of the service, and that all the boys tried to protect him and help him. That was why Dick was checking up on him. I wanted to know why such a thing should happen and this is what Dick told me.

"Why, he just goes ashore whenever he is first class and proceeds to drink with his shipmates until he doesn't know what he's doing. Then you can't get him to return to the ship. As long as his money lasts, he'll stay there. When he goes to sleep and goes into a stupor, he dreams or imagines that he's on the

most wonderful furloughs. Even after he has been brought back to the ship and has sobered up, he remembers every detail of the things that happened on this imaginary trip. At first the executive officer used to soak him hard because he wouldn't return to the ship. He would have to be escorted back by the marines or the master-at-arms. He is such a fine gunner's mate and, outside of this fault of going on imaginary furloughs, there is nothing that can beat him.

"He could have been a warrant gunner long ago if it hadn't been for these periodic binges. Now they let him stay until he must be brought back to save him from a court-martial, and so he won't be declared a deserter. When it is time for him to return to the ship, they send the master-at-arms or the corporal of marines with a couple of marines with him, and they bring O'Leary back to the ship. Then he's just knocked down to fourth class in conduct. He only gets boosted in class once a month, consequently he doesn't get ashore again for four months. They can't even rate him to chief because he is not dependable. They will probably hold him until just shortly before his thirty years are in, and time for retirement, when they will transfer him to the Guardo, where he will do duty and they will rate him chief gunner's mate so that he can be retired with the pay of a chief gunner's mate. His record in the Navy, except for these imaginary furloughs, is very brilliant. Few men have a fine record as he has except for this furlough business. Uncle Sam's Navy does the square thing by a man who has given his all for the Navy.

"That's why I joined the American Navy. I'm from New Zealand, born and raised there, and I went to sea out of New Zealand on the merchant marine. But the first chance I got, I joined the American Navy and I have never regretted it. I am very proud of it! No Navy on earth does what the American Navy does for its men and officers. That is why I always try to

keep track of O'Leary when he is on one of these famous furloughs of his, and you'll find that all the older men on the ship do the same thing.

"Every good saloon keeper in San Diego knows O'Leary. They all know about him and take good care that nothing bad ever happens to him if they can help it. One time, O'Leary made one of those famous furloughs on which he went back to Ireland. He was ashore for only seven days but the adventures he had, the old friends he met, and his folks in Ireland that he saw, would have taken at least three months to accomplish. One of the boys he met on the steamer coming back from his imaginary trip has been paid off and out of the Navy for a long time. He has lived here in San Diego for many years and he would certainly be surprised to learn that he met O'Leary on the steamer coming back from Ireland!

"After O'Leary sobers up, if you go up to him and ask him what kind of trip he had, he will grab you by the blouse and take you over on the chest and sit you down and entertain you for hours telling of the things that he did and the old shipmates that he saw; whether they were married and the number of children they had.

"His story is really a work of art. We get a lot of fun out of listening to him. A bunch of us will get together and get him started, and he will tell about any shipmates anyone asks about. He will know them well and will tell all about them and their families. He will probably say that he has visited at the homes of some of them for two or three days and will even give the names of the children! The truth is, the boys generally ask about someone they know who is still single and still in the Navy. It makes more fun to listen to the fantastic tales he tells about them. The officers are aware of all this and they too are quite amused by his tales."

By this time, we had reached the corner where I was to catch my car, and as my car was coming up the street, Dick went on his way and I proceeded to my uncle's house.

I had a very pleasant time while we stayed in San Diego and the month or six weeks just seemed to fly by. The officers and men all began coming in from their furloughs and everybody was happy. It was the spring of the year and the weather was perfect for pleasure. But what had seemed like a holiday was over and the ship sailed for Mare Island where she went into drydock and got a good overhauling and readying for the next survey trip in the fall. There was work every day: painting and polishing and repairing gear, and a thousand and one other things necessary to be done before we again started south which would probably be late in October when we would be ready to go down for another surveying trip after the danger of hurricanes was over.

The surveyors had brought all their work up-to-date while in San Diego and after they had reported to their superiors, they took their vacations and came back to the ship in time to check their gear and get ready for the next year's work. But in the meantime, they had a good long vacation.

The *Ranger* was a fine old ship, and everybody got along well. There was no dissension, and life was nothing but fun on a ship like that. We worked together and played together. The food was good, and the officers were the finest. She was indeed a real "home." The finest ship afloat that I was ever on. The summer soon passed, and we were ready to go again.

The Cantina Brawl

When the work on the ship was completed and everything was ready for the voyage south, we cast off lines and headed for San Francisco Bay where we dropped anchor for a few days before we headed out the Golden Gate and set our course to the south for San Diego. At San Diego we picked up the rest of the surveyors and the civilians who were going to work with them down in the Gulf, and it was not more than twenty-four hours before we were on our way again.

There was nothing of outstanding interest on the way down. We must have been too early or too late for a good turtle haul, but we did have a day or two when we were lucky enough to find some and haul them aboard. We got enough to take to our friends in La Paz who would have been disappointed if we hadn't brought some turtles to them.

We had a good trip down and sailed quietly into Pichilinque Bay and dropped our anchor. Our friends soon spotted our arrival and it wasn't long before they were there to welcome us as they had done every trip before. Everyone except the police and the soldiers were glad to see us. The people who came to welcome us warned us that the military and the police were still peeved about the incident concerning the miner and his son and that they were nursing their wrath to keep it warm. They warned the boys to be careful when they went ashore and not to stir up any trouble.

Almost at once some of our Yaqui friends showed up and it wasn't but a day or two before canoe after canoe appeared, loaded with Yaquis. We named them the Mosquito Fleet. There were many new faces this time, and some of the old ones were missing, but their numbers didn't diminish. They always looked forward to the coming of the *Ranger* and the survey

parties. It was quite an event in their lives, and of course there were always those tin cans!

Life settled back into the routine of taking out and establishing surveyors and their aides, taking soundings, correcting charts, making new soundings where none had been made before, and correcting mistakes of previous soundings, which was dropping a lead-line to measure the water level. We were always busy and seemed to be out more than on the last trip I had gone on, which was probably a good thing for all of us.

Saturday night the Foo Foo band went to La Paz, along with the rest of the boys, and they gave a concert on the plaza. The parade around the plaza was an old Mexican custom and was very popular with the younger set. The ladies all walk in one direction around the plaza, and the men walk in the opposite direction, making goo-goo eyes at one another and flirting scandalously with all the gaiety of the Latins. It was all in fun and the mothers or other chaperones were watching with eagle eyes.

Our work was about finished, and it was getting close to departure time. In fact, it was to be our last Saturday night ashore, so some of us went to pay our respects and say goodbye to such friends as the Silvas, who had been especially nice to us. Others walked around the plaza for a last look at the *señoritas* and the lustier members of the crew sought out their favorites cantinas. The boys had done well at keeping out of trouble and not having any clashes with the police or soldiers. It looked like we were going to get away without an incident, but that was just too much to expect.

The trouble started in a cantina, as might have been expected if there were to be trouble. They were noisy and boisterous, but not getting into any mischief, when three or four of the police force and a soldier or two went inside. I wasn't there but the boys swore that none of them did anything wrong,

but suddenly the fight was on. One of the soldiers fancied that he had been insulted and made a move toward the man he thought to be the culprit, and fists began to swing. As the battle waxed heavy, the word spread through the town like wildfire and the boys from the ship went running and shouting toward the noise. Edwards and I, coming from the Silvas', knew something was up when we saw everybody headed toward the cantina. All the boys from the ship were running to get there in case our boys were in trouble (which they were sure that it must be the case) and the Mexicans were going there for the excitement. More police came, not because they knew what was going on, but because they knew with the whole town rushing toward the cantina, that there must be trouble afoot.

The trouble started among the crowd of Jack Weir and Jim Garrish and their shipmates. Others joined them as soon as they could get into the building. Fists were flying and the police, who carried clubs but no guns, were swinging those clubs with real abandon, not caring whom they hit. They were crowding our boys back, but those boys were fighting demons when they got started. They had been in many fights before and they knew the game! They could see that they had to get out of there and get more room if they were going to win this one, so Jim made a dive under the billiard table and as he went under, he yanked a leg off the table. Jack Weir went under a card table, which was a sturdy piece of furniture, and he came up with a table leg. The other boys were quick to grasp the idea and they all reached for something to swing or hurl: chairs, stools, or anything suitable that was handy, and they all made a rush for the door. The door was practically blocked by the soldiers, but old Jim was just swinging that big heavy pool table leg around his head and knocking men down like cutting grain with a scythe. Every time Jim would make a swing with that leg he would get two or three of them. The Mexicans gave ground and our boys pushed

forward all the harder until they just seemed to burst right out of that cantina into the street, where they were joined by some more of their shipmates. By this time the fight had evened up and the boys with the table legs and other weapons had taken most of the fight out of their opponents who were losing their desire to fight.

About this time, the chief of police came down the street on horseback, with his swallowtail coattails flying. He felt more official when he wore that coat and a sword. He came riding down the street intending to knock Jim Garrish over, but Jack Weir, sensing his intentions, grabbed the chief's leg as he was going by, and dumped him off his horse. Jim reached down to the fallen chief and took his sword away from him while Jack devested him of his swallow-tail coat. There were handcuffs on his belt, and the boys couldn't resist using them…on the chief himself.

Then they started down the street marching the poor chief in front of them. By this time the tide of battle had turned in favor of our boys where they were jubilantly chasing every cop in town, and when they would catch one they would use the poor fellow's handcuffs on his own wrists or ankles. Before they knew it, every policeman in town was handcuffed. The boys took them all up to the jail: policemen, the chief, and everyone they saw wearing a uniform that did not belong to the United States, and locked them all up.

This melee had started in the wee small hours of the night and it was getting daylight before it was over. Edwards had sent me back to the ship with instructions to report what was going on to the officer of the deck. It was five miles to Pichilinque Bay where the *Ranger* was at anchor, so it took some time to get there.

But it wasn't necessary because the consul had been informed and he had immediately set out to see the captain and

implore him to do something before an international incident developed. He was on the same launch I was on and we boys aboard verified his story. The officer of the deck called the captain immediately and told him what the boys were doing ashore and what they had already done—that they had the whole police force and a company of soldiers locked up in the La Paz jail. The captain ordered our company of marines at once to go and fetch them back.

Well, by the time they got the marines and all their equipment ready, it was past daybreak. The trip back to La Paz was made as fast as the boat could go. On landing, the marines went directly to the jail, ordered all the boys to get down to the dock at once and get into the boats. There was no hesitating about that and the boys did as they were told, some laughing and cutting up, others nursing their wounds, their bumps and bruises which they suddenly noticed now that the excitement had subsided. They quickly filled the waiting launches which immediately shoved off and returned to the ship with their battered but jubilant passengers.

I did not turn in when I got back to the ship but waited up to watch the returning combatants. I knew it would be worth watching and I wanted to hear what had happened after I left town.

Jack Weir was in the first boatload to arrive and Jim Garrish was with him. Jack was standing up in the bow of the boat, proudly wearing the police chief's coat, which being too small for Jack, had split up the back, and the swallowtails were flapping in the breeze, but Jack was just as happy as if it had been fitted by the tailor! He was also wearing the sword which he and Jim had taken from the chief, and he was grinning from ear to ear. Jim had on the fancy hat which had once rested so proudly on the head of that haughty official of the law. The other boys had all helped themselves to the uniforms of the vanquished, or

such parts thereof as had struck their fancy. They were an amazing group and looked for all the world like a comic opera troupe. The captain and first lieutenant stood at the rail and watched them as they came up the side, and they had difficulty in repressing their laughter as they commented that it looked like one of the Central American armies coming aboard. What a parade over the side of the ship! What a sight! They had time between La Paz and Pichilinque to get themselves fixed up in their new finery and they were feeling good. For a long time, they had wanted to give that outfit a good licking and this had been the night.

As they were brought aboard they were devested of their loot—those fine clothes and accoutrements. There was about a boatload of that stuff that went back with the boat when they returned to get any stragglers who were still ashore. Some of the boys had too much of a load on to get away with the first boats, but the marines cleaned up the town and got every one of our boys away. The key to the jail was turned over to the consul and by the time he got up to the jail and had freed its occupants, the last boat with every straggler on board was going full speed up the channel.

Well, sir, that almost caused an international incident. We heard about that straight from Washington…in time. It was a good thing that we didn't have to remain but a little while longer. We were away from there in less than a week. Since there were no telegraphic communications they had to go a long way to reach a telegraph, so we got away without any more trouble. The captain didn't feel so good about it, but the whole crew was all swelled up because we had given them such a good licking! Those Mexican police had been asking for it for a long time and had been needling our boys every time they came ashore.

When we got away this time we struck regular turtle weather north. We had great sport loading up with turtles and when we got back to San Diego all our friends, and practically the whole town, had turtle soup for quite a while.

After we docked at San Diego, the usual procedure of furloughs was followed and when we had been there a month or more, we went to Mare Island for the routine overhaul, repairs, and to scrape the bottom and get painted.

That trip was finished. The captain had to do some fast talking to the Navy Department about that trouble in La Paz, but justice was on our side since it was the Mexicans who jumped our boys and started the fight. We had acted in self-defense. I don't believe the Mexicans ever tried anything like that again. In fact, I don't believe any more survey boats went down there after that. The *Ranger* never did. She was slated to join the fleet.

USS RANGER: THIRD VOYAGE

The Semaphore Challenge

Work went along as usual in the repairs and came a day when we were ready to leave Mare Island. The chief quartermaster was called up before the chief navigator and told that we were to join the fleet the next day; that we were to be taken out of survey duty and that we were to join Rear Admiral Glass's fleet at San Francisco. We often wondered why he wanted that old hay-burner in the fleet. She could make only eight knots with everything favorable! I guess he just wanted to have more ships. It looked that way, anyhow.

The navigator and the chief quartermaster were greatly dismayed about the signal situation. A few months before, the American Navy had adopted the semaphore system of signaling by hand. We had always used the Army and Navy code of wigwag before the adoption of the semaphore system which was already in use in the British Navy. It was so much faster than the wigwag. It took about a third of the time to transmit a message by semaphore as it took to transmit one by wigwag. No one on our ship knew the code! We hadn't bothered to learn it. We had been out surveying. This new state of affairs certainly had us in a bad position. The chief quartermaster told the navigator that he'd go and see what we could do about it, but that he was sure that there was no one on the ship who knew it well enough to use it, if there was anyone who knew it at all. The navigator told him that he had seen Smidders and me fooling with it once or twice after we came up to Mare Island, but that he doubted that we had really done anything with it.

The chief quartermaster called us in and told us what had happened. He said that the captain didn't want to apologize to the admiral for not knowing it because the order had been out for some time to switch to semaphore, but that we had been busy

in survey work and that he had just felt that we could take our own time about learning it.

The chief went on to say that we were now in a jam and that the captain didn't want to put new men in the crew just to get someone who knew the semaphore. Then he asked me what I felt we should do. I told him that I knew a little of it and had an idea what it was. Then he wanted to know if I thought Smidders and I could learn it well enough so that we could send and receive messages when we joined the fleet the next day which would be before noon. Smidders was willing to try it and we volunteered to stay up all night to practice. We said that we couldn't guarantee that we could do it, but we would certainly give it all we had. We felt that we would be able to do it well enough to get by without disgracing the ship very much.

He put two other boys on the bridge as signal boys and relieved us of all our other duties so that we could give our sole time to learning the new code and system. He said they just had to put their faith in us, and Smidders and I promised not to let them down. We would do the job if it busted us!

When the chief quartermaster told the captain what we proposed to do, the captain instructed his own cook to give us a good supper and to put out a good lunch for us when we stopped to rest during the night. He also instructed him to see that there was plenty of hot coffee for us so that after we had worked as hard and as fast as we could to learn the code, we could take a break when we got too tired or began to go stale and refresh ourselves with a cup of hot coffee and a bite to eat. We would work as long as we were able and then stop and eat when we were hungry. We had a good meal before we started to work and then we really turned to.

There were no flags aboard for semaphore use so the first thing we did was to get the second-class gunner's mate by the name of Stoddard, who did tailoring to make extra money, to

come up on deck and we showed him just what kind of flags we would need and asked him to go to work on making four of them right away. We didn't want to waste precious practice time making flags, so we took four handkerchiefs and tied them to four sticks with rags which we had torn into strips. As soon as we had these substitute flags made, we got to work. This was in the afternoon when we started. Occasionally we would quit, have a smoke and a cup of coffee, and rest for ten or fifteen minutes, then we would go after it again.

Smidders was a bright boy and he learned it easily. He had been an apprentice boy, too, and had made his cruise a year earlier than I did as he was a little older than I was. I was always glad that I had something to do with getting him on the *Ranger*. Whatever he learned, he learned it well.

Our practice kept up all night long, learning the code, sending messages in it, and receiving them, going slow at first and gradually increasing speed. It was necessary to read the messages as well as send them. So, we worked on and on, stopping every now and then for a smoke or a cup of coffee, and at midnight we had quite a substantial meal. It was better than usual because the captain had instructed his cook to see that we were well fed. We were hungry by that time and the half-hour's respite was good for us. We relaxed and rested and were eager to go back to work when we were through eating.

As we worked on and on into the small hours of the morning, we began to get tired standing up, so we would sit down on the hatch-combing and do it. The night was long and weary, and I doubt if anyone in the Navy ever learned semaphore faster than we did. We had to learn it well enough to receive messages from the flagship with the Admiral looking on and we didn't want to let our captain down. The flagship knew that we had hardly any practice on the code and we felt pretty sure that they would try to show us up—an old Navy custom.

The ships would always send it as fast as they could to one another and if the signal boy didn't get it, he signaled "CCC" back and then they all laughed at him and maybe they would get up and send it so slow the next time he could hardly tell they were moving their arm. That was to show him up and make him look ignorant. We didn't want to be in that position.

The *Ranger* was due to join the fleet before noon, so after breakfast the lines were let go and we headed for San Francisco. Smidders and I kept right on with our practice. We were getting very good by this time and we could do it fairly fast. The captain watched us and some of the anxiety left him as he watched us go through message after message with apparent ease. But he still couldn't believe that we could match the rest of the fleet.

When we got within flag-signal distance, they hoisted a flag signal instructing us where to anchor in relation to the flagship. The flagship was the armored cruiser New York. It was one of the best ships we had in the Navy at that time. The New York was in the battle of Santiago and was Admiral Sampson's flagship during the battle. Well, the boys were busy getting flags together to send a message back by flag hoist to answer the admiral's signal which was the secret Navy code that was being used then, when all at once a guy jumped on the signal platform with the new regulation semaphore flags, making our call letter, which was "R."

"There it is! There it is!" yelled the chief quartermaster. "You fellows go up and do the best you can." We noted a tone of dismay in his voice.

So, we jumped to the upper bridge. The captain, first lieutenant, and navigator were all there. As the captain looked at us with some little excitement, he asked me if we thought that we could do it. I answered and told him that we were *going* to do it. I knew that we could do it then because we had been doing

it all night and by the time we reached San Francisco we were getting fast and smooth. I was a little faster than Smidders, especially in sending, but not any better than he was. I gave the pencil and paper to him and I said, "I'll get it!"

I got up on the signal platform and answered them, and then, boy! Did that signalman ever perform! This fellow on the Admiral's ship sure did! Fortunately, there were no great big words (I don't think he knew how to spell any big words) and it was a very simple message, but did he burn the air! When he finished and made the signal denoting the end of the message, the captain looked at me hopefully, but I could see that his heart had dropped clear down in his stomach while he was watching. He felt that we were licked as he gazed at the speed of that boy sending the message. He hardly dared ask if I had gotten it, but he took a deep breath and asked, "Did you get it? Did you get all that stuff?" and I answered in the affirmative.

I had told every word to Smidders as it came in. It was a message from the captain of the New York to the captain of the *Ranger* and our captain heaved a big sigh of relief when we handed it to him. Then his face broke into a broad smile and he just beamed as he almost shouted, "You did it! You did it! I wouldn't have believed that you could do it! Good boys!" Then the captain wrote out the answering message and instructed us to send it back, so I called the New York and they answered promptly. They were waiting, and I'm very sure that they were surprised that we were sending an answer instead of asking questions about something we didn't understand in their message. That, of course, was what they were working for, to make us ask for a repeat. The message I sent back was a bit longer than the one they sent me. Boy, I burned it up! I sent that message as fast as I could and did it correctly. The captain's eyes opened in surprise as he watched me, and a funny smile came on his lips. He was rather fascinated. When I finished my

169

message, I stood there, and I could see two or three men running around on the bridge of the New York. They had all been watching the message. There were about three of them taking the message down and they were quite a while before they finally signaled back "repeat."

"What did he say? What did he say?" the captain asked excitedly.

"They didn't get it, sir," I answered smiling, "They asked me to repeat." I couldn't help chuckling a little to myself. That was worth the whole night's work that we had put in. Smidders and I felt good and we forgot all about working all night long.

I repeated the message slowly and as precisely as I could. Of course, they were able to read that. It was a good lesson to them because never again did they try to burn the messages to us. They were good boys from then on. It wasn't long until all the quartermasters and signalmen were using the new semaphore code as well as they were doing on any other ship.

When he left the bridge, the captain said to us, "Boys, I'm not going to forget that." And he didn't forget it, either. Later in the year when we got down to Panama, we were both rated quartermasters, and I wasn't supposed to be rated. I hadn't been a first-class apprentice boy long enough. There was supposed to be a year between each rate, but the captain asked for special dispensation for me. Smidders had his time in, and he was rightly eligible. But we were both rated quartermaster for that little job, so it shows that in those days they didn't forget.

Captain Potter was a fine leader and good to all his men, and we were so glad that we could do something good for him. It reflected to his credit. If we had muffed the semaphore signaling and let the New York show us up, it would have reflected against the ship. There were several quartermasters on the bridge and they all came up and slapped us on the back when it was over. They didn't think we could do it. It just goes to

show that when a crisis comes up, if a person will just go in and give it all he's got, something within him will assure success.

A little later the chief quartermaster came out and he had a worried look on his face. He said, "You wait until night after next. We'll catch hell. They'll send a man up to Mare Island today to investigate who these boys are and if we slipped in a couple of fast signalmen just to humiliate the New York. They'll get word back that nothing of that kind was done. We knew that they suspected that because they were looking at us from the Admiral's signal bridge with their most powerful telescopes to see if anyone knew who our signalmen were, but everyone would turn away shaking his head. Now when they get back from Mare island and report what they have learned, they are going to have an Admiral's night signal drill, and that is when we'll catch hell."

The Admiral had a separate deck of his own which was known as the Admiral's bridge. When drills originated on the Admiral's bridge, all the ships, including the New York, had to participate. The bridge of the New York was the regular bridge on the ship, forward, and separate from the Admiral's bridge.

"So," the quartermaster went on, "night after next when they return, they will throw the book at us."

Sure enough, the chief quartermaster was right. The third night we were at anchor the admiral's bridge called a general signal drill for every ship in the fleet. When the signal drill was called our chief quartermaster came out and said, "Here she comes, boys!" She was a whiz bang. The drill was conducted in such a manner that every contrivance in night signaling was used. The lights were rigged on the forestay just forward of the bridge and consisted of red and white lights arranged in groups and

were operated from the bridge in much the same manner as you would operate a typewriter. There was another type of signal which was shot from a pistol that had a barrel as large as a shotgun aimed high in the sky and it produced multicolor stars. Another method was the use of colored rockets, the various colors having different meanings. The final test was on a dot and dash principle with lights. A light was placed directly behind a board which had a hole in it. A little shutter was operated to make short or long flashes to form the letters or words sent out. The whole test consisted of an article which was extremely difficult to receive with these codes because there was so much technical material and so many figures in it.

When the signal drill was over they announced that the next day at ten o'clock in the morning, the commanders of all ships would report to the admiral and submit the article received, to be checked for accuracy. Our navigator took the article to his private office for transcription, which was part of his regular duties, after which he delivered it in regular typewritten for our Captain Potter to be taken to the meeting on the admiral's bridge the following day.

The next morning the captain, along with all the other commanders, reported to the admiral's bridge. We were all on pins and needles all the time he was gone and were eagerly watching the starboard gangway of the New York for the appearance of our captain after the meeting. We had all the glasses on board, telescopes, and powerful binoculars trained on that gangway. Finally, one of the boys having the largest telescope sang out, "He's smiling, boys!" We all watched the captain descend the gangway to his gig and head toward us. As he approached the Ranger his smile grew broader. Our side-boys met him and piped him aboard, and as he saluted the quarterdeck he started to laugh heartily, and he would probably have grabbed the nearest boy and started to dance, but he knew he was being

watched from that bridge on the New York, so he couldn't do anything that would detract from the dignity of an officer. Then he sang out, "Boys, we were the only ship that got it right. The only ones who got the whole message correct!"

The whole ship broke into cheers. It was as if every man on that ship felt that the honor of the Ranger was at stake, and we were all overjoyed at our own success.

Promotions on our South American Voyage

We cruised up and down the coast of California until sometime in November or early December, then the mighty fleet went out on maneuvers. The ships of the fleet were the *New York*, the light cruiser *Boston*, light cruiser *Philadelphia*, *Marblehead*, *Echo*, and the mighty sea-monster *Ranger*. We were doing all the sea maneuvers, fleet drill, battle practice etc., when we finally got orders from Washington to go down to the Gulf of Fonseca. That is the section of Central America where the boundary lines of Nicaragua, Honduras, and El Salvador come together.

On the way down, we had a very grueling experience. Our course took us across the Gulf of Tehuantepec. The *Ranger* had old horizontal engines and, as I have said before, her horsepower wasn't anything startling.

USS *Boston* 1887 to 1946

Commissioned 1897,
Recommissioned 1903 to 1908 (1914 and 1919)

USS *Marblehead* 1894-1921

There is a wind that blows down there which is called a Tehuantepecer, which comes at night. This violent wind is a seasonal thing and blows from the latter part of October until the spring of the year. On the Isthmus of Tehuantepec there is a low place where there are no high mountains between the Atlantic and the Pacific, and this wind blows across from the Atlantic. It is not a cyclonic, whirling wind such as a hurricane, but a perpendicular wind, and it comes up sometimes to blow

only one night, sometimes for two or three days. It comes off the land and oh, how it can blow! It kicks up a terrific sea. Seafaring men who travel up and down that coast often can tell when one is coming. There is a hazy atmosphere and as the sun sets, it takes on a very peculiar red glow and the whole sea in every direction is covered by a rose-colored haze. This atmospheric condition is a sure indicator that there will be a Tehuantepecer that night.

Well, as the fleet approached the gulf it ran into the storm, and all those larger ships went serenely on their way. They had the power to go through it and no one gave the little old *Ranger* a thought. We didn't have enough power, and we just went backwards and chewed up our own logline. At one time it got so bad that we couldn't hold her head up to the wind and we did not want to get into the trough of it because that would have been exceedingly dangerous. We could have lost the ship that way. So, we set the trysail. That didn't quite hold her, so we finally set the spanker (our aftermost sail) and that held her head up.

We were twenty-four hours behind the rest of the fleet. By that time the admiral began to realize what had happened and he had some uncomfortable moments worrying about us. He dispatched the *Marblehead* to go out and look for us, but just as she was getting underway to go out, we came up. It was just getting twilight as we met her, she signaled us, and we answered. She then told us, by signal, that she was about to go out to look for us. I don't know what they could have done if they hadn't found us. They couldn't have dragged the whole ocean. Anyway, we were mighty thankful to reach there safely. Many ships have been lost in that gulf and if they don't know their stuff, they can get into plenty of trouble.

In later years when I was on the Pacific Mail boats, we used to go down there and at certain times of the year when the

indications were for a blow, we would simply go around, keeping close to the shore. The wind came right off-shore and would blow above us when we hugged the shore. The water was so deep that we could almost touch the bow of the ship at the shore. There were just two reefs that we had to avoid on the whole trip around. These reefs were well charted, and the ships swung out to avoid them. It was a longer trip to keep close to the shore, but it made a better and faster trip out of it. Trying to buck those driving winds only slows a ship down and uses more power trying to go through the heavy seas.

We were directed to an anchorage with the rest of the fleet off the island of Amapola. It was a very picturesque spot and most interesting. By the time we were anchored night had fallen and all was velvety blackness. Three active volcanos were visible and their fiery eruptions against the night sky was a beautiful sight to behold.

Amapola itself was the domain of a fugitive American who had been a bank president and had absconded with a fortune and set up a little kingdom of his own on the island. We had no extradition treaty with those countries at that time, so he was safe as long as he did not go aboard an American ship, which he was extremely careful not to do. Because of his wealth (ill-begotten though it was) he had things his own way, since he was the only rich man there. The plaza was in a state of disrepair when he arrived, so that was one of his first projects. Since the town revolves around the plaza, it was only fitting that it should be cleaned up and beautified. He then built a bandstand and brought all new instruments for a band, and he found a competent leader and organized a band that the town could be

proud to call its own. He encouraged concerts with something going on in the plaza every night. From there he went to other civic improvements. His family joined him there and they all were living in regal splendor, enjoying the slow, easy life of the tropics although he couldn't leave that country.

We had been sent down there because it looked like a war was in the making. We were just sent there for appearances sake and not to take part in quelling any incidents. Our arrival was unexpected, and each country thought one of the others had called on the United States for help and that they were to be attacked. It was quite amusing and much like a comic opera. We went ashore and hobnobbed with the soldiers and our Spanish speaking members of the crew quizzed them but learned little. We tried to find out from the soldiers what the fighting was all about, but they didn't know. In fact, there hadn't been any fighting yet, but they were right on the brink of war. One country had a chip on its shoulder and the other two were looking at it. That's the way most wars were started down there in those days, but our coming turned the tide and they all concluded that they might just as well cut the war out, especially while we were there. We stayed two or three weeks and by that time they had all cooled off and were probably having fandangos together.

After this tremendous war fizzed out and blew over, the diplomats figured that the fleet was no longer needed so it was ordered home. However, Admiral Glass was notified that the ship which was stationed in Panama needed to be relieved, so the *Ranger* was detached from the fleet and ordered to duty there.

There was a revolution in Panama at that time. The section which had rebelled belonged to Columbia, but they were fighting for their independence. We didn't know why we were singled out to go down there, but it was probably because we didn't have power enough to keep up with the rest of the fleet.

Anyway, we were picked to go, and the rest of the fleet sailed northward and home while we plugged along down the coast of Panama.

When we finally arrived, we anchored off Deadman's Island and just lay there. We couldn't go ashore. We couldn't do anything! We were not allowed to eat the fruits that were raised around locally such as papayas and those beautiful luscious-looking bananas! At first, we couldn't buy anything, but later the ban was lifted on the papayas. Our medical officer was a very cautious man and he wasn't taking any chances on our getting any of the tropical diseases.

We had been in Panama a few days before Smidders and I were called up before the captain and we were told that in appreciation for the hard work we had done in learning the new semaphore code just before reaching San Francisco, and the excellent results, we were being rewarded with a petty officer's rating of third-class quartermaster. The captain went on to say that there had been nothing to hold up Smidder's rating as he was being advanced at the regulation rate, but that I was being rated through special consideration. I should have been in another year before being eligible. This little rating ceremony was one of the bright spots in our careers. It was wholly unexpected but mighty nice to have. Besides the added prestige, it carried a raise in pay. We felt good about being petty officers and I was especially gratified in having vindicated myself of the low opinion I believed my shipmates on the *Adams* had of me when they taunted me with, "what could a little runt like you do," and that I wouldn't even be able to keep my clothes washed, and that I would be useless. As far as I know, I was the first petty officer rated from among the one hundred and twenty boys that made our cruise on the *Adams*. I got a lot of satisfaction out of this promotion and wished those boys could know about it.

We were able to take our regular watch with the other quartermasters and at night we stood our watch on the quarterdeck. If there was nothing very important that turned up, the officer of the deck could sleep in. This made us feel important, and we couldn't be blamed for feeling proud because we were young.

Not far from us lay His Majesty's ship Phaeton. She was a large cruiser, but like the *Ranger*, she was outdated as a fighting ship, and for this reason she was homeward bound. She was scheduled to lay in Panama a while before putting down the coast of South America for the Horn or the Straits of Magellan, and then heading for home where she was to be decommissioned permanently. Life would have been very monotonous for us if it hadn't been for this British ship. After the officers had made their calls and acquainted themselves of all their obligations, the crews were permitted to visit back and forth in the evenings if they had nothing else to do. Almost every night there were visiting parties going back and forth between the Phaeton and our ship.

The crew of the British ship boasted of some good talent and they wanted to entertain us, so they got up a party which they called a sing-song. It was a bang-up good one, too. I had the watch that night, so I didn't get to go to the sing-song, but I didn't lack for company.

Standing the night watch was very serious business as far as I was concerned. I walked up and down with the big night glasses tucked under my arm, feeling my responsibility. I could hear the boys over on the Phaeton and they sounded like they were having a real, good time. By and by one of our boys brought

several of the men from the British ship aboard—there must have been four or five of them—and they came up on the bridge. Of course, they were introduced to me and I acknowledged the introductions with all the dignity I could muster. Two of these men were old-timers in the British Navy, and they were almost ready for retirement. When they got a good look at me they were astounded at my youth.

"By Jove!" one of them exclaimed as they went down the ladder, "You know, it is just unbelievable! This kid is a petty officer and his name isn't dry on the books yet! Over in our outfit a fellow works about twenty years to get to be a third-class petty officer. Why didn't I have enough sense to join the American Navy? I could have had a nice little nest egg put away if I had had the chance this kid has!" Which was probably true because I was getting about three times as much money as he was getting. I couldn't help smiling to myself.

I guess when he got back to his own ship he went around telling everybody about what he had seen on our ship, and especially about me, because it wasn't long before there was a regular stream of visitors up on the bridge and they came for no other reason than to look at me, "to get a look at a kid who was a third-class petty officer standing an officer's watch." They were amused. Some of them feigned other interests, but they kept coming back to look at me, but most of them were quite outspoken about it and admitted that they wanted to see me with their own eyes before they could believe the tales the other boys were telling.

The Panama Canal & a Rebel Attack

The boys on the Phaeton gave us a good picture of what was going on in Panama. They said that the people who lived ten or fifteen miles on either side of the old site of the canal, what little there was that had been built by the French. They were trying to sell it to us. They wanted the canal built and they felt that if the United States took it over by purchasing it, that it would get finished. The government of Columbia, who owned Panama, was squabbling about the canal. They had been squabbling about it for ten years. Just about the time we thought we were getting someplace, their political machine would explode, and the new batch of *politicos* would all want their rake-off. It seemed like every government politician wanted to make a million out of it.

Teddy Roosevelt, who was president of the United States at that time, was very anxious to build the canal. He saw the possibilities of cutting out that long voyage around the Horn or through the Straits of Magellan. He was a practical man and he became thoroughly disgusted with the situation in the Isthmus of Panama, but he had his ideas and he went about getting the canal in his own way…and he got it, too! According to the boys on the British ship, the fighting was between the rebels in the little strip on either side of the canal, and the soldiers of Columbia. We were to see more of this later, but for the first few weeks, all the information we had on the canal trouble was what we had garnered from the Phaeton.

It wasn't much more than a week after the sing-song that the British ship pulled up anchor and got under way homeward bound, leaving us alone. We would miss them for a few days because our visits back and forth had done a great deal towards breaking the monotony.

182

The Canal district was alive with people from all over the world. There were a great many who had come from the United States, but the unskilled laborers were mostly from Panama and the West Indies. They were paid fair wages which were higher than any they had ever earned in their lives, but life was hazardous, and the death rate was extremely high. As soon as the United States arrived they set out to kill the mosquitos, the carrier of the deadly yellow fever.

Not too far from where we were anchored, there was a sailing ship which had lost nearly all her crew except the captain or the mate and a couple of other officers and one or two of the crew. They were all victims of yellow fever and had been laid to rest on Deadman's Island.

I could hardly blame our doctor for being so strict about the food we ate and our mingling with people we didn't know anything about. He carefully examined any food that was brought over to us and he supervised the cooking of it, insisting that it be done according to the way he thought it should be prepared to kill any yellow fever germs. He wasn't very popular with the cooks!

Not long after the Phaeton sailed, the monotony of our existence was unexpectedly broken. A shoddy-looking yacht came in, flying the Columbian flag. She looked like she hadn't been painted in forty years. This was a wooden ship which probably had been taken away from the owner. It is very likely that some wealthy man had broken a technical law and the Columbian government had confiscated his boat. This yacht was a good boat, about one hundred and fifty feet long and she had fine lines. Well, in she sailed as proud and important as you

please and anchored about a quarter of a mile off our starboard hand to take troops aboard.

In addition to this yacht, the Columbian government had two old mud-scows and that was the extent of their navy. They were barges normally used to carry away dredged mud. Those boats were equipped with old boilers and they burned whatever they could find to fire them with. I know they couldn't make over six or seven knots at the most. Those boats began to bring over troops, a load at a time, and finally they had that yacht so full of soldiers that I couldn't even imagine where they put them all. I never saw such a crowded boat in my life as that one the night they finished bringing over the soldiers.

We were all intensely interested in the proceedings and there was no doubt but that she was going to take those troops some place to do combat with the rebels, who were Panamanians wanting independence from Columbian rule. We couldn't help wondering where they were going to do all this fighting. We suspected that night that she would get underway early the next morning after getting everything aboard.

I had the morning watch and I came on duty at four o'clock. It was still dark, but I could see some activity on this boat that we'd been watching. If they were only scratching themselves, it would make activity, and the Lord knows, they probably did do plenty of scratching because it was likely that none of them had had a bath in a good long time. So, I had no more than relieved the man on watch and was walking the quarterdeck when I noticed a ship coming out of the Gulf of Panama. She was a fairly large vessel which I judged to be about three thousand tons registry. She looked like a tramp steamer. The red lead stuck out all over her, indicating that they did make some attempt to keep her in some state of repair. It was just getting daylight when I saw her lights coming and as she

approached she went across our bow. A few minutes before she reached us we heard her bugle sound "general quarters." That's the call on a man-of-war calling all hands to battle quarters. It was the same call the Americans used, and my ears stuck right out then. I was all interest. That meant action!

She swung around our bow and came in between us and the transport. Just as she got past us she fired at the transport with her twenty-pounders. They were the heaviest guns down there. The mud-scows the Columbians used for battleships had about six-pounders, but this rebel ship had twenty-pounders in which she used shrapnel!

The firing was so close that it was practically alongside of us and when it started, every officer on our ship was out of his bunk and on the quarterdeck, wearing bathrobes, not taking time to dress. The captain and first lieutenant wanted to know what ship it was, and I told them that as near as I could figure it out, it must be the rebel ship Padilla. I then told them how she came around our bow and came between us and the transport and how her bugler sounded "general quarters" as the Americans did. The officers agreed that it probably was the Padilla. No one on our ship had ever seen her. We had only heard about her and that the Columbians were afraid of her because she had sunk about everything afloat that the Columbian government had— transports and everything else on the Pacific side of Panama.

When the Padilla let go her first salvo {discharge from several pieces simultaneously}, she must have put in at least two twenty-pounders and about four six-pounders and a lot of one-pounders. They all went off about the same time. She let everything go that she could fire on the port side. There were soldiers on the yacht jumping and falling overboard and I suppose getting killed, and the Padilla went right on through, firing all the time until she got clear of our stern and the stern of the transport, then she made a sharp turn and turned right

around and went back, headed the other way on the same route she had taken coming in between us and the Columbian transport again. When she was again in position, the Padilla let go everything she had on the starboard side.

Then we noticed that the transport was listing. Many of the shots must have been below the wind and water level. We could see that she was settling. As soon as the Padilla made her run firing on the starboard side, she headed into the Gulf of Panama, out of the bay and up the Gulf as fast as she could go.

We learned later that the commanding general who was aboard the Columbian transport, was in his room asleep when the firing began. He came rushing up on deck and on the bridge, where he was mortally wounded. Both of his legs were shot off. He was taken below to his stateroom and he went down with the transport and with the hundreds of soldiers who were lost. We never did know exactly how many died. We were told that there were over fourteen hundred aboard, but how they ever got that many aboard her was beyond us, unless she was longer and larger then she appeared to be.

As soon as the Padilla headed out, we called away all our boats and went over to the sinking ship. We saved all that we could find alive. Those who weren't alive went down with the ship or drowned. She sank until there was nothing left of her except her foretopsail. The upper end of her foretopsail mast was sticking out of the water.

The mud-scow battleships of the Columbian government were not to be seen all that day. All the men that we saved—some of them terribly maimed, without an arm or a leg, and many severely wounded—were treated and administered to by our doctor and his corps. They did the best they could for them. There were so many to be cared for and all our medical team worked long and hard.

The wounded men were placed on pallets in the sailing launch and cutters as soon as they were given what help our medical corps could give them, and carried to the dock at Panama City, where they were taken care of by their own government. We had a forty-foot sailing launch and our cutters and our steam launch, and they were busy all day, carrying their loads of suffering humanity to the place designated by the Columbian government. Some of them died en route.

The Columbian government never raised this yacht, nor to my knowledge, made any attempt to recover the bodies. Occasionally one would float up and it would be picked up and taken away for burial. But as far as making any attempt to recover those that went down with the ship, nothing was ever done. The mast stuck out of the water for at least twenty years that I know of.

About two weeks after the attack by the Padilla, we took some American officials, including the American consul, aboard the *Ranger*, pulled up the anchor and headed in the general direction of Point Mala. When we came to the Gulf of Partita we changed our course and headed for Aguadulce, a small town which was the headquarters of the rebels. None of the crew knew what was afoot but I later learned that these officials were sent up there by our government to negotiate with the rebels in an effort to stop the fighting, so the United States could get on with the project of building the canal.

These negotiations took a couple of days and while they were going on, the boys on the ship had a lot of fun. A cutter was put over the side and several of us went up the Chagdus River in it to look for alligators. One of the ship's officers was

with us and his enthusiasm for alligator hunting almost proved our undoing. We were quite a way up the river when we saw what appeared to be a log floating down, but as we drew close to it we were surprised to see it wink its eye. The officer who had a high-powered rifle, was delighted and, I might add, excited.

The vulnerable spot on an alligator is hard to hit, and the man who shoots one should know what he is doing. I do not mean to say that our officer did not know what he was doing, but in his exuberance, he was not as cautious as he should have been. We were a little too close to the beast for safety. When he fired, he hit his mark, but the great beast flipped his tail up and over, and it struck the cutter aft, almost capsizing it. We had some anxious moments but managed to keep the boat upright, although it was damaged by the blow.

The day was hot and before noon we had used all the fresh water we had brought with us, so we filled our canteens with river water for the afternoon trip back to the ship. This was a very foolish thing to do because the water was polluted and every single one of us got the Chagdus fever and were very sick boys. Of course, our doctor who knew more about the dangers which lurked in the food and water of that country than we did, was very upset about all this and he used us as a glaring example of what would happen when his warnings were ignored.

A day or two later, with our officials aboard, we started back for Panama. We were back in the Gulf of Panama before we noticed a ship which seemed to be following us. On looking at her through the big glasses it could be seen that she was the same ship which exterminated the shipload of soldiers. She was that small tramp freighter and could outrun us, and she seemed to be making more speed than we could get out of our ancient boilers. However, she didn't overtake us, which we knew she could have done had she wanted to. When we were within five miles of Deadman's Island, what should we meet out there but

the two mud-scows which were the battleships of the Columbian government, and they had their six-pounders ready for action. The Padilla was coming on fast now, under forced draft, and the battleships started firing at the Padilla. They made a lot of noise, but their shells didn't reach half way to the rebel ship. When the Padilla came closer, she let one of her twenty-pounders go. It came uncomfortably close to one of the mud-scows and they hiked for cover! Each boat had her favorite hiding place and didn't wait for the second round the Padilla fired before getting away from there and lost among the many islands which dotted that area. They were out of sight before the rebel ship could get a shot at them again.

We went into our regular anchorage where we had been before and let go the hook. Shortly afterward the Padilla came in close by and dropped her anchor, too. Her officers tried to communicate with us by voice, but it proved unsatisfactory, so our captain and a couple of the diplomats got in the captain's gig and went over to the Padilla. They were anxious to see more of her. This incident gave them an excuse to go over to her and her captain and to ask them aboard.

As had been suspected, the captain of the Padilla was a white man who had been an officer in either the American or the English Navy. He told our party that we were making it very difficult for them to carry on a war of rebellion and that his ship was having a hard time carrying out their strategy because these little mud-scow battleships of the Columbian Navy would come out of hiding and get behind us. They knew that the Padilla fired at them in that position, they would be taking chances on hitting an American ship, and the Columbians were sure that the rebels would not do this. Of course, this was true, and we were not to be caught napping. We had our guns out, ready for action in either direction had it become necessary.

It appeared that our delegation had not been too cooperative because they hadn't any more than shoved the gig away when the Padilla pulled up her hook and got under way. I suppose she went to hide among the Island where she could watch the Bay of Panama and pounce on any Columbian ship that might show itself.

Protecting the Railroad

After these incidents, things quieted down for a while and our attention was turned to the railroad which ran from Colon from the Caribbean Sea on the east, to Panama City on the Pacific Ocean on the west side of the Isthmus. This railroad, called the Inter-Oceanic Railroad, was built by American capital years before, and the Columbian government had agreed to protect the tracks and guard them from being torn up, and they had promised to protect the trains and guard against any danger to the passengers. Most of the passengers on these trains debarked from their ship at Colon and took the train to Panama where they re-embarked for San Francisco. This eliminated the long, tedious voyage through the Straits of Magellan or around the Horn and saved a great deal of time.

Conditions on the railroad had been going from bad to worse. The Columbian government seemed to have the idea that they owned the railroad and that they could do whatever they liked with it. If they had a big consignment of soldiers to go across the Isthmus, or to be distributed in strategic places along the way close to the railroad, they would just throw the passengers off the train to make room for the soldiers. The railroad officials had been fighting this sort of thing to no avail and word of the situation reached the rebels. They notified our government at Washington what was going on and the rebels did not intend to let this movement of troops by the Columbian government at will, go on any longer. The rebels respected the fact that the railroad was owned by American capital and they didn't bother it nor ride on it. However, they pointed out that the Columbian government was shipping their soldiers on it anytime they wanted to, giving them the advantage of quick transport action, eliminating the necessity of long marches

through the jungles on foot. The rebels warned that if this practice was not discontinued at once, they would blow the railroad to smithereens and there would be no train to ride across the Isthmus.

Our government then notified the Columbians that they would have to discontinue this practice at once or we would have to do something about it. But this did not deter the Columbians, so we got orders to take over the train and protect it. The train made two round trips from Panama City to Colon each day.

Captain of the Machine Gun

When orders reached the *Ranger* to dispatch men and equipment to protect the train consisting of forty to fifty men, including the company of marines, equipped as infantry, they were sent ashore the next morning and took over the guarding of the train. It was my good fortune to be selected as captain of the machine gun, a six mm Colt automatic, mounted in the baggage car. It was a wicked gun when it worked correctly. There was a lot to be desired but in target practice I had done better than anyone else on the ship in firing that gun, so they made me captain of it. Baldy Gass, another apprentice boy, was assigned to duty with me, as second captain. Baldy was a chunky boy, full of fun and a good companion.

The door of the baggage car was wide open, and the gun was pointed outward. I sat on a bicycle seat when I fired the gun. My ammunition was on one side of me and it would pass through the gun to the other side with the empty shells held in place by a canvas belt. This gun shot two-hundred-and fifty times a minute, so it was a busy gun when it worked right. In target practice we put up a canvas with a line of men painted on it. This was held upright and stretched taut, and I was able to cut that canvas right off at the heads, take another bite in the canvas and cut it off in the middle. If the gun worked right, it was wicked indeed. I could stop anything with it and keep on shooting, but it had a habit of sticking. Of course, if a gun doesn't shoot, it isn't any good to anyone. However, it was the best thing we had in the Navy up to that time.

We had our orders when we took over command of the train. No government officials, nor soldiers, nor sailors, nor anyone connected with the Columbian government, could ride on the train unless they had special permission from our officials.

The Columbian army evidently hadn't gotten the word yet. The train left at eight o'clock and we had to be aboard and in our places when it reached the station. We went ashore early in the morning and found the train backed down to the dock where our boats landed, and we loaded our duffel and gear and our machine gun all in the baggage car. We put the Union Jack on the cow-catcher and the American flag on the back platform of the last car. When everything was ready we pulled up about half a mile or so to the station.

As we approached the station we could see a lot of soldiers lined up with packs on their backs, knapsacks, blankets, and so forth, ready to climb aboard. As the trained stopped they came running out, cackling like a flock of magpies or geese, to pile aboard. Just before they got to the train, out stepped our infantry and marines at each platform and some inside the platform with fixed bayonets waiting to see what was going to happen. The Columbians couldn't believe their eyes. They stopped and rubbed their eyes and turned around. The officer in command evidently told them to go aboard but they didn't relish this bayonet business. Our boys were all in position to fight. Finally, they broke ranks and went back, cackling and chattering and that was that. They hung around the station for a little while and then were evidently ordered back to their camp.

The Columbian soldiers had fortifications of sandbags and dirt thrown up along the track, so they could fire on the train. There were some soldiers behind these breastworks and they pointed their guns at us as we went by, and in return we gave them a rather naughty sign with our fingers to our nose. That was all the fighting that ever went on in that incident.

There was a big Irish conductor on the train and he had been on it for many years. That rotund, red-faced fellow was so glad to see us! He had been harassed and badgered plenty and ever since the trouble had started he had taken a beating from

the Columbian soldiers and government. They had forced his passengers off the train and he had been unable to do anything about it. He just had to take it, but it made him furious. He told us all about the indignities he had suffered and what he had gone through, and he could have kissed every one of us he was so glad to see us.

We went across the Isthmus without incident and pulled into the dock at Colon, where we all got out and stretched our legs. There was a Columbian transport there and they had a shipload of soldiers to go back with us. Evidently the news didn't travel so fast. They had not heard that riding on that train was forbidden. Most of them had already reached the dock with their duffel. There must have been about four hundred of them, and they started up the dock toward the train. They had quite a long march from the ship to the train, which gave our lieutenant time to order us all out, machine-gun and all. We lifted it down and got behind a row of cotton bales awaiting shipment on the dock. We put the machine gun on top of the cotton bales, pointing down the pier.

The soldiers were not in formation but just came straggling along and dragging their big, old guns. I don't know what kind of guns they had but they looked like museum pieces to me. The guns with their brass bayonets appeared longer than the soldiers who carried them. They were getting close when our officers who were standing on the top of the bales of cotton, gave them the order to stop and to come no further. The order was given in Spanish to assure it was understood, and that there would be no mistake about it. The men were stopped immediately by their officer in command. He could see that we had something behind those cotton bales and he could see the machine gun on the top. Maybe word had come across the grapevine about keeping the soldiers off the train at Panama, and he could see there were none aboard when the train arrived at the

dock. They fiddled around and argued amongst themselves and in the meantime, we had orders to load our weapons.

We were using the infield gun at that time. It was called the Lee straight-pull and was a very efficient, good gun except that the caliber wasn't as heavy as is used nowadays, but it was very accurate. It shot five times without reloading. They could hear the click of the metal and recognized the noise we made loading and could undoubtedly see the fixed bayonets. By this time their leaders had come to a decision and the men lined up in battle order and their commander gave the order to advance. One fellow would take a step or two and stop. Then the next one would take a step and stop. As they took their first steps to advance we were given the order to aim. They didn't need to understand English to know what the order was because our boys immediately pulled down on them. We had a lot of good shooters aboard our ship.

During survey duty there had been lots of time to practice and they had a chance to learn to be good shots. The soldiers began to hesitate, then they took another look at those guns and bayonets pointing ominously at them and they stopped dead in their tracks, then turned and ran back. Their officers were left stranded with nothing but their shiny swords, so they concluded that they wouldn't try to do the job alone and they went back also and boarded the transport. I never did find out what became of them, but they didn't ride on our train and they never tried it again.

I was plenty scared and I'm sure the other boys were, too. Those soldiers coming up the dock looked like an awful lot of men to me. Fortunately for us, we didn't have to go through with it, and no shots were fired. When we saw that everything was under control and that there would be no more trouble from those Columbian soldiers, we got back aboard the train and headed toward Panama City on the return trip.

This occurrence caused quite a sensation down there and put some respect into the people with whom we had dealings. The trainmen said that the sending back of the troops to their own ship had done more to raise the morale of the people in Colon than anything we could have done.

We had a good trip back with no incidents of note until we were almost back to Panama City. It was about the second or third station before we got there that a large, banana-bellied man came swaggering through our baggage car on his way towards the engine. As he came through the car, he stopped behind me for a minute and looked the Colt automatic machine gun over thoroughly. I was just about to get off my bicycle seat and ask him what he wanted when he turned and continued.

The brakeman was standing in the passageway and, as the man left our car, he came to me and asked me what my orders were. I told him that my orders were to keep all people off the train that belonged to the Columbian government whether they were in or out of uniform. His next question was about the man who had just passed through the car and he wanted to know if I knew the man. I replied that I had no idea who he was and that he was just a one-eyed *hombre* with a little too much curiosity. The brakeman about bowled me over by telling me that this fellow was the second highest general in the Columbian army. That was too much for me and I turned to Baldy and said, "Gass, let's go get 'im!" The brakeman slowed us down, though. He pointed out that the man couldn't get off the train and that he would have to come back. Why not get him then? That seemed sensible.

When he asked what we were going to do we replied that we were going to carry out our orders and that we were going to kick his ass right off the train. Baldy and I both wore .38 Colt sidearms and I told Baldy that when he came through again to grab the general by the back of the neck as he came into the car and that I would frisk him for arms. We had just begun to slow down for the next station when Mr. General came in through the door. As Baldy saw him coming he said to me, "Steve, for God's sake, let me give him a good swift kick in the ass when we put him off! I always have wanted to kick a general, and what a story to tell my grandchildren about the time I kicked a general off the train!"

So, when the general got about halfway down the car we moved in on him. Baldy grabbed his arms from the back and I went over him quickly to see if he had a gun, but I found nothing. Of course, he swelled up and began to look insulted and started to spout off a string of Spanish lingo which meant nothing to us. I told him, "No *sabe* Spanish, only *sabe* American." Baldy and I both knew what he was saying, but we didn't let it show. That brakeman was lounging against the side of the baggage car with a serene smile on his face, just watching developments.

By that time the train had practically slowed to a stop at the station, so we moved him on to the platform where a marine with fixed bayonet stepped down and we went ahead with our plan to give him the old heave-ho, commonly known in the Navy as the deep-six. Baldy got his wish and gave him a good kick in the back side and I got in a fair one myself. That general went off that platform as fast as his legs could carry him and he didn't even look back but kept on going! What a lot of satisfaction we got out of that!

Grandmother's Experience in Panama

By the time we reached Panama the brakeman had told the conductor all about it, and probably with embellishments. The conductor was delighted with the story and came back to congratulate Baldy and me. I told him that justice was a long time in arriving. I said that his ancestors probably had a hand in causing my grandmother and her party so much trouble when they crossed the Isthmus and that this general's ancestors were probably a lot of the bandits, anyway. He readily agreed with me and looked over toward the station.

The station was a corrugated iron building of two stories, and the dilapidated condition of rust and corrosion, attested to the ravages of time. It was full of holes and I asked if they were the result of revolutions. He nodded and said he guessed so, that the bullet holes had been in the building as long as he could remember, and he thought he remembered his father telling stories of fights taking place there. I then told him that my grandmother Stevens and some of her family were in the Panama riot and he nodded and said he had heard of it, but that it was generally not talked about. He seemed interested, so I told him the story as I remembered the way Grandmother had told it to me. The whole guard from the ship took their lunches into the station building to eat as the Navy would not allow the boys to eat any of the food ashore. As the train had stopped and there was no activity for any of us at the moment, I launched into the story grandmother Emeline had told me many times.

Emeline & Husband, Josiah Stevens

My grandfather Josiah Stevens had made several trips between Missouri and the Pacific as captain of the emigration of covered-wagon trains. He was thoroughly familiar with the dangers of these cross-country trips and had many narrow escapes himself, in encounters with the Indians. He knew, too, of the hardships and sickness en route and he didn't want his wife and children subjected to these same experiences. So, he decided to send them by boat to Panama, where they would cross the Isthmus from Colon to the Pacific Ocean on the newly constructed railroad and take another boat north on the Pacific side and thence to San Francisco.

The first passenger train was soon to cross the Isthmus and it was his wish that his family be among the passengers of that epochal journey. He arranged for his wife's two brothers, Lymon "Lime" and Edson Ashley, both experienced Indian fighters, to accompany his wife Emeline and children and the

wife of their next-door neighbor, who wanted to meet her husband in San Francisco, to join them. He booked their passage on the boat which would arrive in time for them to get on that first train. Grandfather knew that the first train, scheduled to depart on January 28, 1855, was a history-making event and he wanted his family to be part of it. Little did he realize what that trip would be, and the terrors that would confront them. Grandmother and the three children would probably have been murdered had not her brothers been with them. It was a mighty fortunate thing for all of them that these two young men were along and armed with their long-barrel, cap and ball .36 caliber Colts {.45 caliber Colt reported in his manuscript was not built yet}.

The boat trip to Colon was without incident and everybody was happy when the first half of the journey came to an end. Everyone was excited about the crossing of the Isthmus on that first passenger train and they were filled with awe and wonder at the new world they were seeing. But their joy was turned to terror a short time later when the train was boarded by a gang of men armed with knives, soon after leaving Colon. As the train slowed down, these ruffians swung aboard, arousing the anxiety of the passengers and soon spreading their fear and trepidation throughout the whole train. Three or four of their band boarded the engine to make sure that the train did not stop or signal any station but would continue in an uninterrupted journey from one coast to the other, thus assuring the rest of the band ample time to rob and strip the passengers of all their valuables and to go through their hand luggage.

They boarded the first and last coaches with the idea of working toward the center coach, but this proved to be an error for the brigands and to the advantage of the passengers, and probably why there were fewer lives lost than would have been had the bandits worked in some other manner. It was but a few

minutes until the passengers in the end coaches began running into the middle coach, screaming with fright and giving warning of the attack. Grandmother's brothers took over at once. They directed that the women and children get under the seats, the backs of which were lifted up for protection. The boys took their stand between the center and either end of the coach with loaded pistols ready. Grandmother and the neighbor lady, both of whom had a lot of experience helping their menfolk loading various kinds of firearms during Indian attacks, took their places by the two brothers to help in this emergency.

These ruthless vandals were not only bent on robbery but on assassination, and they killed without compunction. As many of the passengers as were able to escape into the middle car, crowded into the center of the coach and down behind the seats, and if an assassin dared to open the door of the coach, he was stopped in his tracks by one of those long-barreled Colts. It was not long before the raiders saw that their attempts to enter that coach were futile, so they retreated into the coaches from which they had emerged and looted all the luggage, throwing it off the train when they had examined the contents and taken everything of value and any trinkets they fancied. These poor passengers had only the clothes they wore and such money or jewelry as was concealed on their persons. From time to time an assassin would venture to the door of the center coach, but it was always his undoing and a shot from the gun would discourage any others who had the same idea.

Only one of these bandits managed to get in and out of that coach alive. Just as he cautiously opened the door, little two-year-old Webster, Grandmother's youngest child, who had been entrusted to the care of his older sister Caroline who was nine years old, scooted out into the range of the guns, right by the door that the bandit was opening. Quick as a wink, that bandit grabbed the little fellow and held him close to him, a

202

shield between himself and the defenders. He looked like a mere boy, too young to be associated with such a gang of cutthroats. Caroline was stunned, but only for a moment. She fearlessly ran out into the isle and straight to the bandit, her red braids swinging and her green eyes flashing. It took a great deal of courage to face that bandit who was holding her little brother, but she begged him to give the little fellow back to her. She offered him the pretty ring which was her most treasured possession because it was a going-away gift from her friends in Missouri, but she stripped it from her finger and held it out to him, extending the other hand toward Webster. The bandit understood what she was trying to do, and he grinned at her and winked, and as he patted Webb's tasseled head, he put the child down and held his hand out for the ring. He was careful to keep the children between himself and the shooting irons, and he slipped through the door as quickly as he had come in. Everyone breathed a sigh of relief when he was gone, leaving the children unharmed.

As the train pulled into the station at Panama City, the station agent saw at once that something was amiss, and it was but a moment until he realized what was happening. He quickly arranged for someone to run to the fort to get help, as the government had agreed to protect the railroad. The fort was a mile or more from the depot. There were no telephones nor telegraphs to use in calling for help and transportation was not readily available, so it was assumed that the agent had to send a runner.

When the train came to a halt, the two brothers moved quickly to cover the passengers, holding the brigands and murderers back while the other men hurried the women and children from the train and into the galvanized, iron building which served as a railroad station. They had expected to get help there but when it was seen that there was no help, the men urged

the women and pushed or carried the children up the enclosed stairway which was on the one side of the building, and led to two or three rooms above, used as office space at that time. They were afraid that the knifemen would throw their knives and injure or kill those fleeting the train. There had already been many passengers stabbed on the train, but the guns held the bandits at bay and everybody got safely up those stairs. The Ashley boys were the last ones to ascend as they backed up, step by step, with four guns pointed downward at the robbers who were beginning to move forward, thinking now they had all the passengers trapped in the building with no escape possible.

Everybody was safe upstairs as the rioters entered the building and started up the stairs. Grandmother and her neighbor took their places beside the men to keep the guns loaded for them. They were sure-shots and quick, and they had several men killed or wounded before one of them could throw a knife that far. The bandits kept pressing forward until they realized their numbers were being piled up at the foot of the stairs and the others could not get over the dead and wounded. Suddenly one of the bandits shouted something to his compatriots and they all scrambled to get out of the building and fade away into the jungle. The passengers could hear running feet and then shots and they wondered what new disaster was about to befall them. What a wonder wave of relief swept over these poor, frightened travelers when they realized the soldiers from the fort had come to their rescue.

No one was allowed to go down the stairs until the dead and wounded had been removed and the evidence of carnage had been cleaned up. Finally, the place was acceptable to the commanding officer. He came up the stairs to talk to the group huddled in the upper offices and as he talked, he kept looking for someone. Finally, he asked for the red-headed girl, Caroline. She and little Webb had crawled under a desk and gone to sleep.

Her mother awakened her gently and helped her from under the desk. When the officer smiled at Caroline, she smiled back. After all she had been through one would have thought she would cling to her mother. But not Caroline! There was no sign of her fear on her face. The officer said that one of the wounded men downstairs was asking for her, and would her mother and uncle please come down the stairs with her before the others were allowed to descend. He did not know if the boy would live, and he was granted his request to see the little red-headed girl.

The three went down the stairs with the officer who led them to a pallet on the floor. As Caroline approached the boy he tried to smile, and he was evidently in pain and it was with great effort that he moved his arm and held out his hand to her. As she bent downward she saw that he was giving her precious ring back to her and her heart swelled with joy as she took it from him. She thanked him and told him that she hoped he would get well.

Grandmother was moved to tears by the scene before her and both she and her brothers were moved to compassion for the wounded boy on the bed there on the floor of the depot. Grandmother offered to dress his wounds and do what she could to alleviate his suffering, but the officer said that said that the boy would be moved to the fort where medical treatment was available and that they would take care of him there.

Before the voyagers left for Panama City and the boat they were to take northward, the officer who had rescued them told them about the men who had attacked the train and the reason for it. These men had been making their living with their pack animals. Each owned a string of jackasses, the only animals

used for transportation across the Isthmus at that time. These little animals were sturdy and reliable and sure-footed, and it cost the owners very little to feed them. With the discovery of gold in California their trade had increased by leaps and bounds when men wanted to take a shortcut to California and were willing to pay exorbitant prices to get from one ocean to the other. In only a couple of years they had become wealthy men and had to hire others to help them.

This jackass transportation company had become a booming business and they were unwilling to lose it. At first, they had tried to stop the construction of the railroad and the army had been called upon for protection by the builders. The portage groups had given up and only minor incidents occurred from time to time. Finally, the railroad was finished, and every bit of track had been inspected and both sides of the right-of-way had been examined for ambush plots. The army and the railroad personnel had been lulled into the belief that the protesting natives had accepted the advance of civilization and given up attempts to sabotage their competition.

However, the fire of rebellion smoldered and glowed until it burst into flame when the time came to take their business away from them. Their Latin tempers exploded, and it took only one or two hot-headed leaders to start a rebellion and plant the idea of killing off this iron monster on the very first trip. The little band grew to a big band as mass hysteria gripped the transportation groups. The plan to board the train outside of Colon finally evolved from this smoldering fire and one thing led to another, until they were resolved to kill all the passengers, seize their luggage, and rob them of all their cash and valuables as booty and burn the train when it reached Panama City.

During this uprising, men and boys who had no connection with the brigands were drawn along with them by the mass hysteria they created, and probably paid with their lives for

206

their folly. The plan might have succeeded had it not been for the two Ashley boys who were just cautious enough to keep their weapons and ammunition with them.

⚓

The passengers were kept in the depot throughout the night while the soldiers guarded the building. The bandits had fled into the jungle, taking all their loot that they had taken from the passengers with them. Early in the morning the train was connected and the passengers who were left went aboard the coaches. They were hungry and tired from the events of the day before and had an uncomfortable and restless night without food or much sleep, and they were looking forward to boarding the ship which would take them to San Francisco, where they would get some breakfast in their empty stomachs. The train took them the rest of the way to the dock where they all got off and walked to the gangway of the ship which was ready and waiting for them to go aboard.

The purser was standing at the gangway serenely smiling to welcome them with his hand out to take their tickets, but nobody had any tickets! On learning this, his smile was not quite so genial, but his manner remained suave as he explained that they could not go aboard without tickets or the money to pay their passage to San Francisco. The travelers were shocked! After all that had happened to them, and the losing of all their possessions, and now this! They explained what had happened (as if he hadn't already heard the story!) but he only shook his head and demanded tickets or cash. He was a pompous little cuss and strutted around there like he owned the ship. He began to get a little nasty with the passengers when they began to plead that he let them go aboard. He only shook his head. Then Uncle

Lime came along, and he saw at a glance what was happening. He just picked Mr. Purser by the seat of his pants and the back of his neck, and threw him off the dock, down into the bay and told everybody to go aboard the ship. While the purser sputtered and floundered around in the water and the seamen fished him out, the weary passengers boarded the ship where they were fed and given care. Nothing more was said about payment for passage to San Francisco. That was the last they ever heard of it.

The Guard of the Prisoner Gets the Boot

Well, that was the end of my story and Baldy and I ate the lunches we had brought with us while we continued to guard the train. Our lunches had been put up separately so that we could eat without leaving the doorway of the baggage car and could keep out eye on the train, making sure that nobody molested anything belonging to our outfit while the other boys were in the station building eating.

I had just finished telling my story to the conductor and was listening to his tale of the indignities heaped on him by these barefoot would-be soldiers, and about a lot of other things he had to go through while the revolution had been going on, when I noticed a bare-footed boy in the uniform of a Columbian soldier, carrying an old, long-barreled rifle which had a brass bayonet on its muzzle. He was coming down the side of the track accompanied by another boy about the same age size and age, but unarmed. I drew the attention of the conductor to the pair and asked what was coming down the way. He stretched his neck to look where I indicated, then told us that it was a Columbian soldier exercising a prisoner. The conductor watched them like a hawk, and the gleam in his eyes should have burned a hole right through both of them.

The soldier and his prisoner came along until they were opposite the open door of the baggage car and stood there greatly interested in the Colt machine gun. It seemed to fascinate them and evidently the soldier thought he should see more of it, so he stepped over to the train steps and started to go up to get into the baggage coach. Well, although conductor was a very large man, he was the quickest thing I ever saw on two feet. The boy had taken only one or two steps onto the train when the Irishman's large hand grabbed his blouse at the neck and with

209

his right hand pulled him down, then faced him down the track in the direction from which he had come, and taking aim with the precision of a football player, he planted a well-aimed solid boot in the seat of the soldier's pants and lifted him about two feet off the ground. Had he been playing football and kicking a goal, it would have gone right between the goal posts. It was beautiful, and we were delighted! The poor soldier, who was black, turned almost white he was so scared. He dropped that gun of his and down the cinder path he went like the devil was after him. There was no doubt in Baldy's or my mind that he broke the world's record for the twenty-yard dash.

The prisoner was bewildered and just stood there not knowing what to do under the circumstances. He shifted from one foot to the other and scratched his head trying to make up his mind about what to do. In looking back, Baldy and I concluded that the book of rules he had received when he enlisted, did not cover the situation. At long last he very sheepishly picked up the soldier's gun, and with a scared glance at the conductor, started up the track the way they had come, following the disappearing soldier. We watched them until they vanished around the turn. That was the first time Baldy and I had seen this big conductor really smile. Baldy and I laughed until we couldn't stand up and we got our nice white uniforms all black in the coal slag along the track. We just laughed and laughed until we were almost helpless. This was one of the funniest things I ever saw.

Maybe Taboga Bill

Things went along without anything outstanding happening for about a month. Then one morning when we arrived at the docks of Colon we found a regiment of United States Marines making camp and we learned that they had been sent there to relieve us. We packed up our gear and turned the job over to them, went back to Panama City and embarked for our ship.

Life settled down to the same old routine again under the Panama sun. The only break in the monotony came one morning just about daylight when I had the morning watch on deck. I saw quite a commotion close to the ship right after the ship's cook had dumped some food scraps down the slop-chute. I took it for granted that it was a shark or a large fish of some kind mooching breakfast, so I put the glasses on him and heavenly days! I just about jumped out of my shoes! It was a man-eating shark, and I swear it looked half as long as the ship! The first thing that flashed into my mind was the old legend about Taboga Bill, the shark that had the reputation of taking liberty parties ashore on his back. There is no doubt that I saw the largest shark around the Gulf of Panama, and it was the largest one I ever saw in my life! He was so big that I called several of the boys who were sleeping on deck to jump up and look at him, and most of them did. We never did settle the question about his length. The estimates of his size ran all the way from twenty-five to one hundred feet. It really didn't matter because no one would believe us anyway. But I was always certain that I had the distinction of seeing Taboga Bill.

A New Nation was Born

Things went along smoothly and with the same old monotony for about another month. Then one morning in the midst of lots of smoke, the battleship *Wisconsin* showed up and anchored close by towards Taboga Island. She had a rear admiral and his staff on board. Not only did rumor have it that he had high navel officials with him, but also that he had some officials of the State Department on board. Of course, the scuttlebutt, which was the sea-faring grapevine, is terrific on a ship of that kind and it was really jumping that day.

At eight o'clock when colors were hoisted, and the official salute was fired by us for the admiral, his large steam barge was called away and a great crowd of these officials and the admiral, resplendent in all his gold braid, headed towards the dock nearest the fort, where they spent the greatest part of the day. There was much going back and forth from the fort to the *Wisconsin*. Our officials and the rebel officials were very active for about two weeks thereafter.

The scuttlebutt was working overtime with all the rumors and naturally we were as much if not more, interested in what was going on than the crew of the *Wisconsin*. We felt that the job there and the results therefrom, belonged to us more than it did the *Wisconsin*, so we had visiting parties going aboard the *Wisconsin* whenever the law allowed, besides the pumping of the crews of their small boats for all the information we could get. This went on for about two weeks and then we saw them making two big flags on the quarterdeck of the *Wisconsin*.

Now we were more curious than ever. All the quartermasters' department, tailors, and flag sowers under the supervision of the flag chief-master quartermaster were busy as cats on a tin roof. Of course, our quartermaster had to go to the

212

Wisconsin to find out what was going on. We all managed to get over there at some time and discovered that it was a new flag being constructed. Most of us were lucky enough to run a seam down it as all the sewing was being done by hand. I am sure every quartermaster and signal boy on the *Ranger* put their share of stitches in it. The two flags were the largest size used in the Navy.

After that job was done, everything seemed to stop and wait. We had a glass up on the *Wisconsin* constantly from our bridge, so we wouldn't miss anything. Then one day about noon, it seemed to us that all the civilians belonging on shore got into the admiral's barge. Everything was quiet on the *Wisconsin*. The scuttlebutt got hotter than ever.

The next morning about ten o'clock, we spotted the new flag rolled up and stopped with string so that it would break when given a hard jerk by the halyards and was hauled up to the signal masthead of the *Wisconsin*. Then the quartermaster gang was getting hot. We realized that our officers knew what was going on, and they talked about it down in their wardroom, and we knew more than they thought we did about what was going to happen.

Shortly after the *Wisconsin* had hoisted the rolled-up flag to their signal masthead, the Columbian flag on the fort was pulled down and in its place, went the new Panamanian flag that had been made on the *Wisconsin*.

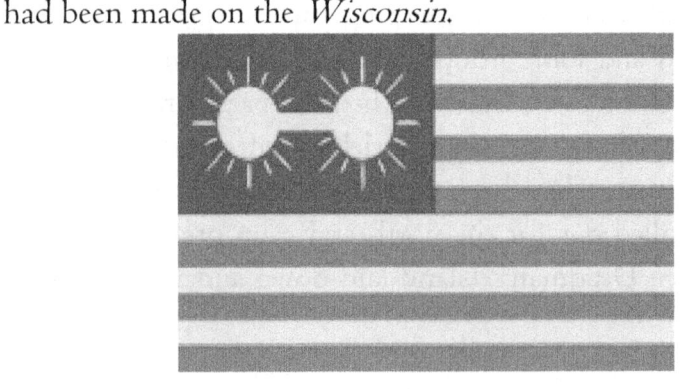

It was a pretty flag, floating there in the breeze. It had no more than reached the peak of the flagstaff of the fort, when the *Wisconsin* broke the flag at their signal masthead and there was just enough breeze blowing to wave it in full. Then bang! Twenty-one guns went off in the proper succession, making a national salute in official recognition of the new flag and country thereof. A new nation had been born: Panama. This is referred to as "Separation Day" on November 3, 1903, which was their independence from the Republic of Columbia. I was nineteen years old at the time and had been in the Navy for four years.

We were all at the rail yelling and cheering on both the *Ranger* and *Wisconsin*, as if we owned this new nation. It was a thrilling and impressive event.

After we had acknowledged and saluted the new flag and new nation, all the officials and the big-wigs of the new republic came aboard the *Wisconsin*. The admiral's barge had been sent in to get the party which also included some lovely and gay *señoritas* and *señoras*. We could guess that this was going to be quite a party. The *Wisconsin's* band was busy from then on—dance music at night and patriotic airs in the daytime.

The scuttlebutt whispered that there was an abundance of champagne and refreshments aboard. This *fiesta* or celebration lasted about three days. Occasionally one of the Panamanian officials would come up on the quarterdeck and sniff the wind and look around and go back down the ladder again to the admiral's quarters. When the party broke up they were all taken ashore, and the scuttlebutt informed us that the treaty with Panama had been signed. A week or so later the *Wisconsin* pulled out for the north and calm prevailed on the Isthmus. Even Deadman's Island laid down and went to sleep again.

If my memory serves me, it was about three months after that the cruiser *Philadelphia* came to relieve us. Six months laying practically dormant in those waters had put so many barnacles on us that we could make only half the speed that we would have made otherwise, and divers had to go down and cut the barnacles off the propeller and the rudder before we left.

Weir's Dead Man's Cocktail

The afternoon before we left Panama City a sailing launch and a steam launch were taken over to Deadman's Island and a large box was put in the sailing launch and towed back to the ship by the steam launch. We hoisted it aboard on the poop deck by the boat davits and it was deposited there and secured to the deck. It proved to be the body of a late paymaster who had died about a year before while on duty on one of our man-of-war ships. It was believed that he died of yellow fever and his body was buried hurriedly in the cemetery on Deadman's Island. The corpse was encased in a coffin and the coffin was placed in a large box which was lined with sheet lead and supposed to be air-tight. The outer box was evidently made by a naval shipwright or carpenter's mate, and the top was attached with large screws.

The next morning, we left Panama and pulled out for the Puget Sound Naval Shipyard at Bremerton, Washington. By this time word had gotten around the ship by way of the scuttlebutt, divulging what was in the large box. Evidently the doctor had told others about the box being full of alcohol to preserve the body, so during the night Jack Weir, with his insatiable curiosity, went back and examined the box. He then went down to Chip's shop (the carpenter's mate) where he found a rubber tube and a wooden plug the same size as the tube. Enlisting the help of one or two of his closest cronies, they went back taking the proper container with them, and a hole was bored in the box, very close to the bottom, about halfway between the head and the foot of the box. They struck "pay dirt" fragrant alcohol which to them the fumes smelled "beautiful." When they had drained off what they wanted, they fitted the wooden plug into the hole and thereby stopped the flow of the precious fluid. In triumph they

casually worked their way forward where they got a fine cloth and they strained the alcohol. They then had the main ingredients of an Eagle Brand condensed-milk cocktail! Ugh! The horrible deed was not discovered the next morning when the ship was washed down. The only thing of a suspicious nature that happened was that Jack and his conspirators were becoming very jovial and frisky and if one would get to windward of them, with a keen sense of smell, the odor of condensed milk and alcohol might be detected.

The odor of this condensed-milk cocktail was well known on the ship because every time we shellacked the lower decks with red shellac, somebody would manage to swipe some shellac and hide it. This consisted of powder that made it red, and alcohol. By pouring water in the mixture and stirring vigorously, the shellac would ball up and separate from the alcohol, allowing the alcohol to be drained off, but it kept its deep red color. However, one can't have everything! Then by making proper negotiations with one of the ship's cooks, they would get ahold of Eagle Brand condensed milk and mix their shellac cocktail. That always happened when we shellacked decks. A little jollification would be held among the chosen few and the event would be highlighted with many a tall tale. Many of Jack Weir's stories were born under such conditions.

The second night out, after we left Panama, the boys proceeded to have their dead man's cocktail. They said that a new country had been born and many officials had celebrated the occasion without any thought or consideration of how the crew's tongues were hanging out, so they were going to have their own celebration, even at the expense of the dead paymaster. Of course, they had some awfully big heads in the morning and the scuttlebutt finally got to the first lieutenant and he and the master-at-arms and some of the marines searched the ship thoroughly to see if there was any alcohol aboard, as the ship's

alcohol chest had not been disturbed. The only thing they found that looked suspicious was a plug at the bottom of the paymaster's coffin box. From then on until we arrived in Bremerton, a sentry was placed at the box…just in case.

It was slow going but we made it home to Bremerton to the Puget Sound Naval Shipyard without further ado. There we received our orders to decommission the *Ranger*. Captain "Handlebar" Hughes had been promoted to rear-admiral and was ordered to take charge of the Bureau of Navigation in Washington, D.C.

Before leaving the ship, the captain called the crew aft to the quarterdeck and gave us a nice "thank you, well done" and told us that if any of us ever needed a favor to write to him. When we walked forward, the chief quartermaster took all the quartermasters and signal boys aft with him and told us that the captain wanted to see us in his wardroom. When we were all assembled there, he said that he wished to especially commend us for our outstanding work on the bridge and he told us that if we need any favors or any information after he got to the Bureau of Navigation, to drop him a line and he would do everything he could to satisfy our request. He shook hands with all of us and wished us well.

We were then sent to the Mare Island Navy Yard on the old steamer "Queen," which was operated by the Pacific Steamship Company. A tug took us off the Queen when she docked and deposited us at the old *Independence* at Mare Island, where we renewed our old acquaintance with the cockroaches who seemed glad to see us.

1890 to 1914
(Decommissioned & recommissioned a few times)

USS *CONCORD*

Hit the Deck...for Real?

We had not been on the *Independence* long before the officers of the *Concord* came over to go through the records of the crew from the *Ranger* for selecting all those they thought it advisable to make up the crew for their ship which was being put into commission.

Going through the records of each man gives the officers an idea of his ability, what he has done in the past and whether he would be useful on their ship. A man who has been useful on one ship might not always be useful on another. He might have characteristics which might prove to be unsuitable for their ship, no matter how good his record. They picked a little less than half of the *Ranger*'s crew to go on the *Concord*. It happened that I was the only quartermaster picked. Of course, in picking a crew like that, sometimes the captain of the *Independence* wouldn't allow them to have every one of the men selected because there might be another ship picking a crew that needed the men as urgently or more so than the ship doing the selecting at the same time.

This was how I was selected for the *Concord*. When I got there, I found that I was the only quartermaster on the ship. The navigating officer called me into his office and said that he couldn't get a certain quartermaster he had tried to draft and didn't like those that were available. He questioned me about what I knew, at the same time looking at my record, which I knew was good. He said, "I see by your record that you are very efficient, but young. Can you take over the department until we can get more quartermasters to our liking?"

I told him that I knew of no reason why I couldn't do it with his advice and counsel, so he sent for the chief boatswain's mate and told him to give me three seamen to stand

quartermaster's watch until we got more quartermasters. The navigator said that a draft of second-class apprentice boys was expected off the *Adams* and he felt that I should get along well with them. He also mentioned that there was already one aboard whose name was Schultz. "If he looks alright to you, take him until we get more men. He can be used as a signal boy. In the meantime, I have a diagram of the dressing-lines that are to be made for dressing ship." Dressing lines are used to bend the flags on holidays and special occasions, commonly called "dressing ship."

The navigator talked the situation over with me and gave me the keys to the quartermaster's storeroom and a list of stores that had already come aboard ship and told me to take charge of all the stores connected with my department and to sign for same as they arrived aboard the ship and instructed me to proceed with the making of the dressing lines, which is a very tedious job.

I went forward and found apprentice boy second class Schultz, and I believe he made one of the last cruises by apprentice boys in the Navy. They did away with that system about that time. From then on, the Navy took boys over eighteen-year old boys for four years' service and called them "landsmen for training." A great many of them sure needed training! I was told some tall tales about these landsmen for training.

It seems that one of these landsmen wrote to his mother, telling her that the Navy was an awfully funny place to be. He said the first night he was on the ship a man blew a whistle in the middle of the night. This whistle was called a boatswain's pipe, but he didn't know why they called it a pipe because he didn't smoke it, he blew it, and he never could see any smoke coming out of it.

This man kept blowing his whistle and called out "All hands on deck!" He wrote that he just stayed there watching the

boys getting out of their hammocks until this great big man with the whistle came up and got under his hammock and bumped him upside down. He hit the deck, bumping his knees and chin. He wrote that he used to think Pa was kind of rough getting him up so early in the morning, but he said Pa never threw him out on his face.

He went on to tell his mother that he put on his pants and went up the stairs (which we referred to as ladders) where he saw the other fellows going up. When he got to the top of the stairs, the big fellow at the head of the stairs sang out again, "All hands on deck!" So, he stepped out on the deck and put both hands on the deck and four or five fellows walked on his hands.

The fellow with the whistle saw him and told him to fall in forward of the foremast. Another fellow with a whistle, who was at the after part of the deck, sang out, "Fall in!" so, he ran over to the railing and started to climb up, but he said he couldn't swim. He said that he knew if he jumped in the water he'd probably, drown, so while he was looking down at the water, getting ready to jump, this first man with the whistle came over and grabbed him by the neck and took him over by the foremast and told him to stand there before he sank the ship.

This fellow with the whistle looked at the boy like he didn't like him, and he said for him not to move from there until he was told to. The landsman told his mother that he was grateful to that big fellow for keeping him from jumping into the water. Then he told her that he found out afterwards that they didn't mean what they said at all. He was doing better now, and he understood what the calls meant.

This story was told to me by a chief boatswain's mate who looked me right in the eye and swore that every word of it was the truth. It sounded fishy to me, but I never batted an eye nor showed any sign of disbelief.

Captain of the Heads

At the time they did away with the apprentice system and took men on as landsmen for training, so getting a crew became frustrating. The ships going in commission needed men very badly and there was no organized training station on the Pacific coast. Consequently, when they could ship a man from Goat Island where the apprentice boys had been trained, or at the receiving ship, *Independence*, and he could be sent to any ship in the fleet the next day, he was a landsman. That very thing happened in a great number of cases, to the detriment of the ship and the morale of the officers and the rest of the crew. Later this situation was rectified by the establishing of boot camps or some semblance of a training system in several places. The men were then sent from those boot camps to the ships.

The chief boatswain's mate said to me, "You don't realize what the situation is since they did away with the apprentice boys. Let me tell you of another letter a rooky wrote his mother." He then went on to tell me the following tale.

On the sailing ships of the old days the ship's toilets for the crew were up in the heads of the ship. The heads of a sailing ship in those days were right where the bow comes together, and the bowsprit goes out over the water. There were generally two toilets—one on either side of the bowsprit. They were officially known as "the heads," but there were no comforts in them like a ship nowadays. The crew never used that place for reading whodunits or catching up on their serial stories, as they do now. These heads were cold and wet, and all around very uncomfortable places. No one ever lingered there any longer than he had to. For this reason, Navy toilets have always been called "the heads" ever since the days of the old sailing ships.

On the gundeck of the *Concord* the heads were large enough to accommodate all the enlisted men of the ship.

The chief boatswain's mate said, "Well, it was not so long ago that I took a man from the new batch of landsmen for training who had been on the ship only a few days, and put him in as captain of the heads, in place of the man who had been there. The boy wrote to his mother that he had been promoted already to Captain of the Heads." That is the ship name for the man who cleans the toilets and takes care of the heads.

"It was not long before the ship's captain received a letter from the boy's mother, thanking him for promoting her son and doing it so quickly after he had joined the ship. She told the captain that she had written her son, warning him not to let the promotion go to his head, and by all means to be good to the men under him. The chief boatswain's mate paused and chuckled a little, then went on, "The captain called me back to his quarters and read that letter to me. How he laughed! But, at the same time he took it seriously being from the boy's mother. Then, with a wink, he told me that we must keep that fellow there for a while because it would break his mother's heart if she thought her son had been demoted. And he told me to keep my eye on him."

Acting Chief Quartermaster

Schultz and I tore loose on getting the quartermaster's department in order as quickly as we could. There had been practically nothing done in the quartermaster's department toward getting her ready to go into commission. The first thing we did was to make up the necessary hand lead-lines, which is quite a difficult job. Then we went back to be sure that the deep-sea sounding machine was up in proper condition to work at any time. We then had to put up the canvas pockets to stow all the signal flags in and put all the signal flags away. Finally, we came to the real tough job where I had to borrow a couple of men from the chief boatswain's mate, and we started making all the dressing lines.

During that time a second-class quartermaster reported for duty. I was very pleased to see him and immediately took him back to the quarterdeck and called for the navigating officer. I introduced him to the navigating officer and told him that this man was one grade senior to me and that I wanted permission to turn the department over to this second-class quartermaster. The navigator asked me, "Aren't you doing all right?"

"I don't know," I answered. "I have never acted as chief quartermaster before. I'm not sure whether I'm doing all right or not."

"I am," he replied. "You're doing fine. We'll have a chief quartermaster show up some of these days, so you just keep on going the way you are."

A day or so after that we had a draft of second-class apprentice boys show up. They were the same ones that Schultz had made his cruise with on the *Adams*. I was entitled to two more signal boys and I thought that by working it properly that I could borrow a couple more of those boys to do

quartermaster's duty until we had our quartermasters show up. Schultz knew them all and he gave me the names of four of them that he said were good, smart boys. I went back to the navigator again and talked him out of two of the boys for signal boys and the loan of two more to act as quartermasters. The chief boatswain's mate wasn't happy about that but could do nothing about it.

Things went along fine. These new boys were just dandy. Of course, we all worked together, and I worked right along with them, doing the same as they did. It wasn't long before we had the bridge and pilot house and all the compasses shining like a ship's bell. Gratings on the bridge were holystoned and bleached; all the painting done that was necessary at that time; and we were proud of our accomplishments. These boys worked hard and took pride in their work.

Then one day a first-class quartermaster, Jimmy Groat, showed up for duty. He was an ex-apprentice boy, probably one of the first ones in the Navy, because he was no spring chicken. He reported to me for duty. I told him that we would go to see the first lieutenant and that I would turn the department over to him. I wasn't going to risk the navigator working shenanigans on me again. I told Groat that I was only a third-class quartermaster, acting as chief until such a time a chief, or someone senior to me arrived. I told him that they might want to rate him chief quartermaster and that with all the service he had, he was undoubtedly entitled to it. He just looked at me and gave me a funny grin. However, I got him to go to the quarterdeck with me to see the first lieutenant.

When we got there the first lieutenant came out and asked me what I wanted. I had a big smile on my face and was as happy as two porpoises. I introduced Jimmy Groat and told him that I had brought Jimmy back, knowing that they probably wanted to make him chief quartermaster and I could turn over

all the keys and everything pertaining to the quartermaster's department to Groat. The first lieutenant looked at me with a broad, benevolent smile, and he asked Groat if he wanted to take over the department. Groat answered in the negative by saying that it was the last thing he wanted to do. He said that he could have been a chief quartermaster years ago if he had wanted that job. He said that his rating suited him just fine and that he hoped to hang on to it until he retired. They both had a big laugh and the first lieutenant asked if Groat had any objections to me acting as chief quartermaster. Groat said he didn't. He said that he had been looking around over the ship for a while and from what he saw and heard, he thought that Stevens was doing a bang-up fine job. Then the lieutenant looked at me again with the same smile and his black handle-bar mustache went up and down two or three times, as if he was very pleased with himself, and he told me to go forward and carry on as I had been doing! He said, "Someday you'll get out of the job."

Charles F. "Handlebar" Hughes

Those handle-bar mustaches became very famous and much loved, for he became the famous "Handle-bar Hughes," rear admiral, commander of the Pacific Fleet. I never met an enlisted man nor anyone else who did not have something fine to say about him.

A few days later Hughes was taking his constitutional walk on the poop-deck and he noted that the after-compass binnacle was a little tarnished from the fog, so seeing young Schultz who had just appeared, he called him and told him to go and tell Stevens that the binnacle needed cleaning and to send a man back to clean it as soon as convenient.

Schultz had finished his work for the day and had stood his watch, and he was just killing time. The rest of the gang were on watch or corking off somewhere. When he came back and told me about the binnacle, I said, "All right," and pulled out the cleaning gearbox and handed it to him and told Schultz to go back and clean it because the rest of the gang were on watch or corking off.

He went back and began to polish and shine up that binnacle and he hadn't been at it long before the first lieutenant, who had watched Schultz, came up to him and asked, "Did Stevens tell you to come back and clean it?"

"Why yes, sir," said Schultz, and he gave the lieutenant a big smile. Schultz always had a smile on tap.

The first lieutenant stood there a minute or two and looked at him, then started to walk up and down the poop-deck again, shaking his head with a puzzled look on his face, as if to denote that it was a new kind of psychology to him.

I must say that all our bunch in the quartermaster's department were a very happy, cooperative lot and turn-to, whenever there was a job to be done. I was never with a finer bunch of boys. They never lost an opportunity to help me when I needed it.

The Belle Got Pinched

Every ship going into commission makes a shakedown cruise to get the ship in good running order and to break in her crew before they join the fleet for duty. The day finally came when we raked up enough crew and had the *Concord* running in acceptable order to make our shakedown cruise. After we were through the Golden Gate, we learned that we were headed for Dutch Harbor in the Aleutian Islands, which meant that we would have to buck strong headwinds all the way.

All went well until about the third day out and then those old boilers seemed to fall to pieces. We had only one chief-boilermaker's mate aboard, and a couple of lesser-rated men to cope with them. The boilers were so bad that we couldn't keep steam up except in one, and it could be seen that it wasn't going to last long. Fortunately, we had enough power to hold her head into the wind and the boiler makers went to work on the boilers. They worked right through many days with practically no sleep, and they finally patched up one. By that time the boiler that had been the best one of the lot, gave up the ghost. Well, we had the one they had just worked on to keep us going and they went to work all over again. This performance kept up practically the whole voyage to Dutch Harbor. Sometimes we would make only three knots an hour and sometimes we made as high as eight. We were mighty glad to tie up at the coal dock at Dutch Harbor.

Dutch Harbor at that time, was a coaling station, and there were a couple of small warehouses and many Eskimo shacks. There were only two or three people working for the United States government who lived in that desolate-looking place.

The desolation didn't matter as far as we were concerned. We didn't have any money and hadn't had any for quite a while.

But just the same, the boys were glad to get off the ship and stretch their legs. The instinct of the blue-jacket in those days was to satisfy his curiosity and to look for women. They went ashore and talked with many of the Eskimos who were able to understand them, but it seemed that there were no young, unmarried Eskimo girls in those parts, which was a sad.

One day one persistent snooper came running aboard with the lovelight shining in his eyes, to get his special shipmate to go with him. It seems that he was on the trail of a beautiful Eskimo lady of easy virtue who was not opposed to making an honest dollar. An honest dollar was important money those days.

I was on the bridge with a couple of signal boys when he came aboard, and when he left with his fellow blue-jacket. One of the signal boys commented, "That fellow, Doe, won't give up. It looks like he has something in sight now. I think I'll run along and follow him to see what he's doing," and so he was on his way. The other signal boy and I watched them with the glasses when they got too far away to see clearly. We watched them go up to a tiny shack on the side hill. It was separated from the other shacks.

When they got up to the shack, they knocked at the door and, sure enough, an Eskimo belle appeared at the door. She was beaded up in great shape. We could also see the signal boy who was stalking them as he came in from the side and kept out of their sight. They talked for a little time to the maiden and then shoved off and came back to the ship and went around among their friends and special cronies, trying to raise some money, but all that they could get was a dollar. What money there had been on the ship had been spent before leaving San Francisco. They were disappointed, but like true denizens of the deep, they never gave up, and they started back again up that hill.

By that time the news was all over the ship that this Eskimo charmer had been found, so quite a bunch of the boys went ashore and just nosed around, making it appear that they were just out for exercise. However, we noted that little by little they were edging closer to this tiny shack on the hillside.

Now it seems that the two boys who went back there had just one round silver dollar between them, so the boy who had discovered this beauty told his shipmate that he would go in to see her first and give her the dollar, then see if he could swipe it back for his friend when he came out. Well, believe it or not, it worked. She stuck the dollar under a little mat on the table by her couch after the ceremonies were over. He came out and told his shipmate the lay of the land and where she had put the dollar. He was well briefed and knew what he was running into when he entered the hall of the ill-fame. He went in and as he held the damsel in his arms, he extracted the dollar from under the mat and paid her with it when he left. She was so pleased and excited over the turn of events that she didn't notice anything.

When he came out there were several more fellows lined up outside waiting for their turn, and they all used the same dollar in the same way. That's the story the boys brought back to us, and we watched through the glasses.

We pulled out of Dutch Harbor as soon as the engineering officer felt that it was safe to do so, considering the boilers. (I might note here that the *Concord* and the *Bennington* were sister ships, and in 1905 there was a tragedy in San Diego Harbor when the boilers of the *Bennington* blew up, killing and injuring scores of enlisted personnel).

The Old Man decided to take the Inner {probably what is commonly referred to as "Inside"} Passage route home to Mare Island where the boilers would all be re-surveyed and gone over again. Taking the Inner Passage route would be safe and easier on the boilers, not to mention the beneficial effect on the morale of the crew.

"Bar" Hunting

We made Kodiak our first stop and anchored there for a couple of days. Everybody went ashore to enjoy the little town and to walk around and get their feet on solid ground once more. When a couple of boys joined me, we walked a few blocks from the center of town where we noticed ahead of us a nice, neat little cottage where there was a small vegetable garden and a few flowers growing around it. Hoeing the garden was a tall, thin man whose white whiskers reached his waist. As we approached, one of the boys, pointing as he spoke, said, "There's a true native son for you!"

The bearded man looked up when he heard our voices and noticed that we were all in uniform. He walked over to the gate and, as we came up, he spoke to us in a nice, pleasant manner of welcome, and asked us if we would want to come in and sit for a few minutes. Since it was such a beautiful, mild day we accepted his invitation and suggested that we just sit on the porch and chat with him for a while. We all found comfortable places in the sun and relaxed to visit with this old-timer. One of the boys who smoked cigars insisted on giving the old gentleman a cigar, which he accepted reluctantly because he had no liquor or refreshments in the house to treat us with.

As we talked he wanted to know all about us, where we came from, and what we had been doing before we arrived at Kodiak. He appeared to be a man of about sixty or seventy years, but despite his age he had a very fine, keen mind. We answered all his queries and before long we were asking him about Alaska and what he had done. As I recall, he said that he was one of the first settlers of Kodiak. There wasn't anything we could ask him about Alaska that he didn't know about, or any place but what he had been there. We learned that he had spent practically

his whole adult life as a prospector and sourdough, and during the times in between his prospecting he had hunted grizzly bears. It seems that grizzly bears were his hobby and he told some tall tales about grizzlies that he had dispatched to the happy hunting grounds, and about the country where he had killed them which was generally where he was prospecting or mining.

He was a young man when he arrived in Alaska during the gold rush and he felt that he could just look any bear in the world in the eye and spit in his face. But unfortunately, his reputation hadn't preceded him and the Kodiak bear, which is the largest and fiercest bear alive, didn't know anything about him. After hearing about the ferocity of the Kodiak bear, the old-timer said he could hardly wait to take time out from his mining and prospecting to get out and show this Kodiak who he was.

About that time the Kodiak bears were building up quite a reputation for themselves and officials of different sections of the country wouldn't allow a tenderfoot sportsman from the outside to hunt Kodiak bear without the proper calibrated gun and a recognized guide. I believe that this practice has continued to this day. He told us that when he got ready to go out and kill him a "bar," he was worked up to the idea of showing the Alaska old-timers how to kill a "bar!" He had heard tales about these Kodiak bears, among them was how a Kodiak bear would follow a man's tracks and tackle him without even being shot at if the beast was feeling grumpy that morning. The old fellow said that he didn't believe such tales. None of the grizzlies ever did that. He had been advised by other sourdoughs who had some experience with this species of bear, that they would hunt a man if they felt like it, and for goodness sake, not to go alone and to never, never tackle two at one time.

⚓

One morning he started out bright and early with his grizzly bear rifle, and a caliber of which was much smaller than the prescribed Kodiak bear gun. He said that he had never failed to get his bear with his gun and that he didn't need any guides to show him how to shoot a bear. He had shot too many. So, he went alone into an area where some friend had told him that bears were often seen. The territory had a beautiful patch of salmon berries in it, so he went there. He found the salmon berries and they were the finest he had ever seen. They were big, luscious juicy things which he couldn't resist. He set his gun down beside a salmon berry bush and started to eat fresh fruit because he hadn't had any for such a long time. He neglected to take as many precautions as he should have done.

The first thing he knew, he heard a twig snap and he looked in that direction and about forty feet from him was the biggest bear that he had ever seen in his life. Right behind him was mamma bear, almost as large. He had to jump over to where he had left his gun, and when he raised it, the bear raised up on his hand feet and he looked as tall as Pikes Peak. He fired for the bear's heart. He knew he had hit the bear because he couldn't miss, but he had evidently been in such a hurry that he had just grazed the vital part of the heart, and Mr. Bear kept coming right for him. He waited this time until the bear got closer before he shot, and when he went to throw a new shell in his gun, the gun jammed. He said that was the first time in all the years that he had owned the gun that it had ever jammed. By that time the bear was on him! He just had time to throw down his gun and reach for his knife, when the bear reached over and grabbed his head at the back of his neck, and he just ripped the scalp right over his head so that it hung over his forehead. From then on,

he knew no more until he was revived in the hospital. Fortunately, he said, the last thing he could dimly remember was to go limp and play dead, which he guessed he almost was. Probably that was the thing that saved him. As it was, he told us, he spent more than a year in the hospital before he was able to get out of bed. He had both arms, one leg, and a hip broken, besides the scalp wounds. His whole body was covered with wounds made by the bear's claws.

After his friend found him, they followed the brush tracks and found the bear, which had died almost at once. They found the bullet had grazed the heart and the bear had bled to death internally. I asked him how many Kodiak bears he had killed since then and he emphatically replied, "None!" He said that he didn't even speak to them when he saw one and laughed at his own joke.

We all enjoyed this story, and the memory of the town of Kodiak always recalls this exciting tale to our minds. We think of that old hunter who had such a bad limp from the broken hip, and his nice little home with its pretty garden, way up there at Kodiak.

Seamen's Games and the World's Fair

The following day we left for Juneau and from there we went to Sitka where we received orders to proceed to Astoria and Portland, Oregon, for the Fourth of July. There we were to hold open house and allow visitors aboard. We were informed that the USS *Marblehead* would join us at Astoria.

We left Sitka and after an uneventful voyage of several days, we arrived off Astoria on the afternoon before the Fourth of July. All the way down we had been practicing many hours on the rowing machine in anticipation of the race we were sure we would have in Astoria.

We found the USS *Marblehead* anchored close to the southern bank of the Columbia River, and we dropped anchor nearby. Immediately our captain paid an official call upon the captain of the *Marblehead* and as soon as he returned to the *Concord*, a committee arranging the sports events for the following day came aboard. They were all civilians who lived in Astoria and were anxious to put on a good program of sporting events. Of course, they wanted some boat races and they had learned that the *Marblehead* had two good crews including one of the men from the ship and one from the apprentice boys.

The committee hadn't had time to reach the shore before we had our apprentice boat and crew over the side. We immediately pulled over, under the bow of the *Marblehead* with our apprentice flag flying at the bow, and we tossed our oars up and down. In Navy sign language this action indicated a challenge to race, and the apprentice flag in the bow showed that it was the apprentice boy crew making the challenge. Immediately the officer of the day came forward and hailed us and said, "Come alongside!" So, we pulled to the port gangway

and as coxswain of the boat, I went aboard and negotiated for the race the next day.

The following day our men were ready for the race. Our men's crew hadn't trained as diligently as I had worked the apprentice boy's crew. However, the only blot on the paper was that our regular number-one apprentice oarsman was stricken with appendicitis and our doctor took him over to the *Marblehead* for the operation, although he loudly acclaimed the fact that he could pull an oar and beat the *Marblehead* anyway. But our doctors didn't believe him, much to his annoyance. Because the *Concord* was so newly commissioned, she was not yet prepared to handle an operation of this kind as well as the *Marblehead*, so it was decided to take the boy to the larger ship, which was a cruiser.

So, there we were with a well-trained crew except for the number-one or bow oarsman. The boys were determined that they wanted to pull that race, so I talked an old-time apprentice, Spud Murphy, into taking the boat as coxswain in my place so I could pull the number one oar. Fortunately, I had done all the training that the boys had done and was in good condition.

Although I was lighter than I should have been, I pulled a good oar. I told the boys that I would take it and that they would have to pull harder because I wasn't as heavy as the rest of them, and I said that would make them win the race. And by the shades of Davy Jones, I believe I did, because we showed them a clean pair of heels during the whole race. Our men's crew got into the races for the sport of it but made a poor showing, but those young, husky apprentice boys who were sent to us from the *Adams*, would be hard to beat in any boat.

There were all kinds of aquatic sporting events such as fishermen's sailing races, fishing for the largest salmon, log rolling contests in the water, and swimming races in which some of our boys entered and made a fine showing. That night there

was a big dance for the crews of both ships, and loggers, fishermen, and blue-jackets mingled hilariously. A good time was certainly had by all.

The next day after the Fourth of July celebration in Astoria, we pulled into Portland on the Columbia river opposite the fairgrounds, where we stayed for about a week. It was 1905 and Portland was hosting the World's Fair. Everyone enjoyed that stay and we all got to go to the World's Fair as often as we wanted to go. The paymaster had paid the crew when we arrived at Astoria, so we had money in our pockets.

About three days after we got to Portland, I was on watch on the bridge during the afternoon and the lieutenant commander, Hughes, affectionately known as "Handlebars," came up on the bridge with me and he looked towards the fairgrounds. From where we lay we could see Ferris wheels, roller coasters which at that time were called scenic railways, and the promenade along the river. As we watched, there seemed to be a blue-jacket with a girl riding high in all those concessions, and along the promenade, too. After watching for a little while, the lieutenant commander turned to me with an amused look on his face and said, "The boys sure seem to be enjoying themselves and having a fine time. I'll bet you that they wish they had that dollar back that they squandered so recklessly in Dutch Harbor."

I almost fell off the signal chest. I had the mistaken idea that he didn't know anything about that dollar deal in Dutch Harbor, but that taught me right then that the officers, and especially the lieutenant commanders, know nearly everything that goes on all the time. I looked so astonished and surprised that he went down the ladder chuckling and shaking all over with laughter. That was one of the things I liked so much about him, that he had a fine vein of humor.

There were people from all over the United States, and more good-looking girls than I had ever seen before, and

everybody was so friendly to the blue-jackets. Here was one place that the boys didn't have to go down to skid row to enjoy themselves. It seems that every younger fellow, and especially the apprentice boys that we had added to our crew when the ship was put in commission, were engaged to be married when they returned to the ship, although they never saw the girls again. It was romance for the boys and romance for the girls. That is what makes the world go 'round.

I had gone back on the poop-deck to see if the patent-log, which measures our speed, had been put up in the correct manner and was ready to stream {use a light, stern anchor} when we got down over the bar at Astoria, just as we were getting up anchor. On a coil of line, looking over toward the shore, sat a young chap, but he was older than the apprentice boys. It seemed as if he was waiting for the exact time that the ship started to move, and I was right. Just at that time the ship's anchor was aweigh, and the propeller started turning over. The ship began to move. At that instant this lad jumped up and started to yell.

"Whee! Whee! Hooray!" he shouted. "All debts paid! All promises off! All marriages null and void! Whee! Whee!"

I walked over to him and asked what had gotten into him and if he was sober. He told me that there was nothing the matter with him and that he had been going through that performance for many years. Now that we were leaving for another port he was about to start a new page. It was his philosophy to promise the girls everything, and in some cases, to marry them, but now that he was leaving port everything was cleaned up and all bets were off.

Shortly after crossing the bar at Astoria, we met a steam-schooner, and she dipped her colors to us. Merchant marine ships do that to men-of-war as a salute, and the men-of-war lower their colors to the deck and hoist them again, which is an acknowledgement of the salute. When their colors were dipped to us I was just coming forward from streaming the log {see nautical terms}, so I was closest to the colors. I started to run back to answer the dip, and when I went from the main deck up the ladder to the poop-deck, I was making knots and my foot slipped half-way up. However, I kept on going and I accomplished the acknowledgement to the salute, but as I did so, I noticed a sharp pain in my right groin. The thought came in my mind that I had probably strained myself while pulling that boat race, but as time passed it kept getting more painful all the time.

The next morning, I went down to sick call after I noticed that a lump had appeared. When the doctor questioned me about my activities, he said that I had undoubtedly ruptured myself when I slipped on the ladder the day before. He said that nothing could be done at that time except to put a compression bandage on me, and that on arrival at Mare Island he would send me to the hospital for an operation. I asked him how long I would be away from the ship and it was then that he told me that I might not get well enough to join my ship before she was ready to sail again. He also said that they might put the ship out of commission because of the rotten condition of her boilers.

I was feeling very low and blue. I had worked hard on her and she was developing into a "home." I was relieved of duty and put on the sick list. That evening after supper I was sitting on the quarterdeck and my friend, lieutenant commander

241

Hughes, came up and noticed me. He called me over to him and said that the doctor had told him that I had some hard luck. I commented that now that the work was all done, and we had a good ship and a good crew, I had to leave her. I was very blue, alright.

"Don't feel too bad about it," he said. "That's the Navy for you. We all get it sometime. This ship may not go to sea again. If they condemn those boilers, they will probably divide this crew up amongst the whole fleet. You just go up and have your operation and get well. And," he continued, "in recognition of the fine work you have done on this ship with that bunch of young apprentice boys, I have advanced your rate to a second-class quartermaster, as of this date. Maybe that will make you feel better. It is shooting you up pretty fast, but the navigator and I both think that you deserve it."

And so, it happened that I went to the hospital at Mare Island with a higher rating than when the ship left a few months before.

1902 to 1919 (first of 3 named *Paul Jones*)

MARE ISLAND HOSPITAL & USS *PAUL JONES*

The Horrifying "Dr. Scrotum"

When we arrived at Mare island there was an ambulance there to meet me and I had my bag and hammock packed, so there was nothing to do but ride up to the hospital in the conveyance sent for me. The following morning the doctors examined me and confirmed the diagnosis made by the doctor on the *Concord.* I wished afterwards that I had refused to have the operation because, as bad luck would have it, the doctor who operated on me had never in all his experience performed a hernia operation.

I had the operation and later one of the hospital apprentices described all that had happened. He said that he could tell that this fellow didn't know what he was doing because, as hospital apprentice, he had assisted in this same operation many times under other doctors. I don't remember the name of the doctor who operated on me, but the hospital apprentices and chief hospital stewards called him "Dr. Scrotum" when nobody was around, so I guess that's what I'll have to call him here.

He was a big, fat slob, and during the operation he didn't even have his head covered to keep the lint and dandruff from his hair from dropping into the incision. He began sweating during the operation and little streamlets of sweat dropped from his brow into the wound. My informant told me he had seen this happen with his own eyes and that everyone present at the operation was horrified. The other doctor attending the operation who was his assistant, looked shocked but could say nothing because he was outranked by Dr. Scrotum. I guess he told the other doctors in the hospital about it, because my friend told me that there was a lot of talk among the doctors about the way Scrotum performed this operation on me. My friend said

that he bet Dr. Scrotum wouldn't perform any more operations at that hospital.

I had been given chloroform for the operation and after it was over I was put in a room by myself, off the ward. In those days they had no women nurses in the Navy and all that work was done by men, called hospital apprentices and stewards. One had been assigned to watch over me and to see that I didn't drink any ice water, as there was a pitcher of ice water on the dresser in my room. This should have been removed but it was overlooked.

Dr. Scrotum never came near me the rest of the day but took the afternoon off and my friend said that he wouldn't be surprised if he hadn't gone off to get drunk. I was all sewn up and was supposed to lie quiet on my back, but when I began coming out of the chloroform I began to vomit. The hospital apprentice took care of me and when I reached the point where there was nothing more to come up, I begged for water. He told me his orders were not to give me anything to drink. Of course, I was not rational and kept insisting that I must have a drink of water and tried to get up. He would shove me back at each attempt.

When I quieted down a little, my attendant stepped out of the room onto the veranda to have a smoke. Evidently, as soon as he had left the room, I wanted a drink again and I got up and walked around the room to see if I could find any water. I found the pitcher of ice water on the dresser across the room, so I brought it over to my bed-stand and proceeded to drink all the water I wanted. Every time I would take a drink, I would vomit some more. I must have had quite a clambake by myself there, walking around with all those new stitches in me and drinking ice water! I had no memory of any of this and didn't know that I had done all these things I shouldn't have done until I was told about it later. Finally, my attendant remembered

about me being under his charge and he leisurely walked in and found me sitting on the edge of my bed with a practically empty pitcher in my hands. Then he got scared. He realized what he had done, and he ran out and got the chief hospital steward of that ward and told him what had happened.

The chief hospital steward tried to get in touch with Dr. Scrotum, but he was unable to find him, so he got ahold of the doctor who had assisted him with the operation. He came right away. The doctor was very upset and concerned because he was afraid that the stitches might have been pulled out and that I might bleed internally. Maybe that did happen, I don't know. All I know is that the wound became infected from the inside and I was in bed about two or three times as long as I should have been for such an operation.

It never did feel right after that, but in those days one doctor protected another if a mistake was made. I complained about the way I felt, but they insisted that I was doing alright. Of course, nothing like that could happen today in our fine Navy with its well-equipped hospitals and excellent doctors who are some of the finest in the country.

I was finally discharged and sent to the *Independence* for duty. I had been there only a couple of days when the skipper of the *Paul Jones*, one of the large destroyers that had just come around the Horn from the east coast, came aboard looking for more crew. He spotted my record and saw that I had a fine record and took high marks in gunnery, and as he had ambitions to win the trophy of the Navy, I suppose I looked good to him. I was "hooked" then and there.

My Diamond of a Friend

The *Paul Jones* was one of the three first four-stack destroyers that was built for our Navy. They had a contact speed of thirty-two knots an hour which in those day, was nothing short of startling. They were fine sea boats and for destroyers, they were the largest and most comfortable we had at that time. Captain Davison had brought her around the Horn with her twosister ships, the *Perry* and the *Preble*.

While I was in the hospital I got acquainted with the chief hospital steward. One day I told him that he looked familiar and I asked him where he lived or worked in the drug business before he went into the Navy. He told me he came from Vacaville, California. I began to laugh, and I told him the name of the drugstore where he had worked. He seemed surprised that I should know, and he told me he had gone to work there when he graduated from college. He admitted that I looked a little familiar to him but said that he had never associated me with that part of the country. Then suddenly he said, "I remember you now. You used to come into town with your mother. You had a buggy pulled by a bay mare. I always admired your mother because she was so pretty, and she always dressed so nice. I sold her lots of gumdrops for you."

That was the beginning of a fine friendship between us while I was on the *Paul Jones*, as he was transferred to that ship just a day or two before we left Mare Island. The destroyers had no doctor aboard, so he was sent to us to oversee the medical department, and he had one hospital apprentice as assistant. His name was Saxton, and everybody called him "Doc" Saxton, although he was not really a medical doctor. I know he must be passing out golden pills to the angels by this time as he has long

since passed away. He was what was known in the Navy of those days as a real shipmate. To illustrate I will tell this incident.

Before we left San Francisco for southern waters with the fleet, it was towards the end of the month, and I suddenly needed forty dollars. I didn't have it and I didn't know where I was going to get it. It was for someone I loved.

Doc, who had been on the Olympia during the Battle of Manila Bay, always wore a fine, large diamond ring, which I had admired when I was in the hospital. It looked to be about two carats, and it was in a beautiful setting. I was joking with him one day and asked him how he conned some woman out of it. He shook his head and he told me it was the most precious thing he owned.

He said that when he got back to New York from Manila, the ship was thrown open for visitors, as everybody wanted to see Dewey's flagship. He said that he happened to be standing by the accommodation ladder one morning when they started to allow the visitors aboard, and he said that a young man and his wife stepped aboard.

They were both remarkable for their fine clothes and cultural bearing and he said that he couldn't resist the temptation to step up to them and ask them if they would like him to show them over the ship. He was dressed in his best chief-petty officer uniform, and they seemed pleased to have him do so. He showed them the "whole works" after they had introduced themselves. He even took them up into the admiral's quarters, and as Admiral Dewey happened to be aboard, he introduced them to the admiral.

They were exceptionally pleased, and after they had inspected the whole ship from keel to truck, which was a circular cap at the head of the mast, they started to tell him how they appreciated what he had done for them, and he said that the

pleasure had been his. They asked if there was anything in the world that they could possibly do for him for his exceptional thoughtfulness and courtesy, and he told them that there wasn't a thing. He said he had everything he needed and that the only thing he needed was lots of good friends. They indicated that they would be pleased to continue his new friendship and he gave Doc his card, which showed they lived on Fifth Avenue. They told him that that was to be his home while he was in New York. Doc said that their friendship was one of the finest of his lifetime.

When the Olympia went out of commission and he was transferred to the torpedo base and thence to the Pacific coast to the Mare Island hospital, they gave a dinner party for him before he shipped out. At his plate was a little box gift wrapped with just the word "Doc" on it. He told how his host got up at the dinner and told the rest of the guests how they came to meet and what pleasure they had together. Then he said to Doc, "Open the little box," which Doc did. In it was this fine diamond ring. He said to Doc, "Like that diamond, I hope our friendship never dims." Doc told me that it was for this reason that he treasured the diamond ring more than anything he owned.

So, when I needed that forty dollars so badly and had no place to turn to get it, and I knew that within a week we were leaving for the south, I was worried and didn't know what to do. I thought of Doc and as payday was about three days off, I thought maybe Doc might know of someplace where I could get the money before payday and I could then give it back. I showed him the letter I had, and I asked Doc for his advice because I didn't know what to do about it.

He said, "You know me, Steve. You know I'm always busted the last few days before payday." Then he took that diamond ring off his finger and he said, "Here, go and get what

you have to have on this. If anything should happen that you can't redeem it before we go, let me know so I won't lose it."

I was speechless. I knew he was the "real article" but I sure didn't think that he would lend that diamond ring to anyone alive. I started to stammer, and tears streamed down my cheeks. He said, "Here now, I know damned well that you would do as much for me."

He got his diamond ring back the minute I got the forty dollars, which was right on time. I handed it back to him and I might have given him an iron ring or something because he just slipped it back on his finger without looking at it! That was the finest thing I ever had done for me in my life.

Bully for Teddy

About the time we were ready to join the fleet in San Francisco Bay, we received word that President Teddy Roosevelt was on his way out to the west coast and would inspect Mare Island Navy Yard and the Pacific fleet. Every good Navy man considered Teddy the father of the new Navy. He was the assistant secretary of the Navy before being elected vice president, and the Navy was his baby. He started building it up and spent most of his time trying to improve the Navy whereby none in the world would be better. It was during his regime as secretary that the battleship Oregon was built; the Olympia and various other modern ships either were built or were begun. He was always after Congress to get more money to bring our Navy up to where it should be. Old-time Navy men told me at the time I went into the Navy that if it hadn't been for Teddy we might never have won those battles that we did—Santiago and Manila Bay.

Consequently, the Navy felt that the president belonged to them and they always spoke of him as "Teddy."

All the ships from Mare Island except the *Preble* left Mare Island and joined the fleet. A few days later I met a quartermaster from the *Preble* who had been at the wheel when she came down from Mare Island. The *Preble* had been held over to bring President Roosevelt down after he had inspected Mare Island. This boy was excited about that trip because "Teddy" had stood beside him all the way down. But, I will give you the story as this lad told it to me.

He began, "When Teddy arrived, he spent one day inspecting the Navy Yard and then early the next morning came aboard the *Preble* accompanied by his retinue and the proverbial secret service men. We were all very excited about this event. I

was acting chief quartermaster with three other quartermasters under me. We spent most of the night "dolling" the bridge, shining up the brass work and so forth. The morning broke bright and clear and they all came down to the ship. Teddy was showing all his teeth with that big smile on his face. The crew were all lined up and, of course, we gave him the twenty-one guns which is the national salute for the president, and the president's flag was broken at the masthead. As you know, we carried that flag at the masthead until he disembarked at San Francisco. When he went aboard the flagship here in the San Francisco Bay it was broken at her masthead and that was when he was given the twenty-one guns there.

"Well, the first thing he said when he shook hands with our captain was, 'This is bully!' That was a word he used a great deal. 'I've been looking forward to riding on one of these ships ever since they were built. I understand that this one is the fastest thing in the Navy.' So, they ushered him up to the bridge. Near the modern three-inch rifle which stands in the center of the bridge, was a large, comfortable chair with an officer's cape draped over it, which was intended for him to sit in. He sized all this up and thanked the captain, but he asked him to take the chairs and all the folderol away. He wanted the bridge clear for the members of the party that were going to be up there with him on the ride to San Francisco.

"I had received orders before they came aboard to take the wheel myself during the trip down, and to have the other quartermasters on the fo'cas'le under the bridge, standing by. You could hear the ship's blowers going then, making steam, because the captain knew that Teddy would expect everything out of the *Preble* that she had in her. She has more horsepower than any battleship to date.

"Those poor secret service men! They were worn to a frazzle. One of them came over to me after we were under way

and said, 'Here, we're going to turn him over to you boys now. We're all tuckered out and we know he is safe with you fellows. Just show us a place where we can all go and get some shuteye.'

"I told them to go into the crew's quarters, that there wouldn't be anybody in there anyway because the boys wouldn't want to miss anything that was going on. That was the best I could do for them unless they wanted me to send someone down to get permission for them to go into the officers' quarters. They said no, that they would rather have the crew's quarters because they would be closer to the president there, and that they were so tired that they could rest anywhere. I guess Teddy was a strenuous proposition to take care of when he was traveling.

"All the lines had been singled up before he came aboard, so all the captain had to do was to sing out, 'Let go all the lines,' and followed this with, 'slow ahead, both engines!' I reached over the wheel and repeated the orders into the two annunciators and we were on our way. Just as soon as the stern was clear, the captain motioned me to put her full speed ahead, and I slammed the annunciators down to full speed for both engines. Boy! That old ship started to hump like a snake. The force-draft was blowing chunks of coal as big as your head out of the stack.

Everything in the channel next to the Navy Yard was all clear for us. As we started, Teddy came up on my steering platform with me and stood beside me. It wasn't long before he had his hand on my shoulder. I sure felt good about that. We were tearing off knots then. The more we tore off, the bigger his smile got, and the more "bullies" he said.

"The president kept asking me about myself—how long I had been in the Navy; how old I was, and about the apprentice system. I told him I was a great believer in the apprentice system. Then he told me that his love for ships and the sea was because he had practically been raised on his family's yacht, mostly around Oyster Bay. He could think of more questions to ask

me, and every time I would tell him something that he especially liked he'd say, 'That's bully! That's bully!' I guess I made the captain and the other officers a bit nervous because he talked to me so much and didn't come down off the platform and talk to them.

"When we were going at our best, the stacks were hot, the paint was peeling off, and we were at our maximum speed, he asked the captain how quickly the ship could be stopped. The captain looked around to make sure that there was nothing coming down the channel, and he sang out to me, 'Full speed astern, both engines!'

"I grabbed the annunciators on either side and slammed them down at reverse! I then took hold of the president's arm and quickly told him to hang on to the stanchions so that he wouldn't fall. Boy! When they put those engines full speed astern, it was as if we had hit a brick wall! All those aboard who had never experienced a maneuver of this kind had something happen to them. Some were thrown with their faces against the bridge stanchion, and there were a lot of black eyes among them when they went to the flagship. Those who had warning or had seen the maneuver before, grabbed something so they wouldn't be thrown forward. We brought her to a full stop, and I thought she was going to break in two a couple of times before she stopped. But she is a strong, sturdy ship, and well built. Of course, such a maneuver is a terrific strain on the hull of the ship.

"Teddy was tickled to death about it. He was like a kid with a new toy! He said excitedly, 'I never would have believed it if I hadn't been on her and seen it for myself. Experiencing that maneuver was worth the whole trip to the Pacific coast.'

"As soon as she came to full stop, we put her on full speed ahead again, and it was remarkable how little time it took to regain our maximum speed. We had the stopwatch on her to know the exact minute we reached the fleet. The boys on the

flagship told us they thought the Navy Yard was on fire and burning up because of the smoke we made.

"When we drew close enough to the flagship we got our signals telling us where to anchor. Immediately the admiral's barge came out and after receiving the President's salute from the flagship, with all the crew manning the rail, the admiral's barge took Teddy and his retinue aboard. The poor secret service men had to go to work again.

"Teddy shook hands with all the crew before he left. The crew was lined up and he went down the line. He never missed a man. Some of the firemen and coal-heavers were up on deck in their dirty work clothes and looked like they had crawled through the coal bin, and were dripping with sweat, but that didn't make any difference to Teddy. They had only an undershirt on the topside, but you couldn't keep them down below if they could get up there to say goodbye to him. And all the time this big grin was shining on everybody and he was telling what a wonderful experience that ride down had been to him. Teddy had the happy faculty of instilling a burning desire in the men to do their best."

Ventura and Louise Sanchez

In a week or so the fleet started south. On the way down from San Francisco to San Diego the flagship sent an order by flag-signal for the *Paul Jones* to anchor off Ventura, California, the next morning. Ventura was having a celebration the day following our arrival and we were to receive visitors and take part in the activities ashore. For the life of me, I cannot be sure what holiday it was, whether it was a local affair, state, or national, but I think that it was national.

Ventura is an open port with a sandy bottom for holding ground to anchor in. They had a small dock which could accommodate small ships but not large enough for our purposes, therefore we anchored far enough out so that we could get the mud-hook up in case of sudden bad weather.

After anchoring, the next morning about nine o'clock, the mayor and his committee came over and everybody was so friendly and invited us to take part in the parade the next day, and a dance was to be held in our honor in the evening. We were also invited to send a baseball team to play their excellent team. I knew the Ventura team would be good—far better than our team would be because we had little or no time to do any real practicing. In those days no holiday was complete without a baseball game, and what a team Ventura had!

Our captain told the mayor that there was no reason why the good people of Ventura couldn't come aboard that day and look the ship over, if they wished to do so. There were several small boats tied up to their dock, so it wasn't long until word got around and folks from town began coming over. They tied their boats up to our boom and when they were through visiting the ship, one of the crew would haul it up to the gangway for

them. They were ranchers and residents of the small seaport town and we enjoyed meeting them.

About two or three o'clock in the afternoon a sudden blow from the south came up, blowing from the sea towards the shore. It started to cloud over, so the first lieutenant, whose name was Dobbs, instructed us to get all the visitors off the ship as fast as possible, but it was only a few minutes before the sea was too rough and we were able to get only one boatload away. We had to hoist anchor right away as the ship began to drag anchor toward the beach. The captain was ashore and that left Dobbs, the first lieutenant, in command. We had to work fast because we had to get under way as soon as the anchor was up to keep the ship off the beach.

Fortunately, when the breeze started to get strong, I had opened the valve and warmed up the steering engine, and the chief engineer had ordered his steam pressure brought up. We had to put right out of there, slowly heading with the wind slightly off the starboard bow, and each minute the velocity of the wind increased. When we put to sea we had twenty visitors still aboard. Some were quite agitated and scared; others thought it a great joke and were thrilled at the prospect of a ride on one of Uncle Sam's ships.

One farmer told me he had tied his team to the hitching rack in town and that he was very perturbed about having to leave them like that. It later turned out that a livery stable owner, hearing about what had happened, took care of his team.

We put the wind on the bow to make the ship ride as easy as possible, and we noticed that some of our spectators and passengers began to disappear and get into sheltered places and sit down on the deck. They gradually lost their color and turned a kind of whitish-green. Those who were so lively on leaving, were losing their enjoyment of the ride. They just lay down wherever they were overcome by this mal de mer. The boys who

257

had bunks in the crew's quarters helped them all they could and felt sorry for them.

There were several very nice, pretty girls among the passengers. I had talked to one of them when she came aboard, and she told me her name was Louise Sanchez. She said that her folks were old-timers in that country and that they owned a ranch on the outskirts of Ventura. She was one of a large family of girls and boys. She said two of her brothers were going to play ball against us the next day. Her family belonged to the Dons of Old Mexico who settled that country before it belonged to the United States. She was very attractive, and I liked her at lot. I asked her if she ever knew anybody in Ventura named "Stevens." She said that there were several Stevens and that she had once had a teacher by the name of Augusta Stevens. I had to laugh at that and she asked if I was any relation to them. I admitted that her teacher was my Aunt Augusta.

"My father was the youngest boy of that Stevens family," I said.

"Oh," she replied, "I think I remember him. He used to work in the printing office of the Ventura Free Press when I was a little girl."

I laughed and said, "Yes, he held the exalted position of printer's devil."

"We knew the whole family," she said.

Three of the six children of Josiah & Emeline: Alice, Webster, Horace (Gaither's father), Emeline (Gaither's grandmother), & Augusta Stevens

I told her that I knew that my relatives had owned a ranch somewhere close to Ventura, but I had never visited them. Then I asked her if she ever knew Judge Thomas Sheppard.

"Indeed, I did!" she exclaimed. "All my family and all our relatives knew Judge Sheppard. He was a very prominent man around Ventura and everybody, including the Mexican people, held him in very high esteem."

"He was on the Superior bench of Ventura County for over ten years," I said, "until he retired from law because he felt that he was getting too deaf to continue."

Then Louise said, "My mother will certainly want to meet you. Was your mother from Ventura, too?"

"Yes," I answered, "she lived there until she was married."

After we got up anchor and things were going along, the first lieutenant was on the bridge and I had a seaman at the wheel, so I went down to look for Louise and I found her huddled by

an after-conning tower. I took her arm and lead her to my forward-conning tower and had her sit down in the folding chair we had there. She was alright and wasn't scared, but she was getting awfully seasick. It was growing darker and darker and, of course, very few of the passengers wanted anything to eat.

The blow had been increasing and the ship was covered with spray. We rigged the lifelines fore and aft. After a while I asked Dodds to let me go down and see how Louise was faring. I told him that she knew all my people and that I might take her down and put her to bed on my bunk in the chief petty officers' quarters, just forward of the wardroom. He gave his permission and I went down. She was so sick that she could hardly hold her head up, so I took her down the ladder to the main deck with my arm around her and she held on to a lifeline. I took her below to the chief petty officers' quarters and there was plenty of room there as some of them had gone ashore on liberty. I covered her up and took her shoes off and gave her a receptacle to use when her stomach turned upside down. I told her that she would be perfectly safe and alright there and that no one would molest her. I then went back on the bridge and told Dodds what I had done, and he had quite a laugh about it.

We went out almost to the Santa Cruz Islands before the weather began to abate. When it did, it calmed down quickly, and we turned around and started back for Ventura. Before long the sea was smooth, and the wind was practically a mere zephyr.

I had a good pull with the chief cook and he used to leave the key to the galley in a secret place where I knew where to find it and in an emergency, I could call him. I went into the galley and saw that they were going to have steak for breakfast, and I knew where they were kept. I then went up on the bridge and asked Dodds how he would like to put a nice broiled steak with toast under his belt.

"Oh," he said, "that would be just perfect. With all the commotion aboard, I didn't get a chance to eat a bite of supper and I could sure use something like that right now."

I told him that I hadn't had my supper either. I said, "I'll make a deal with you. I'll furnish the broiled steak and toast if you will allow me to bring Miss Sanchez, the young lady I was telling you about, up here on the bridge to join us. I'll see that we have a pot of good, hot coffee, too."

He told me to go ahead, so I went back to the galley and I picked out six delicious-looking little steaks and cut enough bread for a couple of pieces of toast apiece. I took all this down to the engine room, and the engineer on watch knew what was up as soon as I showed him the steaks because we had this midnight banquet before. He went into the fireroom and pulled out some red-hot coals and cleaned six shovels and put the coals in the shovels, and he and the fireman proceeded with the culinary work. I went to the galley again and started the coal fire to make a pot of coffee. Not forgetting the man at the wheel, I took enough plates and cups for the four of us on the bridge. By that time the sea was almost as calm as a mill pond and we were running about half speed.

I told Dodds if he would lend me the man at the wheel for a few minutes that I would get my guest up on the bridge, so he took the wheel himself, to relive the helmsman, and we went down to the chief petty officers' quarters and lifted the girl out of the bunk. She was sound asleep. I don't know what ideas flashed through her mind when she found me lifting her to the deck, but I had turned the light on so that she could see plainly who it was. The two of us helped her up the companionway to the main deck. She found that she was over her seasickness and I told her that the storm was over and that we would soon be nearing Ventura. I said that in the meantime, she would be our guest on the bridge and that we would have a cup of hot coffee

for her, which would make her feel much better. By the time she reached the bridge, both her morale and her physical condition had improved.

I introduced her to the first lieutenant and he seated her on the signal chest. I then went down to the galley and brought back the coffee, cream and sugar, and salt and pepper. I had no more than returned to the bridge when the chief engineer came up with four sizzling steaks, done to a turn, and mmmmmmm! They smelled so good with that toast!

When he saw such an attractive young lady, his eyes popped open and he said, "My goodness, I've missed the best part of this party!" So, we introduced him to Louise, but he couldn't stay. He had to leave immediately to get back to his duties below.

I don't think we could cook anything that tastes better than a good steak, broiled over the coals on a fireroom shovel. It has a special flavor of its own. Louise hadn't had anything to eat since breakfast and she really tore into it. The color came back into her cheeks and her eyes sparkled again, and she soon looked like a different person than she had while violently seasick.

By that time, about two-thirty a.m., we were nearing Ventura, so the first lieutenant said, "I'll take the wheel and you and the helmsman go below and wake up all these folks from shore and give them a chance to get thoroughly awake before we put them into boats to take them ashore. Also, have the chief boatswain's mate call "all hands."

Everybody was now over their seasickness, and the waters were almost as smooth as glass. Sparks turned on the searchlight to let the people in town know that the ship was approaching, and we anchored approximately in the same spot where we had anchored before the blow came up. Then we had to get the boats' crews into their boats and get the boats up to the

accommodation ladder. We then helped the people down into the boats. One of our boats carried about eight passengers safely, so that three boats were enough to take everybody ashore. Louise Sanchez was the last to get in the boat. When she left she told the first lieutenant and me that she wished she had been born a man and if she had been, she surely would have been a sailor on a destroyer. She thanked us profusely for what we had done for her and wanted us to be sure and come to the dance that night, which we promised to do.

Right after lunch the breeze began to increase a little and Dodds came along, and he said to me, "Let's get ashore. If she begins to blow again, we don't want to get stuck on here again tonight."

He had the boat's crew haul up to the gangway and we piled into the boat and in a few minutes, we were at the dock, and ashore. Louise Sanchez must have been watching for us because we hadn't walked over a block or two when she came sailing out of a store with all sails set. She hailed us and joined us to walk down to the baseball field. En route she would stop and introduced us to any of her friends we met on the way, and there were lots of them. She told them what heroes we were and the great care we had taken of her on the unscheduled trip to the Santa Cruz Islands the night before. She told them how seasick she got but added that once she was over it she enjoyed every minute of the return trip. Then she described the banquet on the bridge and it seemed to get more delicious each time she repeated it.

When we got to the baseball field the first fellow we ran into was a reporter from the local paper, and she had to lay it all out again to him. The story got better every time she told it. If I could have been discharged from the Navy right then and there, I would undoubtedly have been elected mayor at the next election.

The baseball field was full of boys, young and old, from six years to forty, all practicing baseball. I never in all my life, saw such enthusiasm for baseball as there was in that district. They had about four teams composed of past and future baseball stars. We got a fine grandstand seat close to Homeplate, and Louise saw that every baseball player came over to meet us. The more I saw them practicing, the sorrier I felt for our poor team. They hadn't had a chance to touch a ball for about four months. We had a good pitcher, but he was in the same boat as the rest of the boys, and he was as wild as that man from Borneo. However, we didn't have the heart to refuse to play with them. They were kind enough to let us off easy. The score was only twenty to one, and it could just as easily have been forty to one. But they were too tenderhearted to run it up that much, and besides, hadn't we saved Louise Sanchez's life?

Just before the game started her family swooped down on us, except for the two boys who were on the ball team. I thought at the time when I saw them all, that it was a good thing that I had treated her like a lady should be treated. Her mother was a lovely person and it was not hard to see why her brothers and sisters were all so nice. I didn't blame Louise for being proud of her family.

We enjoyed everything that was going on. They had a barbeque that evening before the dance started. Two steers had been prepared and cooked to a delicious turn over the glowing coals. Long tables had been set up and they groaned with food. Everything in season was on those tables and there were delectable, homemade pies and cakes that appealed to all of us homesick boys who hadn't had anything like that for such a long time. I was complementing Mrs. Sanchez on the quality and the deliciousness of the food, when Louise came along and heard me.

"I'll admit that it is good," she said, "but it can't hold a candle to those steaks we had at two thirty this morning. I'll remember those all my life!"

In due time the dance began, and we partied until sunrise. In those days dances were dances. Everybody went there to dance with everyone. If a man missed dancing with any one lady, he wasn't invited to the next one. He was expected to ask every lady there for a dance. Consequently, there were no such things as wallflowers in those days, and everybody had a wonderful time. At daylight the dance broke up and the boys all headed back to the ship. A large crowd came down to the dock to see us off and to say their farewells. As soon as all of the crew were aboard, we hoisted the mud-hook and set the course for San Diego, where we arrived and joined the fleet without further incident.

Target Practice

We stopped in San Diego for a few days where the crew enjoyed themselves, then worked down the coast of Lower California toward the southern end. There we went through daily fleet maneuvers and drills of all kinds. That was an excellent geographical position to carry on marine drills and maneuvers. We stopped in Magdalena Bay long enough to have small-arms target practice, so we got rid of that daily chore. Every year in those days, a naval vessel of the line was supposed to conduct drills of all kinds pertaining to her efficiency as a fighting ship, especially in target practice, and whenever possible, it was when the fleet ships were all together so that it was witnessed by the admiral and the other vessels. There was a yearly prize given to the ship and to the crew for the top scores in target practice to encourage efficiency in marksmanship.

The gun-pointer of each gun of that class of weaponry on the ship who turned in the highest score, got the greatest reward and was rated as a gun-pointer. Each gun had two gun-pointers, as Ic (first class) and 2c (second class). The highest man was rated Ic and the second highest was rated 2c gun-pointer, and they wore a gunsight insignia on the right arm if they belonged to the starboard watch and on their left arm if it was the port watch. Every man on the ship had a chance to fire and try his skill in practice. He might sometimes be a coal-passer, but generally they were seamen on deck, therefore the men on deck had more chance to practice than the men below.

It meant extra pay per month for the first and second-class gun-pointers, but they had to qualify periodically, or they would lose it, so naturally, the boys were keen about improving their efficiency. We would have a moving target on deck that was twenty or thirty feet from the muzzle of the gun, which was

moved mechanically by hand as the ship would move at two thousand yards. Then on the gun we had .22 rifles lined up without regular gunsight of the gun, and we did our sighting through the gunsights and fired the .22, using the same means of firing as we would in regular practice or battle. That was known as "the Morris tube" method of practice, which I believe was taken from the English Navy. In some cases, we would have the full guns crew loading the dummy shells and ejecting them as they would if firing the gun. It was a wonderful method of improving the efficiency of a gun's crew.

We intended to work south in a leisurely manner until we reached Panama, where the whole fleet was to anchor. Because of our superior speed we were designated as the dispatch boat of the fleet when we left San Diego. This meant that we were to carry all the dispatches to be telegraphed to Washington and to carry the fleet's mail back and forth. We were busy boys on our ship.

There was generally more than one dispatch boat with the fleet in those days, but I believe that the *Perry* and *Preble*, our sister ships, still had work to be done on them and they turned back to Mare Island when we left for the southern waters, so the *Paul Jones* had the duty alone.

Captain Davison {Lt. Gregory Caldwell Davison} was the most brilliant naval officer I ever served under. I had to learn that by degrees, but right from the start I could tell that he had something. He was no Lothario; in fact, he was a little average height and homely as all get out. He was skinny, his head was large, and his large ears stuck out like a pair of wings from it. But, he had plenty inside that head! He was on the ball all the time.

When he took command of the *Paul Jones* he had just finished a thorough course of study with Whitehead Torpedo Company and there wasn't a piece of machinery or metal in that

torpedo that he didn't know, and he probably knew how to make it. He was considered the most brilliant man in torpedoes that the Navy had. Incidentally, he was just as good on gunnery and ballistics as he was on torpedoes. While I was on that ship I saw him perform wonderful work or feats, not only with torpedoes, but with all gunnery.

He brought his own favorite chief gunner's mate and chief torpedo man out with him from the torpedo station on the east coast. They both had courses in their special line--one in the gunnery school and the other in the torpedo school--and they could read the mind of any torpedo! That was all he seemed to live for. I don't believe that half the time Captain Davison ate his meals, and often when I was on the mid-watch at sea, I would go down myself and call the relief officer of the deck when I would find the captain in the wardroom working out problems. No wonder he wasn't fat. He didn't seem to sleep nor eat half of the time. Of course, I hadn't been on the ship long before he went up in my estimation and respect because I always did admire ability and brains. I had to work so hard to get what little I knew.

Captain Davison also brought his own ship's writer with him from the east coast. He had evidently compiled a lot of data for him and had it written up and filed away, and the captain wanted his writer handy to get it for him when he wanted it.

After we left San Diego going south, he called the crew to muster which consisted of about seventy-five to eighty men and told us his plans and how he wanted to operate the ship. He told us that the three-inch and the six pounder semi-automatic guns were still equipped with the old, open-sights and he said that if it was possible within his knowledge of mechanics to change that sight, he was going to devise a sight of his own.

"I'm working on it right now," he said, "because we want the Navy trophy for destroyers and torpedo boats at the coming

yearly target practice in Panama. By hard work and good luck, if we took the trophy of the Navy for all ships, I wouldn't shed any tears over that! I know that is asking an awful lot of a green crew on the first target practice that this ship has ever had, but we're going to work with that aim in view. I feel confident that we will take the trophy of the Navy in torpedo practice because these torpedoes are the latest that the Navy has, and we're going to make them perform for us. So, this won't be a lazy man's ship.

"To do the thing that I have set out to do, every man must give his best if we are going to achieve our goal. I know that the officers are going to work just as hard as you fellows and I are going to work. I am mighty pleased with the crew and the officers and I am glad to find that I have Dodds as first lieutenant under me.

"At the Naval Academy he was first-string quarterback and whipped the Army several times. With that kind of spirit and the material to do it with, we can't miss if we just use all our abilities." It turned out that he was right. We never had time to call our souls our own.

He went around wearing dungarees and a dirty old cap on his head practically all the time. My greatest fear was that some superior officer might come aboard and order him to do something about his appearance because he looked so little like an officer.

Captain Davison had a special machinist in the engine room who had come around from the east coast with him, and this man evidently was one of the best in his line. The two of them immediately got to work on making a new gunsight. This was a peep-sight in back with a rubber shield against the eye to keep the light out, and it was attached to a brass rod which ran forward to the forward sight. On the forward part of the sight they made a ring with crossed wire through it. All this was made

to fit in the slide which held the one sight so that the sight could be adjusted by the old mechanism, raised or lowered or shifted to the one side or the other, as the case might be. It was a beautiful piece of work. The captain, the mechanic, and the chief gunner's mate practically slept with that sight until it was finished, and it proved to be one hundred percent more efficient than the old, original sight. We could shoot more accurately and faster using the new sight.

He also made some changes in the torpedo tube which we had on deck. There were four of them which were the latest model. During the entire trip from San Diego to Panama, he was on deck practically the whole time, working on his beloved gun-sight or torpedo tube. By the time the fleet arrived in Panama, we had practiced many maneuvers at sea on the way down, both night and day; and in the water from the Gulf of Fonseca to Panama, where there were better weather and calm seas than on any other body of water that I ever became acquainted with, our drills became even more intense.

We anchored in the same old anchorage off Deadman's Island that we always used on the *Ranger*, and where the new country of Panama was born. I have been through the Canal, running passenger merchant ships, I would guess around a hundred times, and I never passed by this anchorage without old memories.

There is a very suitable bay for big-gun target practice about twenty-five or thirty-five miles from our anchorage in the Gulf of Panama, and the Navy had shipped timbers down from the north, and all other necessary lumber to build a substantial target for our fleet, expecting it to last if the weather and the worms would allow. The large framework timbers were at least three feet in diameter. As soon as possible, we got to work on the target, which took a little time to build. All the carpenter's mates and warrant carpenters were over there and busier than a

dog with two tails. We did all the running back and forth, taking them over in the morning and bringing them back at night. When we weren't doing that, we were all practicing with the Morris tube and practiced firing with the torpedoes. We didn't even have time to have a smoke.

Finally, this big target was completed, and it was a fine job. The first ship to fire, which was the old *Boston*, proceeded to the target area and remained there until every gun on her had been fired. Each ship that went to target practice took observers and judges from other ships of the fleet who confirmed the results of the operations carried out, making them official. This report was then sent back to the Navy Department in Washington, D.C., to be placed on record.

This target practice went on for about a week or two, the *Paul Jones* leaving the target area early each morning with the dispatches and mail of the ship that was firing, returning in the evening after the mail had come across the Isthmus from Colon on the train. We left the fleet every night when it was dark, and at this distance it didn't take us long at full speed to reach the ship on the range and anchor for the night.

Worry Wort

It started as a normal night. Everybody was tired and glad to get the day over with and get to bed. The night was dark as a black cat and the only lights were the ones which could be seen as we approached the ship laying at anchor. She was anchored about two miles inside the target. I had a nervous feeling that night, a faculty which I have always had, of getting nervous when I thought danger was close. I had a quartermaster at the wheel and we were making full speed of about twenty-five knots an hour. We weren't under forced draft, but we were kicking right along. Captain Davison was on the bridge, as he generally was. I had a restless, nervous feeling all the way after we left the fleet. Finally, it dawned on me what it was. I felt that we were getting close to the target which stood right in the line with the ship, and on every trip before that, we had turned on our searchlights to find the target so that we wouldn't hit it. I finally said to the captain, "Hadn't we better have the electrician up here and turn the searchlights on?"

"Why?" he asked.

I answered that I had the feeling that we were getting close. He looked at his watch and said that we hadn't been long enough time from the fleet to be close to the target. I told him that I knew that, but that I had a feeling that we were getting close to the target, and I said, "The way she is slipping through the water tonight makes me feel that she has made better speed than we counted on."

"Ah," he said, "you are just an old worry wort. There is plenty of time for the searchlight."

That didn't help me at all, nor allay my feelings. We ran along for another five or ten minutes and finally I couldn't stand

it any longer, so I said, "Sir, hadn't I better go down and get the electrician up here?"

This annoyed him very much and he said, "Damn it to hell, if it will make you feel any better, go and get him!"

I was down that bridge ladder in nothing flat. The electrician was sitting in my conning tower that I used as chief quartermaster, and I was so glad to see him there! I grabbed him by the arm and I said, "For God's sake, get on that bridge and turn on that searchlight as soon as you can! I have a feeling that we are getting close to that target."

Sparks was a good egg and a good friend of mine, so he didn't lose any time getting up the ladder. He turned the searchlight on and it was set for dead ahead. As soon as she took hold and the carbon points lit up, the target loomed dead ahead. It seemed to me that we were on top of it. We were too close to stop or back up. The only thing left to do was to squirm by her and hope for the best. If I ever saw a surprised man, it was our Old Man. I imagine his hair stood straight up when he saw that, and he yelled out, "Har' to port!" Then he changed it and reversed it and yelled, "Har' to starboard!" He got excited. The only thing which kept me from getting so excited was the fact that I expected it and he didn't.

The man at the wheel got bewildered. He just stood there confused and didn't know what to do. I jumped for the platform and shoved the man at the wheel away and took my two fingers of the right hand and spun the wheel as fast as I could spin it. She was a very easy-working, small wheel. We held our breath! I couldn't tell whether we had hit the target or not, but she passed on our starboard side, so close that I couldn't put a frog hair between the ship's hull and the target's timbers. As soon as I had her less than the first half of the ship's length clear, I spun the wheel the other way and that threw the stern in the other direction so that we passed clear. As the stern passed her, I

thought I felt the contact of something. However, I straightened her out on her course and turned her back to the man who was at the wheel before I took over. I guess all of us on the bridge were shaking. The Old Man walked back and forth two or three times on that bridge, trying to regain his composure. Then he looked up at me and he said, "Well, you did it, boy! Do you think we touched her?"

"I have a suspicion that we touched her on the starboard quarter," I replied.

"Well, take soundings and we'll soon know."

The carpenter's mate received orders to take soundings every five minutes for the next half hour. Apparently, the hull wasn't hurt. When we anchored I went back on the stern with a strong light to see if I could find anything, and all I could see was the starboard dinghy-boom which looked askew to me like one rung of the Jacob's ladder was broken. We had hit one of the big wire guys {rope} with the end of this little boom. (There was a little boom placed on either side of the stern to tie a boat to and come up the Jacob's ladder when we didn't want to swing out the regular boat boom). There was a solid guy of steel running out from the end of the little boom, and that steel guy at the end of the boom was broken. I went down and had a talk with the Old Man about it and told him what I saw. He said that the best thing to do was to say nothing.

"If we had hit her square, the way she was heading when the searchlight was turned on, the ship would be laying on the bottom now, and perhaps would have blown the forward magazine up, as it contains quite a lot of gun-cotton."

The only humorous part of that incident was the fact that when we got up anchor in the morning and started on our regular run back to the fleet, and were under way for a while, the captain came up to me with the glasses in his hand and asked me if I would look through them and see if I could see anything of the

target. I saw the target alright, but it was up-side-down. He chuckled and said, "My, we must have had rough weather last night to turn that target upside-down!"

I answered that it must have been flipped by a tornado. He responded that he had a never heard of a tornado down there before. We both had a quiet laugh about it and that was the last that any mention was ever made of the incident. However, after that when I began to worry about something, his big ears would prick up.

Eye Trouble

About a week before target practice was over, my eyes got so bad from the glare of the tropical sun down there (I never saw a glare worse than the tropical sun in that locality) that my eyelids got hard and painful and swelled so much that it was difficult to sleep. I had Doc Saxton look at them and he said he thought he knew the cause. He said that it was probably the result of so much target practice with the Morris tube by looking at the glare of the sun on the water. In those days, they had no dark glasses nor shades to put over the gunsights to protect the eyes from the glare, as they have today. Doc went to the skipper and told him about the condition of my eyes and suggested that I should be taken over to the flagship to see their doctor immediately since the results of this condition could turn out to be serious. Captain Davison came running up from the wardroom quite excited about it and told me that they were counting on me for that trophy.

"If you go over there," he said, "and they keep you, it's going to raise hell with us."

I assured him that I wouldn't stay there, even if I had to swim back to our ship, but I told him that I had to have some relief from the pain in my eyes. Doc Saxton took me to the flagship doctor on the old, heavy-armored cruiser New York, who gave me a good examination. I told the doctor that I had to fire in about a week, as I was gun-pointer and that they would throw me overboard if I wasn't there to do it and that I would never be able to go back to that ship if I missed out when it came our turn to try for the trophy.

The doctor said that there had been a lot of the same thing with other gun-pointers in the fleet, and he told me that he thought that he could stop it right away, at least enough so

that I would be able to fire. "But," he said, "it's going to be very painful." He said that it would be a severe dose and asked me if I was willing to stand it. I said that that I guessed that I would have to.

Then he took a sharp pointed pencil of bluestone and turned my eyelid inside out and rubbed it with his bluestone. Holy mackerel! When it started to take hold, the pain was as severe as any I have ever had. Doc Saxton asked him why he didn't give me a drink to ease that pain a little, but he seemed to be dumb, and as I had never yet had a drink in my life, it wasn't made an issue. I just hopped around his operating room, holding my eye and using all the new words I had acquired since joining the Navy. Finally, the pain eased up a bit and he asked me if I was ready for the other eye. I was glad that I had only two eyes! He repeated the same performance on the other eye, only it seemed worse the second time and I was getting shaky by that time. He instructed me to report to him every morning so that he could put some soothing lotion in my eyes. I told him that I couldn't do this because I had to go with the ship on dispatch duty. I also told him that when we were not doing dispatch duty, we were practicing, because we wanted to win the trophy of the Navy. He asked me if I thought we stood any chance to win it and I told him that I knew that we were going to win.

He sat back in his chair and said, "That's the spirit! I wouldn't be surprised to see you do that. I can give this medicine to this chief pharmacist mate and he can do it if you are unable to get over here. But if your eyes don't get better, or if they get any worse, I want him to bring you right over here again and I will bandage your eyes."

He gave Doc the medicine and instructions to put packs on my eyes three or four times a day. Well, by golly, it did the work! My eyes didn't get any worse and I was able to go on with my practice.

The World's Record

We were to be the last ship to fire and we were the busiest ship on the sea. Between running our dispatches back and forth every day and practicing Morris tube, drilling our loaders, and sight-setters in the gun crew for speed, we didn't have any time for anything except the job at hand. Fortunately, we did a lot of practicing while making our dispatch runs. All the time our division officer was keeping his eye open for the fastest loaders on the ship for the six-pounder semi-automatic. The ammunition was fixed so that when they threw the shell in, the powder charge went in behind the shell in the brass case. In other words, it was just like a large rifle bullet and shell, and it took an awfully good man who was strong with a true eye, to slam that shell home immediately after the other shell was ejected. Every second counted. We aimed to shoot that gun as fast as the shells went into the barrel because I had told the captain that I would hold the trigger back after I fired my first shot, and that it was up to the loading crew as to how many shells we got out of that gun. Up to that time, I believe it had never been tested on those guns, but I had practiced it on the .22 of the Morris tube as they called it, and I don't mind admitting that I was pretty good at it.

The firing was finished by the other ships and ours was the only one remaining. We went to the range with our observers and judges with a *Paul Jones* gleam in our eyes. I asked the division officer if he could arrange it so that I would shoot last and he said he thought he could. I knew the boys would be well warmed up by that time. The first guns we fired were the two three-inch guns and the boys did excellently. People began to smile a little then.

We started on our ten six-pounder semiautomatics, a run for each gun at two thousand yards distance from the target. The

first couple of guns didn't do as well as we had expected. Then we seemed to strike our stride and every gun seemed to do a little better than the one before. The boys were beginning to smile and make wisecracks. When a blue-jacket begins to make wisecracks, he is beginning to be efficient.

Finally, it came to our gun and I had to fire because I was acting first gun-pointer. The second gun-pointer had to fire after I was through. As we straightened out and came on the range, I produced a big smile and said, "Come on, boys, let's show Old *John Paul Jones* what we can do for him!"

My gun was located forward next to the crew's quarters. I gave the order to load. On the semi-automatic six pounders in those days the shells were carried by hand to the gun and as the shell was fired, the recoil of the gun opened the breech and threw the shell back against a deflector of brass, which deflected the shell off some distance from the gun.

As we came up, the division officer kept me informed about how much farther we had to go before we could start firing. He finally gave me the order, "Fire when you will!"

He hadn't finished his command before a shell was on its way. Our spotter was on the bridge keeping us informed on how we were doing, as near as he could determine with the powerful binoculars he had. It was considered a hit even if we missed the bullseye if the shell did not go wild, because we were shooting in a space that would hit anything from a destroyer to a battleship, and it was credited as a hit. The next minute seemed to me to be the shortest minute I ever experienced. I never let the trigger go back so that as soon as the shell was thrown home in the gun, she fired. I held her on the target constantly, or as near so as I could. When the string was fired, all I had heard was the spotter saying "Hit, hit, hit," but I couldn't believe that every one of them was a hit, and I couldn't believe that I had done as well as I had hoped to do.

When time was called I fired the last shell. Of course, the breech stayed open because there were no more shells thrown in. I straightened up and stepped away from the gun and looked around me, and I found my division officer with his arms around me, and the captain hurrying down the ladder to do the same thing, and all the crew yelling their heads off! I finally realized that I must have done pretty well. I asked them how many shots I had fired and how many hits I had made, and the captain shouted, "You've done it, boy! You've done it! We won't know for sure until we check with the judges and observers what the exact count was. We have only our own count, and that seems too good to be true, but we know you've done it! We know you have broken the record!"

Then my second pointer fired the next string and did quite well. It was some time before I got the exact report on what the gun did. I had fired twenty-eight shots in a minute, made eighteen bullseyes and the rest were credited as hits.

The captain came running up from the wardroom shouting, "He not only broke the record of our own Navy, but he also broke the world's record!"

Well, I was amazed when I heard him say that and, of course, I felt awfully good to know that I had done so well. We had the records aboard of all the other ships showing what the other ships had done. All the ships carried the same weapons. This was done to stimulate competition. There was nothing in our fleet that came anywhere near the record we had made!

Torpedo Run

We anchored at the target anchorage in preparation for firing torpedoes the next day. That was where the brains of the Old Man and his experts would count. However, everybody was happy that night and we knew the Old Man wouldn't fail us, so she was a happy ship when we turned in that night. Nobody seemed to want to sleep that night because we were so excited and felt so good on what we had accomplished, but after a while we quieted down. We all had a hard day and knew there would be another one tomorrow.

I took a mid-watch on deck, allowing the officer that would have stood it to get more rest and sleep since the other officers were busy computing and all working on torpedoes for the next day. It seemed to me that the Old Man didn't sleep at all during the night. On the midwatch he came up and scanned the weather a couple of times and chatted with me, then went down and did some more computing.

The weather held fine, and it was a perfect day for torpedo practice. We had breakfast a half hour earlier than usual and after breakfast we raised the mud-hook and went to the torpedo range. On the way there, we dropped the target which consisted of one of the four-oared klinker {flat-bottomed} boats with an observer, four oarsmen, and a coxswain. We went to the end of the range and turned around, ready to make the first run.

The klinker boat was used as target. We were supposed to put the torpedo five feet under the boat, which was the standard depth they were supposed to run in those days, and as near amidships of the boat as possible. If the torpedo passed forward of the boat or aft of it, it was a miss, and when the ship is running full speed, and the torpedoes were put where they

would make a hit, it was really something to behold. I don't recall the distance that the boat was from the ship, but the captain had his torpedo ready in the tube, charged. At that time, it was propelled by a beautiful little engine in the torpedo, powered by compressed air and two propellers turning opposite to each other.

In practice the torpedo carried what was known as a practice head. This consisted of a metal head that looked like the warhead, but instead of being filled with gun-cotton as a warhead was, it had nothing more than water in it, bringing the practice head to the same weight as the warhead. The warheads were kept below in the torpedo room and were only broken out and secured to the torpedoes in place of the practice heads in time of war.

A torpedo would be aimed at the target by the man in command of the tube. As it went down the tube it hit a stripper that pulled the trigger and started the engine running, so that when it hit the water the engine was running at full speed. The torpedo was forced out of the tube by the discharge of a powder shell, the force of which was sufficient to send it clear of the tube and the ship, and it was supposed to keep that perfect direction as long as it was running. If it hit a small obstruction and deflected from its course, the gyro-wheel in the ovary would bring it back on its original course. Good torpedo men didn't grow on bushes.

We started our first run and when we were halfway on the run and opposite the target, the captain fired. She seemed to perform alright with the exception that she wasn't quite deep enough, and she was running too shallow. When the torpedo got close to the target-boat, the observer sang out to the crew, "Look out for yourselves, she is running high, and keep your legs up so they won't get hit!" He could tell that she was going to pass right under the boat, and sure enough she did, right at

admiships, but she tore the boat's keel out in doing so! If the boys in the admiships of the boat hadn't had their feet up on the gunwale they probably would have had badly injured legs, or maybe no legs at all. She went clear through the boat and passed on, and stopped where she was set to stop, as near as we could tell. The Old Man was dreadfully disappointed. Although it was a perfect hit, it ran too shallow, detracting from some of the score of that run.

The thing that kept the observer boat from sinking was the fact that she had watertight compartments fore and aft, but she needed a new bottom after that shot. Another boat was dropped over and the bottomless boat was hauled aboard and slung from the davits.

We fired the other nine practice shots and this time we were credited with all hits. I heard that the judges and observers were very lenient with us on penalizing us for the first shot.

We finished up in nice shape and got away from the target range so that we would arrive at the fleet anchorage during daylight, and we had brooms lashed to everything on the ship that stuck out, indicating that we had made a clean sweep. Also, we had our scores hoisted on the signal halyards, in the Navy code. I think we could be forgiven for throwing our chests out and swaggering a little because no crew ever worked harder than that crew did to earn it. As we passed the flagship and made a turn to our anchorage, the flagship crew gave us three cheers and the officer of the deck gave us three whistles, which all helped to reward us for the hard work we put in.

As soon as we anchored we received a signal from the flagship for our commanding officer to report aboard. When he

returned to the ship he had a smile a yard wide, and that night the flagship had signal practice to all vessels and commanders, giving a full account of the scores that we had made on all classes of armor.

The next morning at daylight the fleet weighed anchor and started north for San Diego.

1902 to 1920

MARE ISLAND HOSPITAL & USS *PERRY*

Refusing Surgery by a Butcher

Ever since I had left the hospital and had been on the *Paul Jones*, my operation for the hernia had pained me and kept getting more severe all the time! The swelling and lump was also getting worse. I had confided in Doc Saxton and shown him my condition.

"Although I am not a physician," he said, "I know enough from experience in hospitals to know that rupture has busted and that now you have a worse hernia than when you were first operated on. When we get to San Diego I'll take you to the flagship and do what I can to have you sent to the Mare Island hospital again."

I told him that I didn't want to go back to the Mare Island hospital again and have that same butcher work on me, or any other Navy surgeon work on me. In those days the standard of the Navy surgeons was low. This is not true today. Some of the finest surgeons in the country came out of medical college, did their internship, and then set up offices someplace to practice medicine, but back then if they did not meet with success in breaking into their chosen community, or if they were not considered good enough to get a position in a hospital, the last resort was always the Navy, where, it seemed, they could get a commission and make a living. Consequently, the standard of efficiency in a great many cases was very low. We used to speak of them as "the cross-eyed butchers." Those who didn't know enough to do surgery fell back on good old Epsom salts. It seemed that on some ships when a guy went to sickbay, the doctor would take his temperature and pulse, and then walk right over and pour out a glass of Epsom salts for him. One could always bet on Epsom salts!

A couple of days before we arrived in San Diego, Doc Saxton told the captain about my case, and of course, the captain knew nothing about it. On arrival in San Diego, Saxton took me and some other boys from our ship, to the flagship to see the two doctors there. When they examined me, one of the exclaimed, "My, you have a bad hernia there. We must get you right up to the Mare Island hospital for an operation; otherwise, strangulation might occur."

I told them how I had suffered all the time I was on the ship in Panama, and all the time we were down there, and that I couldn't stay on duty and perform my duties correctly and take all that pain any longer. They told me that the *Bennington* was leaving the next day and was to take all men from the fleet needing hospitalization. They said that they would notify my commanding officer to have me ready to go. I told them that I hated to go to Mare Island and have the same kind of job done on me as the first one, and that I would rather get out of the Navy on a medical discharge and have the operation performed by a civilian doctor—one that I could trust to be good, even if I had to pay for it myself. They tried to reassure me by saying that they didn't know if that same doctor was still at Mare Island, but that he probably wasn't there now; that all that they could do was to send me to the hospital. They had no authority to go further.

The Old Man sent for me when I got back to the ship. Doc Saxton was with me, and Doc told him what the doctors had said. He hadn't known anything about my condition and about my being in pain and had he known he might have been able to have made things easier for me. He asked me why I hadn't told him of the operation when I first came on the ship. I told him that I wasn't a crybaby. He said that he wished that there was some way that he could keep me on his ship.

"If you go to the hospital, I can't hang on to you," he said, "and someone else will get you when you go back to duty after an operation. We are going to miss you like everything, come next target practice."

The next day I was sent to the *Bennington* with my bag, along with the rest of the hospital patients. We were delivered by the *Bennington* on the wharf at Mare Island, where an ambulance met us and took up to the hospital

As I came in and registered, a doctor went by, and I looked at him, and who do you think it was? Yes, you guessed it! None other than the butcher Doctor Scrotum.

I was established in a ward and the next morning the doctors of the hospital, including the senior officer in charge of the hospital, came through on the usual morning inspection. I was a new victim, so they had to know all about me. The senior doctor asked the doctor of the ward what the matter with me was. He started to explain that I had a piece of skin that had broken loose in the groin but didn't amount to much, and that it would be a simple operation to remedy it. He told him that I had previously been operated on for a hernia. The senor doctor then asked where the original operation had been performed and who had performed it. The ward doctor told him that it had been performed at Mare Island and named the operating doctor who was among the group making the rounds. The senior doctor then asked me if I wanted to have another operation for it.

"Absolutely not!" I told him with emphasis. "If they do another job like the first one, I wouldn't have any insides left in me at all!"

The senior officer grinned at me, but old Scrotum would have liked to run a scalpel right through me. He told the senior doctor that it had been a fine job.

I spoke up and said, "The people who witnessed the operation didn't say that it was a fine job. A couple of them told me that it was the worst job they had ever seen, and if you want me to give you the details, I'll do that."

Scrotum spoke up and said, "He's not even ruptured right now."

I quickly told them that every doctor who had looked at me since I had left the hospital after the operation had told me that it was a bad hernia, and probably much worse than before I was operated on. "The doctors on the New York who sent me from San Diego up here to the hospital, called it a bad hernia," I told him, "and you should find that report on my papers of transfer."

The senior doctor turned to old Scrotum and said, "Let me see his papers of transfer."

Scrotum replied that they did not have them there and that he did not know at the moment where they were. The papers must have been *mysteriously* lost because I was told that they were never able to find them.

The next day the senior doctor called me to his office and asked me if I had changed my mind and decided to have an operation. I told him that I had not changed my mind and that I had definitely decided not to have an operation.

"Well," he said, "they will have to survey you and give you a medical discharge, and you won't be able to re-enlist."

I started to laugh and of course, that did not please him. He asked me what I intended to do if I got a medical discharge and I told him that I would go out and have a civilian specialist operate on me, "one who knows what he is doing." I also told him that if the newspapers got hold of this story that I had to come out of the Navy to get the proper operation, that the story would not sit so well with the general public, and I told him that my father happened to be a journalist. I believe that statement

had a lot to do with his actions later. As I have mentioned, those doctors stuck together, no matter what happened.

A week or so passed and I was getting a good rest after our hard work at target practice, and the food was much better than it had been on the ship. I began to feel better and took on a little weight. Then they notified me that a chief hospital steward would take me to San Francisco where I would have a truss fitted to me.

What in the world do I need a truss for if I have no hernia? I thought, but I didn't voice it because I would be very glad to get that truss. All the doctors outside of the Mare Island hospital who had examined me and pronounced it a bad case of hernia, had warned me against strangulation, saying that I should get a truss on there as soon as possible if I did not have an operation at once. The trusses were not as comfortable nor as scientifically made as those of today, but one could do moderate work wearing one, without any danger of strangulation. I was glad to have my anxiety relieved by getting that truss.

I remained at the hospital for about a month, resting, enjoying my truss, and taking on weight from the good hospital food, before I received orders to report to the *Independence* for duty.

The Nightmare Captain of the *Perry*

It was pleasant on the *Independence* and I had nothing to do there but rest. However, had I known what was ahead of me, I wouldn't have slept as well as I did. After putting nearly six years in the Navy and enjoying all of it, getting along as well any anyone could who started as a third-class apprentice boy, the highlights of my career so far included being promoted ahead of time; being interested in my work; liking practically all the crew and officers that I had ever been with; not remembering a disagreeable word or reprimand of an officer during all that time; having trained and coxswained two race boats; managed and helped train two boxing champions of the fleet; played some baseball with the team of the ship; enjoyed the finest fishing; and seeing many interesting sights. Unfortunately, I drew one of the most disagreeable berths and captains of the United States Navy at that time. Instead of being interesting and enjoyable, it was hell from then on until my time was out.

Ever since I had been in the hospital and around the Bay area, I had been hearing stories about the captain of the *Perry* and what a dreadful ship the *Perry* was, and nothing good about her captain, and so on. I heard that she had a full change of crew about every two months and I don't remember the exact number of court-martials for practically nothing that the captain had given his men. It seemed that if the men didn't get court-martialed, their captain made it so miserable for them that they ran away, lots of them staying out of the service entirely; others waited until the ship got out to sea before they reported back to the Guardo.

The *Perry*'s captain was only a two-striper, a little scrawny man with red, shaggy whiskers, and he always looked untidy. I often wondered how he got through Annapolis in that

rig. He was too stingy to go ashore and have his whiskers trimmed by a barber, so he made his colored messenger boy do the job. He didn't have to pay him anything, and it looked like it, too! I said to myself, surely, they can't have men in the Navy like that, in command of ships. But I had to eat them "thar" words before I got through.

He had so many court-martials while his ship was being repaired in the Navy Yard, that Admiral McCullough, who was known as the blue-jackets' admiral, and who was admiral at the Navy Yard at Mare Island, heard about this officer, and to satisfy himself, he came down without being announced and sat in at one of the court-martials. After that, every man who was court-martialed was represented by Admiral McCullough as his counsel. Well, of course, there were no more convictions and I imagine that the captain's record got to Washington because he received notice from the Navy Department, Bureau of Navigation, that there would be no more court-martials conducted by him on his ship approved until the matter was thoroughly investigated. That killed the court-martial business on that ship, but the captain just worked harder at giving the men other punishment and making life hell in general for the whole crew. He had his original ship's writer who had joined the ship when she was commissioned, and oh, how he hated that captain who was generally known as "Pink Whiskers" or "Captain Scraggly."

Ordinarily in the Navy they addressed the commander as "Captain" regardless of his Navy rank, and if they liked him, they would speak of him to one another as "The Skipper," and if they liked and respected him more as time went on, he was always called "The Old Man" regardless of his age.

As events in my life were shaped, one day while I was still on the *Independence*, I was serenely walking up and down by the

quarterdeck, talking to the quartermaster on watch, when a ship down the channel hove-in-sight meaning her sail was in view, and she looked very familiar to me.

"There's my old ship," I said to the quartermaster, "the *Paul Jones*."

"No such luck!" he answered. "That's the pink-whiskered wonder—the hell-ship, *Perry* which is a twin to the *Paul Jones*. But anyway, we won't be worried with him for long. He's so scared of Admiral McCullough that he shakes in his pants when he sees him."

So, I didn't get scared. I didn't know any reason why I should be. Then the quartermaster said, "You better run away right now. You better go ashore and keep on going until that fellow gets out of the Bay area. I understand that he's short a quartermaster. He's always short something, mostly brains, I think. Anyway, you better beat it."

Well, then it did worry me. Sure enough, within an hour that fellow with the pink whiskers came aboard the *Independence* and went into the ship's writer's office. The quartermaster told me that I better go crawl under the sails and hide for two or three days. "I'll try and bring you food and water," he said.

This pink-whiskered man was in the office quite a while before he came out and left the ship. Then the ship's writer came out and when he saw me sitting close to the office he came over to me and said, "I'm sorry, kid, but it looks like you're doomed."

"Well, I'm not afraid of any of them," I said as I looked up at him. "Officers of other ships have always treated me fine, although some of them were considered hard to get along with."

"Well, all I can say is that it's a good thing that you have less than a year to go. He went through the records and spotted you. He saw that you were off the *Paul Jones* and had broken all records on the semi-automatic six pounders, and his mouth

began to water. If I had had warning and had known what he was after, I might have been able to hide those records. But, I think that he had been tipped off by somebody that you were on the *Independence*."

I felt pretty low that night when I turned in, and the next morning I was taken from the *Independence* to the *Perry*, the only man that he had grabbed. When I reported to the officer of the deck, he said, "The captain wants to see you. I'll notify him that you are here."

The captain came out and began to give me a patriotic talk about what a fine ship he had, and everybody was on their toes, and how he expected the same kind of cooperation from me, and that he wanted me to act as chief quartermaster. I was stunned! I had enough sense to just keep my mouth closed and when he finished, I went forward with my bag and hammock to the crew's quarters.

There I found an old sheepherder whom I had met the first time I was ever on the *Independence*. As soon as he learned that I was to be chief quartermaster he said, "Here I'm storekeeper and my storeroom is on the next deck below, down this booby-hatch. The boy who had your job and ran away, used to sleep down there with me. I have two nice mattresses in the storeroom and you'll get more sleep and quiet there than you would in the crew's quarters. If you'd like to join me, I'll be glad to have you."

I thanked him, and I was truly glad to have a place to get out of the way of everybody when I wanted to. I took my gear and went below with the storekeeper who was called "Jack of the Dust." While I was stowing my gear, he began telling me about the crew. He warned me especially about the negro chap who was the captain's mess boy and personal servant and that he was also his stool-pigeon. This mess boy knew that the more indispensable he was to the captain, the better he would be

294

treated, so he took everything he heard to the captain and that the crew knew it.

The mess boy would get in his bunk in the crew's quarters and pretend to be reading, and the crew, with a wink and tongue in cheek, would tell the most blood-curdling stories of how they were going to get rid of the captain. He told about one night when they hatched a really good story about how they were going to coax the captain up on the high fo'c'sle and point down to the bow of the ship. The man with him was to throw his weight against the captain and sort of boost him right over the side, hoping he would hit his head on the anchor, but if he didn't he would drown anyway.

After this recital of the destruction of the captain, the negro got up and casually strolled aft. The boys winked and after he was out of earshot had a good laugh. The boys all knew that the captain heard the story because he would never go up on the fo'c'sle but always sent his junior officer when there were any questions or need for an officer's attention.

The storekeeper was my friend and he wanted me to know what was going on, and he gave it to me straight before I got any other versions to confuse me.

By this time, I had my gear stowed and so I went up on the bridge, and in the conning tower I found the other two quartermasters, and they were all third class and none of them had ever been rated since they had been on the ship. It seemed that they had been there ever since the ship had gone into commission. They looked to me like first-class men. I asked them, "How come none of you boys ever got an advance in rating since you came on this ship?"

"Old Pink Whiskers never advances *anybody*. He wouldn't advance his own mother. Wait until you're with him for a while and you'll understand." They spoke with feeling and I could see how much those quartermasters hated him. I knew

then that this was going to be the toughest job I had ever run into.

I had just had time to settle in when the word was passed by the boatswain's mate, "All hands on deck! Let go lines!" Being exactly like the *Paul Jones*, it was no trick for me to go in and test the steering engine and do the other things preparatory to getting under way. During this operation, I suggested to one of the quartermasters that the ship was not making a long stay at the Navy Yard. He laughed and said that the skipper didn't stay there five minutes longer than he had to because he was too scared of Admiral McCullough.

The Starving Russians

We left Mare Island and went down to San Francisco Bay where we anchored in our regular anchorage. Late in the afternoon, a large three-stack clipper-bow merchant marine-built ship came into port and anchored not far from us. As she came in, we got the glasses on her flag, which was strange to us, and we decided that she was Russian. Naturally, we were very interested in her. She was a big, sleek ship and looked like she had quite a bit of speed in her, but she was as dirty as a pigeon on the outside, cut to rust and lack of paint. She hadn't been anchored more than half an hour before her commander came over in his gig to board us. He was received by side-boys and old Pink Whiskers and the officer of the deck met him at the gangway. They all went below to the wardroom.

The ship's writer, whose office was next to the wardroom, was able to hear all that went on, and, according to him, the Russian commander told quite a story. It seems that his vessel had been converted to a transport. When the Japanese Admiral Togo jumped the Russians off the coast of Japan, this ship started full speed to get out of there. They could tell that the Russians were getting hell knocked out of them, while they were still able to see the progress of the battle, so the skipper just put on all the speed he had and headed for San Francisco.

He said that he didn't believe that he had over ten tons of coal in the bunkers and that it was nip-and-tuck whether they made it to San Francisco, or not. They saw that they were going to run short of coal and they did everything to economize, running at their most efficient speed. Fortunately, they got a nice, fair wind, especially after they passed Honolulu, which was probably all that saved them.

297

According to International Law in those days, a ship at war could come into a neutral country and stay forty-eight hours, I believe, to take on fuel and necessary food supplies, and if they ran over that time, they were supposed to be seized by the neutral country and impounded until the war was over.

This ship immediately notified Russia and reported their whereabouts and predicament and asked for orders. Knowing what I later learned, which was how Togo annihilated that Russian fleet, I don't imagine that the "powers that be" in Russia cared a damn what became of her. It was not until the next day that they got their orders. However, in the meantime, we received orders from the fleet commander to guard her at all times and not allow any official communications to go on with officials of her country. She evidently had been quite a fast and luxurious passenger ship before the Russian government commandeered her for a navy transport.

A rather amusing thing happened when the community officer came aboard our ship. On this class of destroyers that I was on, we ate our meals on the main deck, unprotected by any bulkheads or anything else except a life-railing at the side. When the Russian captain's gig came alongside, we were just eating supper and, boy, you could just see how hungry those fellows were. It was Sunday supper, if I remember right, and we usually got a fairly good meal in port. Everyone had an orange and an apple for their dessert. The Russians were especially attracted by our supper and what we were eating. Some of our boys left the table and were eating their apples or oranges over by the rail. Every Russian in that boat had his eye on us.

One of our boys at the rail made a motion to throw one down to the Russian boys on the boat, and the joyful expression that came over his face was really something to see. It was so pathetic that he threw his orange down to the fellow. The rest of our boys began to take an interest then and they all went to

the rail and threw down all the fruit that they had not taken a bite out of themselves. When they ran out of fruit, they threw cookies, and then they began making sandwiches out of our meat and good fresh bread that was left on the table. Boy, oh boy! I don't suppose those fellows ever played baseball, but they were sure good enough, because they never missed a catch!

The coxswain of the Russian gig could speak a little English and he called up and thanked everybody and said that they hadn't had enough to eat since they left the battle, that they were hungry all the time. To see them tear into that food, well, it was almost laughable, in fact, everybody was laughing on our ship and on the Russian gig. I don't know if Pink Whiskers ever got wind of what happened or not. If he had, he would have tried to get a stomach pump and pump the poor Russians stomachs out! Not that he had anything against the Russians, but it was against Naval regulations.

That night we anchored a little closer to the Russian vessel, and an electrician and a quartermaster were on watch at all times at the searchlight, which was operating back and forth so that no boats could approach her without first getting our permission, and no boats could leave her unknown to us. The next day we received orders from the fleet commander to accompany her to Mare Island Navy Yard where she would be interned.

⚓

The morning after we arrived at the Navy Yard, I reported to the hospital steward, then in charge of the medical corps of the ship, that I was in great pain from my hernia, and asked to be sent back to the hospital for examination but not with my papers, so again I got a free ride in the ambulance to the

hospital, and when I arrived there I went into the office and a doctor whom I knew from past hospitalization, came in and asked me what was the matter with me. I told him that the pain from the hernia was more than I could stand and that I couldn't carry on my duties in that condition. He told me that I had been up there just last month, and he said that he thought they were rid of me. He asked me what they had done to me. I told him that they had sent me to San Francisco with a hospital steward to buy me a truss, which hurt me almost as badly as the hernia did without the truss.

"I see that Dr. Scrotum was the doctor who operated on you the first time," he said.

I admitted that he was correct.

"Well," he said, "I'll get in touch with him. You go in the ward and sit down they'll let you know what to do."

In a little while Dr. Scrotum showed up, looking mad as hell, and wanted to know what I was doing there. I told him that I had been sent up from the ship because I was in such pain with the hernia.

"You haven't any hernia," he demanded.

"Every doctor who has examined me except you has said that it is a hernia," I replied.

"Well, we got you a truss for it anyway. Don't you wear that truss?" he asked.

"Yes, when I am walking around and am on my feet I wear it to prevent a strangulated hernia, but it hurts me almost as bad as when I don't wear any truss."

"I'm not going to order you to the hospital here," he said. "You go back to the ship where you belong. I don't know why you came up here, anyway."

I answered, "Well, I do! I write up the log on that ship and this is going in the log and will be brought out as evidence against you someday." I was riled up and I thought he was going

to take a swipe at me, and I was just ready to go into action myself if he had, although he weighed about two hundred and fifty pounds to my one hundred and forty-nine pounds. I would have enjoyed it while it I lasted. I think I was a little disappointed because he didn't hit me, but he called the ambulance and the ambulance took me back to the ship. Later that day I saw old Doc Scrotum down on the dock talking to Pink Whiskers and I knew that boded no good for me.

My First and Only Reprimand

And so, I was again on the *Perry* when she went back to San Francisco Bay. Pink Whiskers wouldn't stay there one second longer than he had to because he knew Admiral McCullough was having him watched. I was not happy with the outcome of my trip to the hospital and it was my intention to go up to that hospital every time I came into Mare Island during the rest of my cruise, or if old Scrotum was up there, but I was released from the service before I ever got the chance to go there again.

We went to San Francisco, but early the next morning we had to go back to Mare Island because we needed a spare part for the engine room. The ship got away so that we would arrive just as the men were going to work. As I said, Pink Whiskers didn't want to stay around there any longer than he had to.

The ship headed into the wharf at Mare Island to make the spring-lines and head-lines fast both fore and aft. I had been called for the eight-to-twelve morning watch and had put on my high hip boots because the crew was trying to wash down, and that crew was not very careful where they threw the water. I didn't want to get my pants and shoes all wet. Pink Whiskers saw me standing the watch and he said to me, "Take off those boots and put your shoes and socks on."

"Yes, sir," I answered.

Then he dodged down below to the wardroom. The ensign came along at that moment and said to me, "Come out here with me on the dock with the spring-line a moment and give me a hand with it."

"The captain just told me to go and take off my boots and put on my shoes and socks."

"He won't mind if you come along and give me a hand," he said. "It will only take a minute."

"Alright, if he won't mind I'll come out and help you."

After we slackened the spring-line I came aboard, and the captain was standing there watching me. He said, "I told you to take off those boots."

"I intended to do so, sir, and had started when the ensign came by and asked me to help him slacken the spring-line. I told him that I had orders from you to take off my boots and put on my socks and shoes, and he said that you wouldn't mind if I just went over and helped him slacken the spring-line, and so I helped him."

The captain said, "Well, I am now going to bring you before me for disobedience of orders. I told you when you came on this ship that I would spoil that good record of yours. Now I have succeeded."

I turned to the ensign and said, "Then this was all a put-up job, was it?" and they both laughed at me. Then I said, "The men forward are not going to have any love for you for pulling this thing on me. They already call you The Insect."

"Yes," he said, "but I know enough to obey orders, which you didn't do. A man of my rank is used to being called an insect. They always call an ensign an insect."

"Not on the ships I've been on, they didn't," I replied.

And thus, ended my perfect record for obedience and Pink Whiskers succeeded in accomplishing his purpose. It nearly broke my heart because I had always wanted to go through my enlistment with a perfect record.

Target Practice on the *Perry*

After we had been in San Francisco a few days, we received orders from the fleet commander at San Diego to proceed immediately to Magdalena Bay for target practice. We just had time to get down there and complete our practice before our yearly time had expired. That must have hit Pink Whiskers right between the eyes because I fully believe that he thought he was going to get out of the annual target practice that year. Neither he nor the crew had even looked at a gun since the ship had been in commission. We pulled out for Magdalena Bay at once.

After leaving San Francisco I had the equipment of the bridge placed in its usual and proper place. Part of this equipment of the bridge included a large megaphone which the captain used a lot. He loved to stand up on the bridge and bawl the men out in that squeaky voice of his. He had been using that megaphone just before we went through the Golden Gate and instead of setting it down where it belonged, out of the wind and in the shelter of the bridge-dodger, he lazily set it down on the chart board while he was laying his courses out.

That was alright while we were in the shelter of the Gate, but as soon as we hit the roll of the sea and the northwestern blowing down the coast, the megaphone took off. It sailed gracefully off our bridge, out onto the sea where it made a beautiful landing, bobbed a farewell, and sank beneath the sea to finish its career in Davy Jones Locker. Pink Whiskers was startled when it took off and he turned sharply to me and said, "Why did you put that megaphone up there on the chart board?"

"Why, I never touched that megaphone after I put it in its proper place and the ship got under way," I told him, rather indignantly, I'm afraid.

"How did it get up there then, if you didn't put it up there?" he asked.

"The last time you used it you set it up there," I told him, "and I was watching you when you did it."

He didn't like this, and he walked around the three-inch gun on the bridge a couple of times, muttering to himself. He finally came back and cooled off enough to resume his work, but he had to have the last word by saying that he knew very well that I had put it up there. He was probably trying to figure out if he could court-martial me, but because I was the only qualified gun-pointer on his ship that might have had something to do with his changing his mind. Unfortunately, the man at the wheel let his sense of humor get away and every time the captain looked at him, he was laughing, which made the situation even worse.

As soon as we were on our way down the coast, he set about trying to get his division heads to organize gun crews. It was a sorry business and when I saw them in practice at loading, I went into the heads where I would not be seen and leaned my head against my arms and got out all the laughs I had in me.

The biggest part of his crew was not only ignorant of anything pertaining to target practice, but they had no desire to do it. There was no spirit, no incentive, and the effort made was a sorry-looking spectacle. The thought came to my mind that this was the character who spoke to me about beating the record of the *Paul Jones* next target practice! Every time I thought about it, I laughed.

With a fair wind and sea, we made good time to Magdalena Bay and we immediately got ready to get into target practice. It was a dismal affair. At times I almost felt sorry for him. I remember that I had no desire to hit anything, nor even qualify. I would still hold my qualification which, I believe, lasted two years. I was sure that he couldn't take that away from me. Of course, we didn't have the fine new sights that Captain

Davison developed. The *Perry* was using the old-style open sights that the captain of the *Paul Jones* discarded. There were only two six-pounders semi-automatics that qualified at all out of the twelve guns on the ship. I happened to be one of those and I just squeezed in under the wire and qualified, which was very much of a surprise to me because I went at it in a half-hearted way. One other six-pounder qualified.

The three-inch guns made a disgraceful record, but the crew had no practice since they had been on the ship. Ninety percent of them had never fired a big gun in their lives.

After target practice was finished, we got out of the bay and started north again for San Francisco. In a way I felt sorry for Pink Whiskers. The day after leaving Magdalena I was on the bridge doing my usual duties and he came up and said to me, "You didn't do much in this last target practice, did you?"

"No, sir," I replied, looking him right in the eye.

"How was it that you broke the world's record on the *Paul Jones*, firing twenty-eight shots a minute, with eighteen bullseyes and the rest hits?"

I looked squarely at him and said, "There was a great difference between that target practice and this one. One of the main difference was that Captain Davison had special peep-sights made for all the guns and, besides that, Captain Davison gave us inspiration, encouragement, and a great desire to win those trophies. He worked as hard as any of us at long hours of practice."

He looked at me for a long time. I could see the hate-daggers coming out of his eyes. Finally, he gave a couple of ungentlemanly snorts and went down the ladder as fast as he could go, headed for his wardroom. By that time the man at the wheel was shaking with hearty laughter, and even the officer of the deck couldn't conceal his delight, and he let out a snicker,

but when I looked in his direction he hastily tried to wipe the smile off his face.

Mike, the Fireman

All went well on the trip back, as well as could be expected on a hell-ship, or more commonly known as a madhouse. We received word from Mare Island that certain spare parts for the engine were finished. The captain gave liberty that afternoon or evening and a large part of the crew went ashore, including one great, big, red-headed Irish fireman who had a luxurious red mustache. They were given all-night liberty but many of the boys came back to the ship in shore boats manned by a civilian who made his living in this way. I had the deck watch from eight to twelve midnight. A shore boat came alongside with this big Irishman aboard, who was returning from liberty. I noticed that he looked in the captain's quarters as he went by and saw the captain sitting at his table, evidently absorbed in something. When the Irishman reported aboard, I could see that it wasn't all milk that he had been drinking ashore, and I knew that he had lots of trouble with Pink Whiskers. He checked in with me and I gave him a clean bill of arrival.

"I see that old Whiskers is still up," he said as he reported to me.

"I hadn't noticed," I replied. "I guess he is; his light's still burning." I could see that the Irishman had something on his mind and I wasn't anxious to get in an argument with him in the condition he was in, so I dropped the remark that he would have to excuse me as it was time for me to go forward to inspect my prisoners.

We had two men forward in the brig. They had been put in double irons as they had evidently tangled with Pink Whiskers and had incurred his violent displeasure. It was the duty of the officer of the deck to inspect or look in on them once or twice each watch. The time was due for me to do this.

Sometimes their friends smuggled them a bottle of liquor, or something else which was forbidden and for this reason they were inspected at least once each watch, if not more often. I was supposed to have a quartermaster to help me since I was standing the watch for the officer of the deck, but as Pink Whiskers had not assigned one, I had to do everything myself.

I took my time in inspecting the prisoners, chatting a few minutes with them, and then locking the door and going aft. When I got on deck I heard the strangest hollering. It sounded like Pink Whiskers yelling for help or calling for the officer of the deck or quartermaster. I hurried as fast as I could, and I got down there just as Mike, the fireman, was running him around the conning tower, trying to catch him. I grabbed Mike by the arm and managed to stop him, and I asked him what he was doing, chasing the captain around like that.

"Well, if I had caught him I was going to throw him overboard! And I will yet, before I get off this ship!"

In the meantime, Pink Whiskers had darted below to his stateroom and locked the door. I took Mike forward by the arm and got him to the crew's quarters and talked to him, telling him that he would get into very serious trouble if he didn't undress and get in his bunk and be quiet as a mouse.

He started to laugh. "I caught him in the wardroom and chased him around the table and told him that I was going to throw him overboard and drown him. I told him that he wouldn't make life so miserable on any other ship again. He started to yell for help, calling for the quartermaster and the officer of the deck, then he made it to the door and dashed up the companionway and around the conning tower, yelling the whole time," and Mike just laughed softly to himself, as if he relished every bit of the picture he painted. It was a lucky thing for Mike that the other officer was ashore just then. I left Mike

feeling satisfied with himself and settling down for the night, and I went aft to the conning tower and resumed my watch.

Soon Pink Whiskers stuck his nose around the conning tower to make sure that the wild Irishman wasn't around, and he asked me where I was when he was attacked by that wild man. I told him that Mike had reported in, so I went forward to inspect the prisoners. He asked me if I knew that Mike was looking for him to attack him, and I assured him that I knew nothing of Mike's plan and thought that he was going forward to go to bed. He strode over to the rough logbook, then turned around sharply and asked me who else had seen all this. I told him that I was the only one who knew anything about it and that I knew only what he had told me. He gave me one of his long, searching looks, as if to tell me that I was the biggest liar on earth. When I asked him if he wanted it written up in the log, he studied and studied for quite a while, then he said, "No. Unless I give you orders, say nothing about it." He then turned and went below. Of course, the crew all got it from the scuttlebutt the next morning, but I don't think he knew it.

Going Like Hell, Love Dick

A day or so after this, we had a payday and after everyone had been paid, Dick Lowe, one of the ship's crew, came to me and said, "I'm going on liberty when the liberty party goes ashore. Keep your eyes on Pink Whiskers and the messenger boys."

"What's up?" I asked him.

He just reached over and shook my hand and said, "Goodbye, Steve, and good luck to you. I'll let you figure it out for yourself."

It dawned on me then, what was going to happen. After the liberty party went ashore and along towards evening, a shore-boat came pulling over toward the ship from the San Francisco landing, with a messenger boy in it. Pink Whiskers was expecting a telegram from either Washington or the fleet commander, with orders. The messenger boy came up on the gangway and handed the message to Pink Whiskers and had him sign for it and he said it was sent "collect." The officer grumbled about it but paid for it. It was not the usual procedure, but it happened sometimes. The messenger waited in case there was to be an answer, and Pink Whiskers read the message. I could tell from his expression that he was very displeased, and he crumpled the message up and threw it down by the conning tower and it rolled underneath as he turned on his heel and went below. After he was gone, I went over and fished the message out and looked at it. It said, "Two hundred miles away and going like hell! Love, Dick Lowe."

The messenger boy went ashore and in about two hours another boat came out with a messenger boy aboard and he came up the gangway with a message for the captain. The quartermaster on watch went down and told him that there was

311

a boy up there with a telegram, so he came up, and after paying the charges he took the message and tore it open, read it, and crumpled it up and threw it away. It landed near the torpedo tube, but he was indifferent as to where it landed, and he hastened below again. I retrieved this message, too. This one was just like the other one only he was "three hundred miles away and going like hell—Love, Dick." I took both messages forward with me and the crew enjoyed them immensely. The only trouble was that his stool-pigeon, the negro mess-boy, heard it and got up and went aft. I knew that the messages wouldn't get into my hands again.

Now, everybody was looking out for the shore-boats with messenger boys. In another couple of hours here came another boat with a messenger boy, and again the captain had to pay for that message, but this time he didn't crush it in a ball and throw it on deck. He told the messenger boy that he would receive no more messages collect. Well, the boy said that he just received them from the office and if they told him to take them over to the ship, he would be disobeying orders if he didn't bring them over.

"Well," said Pink Whiskers, "I won't pay for any more of them!"

So, it went along for about three hours more and the boat came over with a messenger boy in it. I noticed that this boy was rather mean-looking and large for a messenger boy. He came up the gangway and the quartermaster went below and told Pink Whiskers that there was a boy up there with a telegram for him—collect. He told the quartermaster that he wouldn't receive them and to send it back to the telegraph office. The quartermaster delivered that message to the messenger boy and the messenger boy said, "You tell him that he had better come up here and receive this message. That is what I was sent over

here for, to deliver this message to him, and I'm going to stay here until he receives it, if I have to stay here all night."

The quartermaster went down and told the captain what the messenger boy had said, and he finally came up. The messenger boy looked very tough like he might be from Telegraph Hill. I wouldn't have liked to tangle with him myself. He looked like he could lick his weight in wildcats. Pink Whiskers sized him up and he dug in his pocket and gave the boy the money for the message. He opened the telegram and it was another one, although he didn't throw it where we could look at it. He asked the messenger boy to wait a minute while he went below to write out a communication for him to take back to the telegraph office. I presume that he instructed the telegraph office to refuse any more telegrams which came collect, signed by that particular party. The messenger boy left, and we didn't have any more of them come out to the ship that night. It was lots of fun while it lasted.

The next morning about nine o'clock a boat came over with a messenger boy in it, and this message wasn't collect. Pink Whiskers came up and signed for it and glanced at it, and he told the messenger boy that there would be no reply, and he went below. It wasn't long before the scuttlebutt informed us that it was orders from the Navy Department in Washington, D.C., ordering us to go north, making Ketchikan the first port of call and instructing us to spend the Fourth of July there.

Fourth of July in Ketchikan

We learned that there was a tentative schedule for Alaska by way of the Inland Passage, as far as Skagway, which is practically the end of the of the Inland Passage. There was immediate activity aboard the ship as we prepared for sea. Some of the boys didn't come back when their liberty was up at seven o'clock that morning. They must have gotten word that we were going to sea and they conveniently missed the boat, hoping that they could report back to the *Independence* after the boat had left, and maybe be sent to another ship, which is just what happened to most of them. Therefore, we were short-handed when we left.

One would have had to be on destroyers to really understand how uncomfortable they can be at sea in heavy weather, especially heading into it. The modern destroyer of today is built to overcome those difficulties, but we had practically no protection from the sea on deck in heavy weather. As soon as we were out of the Gate, we plunged right into that old nor'wester that blows so hard during the summer months. All we could do was rig lifelines on deck so any of the crew would have something more to hold on to in case he was washed to the side of the ship. Then we just settled down to plugging along into it, and not at full speed, either. I could stand at the forward conning tower and watch her wiggle up and down like a snake. The sea was so heavy, and the wind so strong, that we had to abandon the top bridge because it was covered with water and spray, having to do our steering in the forward conning tower where there was another wheel for just this purpose. Of course, no tables were set for meals. The corn wooly {creamed chip beef} would have been washed overboard and undoubtedly would have resulted in a lot of sick sharks!

The galley was amidships and each one of us took his plate and cup to the galley where the cook doled out our food onto the plate, then we'd make a run for it to get under cover, away from the sea, as the deck was awash most of the time. Most of the crew went into the crews' quarters and wound a leg around a stanchion, then disregarding all the table manners, would get their food downed. In those day the proverbial tin can, as destroyers were called, were considered the most uncomfortable navy ships afloat.

Generally, at that time of the year this strong northwester and heavy sea would last about three days and then ease up to get a rest to stir up another one. We picked up an Inland Passage pilot at Port Angeles. He took us safely to our anchorage in Ketchikan, where we arrived in the early afternoon of July the third. After a miserable, rough trip up the coast, we were very thankful to reach the Inland Passage where we could be in smooth weather and dry off. I think that if the boys could have run away at Ketchikan and gotten away from there, we would have lost about half the crew. We had a large percentage of rookies and green men aboard, and many of them were seasick the whole trip up. Some of them never ate a bite of anything during the trip north and just subsisted on hot coffee.

A short time after we anchored at Ketchikan, all kinds of small boats and canoes, some made from animal skins called *wikiups,* came swarming out to the ship, bringing a great big welcoming smile on their faces. There were Indian men and women, cannery workers, loggers, and fishermen. All had come to Ketchikan for the Fourth of July. I never saw such a nondescript bunch of boats around one poor old tin can like that destroyer. We couldn't keep them off the boat. They swarmed up on the boat from all directions. There was no use telling them to get off because they wouldn't. They just wanted to shake hands and be friendly. A great many of the men who came

over had a quart of whisky in the hip pocket and they saw no reason why we shouldn't have a drink with them.

Pink Whiskers nearly went crazy. He ordered the officer of the deck to have them all put off; he wanted to wash down and clean up the ship, but he might as well have talked to a totem pole for all the attention they paid to him. He went up the deck with his other officer, ordering the people ashore, but they would just stick out their hands and want to shake hands. The other officer saw the funny side of it and began to laugh. He just couldn't help himself. Finally, Pink Whiskers turned about and went down to his wardroom. Of course, they wanted the boys to come ashore with them, but Pink Whiskers had ruled against any liberty that night because he wanted to get the ship cleaned up. When the men of the crew came to ask the officer of the deck if they could have liberty that night, they were told of the orders the captain had given. The boatswain's mate turned on the hose and the deckhands made the best attempt they could to wash the ship down and get some of the grime off her, but it was a poor job.

Finally, it began getting late and the crowd started leaving in their little boats and headed for shore. It didn't take an FBI man or a secret service operator to tell that some of those little boats had one of our crew covered up and out of sight in them. I know very well that there was quite a number of them that went ashore. They didn't have to take any money with them. Their money wasn't worth anything up there where the people seemed to feel that they had asked the Navy Department to send this man-of-war up for the Fourth of July celebration, and by the shades of *John Paul Jones*, it was theirs while it was there. I know that the quartermaster on the morning watch (four to eight) told me that it was amazing how many little boats came out and delivered somebody aboard about daylight. I don't

know what would have happened if Pink Whiskers had free reign to court-martial everybody. That was one time he was stumped!

We got the ship cleaned up that morning before breakfast and all those men that could be spared could go ashore about nine o'clock to participate in the sporting events. It was great fun watching them try to catch the greased pig or climb a pole which was attached to the end of the wharf and slanted out over the water. It was well-greased, too. They must have used at least half a whale to grease that pole. More than one contestant got a good dunking when he slipped off. The fellow who could climb out on the pole and bring back the apple that was stuck out there, won a quart of whiskey for the prize and received thunderous applause from the crowd that had gathered to watch the fun.

I didn't go ashore. I felt that I might just as well give my place up to one of the boys who really wanted to go and take part in the fun. My time would be up in about a month, so I didn't care much about going ashore. But from all appearances, they must have all had a wonderful time. All day long these nondescript small boats came alongside, filled with civilian men and women, and they came aboard and went all over the ship. Pink Whiskers had a guard posted at the top of the stairs leading to the wardroom but that did about as much good as if he had posted a totem pole there. The guard would try to stop them by putting his hand out, and they would immediately grab it and shake hands with him, then scoot down into the officers' quarters.

Finally, when the other officer asked Pink Whiskers if he could go ashore since he was not doing any good aboard, the captain said, "Yes, let us both get off the ship before I go crazy. I'll see if the pilot will stay aboard and I'll order one engineer to stay aboard, the boatswain's mate, and the chief quartermaster, and we'll just get off the ship ourselves. But lock everything up

that you value in your room." All of which was done, and they went ashore.

The pilot came aft to the quarter deck where there were some chairs, and started to talk to me, as I had the deck. His conversation was very interesting because he told me he had started when he was a youngster, as an apprentice pilot, and I think that at that time they had to spend seven years under the direction of the other pilots before they could take a ship alone. The waters of the Inland Passage are very treacherous at times and in places the channel is quite narrow and deep. In some of those dangerous places there were jagged rocks that they would hit if they were too far out of the channel. Therefore, it takes the finest piloting that I have ever seen up there, especially when the weather is thick and misty or hazy. The channel was not well marked by navigation lights and lighthouses, either.

In foggy weather the pilot keeps right on going unless the captain demands that he anchor, which is rarely done. The pilot will navigate by the echo of the steam whistle. He will ask everyone on the bridge to be as quiet as possible, then he will lean out forward over the bridge-dodger and sound a long blast of the whistle. He then puts his hand to his ear and listens for the echo. There is one thing the average person is not aware of and that is that the fog makes an echo. Some of these places where he passed through by the echo may have a tide of eight or nine knots running, although they try to hit those dangerous places at a safer speed when a tide is running. The ordinary sea-faring navigator is thrilled the first time he makes that trip under the tutelage of a good, experienced pilot.

The bones of many ships lie at the bottom of that Inland Passage. I remember in my span of sea-faring life, many tragedies of ships hitting the rocks or other mishaps on the Inland Passage. In a great number of them it was not just the ship that was lost, but also the passengers and crew. Believe me, I never did crave

to run up the Inland Passage in command of a ship. I turned down several opportunities.

I asked him why he didn't go ashore with the bunch and participate in the celebration and he said, "Those kinds of celebrations are not new to me, and I want a clear head when I wake up in the morning. I know practically every Old Timer over in that town tonight, and they would want me to make the rounds with them. I had better turn in and get a good rest and if anything should not be alright, call me at once and I will give you a hand. Those festivities will probably last all night."

The Furry Hospitality Gifts

About twelve-thirty the boys began drifting back to the ship. We had one of our boats ashore with a crew to row them back, but it seemed like every other boat in Alaska was down there to help bring them back if they wished to come. The first boat to come back was one of our cutters with five or six boys in the boat. There was something else in that boat which walked like a man but wasn't a man. I thought when I first saw it that it might be a Russian, but it turned out to be a half-grown bear. As the evening progressed everyone became more exuberant. Besides buying drinks for the boys and providing a band and music for dancing, they served them all the local goodies that are a part of that country, such as smoked salmon, all kinds of pickled fish, and venison roast. When the boys were ready to leave, these hospitable people insisted on giving their pet bear for a ship's mascot. It seemed that the giving away their pet bear was the ultimate in hospitality. They might give you their wife, but the supreme sacrifice was their pet bear.

The boys started up the gangway and two boys had the bear with a line on each side of its neck. The rest of the boys were pushing from behind. The bear's education in maritime affairs had been sadly neglected. It was very evident that there was no Annapolis for bears in Alaska. This bear was at a good-natured age and he had undoubtedly been well-treated because he was willing to do his part and oblige the boys.

When they got him up on deck, I questioned the boys, "What did you do, swipe somebody's bear?"

"No," they answered. "He's to be our mascot! The owner of the Malamute Saloon owned him and kept him tied up in the backyard of the saloon. He's everybody's friend."

"Well," I suggested, "it seems to me that we have enough whiskers on this ship without importing some more from shore."

"But this fellow's whiskers are black, not pink, so he'll be alright. We'll be the only ship in the fleet that has a mascot like this."

I didn't know what to do. I hadn't had any orders *not* to allow bears aboard the ship. It seemed that everything else was allowed aboard. I told the boys to tie him up well, forward of the engine-room hatch. I had a feeling that things would be popping when Pink Whiskers got aboard. This was only the beginning!

From then on until three or three-thirty in the morning when it was beginning to get light, every boat that came with a liberty party on it, whether it was our own boat or a fisherman's boat, brought a bear mascot back on it. Things were so muddled up by that time that I never did keep track of how many came aboard. Despite all that I could do or say, they wouldn't take them back, and they had to be tied up some place, so we had bears on deck, tied up from stern to bow. You couldn't walk anywhere on deck without shoving a bear out of the way. Some of them looked like they didn't have very sweet dispositions, either. Two or three of them got loose from their lines and went into the crews' quarters and occupied empty bunks. The whole ship was just lousy with bears. I had never imagined that anything like that could happen, but there it was! One or two of them got lonesome for human companionship and came back on the quarterdeck where I was on watch and curled up on the deck and went to sleep. They were sociable bears who had grown up among people and liked to feel that there was a friendly man close by.

It was about three-thirty in the morning when a "whiteall" came out to the ship. It appeared to be one of the official boats of the Port as it was nicely kept and very clean.

The men at the oars were unknown to me but our captain was sitting in the stern, steering it. I suspected that Pink Whiskers had been entertained by some of the Port officials. I hailed the boat and he answered with the name of the ship, "*Perry*," which meant that he was the captain of the *Perry*. He thanked the men who had rowed him over to the ship and came up the gangway, looking at me to see if I was sober, I suppose, or if everything was in order. He immediately stepped on a bear. I was able to grab him by the arm and keep him from busting his head on the deck, and the bear came up and started to lick him in the face. This one was only a small cub and very friendly and affectionate, but it nearly scared the pants off the captain.

"My God! Where did that thing come from?" he screamed.

"The boys brought it over with them from the shore for a mascot," I told him.

He straightened up and looked up the deck, and by that time some of the other bears were moving around a little, and everywhere he looked there were bears. He seemed a little shaken at the sight of so many.

"My God! Why did you let all these things come aboard?"

"I couldn't stop them, sir," I replied.

"You mean they swam over and came aboard?" he asked.

"No, sir. They were brought aboard by the sailors, and they brought each one aboard, saying that some certain party in Ketchikan had sent it over to you, sir, for a mascot for the ship, and that they did nothing more than to grant the man a favor by bringing it over to you."

"Lord!" he exclaimed as he walked over and sat down in one of the chairs on the quarterdeck. "This is the damnedest thing that ever happened to me in all my life."

"I got the impression from what the boys said that the people who sent the bears over by them had contacted you and would be very much insulted and hurt if you did not receive them. There was nothing else to do but receive them since I had no orders against receiving bears."

"Has the other officer come aboard yet?" he asked.

"No, sir, and I hope that they don't bring any bears in his boat," I replied.

"If he does, I'll have him court-martialed! Call me just as soon as he comes aboard. We'll have the march of the bears!"

"Aye, aye, sir," I replied meekly.

He looked at me with a very peculiar look which I could not fathom, but he didn't say anything more. I was in hopes that some of the bears had gone down in the wardroom and occupied the lounges and available beds down there, but I was never able to find out if any did.

Since no one had come to relieve me, I was still on watch when the other officer came aboard about six o'clock. I told him that the captain had left orders to be called when he arrived. This was quite upsetting to him and he asked me what was wrong, saying that there was no set time for his return and that he did not think he was expected to return before breakfast.

"I don't know what's wrong, sir." I said.

He had probably consumed quite a lot of bilge water, otherwise known as whiskey, because when he walked over to sit down in the comfortable, big chair on the quarterdeck, he laid down on a sleeping cub. The cub let out a howl and his feeling seemed to be deeply hurt. The officer jumped up about four feet in the air and shrieked, "What's that?"

"It's just a bear cub, sir. He won't hurt you."

He stood there a moment, sort of collecting himself, before he began to take notice of the situation. As he gazed up and down the deck a look of wonderment spread over his

323

countenance. Then he asked me what was meant by all the bears around and how they came aboard. Such an opportunity was just too good to pass up and I told him they had been brought aboard by the inhabitants to be shipped north to Skagway as there were rumors that there was a grave scarcity of beasts up there. I suggested that it might be government orders. He just stood there with his mouth open and I went below and called the captain.

When the captain came on deck he had the pilot with him. They both stood there surveying the situation and the captain asked how we were going to get those things off the ship without throwing them overboard.

"A couple of miles up the channel there is a little cove where we can lay-to," the pilot told him. "You can take them ashore in the boats."

"It wouldn't do to throw them overboard?" Pink Whiskers asked hopefully.

"No indeed," the pilot answered. "They might get wind of it in Ketchikan and take offense. We fellow at sea need all the friends we can get ashore. Besides, the bears might bite or harm somebody while being thrown overboard. No, that wouldn't do."

When we reached the cove, the boats were lowered, and the bears were taken ashore, as the pilot had suggested. When we got close to shore it was not hard to get them out of the boats and they all clambered up the beach and headed into the woods. I never found out whether the town learned what had become of their bears as we did not stop there on the way back, but I like to think that at least some of those bears headed for Ketchikan and home.

Totems, a Train Ride, & a Glacier

We then proceeded up the Passage where we stopped at a place where there was an Indian school which had been established for the education of Indian girls. This school was in a beautiful spot overlooking a sheltered cove. The officers and a lot of the men went ashore and were cordially welcomed by the teachers and pupils who proudly showed them around the school. This was a fine school and had been founded with the intention of teaching the girls to be better homemakers.

Right in front of the school and looking out over the cove, was the largest and finest, awe-inspiring totem pole that I ever saw in Alaska. Every little village or group of families had their totem pole, which is a history of their family. Some of the carving was superb. I never saw one finer that this one at the Indian school.

We stopped at all the main towns or cities on the way up, including Juneau, where the Treadwell mine was in full operation. The main part of the mine was under the bay, deep under water. At that time, they claimed that it was the largest gold mine in the world. We leisurely poked along until we anchored at Skagway, which at the time of the gold rush was about the biggest place in Alaska because it was close to Chilkoot Pass. There was a railway which had been built and operated by the government. The other terminal was the White Pass, where both gold and coal were mined.

The officials of the railroad invited all the officers and men who wished to take the trip up and back the next day, to send in their names. Well, I saw a chance to get a good ride for nothing, so I put my name down. It was beautiful ride with scenery which is beyond description. In fact, the scenery all the way up along the Inland Passage is beyond description and,

although I have been all over the world several times, I have never found anything more beautiful than is found in Alaska on the Inland Passage during the months of July and August. Everybody who made the trip was awed by the grandeur of the scenery. When we got to the end of the line we were invited into the station-house to have a cup of coffee while they turned the train around.

As I got off the car I was on, I looked up to the end of the track that we were on, what do you think I saw? It was a sign which said, "LOS ANGELES CITY LIMITS!" The boys wanted to pull it up and take it back to the ship with them, but the brakeman told them not to touch it because they would be in a lot of trouble. The railroad was rather proud of that sign.

The next day the ship proceeded over to a place opposite to the Muir Glacier and we worked our way slowly among the icebergs to a place as close as we dared to get to it. What a thrill to be so close to a real glacier! Some of the boys were grouching because we didn't go in closer but, as the pilot explained, it was no place for tin cans like our destroyer around icebergs as only about one-eighth of the iceberg is visible above the water.

{Per research, the Muir Glacier is no longer visible as it receded more than 50 kilometers from his visit.}

The End of My Apprentice Boy Adventure

When we left there, we headed down the Passage and proceeded to Seattle without incident. On arriving at our anchorage in Seattle, we found the USS *Marblehead* anchored nearby. I learned that she was scheduled to leave in two or three days for Port Harford, which was the port for San Luis Obispo, California. There was a narrow-gage, jerkwater railroad from the dock at Port Harford to the town of San Luis Obispo, about ten or twelve miles inland, where it connected with the Southern Pacific Railroad.

Since I had enlisted in San Francisco, the government was obliged to return me to San Francisco at their expense. No one knew when our ship would leave for San Francisco, so since the termination of enlistment would come at about the day the *Marblehead* would arrive at Port Harford, I put the proposition up to Pink Whiskers to let me go down on the *Marblehead* and let me be paid off from the *Marblehead* at that port, thereby saving the government the expense of sending me from Seattle to San Francisco. He agreed to this and notified the commander of the *Marblehead* that they were sending me to be paid off on arrival at Port Harford.

The *Marblehead* sent word that she was leaving the next day and for me to come aboard. I packed my bag and hammock and went below to get my transfer papers. The captain was sitting at his desk in the wardroom when I reported to him and he handed over my papers necessary for discharge, which I was able to take to the *Marblehead* with me. He looked hard at me and I returned the gaze. I'd have given anything to know what he was thinking and maybe he felt the same way about me. However, he got up and stuck out his hand and said, "Well,

goodbye. I suppose that with your good record and good marks that you will undoubtedly re-enlist."

I looked straight into his eyes and said, "No, sir. Not while you're in the Navy."

Well, that was quite a shock to him. I guess he was debating whether to change his mind in hopes of getting something on me on the way down to San Francisco so that he could court-martial me. I think that statement knocked him speechless, and he knew very well that I meant it, too. He dropped my hand like it was a hot potato and turn his back on me and walked to the other side of the wardroom. I picked up my papers and went up on the main deck where there was a boat's crew waiting at the gangway. After shaking hands with about everybody, I got into the boat, and everyone lined the rail and yelled goodbye and good luck. I saw all the crew members on the ship there except Pink Whiskers, as the boat pulled away. I don't believe he could face it.

I went aboard the *Marblehead* and the next day we left for the south. The voyage down was very pleasant and agreeable. I went to the chief quartermaster and offered to stand a watch for him on the way down, but being an ex-apprentice boy himself, he told me that anybody who had done nearly six years apprenticeship, shouldn't have to work his way down on the ship to get home and to take it easy and enjoy myself.

We arrived in Port Harford late in the afternoon and the train didn't leave for San Luis Obispo for two or three hours, so I rested on my hammock and bag waiting for the train. In San Luis Obispo I had a couple of hours to wait there for the train

which was to take me to Los Angeles where my family was now living.

During this wait I reviewed the past six years from 1899 to August of 1905, and found pleasure in the memories I had. When that train whistle blew, and I got aboard that Southern Pacific train, I was proud of the uniform I wore and the fact that I had been an apprentice boy and had acquitted myself well. I was glad then for the apprentice training and felt that it had given me something I could have gained in no other way. I still believe that training of this kind could be the answer to some of the teenage problems which confront us today.

REFERENCES

Names of Sails

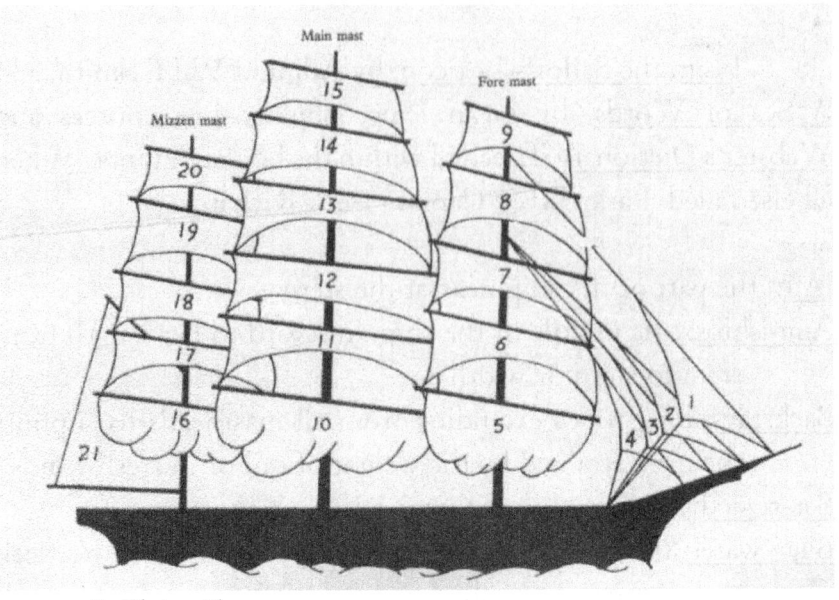

1 Flying jib
2 Outer jib
3 Inner jib
4 Fore topmast staysail
5 Foresail
6 Lower fore topsail
7 Upper fore topsail
8 Fore topgallant sail
9 Fore royal
10 Mainsail
11 Lower main topsail
12 Upper main topsail
13 Lower main topgallant sail
14 Upper main topgallant sail
15 Main royal
16 Cross-jack
17 Lower mizzen topsail
18 Upper mizzen topsail
19 Mizzen topgallant
20 Mizzen royal
21 Driver or spanker

Nautical Terms

From the Sailor's Lexicon, by Admiral W.H. Smith, and A Sea of Words, by Dean King, plus on-line sources and Webster's Dictionary if needed within the book contents. When all else failed, I asked Ret. Captain Nick Richards.

Aft: the part of the ship nearest the stern

Amidships: the middle of the ship, in regard to her length from stem to stern or width

Backstays: long ropes extending from all mastheads to support the mast strained by the weight of sail or in fresh winds

Bar-rigged: a sailing ship with cross-bars on the masts

Bilge water: the rain or sea water that runs down a ship's deck and remains in the ship's bilge until it is pumped out

Bowsprit: a large spar projecting over the stem; beyond it extends the jib-boom (a light sail); and beyond that is flying jib-boom

Companionway: A raised and windowed hatchway in the ship's deck, with a ladder leading below to the main cabin

Conning tower: a heavily armored pilot house on a warship

Forecastle: A partial deck, above the upper deck and at the head of the vessel; traditionally the sailors' living quarters.

Guardo: Navy nickname for Mare Island

Guardo: What sailors called Mare Island.

Gun-cotton: an explosive compound made or ordinary cotton with nitric and sulfuric acid and water.

Fore and Aft: from stem to stern

Heave the lead (lead refers to a metal): to take soundings with the hand lead-line

Jackstay: an iron rod bolted clear of the mainmast, to which the luff of the mainsail is laced

Klinker: a flat-bottomed boat

Lead-line: a line attached to the upper end of the sounding-lead

Leadsman: the man who heaves the lead-line

Messenger Line: a cable line used to unmoor or haul up an anchor or throw to another ship.

Mudhook: Probably slang for small anchor in shallow water (please update me as I cannot find the term)

Parcelling: winding tarred canvass around a rope

Ratlines: small lines which travers the shrouds of a ship placed horizontally 15 or 16 inches apart forming a series of steps or ladders

Ship's writer: In the Navy, a writer describes all those positions involved in administration and accountancy. It has nothing to do with being a journalist or author.

Soundings: Ascertaining the depth of the sea by means of a lead-line in shallow waters where the lead-line will reach the bottom.

Streaming the Log: The crew would lower a specially crafted piece of wood on a line and let it float freely down the side of the ship. They would measure the distance it traveled to a specific spot to determine the speed in knots.

Worming: To protect a section of rope from chafing by wrapping marline or other small stuff around it and stitching a covering of canvas (parceling) over all.

Yard: A long and narrow wooden spar, slung from the mast in a square-rigged ship.

Yardarm: Either of the ends of a yard where signal flags were flown in a square-rigged ship.

Apprentice Boy System
Based on an article By Lt. A.B. Wychoff

The initial program began in 1837 for boys between the ages of 13 and 18 and was abandoned in 1843. There were many issues with this program that failed, however, after the success of the apprentice system in European navies, the program was revived on April 8, 1875, until 1904, with updated policies. Some small lads could be accepted, for example, a boy 16 years old had a minimum height restriction of 5'1" and weight of 90 pounds.

Their character had to be well above average for a pay of $9.00 per month. In 1897 the apprentice boys served on the cruiser training ships *Essex, Adams,* and *Alliance* which were bark-rigged and wooden-hulled, 185 feet long and 1,375 tons. Wychoff said that the boys were stationed in one part of the ship for three months

The cruiser training ships made a summer and a winter cruise and after making both cruises the apprentices were transferred to a cruising ship of war. The boys were advanced to apprentice second class with a pay raise to $10.00 a month. After one year's service, they advanced to apprentice first class and were paid $11.00.

The ships' regular crews were mature men specially adapted for that service selected for their character, intelligence, and professional qualifications.

Wyckoff said, "In view of the difficult entrance requirements, the low pay, and the varied duty they were subjected to, the question often was asked why a youngster would want to become an apprentice. One of those reasons was that they received a good education for the time, and at the same time received systematic instruction in seamanship."

The program ended in December 1904, just as Gaither Stevens had served his six years and felt that the program generated some of the Navy's finest leaders.

Brief Family History

Gather's grandparents: Josiah Stevens born Nov. 18, 1815, married to Emeline Ashley

Gaither's parents: Horace Greely Stevens, born March 10, 1860, married Marguerite (Maggie) A. Sheppard. Horace was a journalist and bravely co-wrote the book *Looters of the Public Domain* with S.A.D. Puter in 1907 "Embracing a complete exposure of the fraudulent system of acquiring titles to the public lands of the United States."

Horace Greeley Stevens

Gaither "Steve" Stevens born August 2, 1884, married Elmira Poundstone, divorced and married Helen Anderson until their deaths. Gaither died March 12, 1962

Gaither's children: Eugene (father to Nan and Wendy); Horace "Hod" Gaither (no children); Daughters Frances and Myra (Terrie's mother). Step-son with Helen, was Tom who took Stevens as his last name.

Family dinner honoring Gaither Stevens

(in relation to Terrie)

Left to right: Bob & cousin Nan Bullough (Gaither's grand-daughter), "Chick" (Hod's wife), David Bennett (Terrie's brother), Helen (Gaither's 2nd wife); Marion "Benny" Bennett (Terrie's father); cousin Gary Connolly (Aunt Fran's son); Myra Bennet (Terrie's mom and Gaither's daughter); Gaither, Terrie, Aunt Fran (Gaither's daughter); Uncle Hod (Gaither's son) cousin Wendy (Gaither's grand-daughter); Adelbert Johnson (married to Gaither's ex-wife Elmira); Elmira Johnson (Terrie's grandmother & Gaither's first wife); Bud Connolly (Aunt Fran's husband); and Aunt Charlotte (Wendy and Nan's mother) married to Gaither's son Eugene "Uncle Gene" (not in photo)

I have the genealogy of the Stevens family back to 1605, however, I am going back only a couple of generations while I am building the family history on Ancestry.com under my family tree.

About the Presenter/Editor

Terrie Biggs has been writing creative non-fiction for years. Terrie resides in La Grande, Oregon, with her husband Dan. Their children are adults. She has a lifetime passion for kitchen design and owns her own business. Her published books are also in the Amazon Kindle store.

Check out her books at http://www.NovelsbyTerrie.com or visit her "Terrie Biggs" page on Amazon. See progress and updates on Novels by Terrie Facebook page.

Reviews on Amazon are encouraged and appreciated very much, and so are comments or corrections. One review can encourage hundreds of readers.
Email: novelsbyterrie@gmail.com

4647828ZR00193